Affirmative Action
in
Antidiscrimination
Law and Policy

SUNY series in American Constitutionalism
Robert J. Spitzer, editor

Affirmative Action in Antidiscrimination Law and Policy

An Overview and Synthesis

Samuel Leiter
William M. Leiter

State University of New York Press

Published by
State University of New York Press, Albany

For information, address State University of New York Press,
90 State Street, Suite 700, Albany, NY 12207

Production by Marilyn P. Semerad
Marketing by Patrick Durocher

Library of Congress Cataloging-in-Publication Data

Leiter, Samuel, 1922–
    Affirmative action in anti-discrimination law and policy : an overview
and synthesis / Samuel and William Leiter.
        p. cm. — (SUNY series in American constitutionalism)
Includes bibliographical references and index.
    ISBN 0-7914-5509-2 (hc : acid free) — ISBN 0-7914-5510-6 (pb : acid
free)
    1. Affirmative action programs—Law and legislation—United States.
    2. Discrimination in employment—Law and legislation—United States.
    3. Discrimination—Law and legislation—United States. I. Leiter,
William M., 1934– II. Title. III. Series.
    KF4755.5 .L45 2002
    344.7301'133—dc21
                                                        2002002514

10 9 8 7 6 5 4 3 2 1

*In memory of our beloved
sister Lillian*

Contents

———✦✦✦———

Acknowledgments

—◦◊◦—

Many thanks to family members and colleagues who assisted our efforts. The library facilities and librarians at California State University—Long Beach provided wonderful help in the production of this volume. Thanks are also extended to FindLaw—a computer web site—for permission to download and reproduce extended excerpts of U.S. Supreme Court opinions from that source. Additionally, Sage Publications, Inc. granted the authors permission to reproduce a portion of their essay (see pages 119–124 herein): *Affirmative Action and the Presidential Role in Modern Civil Rights Reform: A Sampler of Books of the 1990s,* 29 Presidential Studies Quarterly 175, 184–188 (March, 1999) © Center For The Study Of The Presidency.

Chapter One

—*·/I/·*—

Introduction

The Topic

The subject of this treatise/casebook is the legal and ideological controversy over the application of affirmative action policy to combat discrimination based on race, national origin/ethnicity, and gender. Racism, sexism, and ethnic discrimination have long represented a seemingly intractable problem. Affirmative action was conceived as an attack on this ingrained problem but today it is widely misunderstood. We feel the time is ripe for the comprehensive review that we attempt in this book. To maintain our primary focus, we have left for another day examination of the more recent—still evolving—initiatives against discrimination based on age, disability, and genetic testing.

Affirmative action differs from other antidiscrimination initiatives in that (1) it targets *societal* bias (as manifested in public and private action), not individual malefactors; (2) it mandates race, ethnic, and gender-conscious remedies for the disproportionately adverse effects—the so-called *disparate impact*—of societal discrimination on protected groups, whether or not specific discriminatory intent on the part of individual defendants can be isolated; and (3) it seeks to integrate institutions by race, ethnicity, and gender.[1] As will be seen, the doctrine of *disparate impact* is a particularly central reason for the quarrel over affirmative action, and thus is a central theme of this book.

Affirmative action connotes remedial consideration of race, ethnicity, or sex as a factor, among others, in decision making about outreach, jobs, government contracting, K-12 student assignment, university admission, voting rights, and housing. The goal of this process is to redress the disadvantage under which members of disparately impacted groups are said to labor. The relative weight accorded to the race, national origin/ethnicity, or sex factor varies from program to program; thus affirmative action remedies range from disseminating job information to preferential employment and admissions

1

practices, classroom integration, the creation of majority-minority legislative districts, and court-ordered quotas in egregious discrimination cases.

Opponents of affirmative action generally portray it as a radical departure from equal opportunity's original goal. In their version, the founding fathers of modern civil rights reform conceived of racial, ethnic, and gender discrimination as *intentional* maltreatment—*disparate treatment*, so-called—and strictly limited the remedy to parity—*equal treatment*, as it came to be known. Affirmative action came into being by displacing these time-honored precepts with the revolutionary notion that the *group* effects of societal bias warrant government intervention, wholly apart from the question of intent. The upshot, according to the critics, has been the ascendancy of protected-group preferences and antimeritocratic equality of *results*.

In this book, we endeavor to present an evenhanded account of these claims, and the counterclaims of affirmative action's advocates in the spheres of employment, contracting, education, voting rights, and housing. We focus on affirmative action as the remedy for the effects of *both* facially neutral practices that disparately impact minorities and women; and government-sanctioned (de jure/intentional) segregation of protected groups in education and housing.[2] (See chapters 3, 4, 5, 6, and 7 in this volume.) In addition, we visit the alternative rationale of *diversity*, that is, increased nonremedial inclusion of protected groups in the economy and education.

A Thumbnail History

Affirmative action came to the fore about half a century ago, at the beginning of a new era in civil rights reform. Prior reform initiatives had dealt mainly with intentional racial maltreatment of individuals and other traditional barriers to equal treatment. However, during our recent tumultuous confrontation with the nation's racist past, the ideology of reform took on a far more proactive cast. True equality, it was said, would be unattainable without some form of compensation for the inherited disadvantage of disparately impacted minorities and females.[3] Under the umbrella-label of *affirmative action,* providing such special assistance on the basis of group membership—rather than individual victimization—displaced *equal treatment* as the hallmark of federal policy.

From the late 1960s, affirmative action fostered a nationwide torrent of court-orders, government programs, and voluntary plans, which provided benefits ranging from outreach and special training; hiring goals and timetables; preferences in hiring, promotion, and university admission; public school integration; political representation; and—to a limited degree—"balanced" housing. More than any other recent experiment in social engineering, this profusion of minority and female privilege evoked public outcry against claimed overinclusiveness, violations of the merit principle, and "reverse discrimination." Nonetheless, with the spirited support of the courts until the end of the 1980s, affirmative action set the standard for equal opportunity in the public and private economies, and society as a whole. By the 1990s, the early limitation of "protected groups" to blacks had yielded to widespread coverage of Hispanics, women, American Indians, and Asians. In its heyday, affirmative action represented the centerpiece of America's most ambitious, most promising, attempt to overcome the scourge of race, ethnic, and gender bias. (For a sampler of the extensive federal program, see the appendix to this chapter.)

The promise has not been fulfilled. Affirmative action has surely worked important policy changes, but there is no avoiding the fact that antiminority discrimination and sexism remain forces to be reckoned with. Whether affirmative action is up to this task is open to increasingly serious question. A series of adverse court rulings and state referenda in the 1990s have raised doubts about its legality. Public opposition is great. One cannot discount the possibility that affirmative action will soon be discarded or emasculated. The day may come when we have learned how to handle our racial/ethnic, and gender differences; what the history of affirmative action teaches is that such a day is not yet upon us.

The Book

Affirmative action is indisputably the flash point of America's civil rights agenda. The affirmative action literature is voluminous, but no comprehensive account of its major legal/public policy dimensions exists. This book aims to fill the gap.

The book covers affirmative action's origins and growth; the reasons for its current predicament; its impact on American society, and its future antidiscrimination role, if any. We have immersed ourselves in the literature of discrete disciplines that deal with these subjects: law, history, economics, statistics, sociology, political science, urban studies, and criminology. Our text integrates the relevant legal materials (constitutional and statutory provisions, regulations, and case law) with analysis and commentary that draw upon the ranking specialists (academic and otherwise) in the cited fields of study. We are convinced that affirmative action would make an outstanding case study in constitutional law, and respectfully offer our treatment as a model for constitutional studies. Though the subject is intricate, our goal is simple: to further a better understanding of affirmative action's complexities through an evenhanded presentation of its roots, substantive components and diverse applications, eye-crossing issues, and endlessly debated impact.

In chapter 2 of this interdisciplinary synthesis, we examine the government's abortive attempt to eradicate the effects of racial discrimination after the Civil War. We also discuss the women's rights movement, and examine the question of which groups should be covered by affirmative action. Chapter 3 deals with the genesis and operations of affirmative action in employment. Chapters 4 and 5 describe affirmative action's role in education. In chapter 6, we recount affirmative action's record in countering voting-rights discrimination. Chapter 7 treats America's limited efforts to deploy affirmative action against residential segregation. In chapter 8, we raise central legal questions and summarize primary ideological claims including those made by a representative sample of distinguished disputants.

This book highlights affirmative action's legal dimensions. Here there has been no "separation of powers." Rather, the separate institutions of our national government—the courts, the bureaucracy, and the legislature—have all been involved in saying what law is. Often, the study of lawmaking is artificially truncated because our texts and courses focus on one branch to the neglect of others. Our study attempts to reduce this myopia. Further, it underscores the lack of guidance provided by Congress and the Supreme Court in critical areas. Thus, Congress—in equal employment opportunity (Title VII[4])—did not formally adopt disparate-impact theory until some two decades after the courts and the administrators had nourished it into a flourishing concern. (And Congress has yet to define what it means by the concept.) Likewise, it was not until 1968 that the Supreme Court ruled that its 1954 decision to end racial segregation in the public schools also required racial integration. The merit of governmental ambiguity is a question that should also be explored in connection with the bureaucracy. At the heart of major affirmative action programs is the administrative requirement that good faith efforts be employed to provide compensatory benefits to protected groups. What constitutes good faith depends on the differing values of the scrutinizing bureaucrats who may impose serious sanctions for what are viewed as deviations from that slippery standard.

Our interdisciplinary approach argues that a central reason for affirmative action's current predicament is uncertainty over the objective of antidiscrimination law. Had Congress, in the beginning, defined *discrimination* in Title VII, we might have been spared the fevered dispute over whether that law contemplates affirmative remediation (*equal results*) or only discrimination cessation (*equal treatment*). However, as we show in chapter 3, this fundamental substantive issue was left open. The concept of affirmative action as a remedy for disparate impact came into being as a court-sanctioned administrative interpretation of this legislative gap. In effect, the bureaucracy, with the courts' blessings, took it upon itself to complete Congress' unfinished business. It seems fair to say that Congress was primarily responsible for the legal muddle that is reflected in the conflicting rulings that the Supreme Court, over time, has issued in interpreting Title VII. (See pages 79–83, 225–231 in this volume for a delineation of the continuing issues.) For its part, as will be seen, the Supreme Court has magnified the legal muddle on the constitutional level by initially failing to muster a majority on the issue of the proper standard of affirmative action judicial review. Further, the Court has refused both to clarify critical aspects of that standard and to determine the validity of nonremedial affirmative action.

We believe that this lamentable state of affairs is directly attributable to the government's consistent departures from constitutional norms. The repeated failure of both Congress and the Supreme Court to discharge their responsibilities, coupled with the bureaucracy's immersion in the legislative sphere, have challenged the principle of separation of powers, and have deprived the public of sorely needed guidance. In our view, this perspective on affirmative action deserves greater emphasis.

Remembrance of Things Past

Affirmative action is not our first equal opportunity program. We see it as a revival of the ill-fated attempt to make citizens out of slaves after the Civil War. The past is prologue, and it is the past that we will turn to in chapter 2.

Note on Citations

Except where incorporated in this volume, citations in public documents extracted herein have been omitted without notification. Where the footnotes of these documents were reproduced, their numbers were changed to follow the order of the authors' citations.

The authors' citations conform with *The University of Chicago Manual of Legal Citations* (Bancroft-Whitney, 1989). Unless otherwise noted, where citations from other documents are reproduced in this volume, the style of the original was maintained.

Newspaper articles cited by the authors may be paginated differently in library newspaper indexes.

The bracketed numbers located in excerpts from U. S. Supreme Court opinions (introduced by boldface titles) refer to page numbers in the *United States Reports*. There are also bracketed references to pages in the *Federal Reporter* and *Federal Register* in this volume's extended excerpts reproduced from these sources and introduced with boldfaced titles.

Appendix to Chapter One

——◦◦◦——

A Sampler of Federal Affirmative Action Programs Explicitly Mandated or Authorized by Statute or Administrative Regulation

This sampler consists of excerpts from two sources: The portions titled "Equal Employment Opportunity Laws," and "Grants and Other Assistance" are from the Congressional Research Service.[5] The materials under the titles of "Military Recruiting" and "Federal Procurement Policies and Practices" are from a report to President Clinton.[6]

Equal Employment Opportunity Laws

. . . The evolution of federal law and policy regarding affirmative action in employment may be traced to a series of executive orders dating to the 1960's which prohibit discrimination and require affirmative action by contractors with the federal government. The Office of Federal Contract Compliance Programs, an arm of the U.S. Department of Labor, currently enforces the E.O. [Executive Order] 11246, as amended, by means of a regulatory program requiring larger federal contractors, those with procurement or construction contracts in excess of $50,000, to make a "good faith effort" to attain "goals and timetables" to remedy underutilization of minorities and women. . . .

Public and private employers with 15 or more employees are also subject to a comprehensive code of equal employment opportunity regulation under Title VII of the 1964 Civil Rights Act.[7] Except as may be
imposed by court order to remedy "egregious" violations of the law, or
by consent decree to settle pending claims, however, there is no general
statutory obligation on employers to adopt affirmative action measures.
But the EEOC [Equal Employment Opportunities Commission] has issued guidelines to protect employers and unions from charges of "reverse discrimination" when they voluntarily take action to correct the
effects of past discrimination.[8] [See appendices 1 and 2 in chapter 3 in
this volume.] Federal departments and agencies, by contrast, are required to periodically formulate affirmative action plans for their employees and a "minority recruitment program" to eliminate minority
"underrepresentation" in specific federal job categories.

Section 717 of [the] 1972 Amendments to Title VII of the 1964 Civil Rights
Act empowers the Equal Employment Opportunity Commission to enforce
nondiscrimination policy in federal employment by "necessary and appropriate" rules, regulations, and orders and through "appropriate remedies,
including reinstatement or hiring of employees, with or without back-pay."[9]
Each federal department and agency, in turn, is required to prepare annually
a "national and regional equal employment opportunity plan" for submission to the EEOC as part of "an affirmative program of equal employment
opportunity for all . . . employees and applicants for employment."[10]

Section 717 was reinforced in 1978 when Congress enacted major federal
civil service reforms including a mandate for immediate development of a
"minority recruitment program" designed to eliminate "underrepresentation"
of minority groups in specific federal job categories.[11] The EEOC and Office
of Personnel Management have issued rules to guide implementation and
monitoring of minority recruitment programs by individual federal agencies.
Among various other specified requirements, each agency plan "must include annual specific determinations of underrepresentation for each group
and must be accompanied by quantifiable indices by which progress toward
eliminating underrepresentation can be measured."[12]

In addition, the following [are among the] statutes and regulations [that]
relate to employment policies of the federal government or under federal
grant and assistance programs:

5 U.S.C. § 4313(5): Performance appraisal in the Senior Executive
Services to take account of individuals' "meeting affirmative action goals,
achievement of equal employment opportunity requirements, and compliance with merit principles. . . ."

5 U.S.C. § 7201: Establishes a "Minority Recruitment Program" for the Executive Branch and directs each Executive agency, "to the maximum extent possible," to "conduct a continuing program for the recruitment of members of minorities for positions in the agency . . . in a manner designed to eliminate underrepresentation of minorities in the various categories of civil service employment within the Federal service, with special efforts directed at recruiting in minority communities, in educational institutions, and from other sources from which minorities can be recruited."

22 U.S.C. § 4141(b): Establishes the Foreign Service Internship Program "to promote the Foreign Service as a viable and rewarding career opportunity for qualified individuals who reflect the cultural and ethnic diversity of the United States. . . ."

42 U.S.C. § 282(h): The Secretary of HHS [Health and Human Services], and the National Institutes of Health, "shall, in conducting and supporting programs for research, research training, recruitment, and other activities, provide for an increase in the number of women and individuals from disadvantaged backgrounds (including racial and ethnic minorities) in the fields of biomedical and behavioral research." . . .

41 C.F.R. Part 60 (1994): Sets forth the body of administrative rules issued by the Office of Federal Contract Compliance Programs [OFCCP] within the Department of Labor to enforce the affirmative action requirements of E.O. 11246 on federal procurement and construction contractors. All contractors and subcontractors with federal contracts in excess of $10,000 are prohibited by the Executive Order from discriminating and required to take affirmative action in the employ[ment] of minority groups and women. Federal contractors and subcontractors with 50 or more employees and government contracts of $50,000 or more must develop written affirmative action compliance programs for each of their facilities. OFCCP rules direct these larger contractors to conduct a "utilization analysis" of all major job classifications and explain any underutilization of minorities and women by job category when compared with the availability of qualified members of these groups in the relevant labor area. Based on this analysis, the contractor's affirmative action plan must set forth appropriate goals and timetables to which the contractor must direct its "good faith efforts" to correct deficiencies. In addition, OFCCP has established nationwide hiring goals of 6.9 percent for women in construction, and regional and local goals for minorities in construction, which are set out in an appendix to the agency's affirmative action in construction regulations. 41 C.F.R. [§] 60-4. [OFCCP's current affirmative action regulations covering larger service and supply contracts are excerpted in appendix 3 in chapter 3 of this volume.]

48 C.F.R. [§] 22.804 (1994): Affirmative action program under Federal Acquisition Regulations requires written affirmative action plans of federal nonconstruction prime and subcontractors with 50 or more employees that comply with DOL [Department of Labor] regulations to assure equal opportunity in employment to minorities and women.

48 C.F.R. [§§] 52.222-23, 52.222-27 (1994): Prescribes clause for inclusion of federal contracts that requires "[g]oals for minority and female participation, expressed in percentage terms for the Contractor's aggregate workforce in each trade on all construction work in the covered area" and "to make a good faith effort to achieve each goal under the plan in each trade in which it has employees." . . .

[Military Recruiting]

. . . Because minorities are overrepresented in the enlisted ranks and underrepresented in the officer corps, . . . the armed forces have focused recently on the officer "pipeline." The services employ a number of tools:

Goals and Timetables: The Navy and the Marine Corps, historically less successful than the other services in this arena, have responded in recent months by setting *explicit goals* to increase minority representation in the officer corps. Both services seek to ensure that, in terms of race and ethnicity, the group of officers commissioned in the year 2000 roughly reflects the overall population: 12 percent African American, 12 percent Hispanic, and 5 percent Asian. Department of the Navy officials point out that this represents a significantly more aggressive goal than had been the case, when the focus for comparison had been on college graduates; the more aggressive goal implies vigorous outreach and other efforts. . . . Moreover, the Navy and the Marine Corps have set specific year-by-year targets for meeting the 12/12/5 goal.

Outreach, Recruiting, & Training: All of the services target outreach and recruiting activities through ROTC [the Reserve Officers Training Corps], the service academies, and other channels. Also, the services have made *special, race-conscious (though not racially exclusive) efforts to recruit officer candidates.* For example, the Army operates a very successful "preparatory school" for students nominated to West Point whose academic readiness is thought to be marginal; the enrollees are disproportionately but . . . no[t] exclusively minority.

Selection Procedures: All of the services emphasize racial and gender diversity in their promotion procedures. The Army, for example: instructs officer promotion boards to "be alert to the possibility of past personal or institutional discrimination—either intentional or inadvertent;" [and] sets as a *goal that promotion rates for each minority and gender group [are] at least equal [to] promotion rates for the overall eligible population.* . . . [I]f, for example, a selection board has a general guideline that 44 percent of eligible lieutenant colonels be promoted to colonel, the flexible goal is that promotions of minorities and women be at that same rate. . . . [The procedure] establishes a *"second look" process* under which the files for candidates from underrepresented groups who are not selected upon initial consideration are reconsidered with an eye toward identifying any past discrimination; and [the procedure] instructs members of a promotion board carefully so that the process does not force promotion boards to use quotas. . . .

Management Tools: These include performance standards, reporting requirements, and training and analytic capacity.—Personnel evaluations include matters related to effectiveness in EO [Equal Opportunity] matters. [Department of Defense] DoD maintains the Defense Equal Opportunity Management Institute, which trains EO personnel, advises DoD on EO policy, and conducts related research.—DoD conducts various surveys and studies to monitor equal opportunity initiatives and the views of personnel.—Most important, DoD requires each service to maintain and review affirmative action plans and to complete an annual "Military Equal Opportunity Assessment" (MEOA). The MEOA reports whether various equal opportunity objectives were met and identifies problems such as harassment and discrimination.

The MEOA includes both data and narrative assessments of progress in 10 areas. One of these is recruitment and accessions (*i.e.,* commissioning of officers). Other areas include . . . completion of officer and enlisted professional military education (*e.g.,* the war colleges and noncommissioned officer academies), augmentation of officers into the Regular component, [and] assignment to billets that are Service defined as career-enhancing. . . . In addition to these formal efforts, the Services support the efforts of non-profit service organizations, such as the Air Force Cadet Officer Mentor Action Program, that strengthen professional and leadership development through mentorship, assist in the transition to military life, and support the establishing of networks. . . .

[Grants and Other Assistance]

. . . 7 U.S.C. § 3154(c): The Secretary of Agriculture is authorized "to set aside a portion of funds" appropriated for certain research on the production and marketing of alcohols and industrial hydrocarbons for grants to colleges and universities to achieve "the objective of full participation of minority groups." . . .

7 C.F.R. § 1944. 671(b) (1994): Equal Opportunity and outreach requirements applicable to . . . [Department of Agriculture] Housing Preservation Grants program state that "[a]s a measure of compliance, the percentage of the individuals served by the HPG [Housing Preservation Grants] grantee should be in proportion to the percentages of the population of the service area by race/national origin." . . .

7 C.F.R. §§ 3403.1, 3403.2 (1994): [A goal of the] USDA [United States Department of Agriculture] regulations . . . is to " . . . encourage minority and disadvantaged [participation] in technological innovation." For purposes of this program [a] "minority and disadvantaged individual is defined as a member of any of the following groups: Black Americans, Hispanic Americans, Native Americans, Asian Pacific Americans, or Subcontinent Asian Americans." . . .

12 U.S.C. § 144la (r-w): Provides for various incentives, including "preference points" on proposals and minority capital assistance programs, to preserve and expand bank ownership by minorities and women; authorizes establishment of Resolution Trust Corporation [RTC] guidelines to achieve parity in distribution of RTC contracts, and "reasonable goals" for subcontracting to minority and women-owned businesses and firms; and provides a "[m]inority preference in acquisition of institutions in predominantly minority neighborhoods." . . .

12 U.S.C. § 2907: Any donation or sale on favorable terms of [a] bank branch in [a] minority neighborhood to minority or women-owned depository institutions shall be a factor in determining the seller or donor institution's compliance with the Community Reinvestment Act. . . .

15 C.F.R. § 917.11(d) (1994): A "factor considered" in the approval of proposals under the Sea Grant Matched Funding Program "will be the potential of the proposed program to stimulate interest in marine related careers among . . . minorities, women, and the handicapped whose previous background or training might not have generated such an interest." . . .

47 C.F.R. § 73.3555(d)(2)(ii) (1994): Federal Communications Commission (FCC) multiple ownership rules provide exemption for "minority-controlled" broadcast facilities from certain restrictions on the granting or transfer of commercial TV broadcast stations which result in an aggregate national audience exceeding twenty-five percent. "*Minority* means Black, Hispanic, American Indian, Alaska Native, Asian and Pacific Islander." . . .

68 F.C.C. 2d 381, 411-412 (1978). FCC policy awards a quality enhancement credit for minority ownership and participation in station management in the comparative licensing process. When faced with mutually exclusive applications for the same broadcast channel, the FCC initiates a proceeding to compare the merits of the competing applicants based on specific factors including: diversification of control of mass media communications, full time participation in station management by owners, proposed program service, past broadcast record, efficient use of frequency, and character of the applicant. Under the FCC's preference policy, ownership and active participation in station management by members of a minority group are considered a plus to be weighed in with the other comparative factors.

68 F.C.C. 2d 983 (1978): FCC "Distress Sale" Policy. Under this policy, existing licensees in jeopardy of having their licenses revoked or whose licenses have been designated for a renewal hearing are given the option of selling the license to a minority-owned or controlled firm for up to seventy-five percent of fair market value. The minority-assignee must meet the basic qualifications necessary to hold a license under FCC regulations and must be approved by the FCC before the transfer is consummated. . . .

20 U.S.C. § 1047: Authorizes grants and contracts by the Department of Education (ED) with "historically black colleges and universit[ies]" and other institutions of higher education serving a "high percentage of minority students" for the purpose of strengthening their library and information science programs, and establishing fellowships and traineeships for that purpose.

20 U.S.C. § 1063b: Authorizes ED grants to specified postgraduate institutions "determined by the Secretary [of Education] to be making substantial contributions to the legal, medical, dental, veterinary, or other graduate education opportunities for Black Americans."

20 U.S.C. § 1069f(c): Reservation of 25% of the excess of certain educational appropriations for allocation "among eligible institutions at which at least 60 percent of the students are African Americans, Hispanic Americans, Native Americans, Asian Americans . . . Native Hawaiians, or Pacific Islanders, or any combination thereof."

20 U.S.C. § 1070a-41: "Priority" in selection for Model Program Community Partnership and Counseling Grants given to program proposals "directed at areas which have a high proportion of minority, limited English proficiency, economically disadvantaged, disabled, nontraditional, or at-risk students. . . ."

20 U.S.C. §1112d(d): "Special consideration" to be given [to] "historically Black colleges and universities" and to institutions having at least 50% minority enrollment in making grants for teacher training and placement.

20 U.S.C.S. § 1132b-2: In awarding facilities improvement grants, the ED [Education] Secretary or each State higher education agency "shall give priority to institutions of higher education that serve large numbers or percentages of minority or disadvantaged students."

20 U.S.C. § 1134e: In making grants for post-graduate study, the . . . Secretary [of Education] shall "consider the need to prepare a larger number of women and individuals from minority groups, especially from among such groups which have been traditionally underrepresented in professional and academic careers," and shall accord a "priority" for awards to "individuals from minority groups and women" pursuing study in specified professional and career fields.

20 U.S.C. § 1134s: The ED Secretary "shall carry out a program to assist minority, low-income, or educationally disadvantaged college students" to pursue a degree and career in law through an annual grant or contract.

20 U.S.C. §§ 1135c, 1135d: The ED Secretary shall "carry out a program of making grants to institutions of higher education that are designed to provide and improve support programs for minority students enrolled in science and engineering programs as institutions with a significant minority enrollment. . . ." Eligibility for such grants is limited to "minority institutions" (minority enrollment in excess of 50%) or other public or private nonprofit institutions with at least 10 percent minority enrollment.

20 U.S.C. § 1409(j)(2): The ED Secretary "shall develop a plan for providing outreach services" to historically Black colleges and universities, other higher educational institutions with at least 25% minority student enrollment, and "underrepresented populations" in order to "increase the participation of such entities" in competitions for certain grants, contracts, and cooperative agreements.

20 U.S.C. § 1431(a)(3): "Priority consideration" for fellowships and traineeships in special education and related services shall be given to "individuals from disadvantaged backgrounds, including minority and individuals with disabilities who are underrepresented in the teaching profession or in the specialization in which they are being trained."

20 U.S.C. § 2986(b): A portion of state allotment of critical skills improvement funds to be distributed for various purposes, including "re-

cruitment or retraining of minority teachers to become mathematics and science teachers."

20 U.S.C. § 3156(a): Program to assist local educational agencies "which have significant percentages of minority students" to conduct "alternative curriculum" schools which "reflect a minority composition of at least 50 percent" and contribute to school desegregation efforts.

20 U.S.C. § 3916: Fifteen percent of National Science Foundation funds available for science and engineering education is to be allocated to faculty exchange and other programs involving higher educational institutions with "an enrollment which includes a substantial percentage of students who are members of a minority group."

20 U.S.C. § 5205(d): No less than 10 percent of Eisenhower Exchange Fellowship Program funds "shall be available only for participation by individuals who are representative of United States minority populations."

20 U.S.C. § 6031(c) (5): ED "shall establish and maintain initiatives and programs to increase the participation" of "researchers who are women, African-American, Hispanic, American Indian and Alaskan Native, or other ethnic minorities" in the activities of various authorized educational institutes.

42 U.S.C. § 292g (d)(3): For a three-year period beginning on October 13, 1992, historically black colleges and universities are exempted from provision rendering certain institutions ineligible for student loan program based on high loan default rate.

42 U.S.C. § 293a: "Special consideration" in scholarship grant program to be given "health profession schools that have enrollments of underrepresented minorities above the national average for health profession schools."

42 U.S.C. § 293b(3): Institutional eligibility for faculty fellowship program based on "ability to . . . identify, recruit and select individuals from underrepresented minorities in the health profession" with potential for teaching and educational administration.

42 U.S.C. § 1862d: At least 12 percent of amounts appropriated for the Academic Research Facilities Modernization Program shall be reserved for historically Black colleges and universities and other institutions which enroll a substantial percentage of Black American, Hispanic American, or Native American students.

34 C.F.R. § 74.12 (1994): Department of Education (ED) Uniform Administrative Requirements for Grants to Institutions of Higher Education,

Hospitals, and Nonprofit Organizations "encourage" ED grantees and subgrantees to use minority-owned banks. . . .

34 C.F.R. § 318.11(a)(15), (16) (1994): Includes "[t]raining minorities and individuals with disabilities" and "minority institutions" among several optional funding priorities under special education training program.

34 C.F.R. § 461.33(a)(2)(ii) (1994): "[P]articular emphasis" placed on training "minority" adult educators under one aspect of adult education demonstration grant program.

34 C.F.R. Part 607, § 607.2(b) (1994): An institution of higher education is eligible to receive a grant under the Strengthening Institutions Program even if it does not satisfy certain other generally applicable state authorization or accreditation requirements if its student enrollment consists of specified percentages of designated minority groups.

34 C.F.R. Parts 608, 609 (1994): "The Strengthening Historically Black Colleges and Universities Program . . . provides grants to Historically Black Colleges and Universities to assist these institutions in establishing and strengthening their physical plants, academic resources and student services so that they may continue to participate in fulfilling the goal of equality of educational opportunity." (§ 608.1).

34 C.F.R. § 637.1 (1994): "The Minority Science Improvement Program is designed to effect long-range improvement in science education at predominantly minority institutions and to increase the flow of underrepresented ethnic minorities, particularly minority women, into scientific careers."

34 C.F.R. § 641.1 (1994): "The Faculty Development Fellowship Program provides grants to institutions of higher education . . . and nonprofit organizations to fund fellowships for individuals from underrepresented minority groups to enter or continue in the higher education professorate." . . .

42 U.S.C. § 3027: State plans for grant programs on aging "shall provide assurances that special efforts will be made to provide technical assistance to minority providers of services."

42 U.S.C. § 3035d: Provides that the Assistant [Health and Human Services] HHS Secretary "shall carry out, directly or through grants or contracts, special training program and technical assistance designed to improve services to minorities" under the Older Americans Act.

42 C.F.R. § 52c.2 (1994): Minority Biomedical Research Support Program makes grants to higher educational institutions with 50 percent or other "significant proportion" of ethnic minority enrollment.

42 C.F.R. § 62.57(h) (1994): Among factors considered in making certain State loan repayment grants to State applicants is "[t]he extent to which special consideration will be extended to medically underserved areas with large minority populations."

42 C.F.R. § 64a.105(d)(2) (1994): "Preferred service" for purposes of obligated service requirement for mental health traineeships includes service in any public or private nonprofit entity serving 50 percent or more specified racial or ethnic minorities. . . .

29 U.S.C. § 718b(b): Directs the [Department of Labor] Commissioner of the Rehabilitation Services Administration to develop an "outreach" policy for "recruitment of minorities into the field of vocational rehabilitation, counseling and related disciplines" and for "financially assisting Historically Black Colleges and Universities, Hispanic-serving institutions of higher education, and other institutions of higher education whose minority enrollment is at least 50 percent."

29 U.S.C. § 771a: Authorizes [Department of Labor] grants for personnel projects relating to training, traineeships and related activities to historically Black colleges and universities and other higher educational institutions with at least 50% minority student enrollment. . . .

P.L. 103-306, 108 Stat. 1608, § 555 (1994): Provides for a 10 percent setaside of the aggregate amount of certain appropriations to the Agency for International Development—the Development Assistance Fund, Population Development Assistance, and the Development Fund for Africa—for socially and economically disadvantaged U.S. businesses and private voluntary organizations, historically black colleges and universities, and higher educational institutions with more that 40 percent Hispanic student enrollment. . . .

Federal Procurement Policies and Practices

. . . Throughout the federal government, several programs seek to increase procurement and contracting with minority- and women-owned businesses. The largest of these efforts are government-wide programs overseen by the [Small Business Administration] SBA; this overall effort is supplemented in some cases by agency-specific initiatives. Under these programs taken as a whole, some procurement contracts are set aside for sole-source or sheltered competition contracting, eligibility for which is targeted to minority-owned businesses (and in some cases nonminority women-owned businesses), but by statute available more broadly to "socially and economically disadvantaged" individuals. There is also a broad, race-neutral, sheltered competition or set aside for small businesses generally. This operates separately and has a lower priority than the more targeted efforts; still, over 93 percent of procurements are with non-minority firms. . . .

Policies & Practices

Government-Wide Efforts

Goals: Federal law establishes several overall, national goals to encourage broader participation in federal procurement: 20 percent for small businesses; 5 percent for small disadvantaged businesses (SDB's); and 5 percent for women-owned businesses. . . . The goal for women was added in the 1994 procurement reform legislation, the Federal Acquisition and Simplification Act. Racial minorities are presumed to be "socially disadvantaged" for purposes of the government-wide SDB program, mirroring the statutory presumption in the SBA's § 8(a) program described below. . . . [This contentious presumption of disadvantaged status is discussed at length in chapter 2, pages 34–36.] The SBA consults with each agency to set annual agency-level goals to ensure progress toward the overall goal. (For contracts and firms above certain thresholds, the law requires subcontracting plans in furtherance of these goals.) The goals are themselves flexible, and hence relatively non-controversial. The government-wide SDB goal was met for the first time in 1993.

Sole-source contracting: Under the **§ 8(a) program,** which is statutorily mandated, small SDBs can secure smaller contracts (usually less than $3 million) without open competition. This "sole sourcing" is accomplished when an agency contracts with SBA, which in turn subcontracts with the SDB.

For a company to participate in the § 8(a) program, SBA must certify that the firm is controlled and operated by **socially *and* economically disadvantaged persons.** By statute, persons from certain racial and ethnic groups . . . are presumed to be socially disadvantaged; persons are considered economically disadvantaged if they face "diminished capital and credit opportunities"—measured by asset and net-worth standards. [For a discussion and critique of the 8(a) program, see pages 34–36 in this volume.]

In FY [fiscal year] 1994, the § 8(a) program accounted for about 2.7 percent of all government procurement—about $4.9 billion. The number of certified § 8(a) firms grew from 3,673 in 1990 to 5,833 in 1994, of which 47 percent received contract actions.

Once a firm is certified and brought into the § 8(a) program, the 1987 amendments to the statute establish both a "graduation" period of nine years and a requirement that, over time, firms achieve an increasing mix of business from outside the § 8(a) program and outside federal contracting.[13] Under the [first Bush] Administration, the SBA did not aggressively implement these 1987 statutory changes, but it has now done so. Moreover, in recent years there has been increasing emphasis on using competition among [§] 8(a) and SDB firms rather than sole-source procurements.

Bid price preferences: Procurement reforms enacted by Congress last year [1994] authorize government-wide use of the 10 percent bid preference for SDBs which previously was a tool available primarily at DOD [Department of Defense] (the so-called "§1207 program"—see below). . . . These regulations could have a significant effect on procurement by SDBs in those agencies that do not use an effective set-aside scheme such as DOD's "rule of two," described below.

Agency-Specific Efforts

Department of Defense: In addition to participating in the goal-setting and § 8(a) efforts, DOD has two additional efforts, which are significant because DOD executes roughly two-thirds by amount of all federal prime contracts. These additional programs are part of DOD's effort to meet its share of the government-wide goals mentioned above.

SDB shelters or rule-of-two set-asides: Contracting officers are authorized to limit bidding on a particular contract to small disadvantaged businesses (SDBs) if two or more such firms are potential bidders and the officer determines the prevailing bid will likely be within 10 percent of the fair market price.

SDB 10 percent bid preferences: Whenever there is full and open competition and procurement is based on price factors alone, contracting officers nationally add 10 percent to the price of *non-SDB* bidders, and then award the contract on the basis of the revised bids. (This is the "§ 1207" program. Although the applicable statute merely makes this tool *available* to DOD as a means of achieving its contracting goals, the Department's procurement regulations mandate its use.)[14]

Comparative usefulness of tools: Over 60 percent of DOD's contracting with SDBs occurs through either this "rule of two" set-aside or through the § 8(a) program; the 10 percent bid price preference has been little-used in recent years because regulations require that the "rule of two" be used whenever possible, as it generally is.

Department of Transportation [DOT]: In addition to participating in the goal-setting and § 8(a) efforts, DOT manages an effort to encourage business with minority-*and* women-owned firms through its grants to state and local entities.[15]

Subcontracting preferences: In addition to setting goals for subcontracting with women- and minority-owned firms, DOT requires that grant recipients (usually state or local authorities) provide an additional payment to contractors who attain certain levels of contracting with women- or minority-owned subcontractors and who provide certain technical assistance to those subcontractors. The payment is designed to compensate the prime contractor for additional costs for assisting the subcontractors. This compensation incentive is up to 1.5 to 2.0 percent of the total contract.[16]

Graduation from sheltered competition: Unlike the § 8(a) program, the DOD and DOT programs do not require that firms graduate from preferences, or that firms have a mix of federal procurement and other business. There is, of course, the "natural" graduation which occurs if a firm becomes bigger than the "small" business size standard established by the Small Business Act, or the owner's wealth rises above the applicable threshold.[17]

Certification of eligibility[:] [I]n these programs [the certification process] differs from SBA's certification for participation in the government-wide § 8(a) program. In the DOD programs, the firms self-certify that they are qualified; in the DOT program, the state/local grant recipient is responsible for certifying the subcontractor's status.[18]

Complementary Programs: Technical & Other Assistance

A number of agencies have other programs to assist women- and minority-owned firms seeking procurement opportunities. These include:

SBA maintains several programs that serve small businesses generally, by providing technical assistance, loan guarantees, and equity capital through Small Business Investment Companies (SBICs).

The Minority Business Development Administration (MBDA) at [The Department of] Commerce provides technical assistance and support for women- and minority-owned firms.

Several agencies maintain *"Mentor-Protégé"* programs which encourage majority firms to advise and nurture new and growing minority-owned firms by providing managerial and technical assistance.

SBA's Surety Bond Program provides up to a 90 percent guarantee for bonds required of contractors and subcontractors on many public and private construction contracts, thereby lowering the small firm's cost of doing business. In FY 1994, SBA approved more than 22,000 bid bond guarantees, resulting in 6,591 final bonds, for a total bond guarantee amount of $1.08 billion. Although this program is not specifically targeted, 24 percent of bonds went to minority firms; nearly half of these were African-American, and one-quarter were Hispanic. . . .

Authors' Note[19]: Mending Affirmative Action and the Clinton Administration

In 1995, the Supreme Court—in *Adarand v. Peña*[20]—subjected racial/ethnic affirmative action to the highest standard of judicial review: strict scrutiny. (Discussed at pages 70–79 below.) Following the opinion, President Clinton announced his policy of mending not ending affirmative action, a mending that would conform to the dictates of *Adarand*.[21] A major initiative here was announced in mid-1998, and was to be phased in during the last years of the administration. This policy concerned the much-criticized federal procurement efforts affecting Small Disadvantaged Businesses described in the report just excerpted. The administration remained strident in its defense of affirmative action for Minority Business Enterprises (MBEs) which have been very heavily represented in SDB undertakings.[22] (For a critique of MBE programs, see pages 34–36 below.) The administration argued that government had a *compelling* interest in ameliorating America's systemic discrimination that had hobbled minorities and minority enterprise. But there was a constitutional requirement enunciated in *Adarand* to narrowly target affirmative assistance to those situations where there was evidence that MBEs had suffered from discrimination.

To that end, the administration inaugurated a "benchmark" policy involving the determination of minority business *capacity* (as gauged by factors like size and age) in an extensive array of industries providing goods and services to the federal government. Minority capacity was to be measured against governmental *utilization* of that capacity in terms of dollars expended for their services. Where a significant discrepancy existed between capacity and utilization in a particular industry, MBEs were to be granted "price evaluation credits" of 10%, that is, MBE bids were to be considered 10% lower than those actually submitted for the purpose of boosting their competitiveness. Thus, MBEs were slated to get a bid-boost in the electronic equipment field (where minority firms received 1.2% of federal contracts although they held 7.6% of that industry in terms of their capacity); and the wholesale durable goods sector (where minority capacity was 33.1%, and utilization 26.6%). There was no appreciable discrimination in a number of industries including food processing, social services, and management consulting. Firms controlled by members of minority groups were presumed to be socially disadvantaged in the Clinton program if "underutilized." But MBE owners— to be eligible for benchmark credits—had to demonstrate economic disadvantage, which involved a "wealth cap," net worth requirement of $750,000 excluding business and home equity. (For further discussion of group eligibility for affirmative action, see pages 34–38 below.)

The benchmark system was to *guide* federal administrators. Flexibility and administrative discretion were assured. Where "price-credits" failed to end underutilization, set-asides could be reinstituted. Further, a number of agencies were not subject to the "price-credit" system. For example, the Small Business Administration was still to employ the above-described "sole-source" contracting procedure. Likewise, federal grant-in-aid recipients like states and localities were exempt from required benchmark use.

The following includes other affirmative action changes made during the Clinton years: The Department of Defense Rule of Two was rescinded (see the Department of Defense procurement policy just discussed); the Federal Communications Commission promised not to consider minority-utilization in license applications as it was charged with doing in the past; and various programs for increasing minority teachers, scientists, foreign service officers, and managers of public broadcasting stations reportedly have been, or were supposed to be, reduced in size.

Chapter Two

─❦─

The Roots of Affirmative Action, the Women's Movement, and the Groups Covered by Affirmative Action

Reconstruction and the Origins of Affirmative Action

Reconstruction's Enduring Achievement

Affirmative action first cropped up in the modern era as a theory for advancing education, work, and voting opportunities for disadvantaged minorities.[1] Affirmative action's initial agenda was to complete the task that post-Civil War Reconstruction had undertaken, but abandoned, a full century earlier, namely, the integration of America's black community into the economic and political mainstream. Affirmative action's operational concept was the achievement of nonracial civic equality—a notion that Reconstruction had inserted into our constitutional order. In this sense, affirmative action as a legal right originated in the Reconstruction era.[2]

Indeed, the inception of modern affirmative action might best be understood as a continuation or revival of Reconstruction. In the aftermath of the Civil War, as in recent history, the overriding antidiscrimination issue was whether to take "special action" in order to counteract the effects of historical discrimination. Then the specific problem was how to emancipate the slaves whom the Thirteenth Amendment had liberated in 1865. Should—the critical question was— these "freedmen" "be viewed as individuals ready to take their place as citizens and participants in the competitive marketplace, or [should] their unique historical experience oblige the federal government to take *special action* on their behalf ?"[3] After a titanic struggle with President Andrew Johnson, the Republican majority in Congress opted for a form of federal intervention based on the principle of equal citizenship.[4]

This decision was one of the most significant events in our entire constitutional history. In contemporary constitutional theory, equality is a fundamental principle of our democracy. At the moment of birth, every American-born person is deemed the equal of every other American in civil rights and obligations. It is a given that civic equality—freedom as a universal entitlement—and the right to vote are the quintessential prerequisites of American freedom.

But, it was not ever thus. In fact, it was not until Reconstruction that the seminal notion of federally protected equality for whites and blacks entered the constitutional landscape. In drafting the Constitution, the Founding Fathers "left [many] important matters ambiguous, including . . . the constitutional status of slavery, and the issue of racial criteria for citizenship."[5] During its infancy and adolescence, the new republic allowed white supremacy and a racial concept of citizenship to become its predominant institutional mode. For nominally "free" northern blacks, the antebellum years were a time of political disenfranchisement, social segregation, and severe economic privation.[6] And in the South, the plantation economy— long the epitome of institutionalized racial subordination—continued to flourish under the aegis of state "slave codes." On the eve of war, the system's four million black chattel slaves lived in legally sanctioned, servile bondage to their white owners, without personal freedom, or political democracy, and with only a much-attenuated opportunity for self-improvement.[7] In the words of the chief justice of the United States, Negro slaves and those who had slave ancestors were an "inferior" race, fit only for domination by whites, with no rights that the white man was bound to respect, and incapable of United States citizenship.[8]

To their everlasting credit, the makers of post-Civil War policy repudiated this view. In order to change the freedmen's legal status and integrate them, Congress installed civic equality as the explicit constitutional standard of citizenship.[9] The Thirteenth Amendment (1865) abolished slavery. The Fourteenth (1868) declared all American-born persons national and state citizens, and prohibited state violation of three general groupings of civil rights ("privileges and immunities," "equal protection," and "due process"). The Fifteenth (1870) prohibited federal and state violation of the right to vote "on account of race, color, or previous condition of servitude."

Congress enacted legislation to enforce the new constitutional mandates.[10] The prototypical civil rights statute of the period was the Civil Rights Act of

1866,[11] the enforcement statute for the Thirteenth Amendment that declared any American-born person a citizen, regardless of race or color; provided that all citizens were entitled to "equal protection" of laws relating to persons or property, and had equal rights to sue, testify, contract, and own property; and authorized criminal prosecution of violators acting "under color of law," namely, the officers of the states and their subdivisions. Further, the Military and Reconstruction Act of 1867[12] placed the defeated South under military occupation pending readmission to the Union, and required the former secessionist states, as the price of readmission, to enact constitutional guarantees of black suffrage and to ratify the Fourteenth Amendment.[13] By 1870, the South complied and rejoined the fold.

There is no question that Reconstruction effected permanent constitutional and political change. By coupling a national commitment to color-blind birthplace citizenship with a prohibition of invidious discrimination, it transformed the Constitution into a "vehicle through which members of vulnerable minorities could stake a claim to substantive freedom and seek protection against misconduct by all levels of government."[14] Moreover, by endowing the federal government with the power to "define and protect citizens' rights,"[15] Reconstruction laid much of the groundwork for a "vast expansion of federal legislative power over matters which had been subject to state common law rules, including the law of employment,"[16] and voting.[17] It was in the exercise of this power—strengthened, starting in the late 1930s, by the Supreme Court's very liberal reading of the national commerce power under the Constitution—that the federal government produced the civil rights laws and regulations of the 1960s that outlawed various forms of invidious racial, national origin (ethnic/ancestral), and gender discrimination in the public and private sectors. Thus, the Civil Rights Act of 1964[18] prohibited race, color, and national origin discrimination in public facilities and accommodations (Title II[19]); in activities subsidized by federal funds (Title VI[20]); and in employment (Title VII[21]). Title VII also barred sex discrimination. President Lyndon Johnson's Executive Order 11246 of 1965 (EO 11246) prohibited discrimination in government contracting and federal employment on account of race, religion, or national origin. And the Voting Rights Act of 1965[22] was structured squarely on the Fifteenth Amendment. Early dimensions of affirmative action emerged as a legal theory for applying Title VII and EO 11246, and in implementing the Voting Rights Act. A later Civil Rights Act was enacted, in 1968, to battle racial discrimination in housing.[23] These statutes, and their associated administrative regulations, attempted to further Reconstruction's historic act of expunging racism from our legal edifice. The extent to which they have eradicated its real-world effects is a different matter. In this connection, it is appropriate to glance at the other side of the Reconstruction story.

Reconstruction's Tragic Failure

For all of Reconstruction's truly monumental long-term achievements, in its own time it proved unsuccessful. The program "promise[d] that the ideal of equal citizenship would be converted into a set of enforceable legal rights."[24] The South's quick return to the Union, and a concurrent flurry of black political and entrepreneurial activity,[25] seemed to augur well. But it was not to be. When the federal occupation force was withdrawn in 1877, thereby formally terminating Reconstruction,[26] its promise had not been fulfilled. Notwithstanding their newly mandated franchise, the great mass of former slaves reverted to a status of political and economic dependency. This is considered Reconstruction's "greatest [short-term] failure."[27]

The debacle is attributable to an unusual combination of systemic policy flaws; reactionary Supreme Court rulings; the South's refusal to accept defeat; and the North's inability, or unwillingness, to stay the course. To begin, as Professor Eric Foner has shown in his great study, the scheme of Congressional Reconstruction was "an incongruous mixture of idealism and political expediency."[28] Because "most Republicans still believed the states retained rights beyond the scope of federal intervention,"[29] this potent states' rights lobby was able to impede the creation of constitutionally specific rights in the contemplated post-Civil War amendments,[30] and thus limit the national government's power to intervene directly against civil rights violations.[31] The Fourteenth and Fifteenth Amendments—the great exemplars of Reconstruction ideology—do not enumerate *specific* national rights, or otherwise challenge the states' claim of very extensive civil rights jurisdiction.[32] It may be, as some suggest, that the framers deliberately opted for rhetorical effect over legalistic precision;[33] but, if so, they paid a heavy price indeed. Not only did their vagueness invite the nineteenth-century High Court to limit racial equality (see below), but it also raised serious doubts about the significance of the federal role. Some authorities suggest that Reconstruction's true purpose was to authorize the federal government to ensure that the states enforced their own laws.[34] Thus, in Professor Michael L. Benedict's view, the framers opted to protect black rights in a way that preserved traditional states' rights as much as possible.[35]

In any case, Congressional Reconstruction suffered from a far more serious defect. The policy "made no economic provisions for the freedmen."[36] The Republicans scorned public "economic underpinning," anticipating that "once accorded equal rights, the freedmen would find their social level and assume responsibility for their own fate."[37] This self-help scenario combined two elements. First, the then prevailing "free labor" model of *equal opportunity*: "a classless utopia [in which] . . . industrious and frugal laborers could save money, purchase their own homes, and eventually acquire a farm or shop, thereby escaping the status of wage labor and assimilating into the republic of property holders."[38] Second, the sovereign power of the franchise. In Reconstruction theory, the right to vote *by itself* would enable the freedmen to market their occupational and vocational skills, and by diligent labor become independent, productive, self-respecting citizens and property holders.[39] Moreover, exercise of the franchise over time would ensure acquisition of self-sufficiency within the federal system.[40] In short, what Reconstruction's version of equal opportunity offered the freedmen focused upon a guarantee of political, but not economic autonomy.

In the end, neither was forthcoming. The prospect of political emancipation, seemingly at hand when the freedmen gained the vote, was a mirage. The newly enfranchised freedmen came to be excluded from effective political activity by violence, fraud, and "structural discrimination" (poll taxes, literacy tests, gerrymanders, etc.).[41] By the turn of the century, their incipient political strength was neutralized, thanks in no small measure to the lack of timely northern intervention.[42]

In addition, most of the former slaves never enjoyed any true employment or entrepreneurial opportunity, and for this the blame belongs equally to the North and the South. The "vast majority" of blacks emerged from slavery without the resources for acquiring land, "confronting a white community united in the refusal to advance credit or sell them property."[43] They yearned for economic independence,[44] but they got little long-term assistance from their erstwhile liberators. Indeed the architects of Reconstruction forfeited virtually every chance to help the freedmen become self-sufficient. For example, in 1867 Congress reneged on a wartime promise to settle the slaves on occupied Confederate land.[45]

Most freedmen were accordingly compelled to "enter . . . the world of free labor as wage or share workers on land owned by whites,"[46] under conditions dictated by their employers (often their former owners), and without bargaining rights or government protection.[47] In other words, the economic posture of the "emancipated" plantation slaves did not essentially change.[48] The fact that they were barred, on account of their race, from applying their considerable skills as craftsmen, farmers, and domestics in the open market[49] was proof positive of Reconstruction's failure.

The End of Reconstruction

Reconstruction's goal was to "give the Negroes [full citizenship, i.e.,] civil rights and the ballot, and get white men accustomed to treating Negroes as equals, at least politically and legally . . . in effect, to revolutionize the relations of the two races."[50] By 1877, however, the country was in full "political and judicial retreat" from this goal.[51] And later in the century, it was apparent that the "program" had collapsed. Beyond the grant of citizenship and the paper right to vote, *none* of Reconstruction's equal opportunity goals had been achieved. No independent black workforce or property-holding class had come into being. On the contrary, the great mass of former slaves remained an impoverished, dependent, and disenfranchised rural proletariat. To be sure, they were now U.S. citizens; but this citizenship was legally unequal, due to the Supreme Court's myopic acknowledgment of it.[52]

For the North as well as the South, the great tragedy was not so much that a bold experiment in racial politics had failed, but that, notwithstanding the terrible carnage of the War, the time-hallowed primacy of racial subordination in our culture had been decisively reconfirmed. Racialization of the nation as a whole was well under way, on a hitherto unseen scale, and with retrograde cultural and political consequences that have persisted to this day.[53]

White Supremacy and the Origins of Disparate Impact

Definitions

The eye of the storm over affirmative action is the doctrine of *disparate impact*. This is the sophisticated, conceptual model of discrimination on which affirmative action is centrally based. Disparate-impact theory demands legal relief for the effects of societal bias on groups; the contrasting common law theory of *disparate treatment* restricts legal liability to cases of intentional discrimination against specific individuals. The contrast is most clearly visible in the area of legal proof. *Disparate impact* insists that (1) proof of discriminatory intent, and identification of victims, both requisite at common law, is *unnecessary* in cases of alleged group discrimination; (2) such allegations can be sustained by statistical demonstration that the complaining group has suffered from societal bias; (3) given such demonstration, compensatory remedies are in order for members of the impacted group solely on the basis of their membership; and (4) employers and governing officials who do not take "good faith" steps, or other mandated requirements to remove the effects of disparate-impact discrimination, may be responsible for violating antidiscrimination laws.[54]

Affirmative action's disparate-impact pillar has been under heavy fire from the moment of its advent in the 1950s. Detractors claim that the notions of group rights and compensatory relief (*equal results*) are unconstitutional, illegal, immoral, unfair, and counterproductive.[55] Proponents rebut these claims and assert that affirmative action is the only way to the "Promised Land."[56] The various manifestations of this controversy are treated throughout this volume.

Here we deal with disparate impact's historical source. We believe that the plight of the black community during the peak period of white supremacy dramatically illustrates the invidiously systemic bias that affirmative action was designed to correct.

The Apotheosis of White Supremacy

The nation's "retreat" from Reconstruction began even before its official demise, and was completed during the 1890s.[57] By the turn of the century, "the ideals of color-blind citizenship and freedom as a universal entitlement had been repudiated."[58] Through a stream of rulings that culminated in the legendary *Plessy v. Ferguson* decision in 1896, the Supreme Court had displaced equality before the law for blacks with protection of corporate interests ("liberty of contract") as the basis for interpreting the Fourteenth Amendment.[59]

Plessy v. Ferguson is more than a century old, but remains one of the most controversial decisions in civil rights law. In this case involving state-mandated racial segregation of railroad passenger cars (a Jim Crow commonplace), the Court decided that the equal protection clause does not outlaw segregation that equalizes separate facilities or services. The majority said that the equal protection clause "was undoubtedly [intended] to enforce the absolute equality of the two races before the law, but in the nature of things it could not have been intended to abolish distinctions based on color."[60] This celebrated statement of the "separate but equal" thesis evoked an equally famous rebuttal by Justice Harlan, whose dissent argued that segregation is discriminatory per se, because the Constitution is "color-blind, and neither knows nor tolerates classes among citizens."[61]

The majority's decision in *Plessy* conformed with a long line of cases in which the nineteenth-century High Court dampened Reconstruction's civil rights ideology: (1) The *Slaughterhouse Cases* (1873)[62]—held that the privileges and immunities protected by the Fourteenth Amendment do not include the "fundamental rights of citizenship," since these derive solely from the states. (2) *U.S. v. Cruikshank* (1876)[63] and *U.S. v. Reese* (1876)[64]—held that the Fifteenth Amendment does not confer a right to vote enforceable by criminal sanctions, but only "exemption" from discrimination in the exercise of that right under state law. (3) Jury cases—so long as the exclusion of blacks from juries was not "open"—that is, not governmentally mandated— the equal protection clause is not breached by de facto exclusion of blacks from jury service (See *Virginia v. Rives* [1880]).[65] However, jury exclusion officially imposed by government was unconstitutional (See *Strauder v. West Virginia* [1880]).[66] (4) The *Civil Rights Cases* (1883)[67]—held that the Civil Rights Act of 1875, desegregating privately owned public accommodations, violated the reservation of nondelegated powers to the states under the Tenth Amendment.[68] The Fourteenth Amendment, which authorized that statute, applied only to *state* and not *private* action.

Plessy was overruled by the High Court in the *Brown v. Board of Education* school segregation case in 1954.[69] Nonetheless, *Plessy* not only raised the most profound analytical questions about the meaning of "equality," but it also framed the unresolved civil rights disputes of our time. Some consider it a "betrayal" of our ideals, but, given the "vagueness" of the great amendments, one is tempted to wonder whether such demonizing begs the question.[70] In any case, the segregation thesis (i.e., that the races are "better off" apart) is still powerful, and it would be rash to discount the possibility that *Plessy* may yet rise from the dead and once again become the law of the land.

Reconstruction's erosion went far beyond the realm of constitutional law.[71] Suffice it to say that the "polity and economy were more thoroughly racialized at the dawn of the twentieth century than at any other point in American history,"[72] and remained in that condition through the end of World War II.[73] It is an astonishing fact that an obsession with the superiority of whiteness helped define America for the seventy-five odd years during which it passed from the ghastly bloodletting of the Civil War through the convulsions of capitalist industrialization and the Armageddons of world war and economic depression, and became a troubled racial melting pot.

Jim Crow

In the post-Reconstruction South, white supremacy was practiced in the form of a quasi-religious, state-mandated caste system. The credo of the system was the thoroughgoing degradation of the black man, the annihilation of his personal autonomy. In Professor Leon F. Litwack's apt summary, "To maintain and underscore its absolute supremacy, the white South systematically disenfranchised black men, imposed rigid patterns of racial segregation, manipulated the judicial system and sustained extraordinary levels of violence and brutality."[74]

These practices produced the classic forms of disparate impact. For example, because of educational segregation, generations of blacks were either illiterate or grossly undereducated, by comparison to their white counterparts. As a result of this socially imposed racial disparity, blacks as a class were frequently deprived of the right to vote, or the opportunity of finding desirable employment. Societal discrimination against blacks as a group was endemic in employment, education, voting, housing, administration of justice, and access to public facilities. It was in the areas of voting and employment that the Supreme Court, for the first time, accepted the notion of disparate-impact remediation for group discrimination.[75] And disparate-impact theory remained the main vehicle for affirmative action.

The Great Migration

Disparate-impact discrimination has by no means been confined to the South. The post-World War II industrial boom inspired a wave of black migration to the urban centers of the North and Midwest that reached flood tide in the 1950s.[76] This was a period of massive social change for some two million black citizens, and the migration provided them with a higher standard of living and greater recognition of their civil rights. Nonetheless, barriers resulting from systemic racism prevailed throughout the nation. It should be emphasized that race discrimination was a fixture in the North long before the Civil War. The tremendous influx of southern blacks in the twentieth century touched off an explosion of racial exclusion. For much of this century, northern urban blacks were routinely excluded from higher-status jobs and training by racist employers and labor unions. Because of limited resources, they were unable to establish a significant number of small businesses.[77] Like their brethren in the South, they were often confined to inferior segregated schools and housing. The black influx produced an exodus of whites and good jobs. The central cities, inhabited, in large measure, by low-paid or unemployed blacks, developed the symptoms that have blossomed into the urban crisis of our own time: concentrated poverty and welfare dependency; dysfunctional families; drug addiction and high crime rates; inadequate health care and sanitation; inferior housing and education; and exploitative retail services.[78]

The Legacy of White Supremacy

Disparate impact's discrimination curse has not been limited to slaves' descendants; women and various nonblack minorities, too, have long suffered its "whips and scorns."[79] But it is undisputable that the black community's experience in discrimination's sad history was especially tragic.[80] In the words of a respected authority:

> [A]fter emancipation, as before the ending of slavery, the role of the black population remained different and separate from that of the rest of the population. . . . Unlike other groups the range of employment opportunities available to the black labor force was narrowly constrained. Freedom for African Americans therefore was subject to many more obstacles than . . . for other population subgroups. . . . [W]hile a free market ideology in principle is color-blind, the denial of employment to African Americans in the North and the denial of full legal and civil rights in the South was the dominant reality experienced by the black population.[81]

In chapter 3, we will show that the original formulation of employment affirmative action policy was predicated on the disproportionate effects of white supremacy on the black population.

The Women's Movement: The First and Second "Waves"

It is a truism to note that minority and nonminority women have also been subjugated by unique disparate-impact limitations. The cultural dominance of patriarchal thinking in our society served to pressure females into family-maintenance undertakings, while greatly limiting their presence in the arts and sciences. The vast world of high and low jobs was left to be filled primarily by males.[82] Restrictions on females were staples of nineteenth-century law that regarded married women as "civilly dead," to use the language of that era's feminist movement.[83] The common law of that time considered spouses to be one, and that *one* was the husband. On their own, married women could not contract, own, and will property, or acquire guardianship over their children after divorce.[84] Exemplifying gender shackles was the prohibition on the right to vote.

Historians locate the inaugural of America's "first-wave" women's-rights movement in the 1840s when it focused on equalization of legal treatment. Some feminists of that day went further by urging that females be allowed and encouraged to pursue careers other than homemaking and child rearing— a theme much trumpeted in feminism's "second wave" starting in the 1960s.[85]

In antebellum times, feminists served as "foot soldiers" for abolitionism, among other reasons, because freeing the slaves, it was thought, would help release women from their subordinate status. But females reaped few benefits, since "Reconstruction left the law of marriage and conventions of gender relations largely intact."[86]

Between the 1870s and 1920, feminist activism was roughly bifurcated: the single-issue "suffragists" who committed themselves almost solely to obtaining the vote; and the "social feminists" who (in addition to suffrage) were interested in social welfare reform, including protecting working females against exploitation.[87] While the suffragists were successful in removing gender barriers to voting in public elections through the Nineteenth Amendment's ban on using sex to deny or abridge the right to vote, social feminists helped persuade the state legislatures to enact laws for women workers establishing minimum wages and maximum hours; excluding them from dangerous work (e.g., mining and foundry positions); and requiring that they be given rest periods at the workplace.[88]

After the 1920 ratification of the Nineteenth Amendment, feminist fervor dissolved, leaving the movement largely moribund until the 1960s[89]—

apparently, in part, a case of all passion spent after the vehement battle for the vote. The absence of zealotry did not end disputes among women's organizations. Those peopled by the higher-income and college-educated tended to support earlier versions of the Equal Rights Amendment that would have attempted to constitutionally impose strict gender equality. Groups championing lower-income females opposed such equalization, fearing the undermining of the protective-labor codes.[90]

While feminism slept, the black rights cause—feeding on common grievances, and driven by an ideology that improvement was both essential and achievable—grew increasingly restive and robust. One result was the fusillade of 1960s rights legislation. The very robustness of the African-American movement helped spark the birth of "second-wave" feminism.[91] Of course, there were other reasons for the renaissance, including the writing of Betty Friedan, and the "consciousness-raising" efforts of groups like the National Organization of Women (NOW) which—at its inception—was headed by Friedan.[92] Some central points in Friedan's thinking are summarized in the following excerpt from her earlier "second-wave" writing:

> Thanks to the early feminists, we who have mounted the second stage of the feminist revolution have grown up with the right to vote, . . . with the right to higher education and to employment, and with some, not all, of the legal right to equality . . . [But] even those of us who have managed to achieve a precarious success in a given field still walk as freaks in "man's world" since every profession—politics, the church, teaching—is still structured as man's world . . . Women, almost too visible as sex objects in this country today, are at the same time invisible people. As the Negro was the invisible man, so women are the invisible people in America today. To be taken seriously as people, women have to share in the decisions of government, of politics, of the church—not just to cook the church supper, but to preach the sermon; not just to look up the zip codes and address the envelopes, but to make the political decisions; not just to do the housework of industry, but to make some of the executive decisions . . . If we are going to address ourselves to the need for changing the social institutions that will permit women to be free and equal individuals, participating actively in their society and changing that society—with men—then we must talk in terms of what is possible, and not accept what is as what must be . . . We need not accept marriage as it's currently structured with the implicit idea of man, the breadwinner, and woman, the housewife. There are many different ways we could posit marriage. To enable *all* women, not just the exceptional few, to participate in society we must confront the fact of life . . . that women do give birth to children. But we must challenge the idea that a woman is primarily responsible for raising children. Man and society have to be

educated to accept their responsibility for that role as well . . . If more than a very few women are to enjoy equality, we have an absolute responsibility to get serious political priority for childcare centres, to make it possible for women not to have to bow out of society for ten or fifteen years when they have children. Or else we are going to be talking of equal opportunities for a few.[93]

In chapter 3, at page 51, we contrast the black and feminist attitudes toward affirmative action.

Which Groups Should Be Eligible for Affirmative Action Benefits?

The scope of affirmative action's coverage is the subject of persistent controversy. Since its inception in the mid-1950s as a remedy for discrimination against blacks, many of its programs have come to include women and a number of diverse racial and ethnic "minorities." Some critics maintain that the expanded coverage has been "overinclusive," that is, many of its beneficiaries were not disparately impacted or disadvantaged, and hence not eligible to participate under a fairly administered, equal opportunity standard.[94]

George R. La Noue and John C. Sullivan (cited here as L/S) have forcefully stated the overinclusion critique in their recent reviews of presumptive-eligibility determinations under federal "minority business enterprises" (MBE) programs.[95] In essence, these statutory programs set aside lucrative procurement and construction contracts for the benefit of firms owned by members of "socially and economically disadvantaged" groups.[96] The centerpiece of these programs is Section 8(a) of the Small Business Act,[97] which in 1978 conferred *presumptive eligibility* for such preferences on "Black Americans, Hispanic Americans, and Native Americans," and, prospectively, on *other groups* that the Small Business Administration (SBA) might designate from time to time.[98] Under current federal regulations, any citizen or legal resident who can identify with any of the following groups is presumptively eligible:

> *Black Americans; Hispanic Americans; Native Americans* (American Indians, Eskimos, Aleuts, or Native Hawaiians); *Asian-Pacific Americans* (persons with origins from Burma, Thailand, Malaysia, Indonesia, Singapore, Brunei, Japan, China [including Hong Kong], Taiwan, Laos, Cambodia [Kampuchea], Vietnam, Korea, The Philippines, U.S. Trust Territory of the Pacific Islands [Republic of Palau], Republic of the Marshall Islands, Federated States of Micronesia, The Commonwealth of Northern Mariana Islands, Guam, Samoa, Macao, Fiji, Tonga, Kiribati, Tuvalu, or Nauru); [and] *Subcontinent-Asian Americans* (persons with

origins from India, Pakistan, Bangladesh, Sri Lanka, Bhutan, the Maldives Islands, or Nepal).[99]

The exponential growth of the eligibility list reflects a series of inclusion and exclusion determinations by SBA during the 1970s and 1980s.[100] L/S assert that Congress lacked both the "political will" and the "information to draw clear cut lines of inclusion/exclusion."[101] Moreover, in their view, SBA's decisions have not been based on objective measurement of "actual discrimination" or "comparative social disadvantage,"[102] but rather on bureaucratic convenience and political pressure.[103]

L/S offer a number of particulars in support of this indictment. First, while Section 8 articulates separate "social" (racial/ethnic bias) and "economic" (income limits) components for "disadvantage,"[104] SBA considers these definitions imprecise, indeed questions whether "a precise definition is appropriate."[105] SBA accepts applicants' " 'representation' " of economic disadvantage, absent contrary evidence. In practice, the criteria of eligibility "for almost everyone are the racial and ethnic presumptions of social disadvantage."[106]

Second, SBA's inclusion decisions are not in keeping with objective socioeconomic data. Measured by the standard demographic indicators of business-formation rates, education, and income, some groups on the presumptive-eligibility list are at the socioeconomic bottom of our society, others at the top. Disparities of this kind and magnitude cannot be satisfactorily explained by any theory of discrimination or disadvantage. On the contrary, they clearly indicate unjustified overinclusiveness in preferential access to the highly prized benefits of MBE-eligibility. A prime example is the "Asian-Pacific American" category, which contains groups deriving from twenty-five different counties and enormously different cultures. According to post-1990 census regression analysis of comparative business formation rates in affirmative action and nonaffirmative action groups, Korean Americans stood at the very top of *all* groups surveyed, Laotian Americans at the very bottom, Chinese and Japanese Americans at the mean. These statistics show that treating Asian Americans as a single category is "clearly overinclusive." Similarly, in the "Hispanic-American" category, which contains distinct cultural differences between persons deriving from Spain and those from Central or Latin America, Cubans stood well above the mean in business formation, Central and Mexican Americans considerably below it.[107]

Third, there is no "principled basis" or "consistent rationale" for SBA's decisions.[108] In making racial and ethnic decisions to grant, or withhold, presumptive eligibility, the agency has not gathered any statistical data, sought any uniform measurement of educational or economic achievement, or supplied any consistent definition of group-eligibility standards.[109] The agency does not require that a presumptively eligible person has suffered discrimination by the federal government, nor does it attempt to verify whether an applicant has actually suffered any form of discrimination.[110] Although many of SBA's inclusions are attributable to lobbying by politicians and advocacy groups (e.g., the addition of the Asian-American category to the presumptive list in 1979),[111] it has not conducted periodic reviews of social disadvantage. Once a person identifies with a group that is presumptively socially disadvantaged, he will always be deemed socially disadvantaged regardless of personal achievement.[112] The agency's policy has been *under*inclusive, as well as *over*inclusive, since, from time to time, it has failed to include, or has rejected, groups whose socioeconomic profiles were not significantly different from some included groups.[113]

To L/S, the MBE program is the preeminent model for public and private sector affirmative action.[114] They conclude that SBA's administration of presumptive eligibility has been totally "political," based on racial and ethnic stereotypes that are out of touch with current demographic reality, and inconsistent with the past discrimination requirements of strict scrutiny established by the Supreme Court's opinions.[115] (These opinions are discussed at pages 70–79.) They maintain that, in modern America, *any* group measure of social disadvantage will be "crude and overinclusive"; and they call for replacement of presumptive eligibility with a policy "that targets aspiring entrepreneurs of any race or ethnicity who have endured measurable disadvantage."[116]

One need not take L/S' assault on Congress and the bureaucracy, or their disavowal of disparate impact/group remediation, or their view of strict scrutiny, at full face value in order to see that they have raised some troubling questions about race/ethnic-based affirmative action. They argue, in effect, that, as currently administered, MBE programs benefit many nondiscriminatees who have no valid claim to *any* preferences, much less presumptive entitlement. This contention cannot be dismissed out of hand. In casting doubt on the validity of group-eligibility now available to many recently arrived immigrants,[117] L/S express widespread concern over this form of overinclusiveness. No less an authority than civil rights historian Professor Hugh Davis Graham shared this concern. He argued that millions of noncitizens can participate in affirmative action, and this operates to disadvantage African Americans whose welfare was the original purpose of affirmative action. This sad situation has bred interminority conflict, and weakened affirmative action's moral imperative.[118]

L/S have made a powerful case for a complete evaluatory examination of affirmative action methodology. If SBA is out of touch with socioeconomic reality, then what of the Equal Employment Opportunities Commission (EEOC), a major progenitor of affirmative action in employment, and now its major overseer? EEOC has promoted widespread adoption of its current affirmative action guidelines that require all "users" (e.g., covered employers and unions) to maintain records by sex, and the following races and ethnic groups: blacks (Negroes); American Indians (including Alaskan

Natives); Asians (including Pacific Islanders); Hispanics (including Mexicans, Puerto Ricans, Cubans, Central or South Americans, or others of Spanish origin or culture regardless of race); and whites (Caucasians) other than Hispanic.[119] On its face, this listing appears to replicate the gross overinclusiveness which L/S found in SBA practice. The records are meant to be, and have been, an important engine of employment affirmative action by encouraging the granting of employment opportunities to "underutilized" minorities and women. (See appendixes 2 and 3 of chapter 3 for the EEOC regulations, and those of the Office of Federal Contract Compliance Programs.)

That said, other views on this matter should be considered. Writing in the mid-1990s, Professor Christopher Edley Jr. argues that the case remains strong for designating blacks, Hispanics, and Asians as protected groups.[120] "Even the comparative 'success,'" he writes, "of Japanese Americans and many immigrants from the Indian subcontinent has not immunized from discrimination those subgroups, much less the larger diverse community of Asian and Pacific Islanders."[121] Thus, none of these groups—along with recent black immigrants from the Caribbean—should be excluded. Liberal inclusiveness should guide us. "We are whom we include."[122]

Nonetheless, Edley urges careful research in order to determine how much preferential treatment should be afforded various groups. Such a study should concern itself with the following questions: Is it to be expected that a group will receive equal treatment without affirmative action? (Edley maintains, for example, that newly arrived Swedes will not be subject to discrimination, unlike Mexican immigrants.) How closely does economic need correlate with group membership? To what extent was coming to America voluntary? (Edley thinks that voluntary immigrants "have a lesser claim on our solicitude."[123])

Questions of the Edley-kind prompted his Harvard colleague—Orlando Patterson—to propose an attenuated affirmative action policy. Patterson acknowledges that affirmative action has flaws, but would nevertheless maintain protected-group preferences for the next fifteen years, phasing it out and ultimately replacing it with class-based preferences[124] "for all American-born persons from poor families."[125]

This phase out stance plainly reflects Patterson's internal struggle with the powerful pros and cons of the affirmative action controversy. On the one hand, he believes that affirmative action, because it has secured the inclusion of excluded groups, deserves major credit for black America's good fortune. Given that democracy is "quintessentially about inclusion,"[126] the circumstances argue for affirmative action's limited continuation notwithstanding its demonstrable flaws.[127] Patterson thus distances himself from the critics in this regard. He dismisses the "reverse discrimination" thesis as a "concoction,"[128] and scornfully decries the invocation of merit and color-blindness by affirmative action's detractors.[129] By the same token, however, he forthrightly acknowledges both the necessity and the difficulty of reconciling group rights and individual rights in our ideological framework that traditionally accented the latter, while the former is approached with great reluctance.[130] His final position that affirmative action is defensible only as a "medium-term" solution[131] apparently represents an attempt to chart a middle course between the extreme positions in the preferential affirmative action quarrel. The Patterson proposal then—to use an old metaphor for the predicament of a navigator trying to avoid one danger without coming too close to another—is to steer between Scylla (a mythological sea monster) and Charybdis (a mythological whirlpool).

Patterson's proposal for phasing out affirmative action in fifteen years is studded with obvious administrative and equity issues. Initially, the only eligible Hispanics would be Puerto Ricans and Mexican Americans of second or later generations. First-generation black immigrants from anywhere are ineligible *except* for diversity purposes. All Asians are to be excluded save for the Chinese descended from the pre-1923 immigration. In five years, members of families with more than an annual $75,000 income (in 1997 dollars) would no longer qualify. In ten years, only minorities and females from lower-class backgrounds would be eligible.[132] At the end of fifteen years, affirmative action would be restricted to "American-born persons from poor families."[133]

Among the significant issues in this proposal left unaddressed by Patterson are the following: What is the justification for restricting the antipoverty program to Native Americans to the presumed exclusion of naturalized citizens? Would American Indians qualify? Patterson derides chauvinism,[134] but is there not a streak of that attitude in this proposal?

Chapter Three

⟹⟸

The Career of Affirmative Action in Employment

Prologue

The antidiscrimination ferment of the 1950s and 1960s sparked a radical shift in national policy, for which the modern civil rights movement deserves a lion's share of credit.

During the nineteenth century, American blacks generally refrained from organized civil resistance, preferring to cultivate various strategies of accommodation with the white majority. An example is Booker T. Washington's "self-help" regimen through vocational education and entrepreneurship.[1]

The modern movement began early in the twentieth century with a period of interracial lobbying, litigation, and public advocacy. The flagship of this phase was the National Association for the Advancement of Colored People, formed in 1910 to combat Jim Crow. Its Legal Defense Fund scored notable antisegregation victories in the 1930s and 1940s, then planned and won the legendary antisegregation *Brown v. Board of Education* case in 1954.[2] This period also witnessed the beginnings of presidential antidiscrimination politics conducted through executive order. To avert threatened black demonstrations during the labor crisis of World War II, President Roosevelt proclaimed a new policy of nondiscrimination in federal employment and defense contracting, to be administered by a Fair Employment Practice Commission (FEPC).[3] Black protests over military segregation and exclusion from the phenomenal post-World War II boom drove President Truman to desegregate the armed forces in 1948, and brought about the creation of numerous state and local FEPCs.[4] The African-American civil rights movement became part of the Washington "Beltway" establishment in 1949 with the formation of the Leadership Conference on Civil Rights, a permanent, Washington-based coalition of

39

civil rights and labor activists.[5] These were the "little acorns" of modern civil rights reform.

The second phase of this civil rights movement was outright black insurgency, waged as Gandhiesque nonviolent civil disobedience. This was a war of protest against the iron grip of Jim Crow in the South. After the celebrated 1955 bus boycott in Montgomery, Alabama, the tactics in this war ranged from "freedom rides," voter registration drives, and "sit-ins" to massive public demonstrations in the South's major cities. Often, these were met with savage attacks by some local police, countless arrests and jail sentences, church burnings, assassinations, and race riots in the North as well as in the South. By design, or otherwise, these protests dramatized the absurdity and inhumanity of racial discrimination, and the imperative need for federal intervention. In 1963, they culminated in Martin Luther King Jr.'s bloody confrontation with the Birmingham, Alabama, police, followed by his storied march on Washington and "I Have a Dream" oration.[6]

The Shift in National Policy

In March, 1961, President Kennedy issued an Executive Order directing federal contractors to refrain from discrimination, and to "take *affirmative action* to ensure that applicants are employed and that employees are treated . . . without regard to their race, creed, color, or national origin."[7]

In June, 1963, in the wake of King's Birmingham march, Kennedy filed a bill to prohibit racial discrimination in public accommodations, education, voting, federally funded programs, and to establish a Community Relations Service for the purpose of mediating racial disputes. During hearings in the House, the Leadership Conference on Civil Rights secured insertion of a ban on employment discrimination.[8] At that point, the campaign for equal employment opportunity legislation became the focus of the drive for civil rights reform.[9]

Congressional hearings on the bill lasted for more than a year, the longest such period in our history. On July 2, 1964, under President Johnson, it was enacted as the Civil Rights Act of 1964[10] (CRA 1964) effective July 2, 1965, its Title VII provisions regarding equal employment opportunity to be administered by a newly created Equal Employment Opportunity Commission (EEOC).[11] This was our first comprehensive legislative attack on the scourge of racism in the twentieth century.[12]

By August, 1965, the pace of reform accelerated dramatically. In that month, following on the effective date of the new 1964 Civil Rights Act, Congress enacted a Voting Rights Act (VRA) that LBJ had filed only five months earlier. The Act[13] prohibited race or color-based denial of voting rights, and invalidated literacy, character, or educational tests, particularly in the South as preconditions for voting—an early example of remedial affirmative action meant to soften the disparate, historical denial of black voting rights. Responsibility for enforcing the 1965 voting law was assigned to the Office of Civil Rights in the Department of Justice. (See chapter 6 in this volume.)

In September, 1965, President Johnson reissued JFK's 1961 federal-contracting order as Executive Order 11246. This order retained Kennedy's affirmative action mandate verbatim, added a ban on sex discrimination, and assigned its administration to the Office of Federal Contract Compliance Programs (OFCCP)—what was to become the key affirmative action enforcement branch of the Department of Labor.[14] The stage was now set for the emergence of employment affirmative action as an overriding issue in a climactic war over how to administer civil rights reform.

It is customary to characterize the war as a dispute over "goals." Should the goal be to end racial discrimination, or to ensure racial equality—to equalize "opportunity," or to equalize "results"? In our view, this characterization overlooks the problems faced by the working administrators. When the bureaucracies at EEOC and OFCCP began to implement their new mandates, the problem that surfaced immediately was not defining "goals." That job had already been accomplished in the century that followed Reconstruction. In the view of the implementing bureaucrats, the disparity between blacks and whites in every walk of life was so enormous that—even by the most minimal standards of civic equality—the task of "ending" discrimination necessarily implied an obligation to ensure improvement. In other words, history had mandated the "goal" of equalizing both "opportunity" and "results." What confronted the administrators in 1965 was the daunting job of finding the right means to that end. As a general approach, they adopted the notion of race, ethnic, and gender-conscious compensatory remediation as the basis for allocating minority access to jobs, entrepreneurial opportunities, education, and electoral-procedure reform. The bureaucrats' decision won initial court approval, and touched off an ideological war over constitutionality, fairness, and effectiveness. This war is still ongoing, its outcome uncertain. Lamentably, "the unifying moral vision of civil rights" has given way to a "divisive nightmare of race."[15]

Let us now explore the equal employment opportunity (EEO) front in greater detail.

Title VII and Employment Discrimination

Title VII

Title VII, *Equal Employment Opportunity*, is a central dimension of the 1964 CRA's eleven titles, reflecting the fact that employment discrimination has always been a prime target of civil rights advocacy.[16] It has "dwarfed all the other titles combined, frequently generating a huge backlog of cases in the . . . EEOC, and leading to thousands of judicial decisions."[17] Title VII has been judicially determined to be a permissible exercise of Congress' constitutional power to regulate commerce; thus it reaches the enormous private sector labor market as well as public employment.[18]

The specific goal of this law was to eliminate the gross disparities between whites and minorities, and between men and women, in employment, income, and types of work.[19] Currently, Title VII covers most private employers with fifteen or more employees; labor unions with fifteen or more members; employment agencies; and federal, state, and local governments. Under the caption "unlawful employment practices" covered employers are forbidden to engage in the following "unfair employment practice(s)":

Section 703(a)(1)(2)

(1) to fail or refuse to hire or to discharge . . . or otherwise discriminate against any individual with respect to his compensation, terms, conditions, or privileges of employment because of race, color, religion, sex, or national origin.

(2) to limit, segregate, or classify . . . employees in any way which would deprive . . . any individual of employment opportunities or otherwise adversely affect his status as an employee because of race, color, religion, sex, or national origin.[20]

Two additional particularly controversial provisions in the Act are Sections 703(j) and 706(g):

Section 703(j)

The "no preference" clause, providing in pertinent part that:

Nothing in this title shall be interpreted to require any employer . . . [or] labor organization . . . to grant preferential treatment to any individual or to any group on account of an imbalance which may exist with respect to the total number or percentage of persons of any race, color, religion, sex, or national origin employed by any employer . . . [or] admitted to membership . . . by any labor organization . . . in comparison with the total number or percentage of persons of such race, color, religion, sex, or national origin in any community, State, section, or other area, or in the available work force in any community, State, section, or other area.[21]

Section 706(g)

This is the enforcement clause, providing in pertinent part that:

If the court finds that the respondent has intentionally engaged in an unlawful employment practice . . . the court may enjoin the respondent from engaging in such . . . practice, and order such affirmative action as may be appropriate, which may include reinstatement or hiring of employees, with or without back pay.[22]

The Genesis of Employment Affirmative Action: The EEOC and Disparate-Impact Theory

When the EEOC opened for business on July 2, 1965, it enjoyed none of the quasi-judicial prerogatives that independent regulatory agencies normally exercise. It could not conduct adversary hearings; issue cease-and-desist orders; or seek court enforcement of such orders. It did not have the right to issue and enforce substantive rules and regulations. It did not even have the right to file and prosecute lawsuits on its own initiative. The entire package of enforcement and regulatory powers had been withheld by Congress in order to secure Title VII's passage. Thus, it came to pass that, apart from limited administrative functions, the new Commission was restricted by statute to investigating, and attempting to conciliate, individual complaints.[23]

Over the years, EEOC has devoted the great bulk of its efforts to its prescribed task of treating individual complaints.[24] But it has always aspired to a role that transcended its initial statutory mandate. As Alfred W. Blumrosen, who held an important position on the early EEOC legal staff, has written, "From its inception, the EEOC attempted to develop a self-initiated program to investigate systemic discrimination independently of complaints."[25] If, as he believes, the Commission has failed to develop "an effective program" for policing systemic discrimination in this country,[26] it has not been for lack of trying. By design or otherwise, much of the thrust of the operating policies which the agency adopted in 1965 and 1966 was based on the notion that the discrimination affecting blacks was rampant (though often unconscious) in white America—in short, it was systemic. It was in these policies that EEOC planted the seeds of employment affirmative action. The following is an itemized summary of these seed-policies, and of their underlying rationale, as set out by Blumrosen in his authoritative *Modern Law* treatise:

• *Title VII, Blumrosen argues, was intended to improve the economic position of minorities in the workplace, not merely to provide "equal treatment" as a remedy for intentional discriminatory practices.*[27] The EEOC's task in interpreting Title VII was to determine the relationship between the language of the new law and the "desired alteration of existing behavior."[28] Title VII does not contain any statement of Congress' intent, nor does it define its key terms (e.g., *discrimination*) so as to permit reasonable inferences of that intent.[29] However, the legislative history of Congress' constant stress on the indicators underscoring the grossly inferior position of blacks in employment warrants the conclusion that: "In its broadest sense, the 'legislative purpose' was to improve the objective condition of minority groups, as defined by these indicators."[30]

- *Discrimination—to continue the Blumrosen thesis—under Title VII includes both adverse effects (disparate impacts) on groups and intentional maltreatment of individuals.*[31] Early on, in Blumrosen's view, EEOC developed a policy of applying the concept of "group interest" in processing individual complaints based on employer practices with group-wide impact such as seniority systems and testing. Such complaints were treated as vehicles for group remedies. What the policy targeted were the *effects* of the practices on designated minorities and females. The EEOC could have interpreted the law as requiring proof of discriminatory intent, but chose not to do so, in order to avoid the difficult task of proving intent, and to prevent employers from relying on *good intent* in restricting minority opportunities. The *effects* test is in keeping with the sense in which *discrimination* was used during the debate over the enactment of the 1964 Civil Rights Act, and is aimed at maximizing the impact of the law on industrial practices.[32]

- *Practices—the EEOC concluded—which adversely affect (have a disparate impact on) protected groups are illegal unless they can be justified.*[33]

In 1966, the EEOC initiated a national reporting system requiring covered employers, unions, and apprenticeship committees to file annual reports identifying the number of employees, union members, and apprentices by job category, and by race, sex, and national origin.[34] From the beginning, these data have been analyzed statistically in terms of the standard indicators of discrimination: relative occupational distribution, relative wage and salary income, and relative unemployment rate. Also, according to Blumrosen, from the beginning, the statistics confirmed widespread protected-group disparities of such magnitude as to compel the conclusion on the part of the EEOC that they could only have been caused by racial, ethnic, and gender discrimination. These data were used by EEOC and by other agencies in their quest for remedial action, such as the establishment of minority-hiring goals and timetables.[35] Absent justification, serious, statistically demonstrated racial, ethnic, and gender disparities, in and of themselves, were interpreted as violating Title VII and as requiring remediation.[36]

The Gospel According to Griggs

During the late 1960s, the seeds of employment affirmative action matured slowly. EEOC refined the emerging *adverse-effects/disparate-impact* doctrine by incorporating it both in guidelines for interpreting Title VII's testing provisions, and in supportive amicus briefs in court cases which it then lacked authority to prosecute on its own.[37] It worked in constant conjunction with the

Leadership Conference on Civil Rights and its affiliates, if not, as some suggest, under their virtually direct tutelage.[38]

In 1971, it all came together in *Griggs v. Duke Power Co.*[39] that "lent blanket judicial approval to"[40] EEOC's disparate-impact interpretation of Title VII. As of the Act's 1965 effective date, the defendant-employer, a large electric utility, abandoned a long-standing practice of segregating black employees in low-paying laboring jobs. But it continued to implement a policy, initiated in 1955, under which access to high-paying "white" jobs was made available to all applicants, white or black, who held high school diplomas and/or passed two professionally developed general aptitude tests. The tests were not "job-related" in the sense of the EEOC's testing guidelines.[41] The thirteen African-American plaintiffs had been hired without diplomas into segregated jobs at various dates before and after 1955; all of them claimed that the requirements were discriminatory because they made it difficult to move from segregated jobs into previously white jobs.[42] An extended excerpt from *Griggs* follows:

Griggs v. Duke Power Co., **401 U.S. 424 (1971)**

Mr. Chief Justice Burger delivered the opinion of the Court.

. . . [428] The Court of Appeals was confronted with a question of first impression, as are we, concerning the meaning of Title VII. After careful analysis a majority of that court concluded that a subjective test of the employer's intent should govern, particularly in a close case, and that in this case there was no showing of a discriminatory purpose in the adoption of the diploma and test requirements. On this basis, the Court of Appeals concluded there was no violation of the Act.

[429] The Court of Appeals reversed the District Court in part, rejecting the holding that residual discrimination arising from prior employment practices was insulated from remedial action. The Court of Appeals noted, however, that the District Court was correct in its conclusion that there was no showing of a racial purpose or invidious intent in the adoption of the high school diploma requirement or general intelligence test and that these standards had been applied fairly to whites and Negroes alike. It held that, in the absence of a discriminatory purpose, use of such requirements was permitted by the Act. In so doing, the Court of Appeals rejected the claim that because these two requirements operated to render ineligible a markedly disproportionate number of Negroes, they were unlawful under Title VII unless shown to be job related. We granted the writ on these claims.

The objective of Congress in the enactment of Title VII is plain from the language of the statute. It was to achieve equality of employment opportunities and remove [430] barriers that have operated in the past to favor an identifiable group of white employees over other employees. Under the Act, practices, procedures, or tests neutral on their face, and even neutral in terms of intent, cannot be maintained if they operate to "freeze" the status quo of prior discriminatory employment practices.

The Court of Appeals' opinion, and the partial dissent, agreed that, on the record in the present case, "whites register far better on the Company's alternative requirements" than Negroes. This consequence would appear to be directly traceable to race. Basic intelligence must have the means of articulation to manifest itself fairly in a testing process. Because they are Negroes, petitioners have long received inferior education in segregated schools and this Court expressly recognized these differences in *Gaston County v. United States,* 395 U.S. 285 (1969). There, because of the inferior education received by Negroes in North Carolina, this Court barred the institution of a literacy test for voter registration on the ground that the test would abridge the right to vote indirectly on account of race. Congress did not intend by Title VII, however, to guarantee a job to every person regardless of qualifications. In short, the Act does not command that any [431] person be hired simply because he was formerly the subject of discrimination, or because he is a member of a minority group. Discriminatory preference for any group, minority or majority, is precisely and only what Congress has proscribed. What is required by Congress is the removal of artificial, arbitrary, and unnecessary barriers to employment when the barriers operate invidiously to discriminate on the basis of racial or other impermissible classification. . . .

. . . The Act proscribes not only overt discrimination but also practices that are fair in form, but discriminatory in operation. The touchstone is business necessity. If an employment practice which operates to exclude Negroes cannot be shown to be related to job performance, the practice is prohibited.

On the record before us, neither the high school completion requirement nor the general intelligence test is shown to bear a demonstrable relationship to successful performance of the jobs for which it was used. Both were adopted, as the Court of Appeals noted, without meaningful study of their relationship to job-performance ability. Rather, a vice president of the Company testified, the requirements were instituted on the Company's judgment that they generally would improve the overall quality of the work force.

The evidence, however, shows that employees who have not completed high school or taken the tests have continued to perform satisfactorily and make progress in departments for which the high school and test criteria [432] are now used. The promotion record of present employees who would not be able to meet the new criteria thus suggests the possibility that the requirements may not be needed even for the limited purpose of preserving the avowed policy of advancement within the Company. In the context of this case, it is unnecessary to reach the question whether testing requirements that take into account capability for the next succeeding position or related future promotion might be utilized upon a showing that such long-range requirements fulfill a genuine business need. In the present case the Company has made no such showing.

The Court of Appeals held that the Company had adopted the diploma and test requirements without any "intention to discriminate against Negro employees." We do not suggest that either the District Court or the Court of Appeals erred in examining the employer's intent; but good intent or absence of discriminatory intent does not redeem employment procedures or testing mechanisms that operate as "built-in headwinds" for minority groups and are unrelated to measuring job capability.

The Company's lack of discriminatory intent is suggested by special efforts to help the undereducated employees through Company financing of two-thirds the cost of tuition for high school training. But Congress directed the thrust of the Act to the *consequences* of employment practices, not simply the motivation. More than that, Congress has placed on the employer the burden of showing that any given requirement must have a manifest relationship to the employment in question.

[433] The facts of this case demonstrate the inadequacy of broad and general testing devices as well as the infirmity of using diplomas or degrees as fixed measures of capability. History is filled with examples of men and women who rendered highly effective performance without the conventional badges of accomplishment in terms of certificates, diplomas, or degrees. Diplomas and tests are useful servants, but Congress has mandated the commonsense proposition that they are not to become masters of reality. . . .

[436] Nothing in the Act precludes the use of testing or measuring procedures; obviously they are useful. What Congress has forbidden is giving these devices and mechanisms controlling force unless they are demonstrably a reasonable measure of job performance. Congress has not commanded that the less qualified be preferred over the better qualified simply because of minority origins. Far from disparaging job qualifications as such, Congress has made such qualifications the controlling factor, so that race, religion, nationality, and sex become irrelevant. What Congress

has commanded is that any tests used must measure the person for the job and not the person in the abstract.

The judgment of the Court of Appeals is, as to that portion of the judgment appealed from, reversed.

The Supreme Court's decision in *Griggs* is a Holy Writ of affirmative action: In Blumrosen's words,

> The *Griggs* decision flows from an understanding of the legislative purpose. It constitutes a creative judicial interpretation in an area where Congress had not been clear as to the means to be used to improve the status of minorities. And it confirmed to some extent, the administrative agency judgments which sought to produce the maximum impact for the statute. . . . [T]hree different concepts of discrimination were used in *Griggs* as it worked its way through the courts. The district court applied an "intent to discriminate" concept, the court of appeals applied an "equal treatment" concept with respect to some of the black plaintiffs, and the Supreme Court developed the "adverse effect" or "disparate impact" concept.[43]

In the wake of *Griggs,* the EEOC has encouraged private employers under its jurisdiction and other "users" (like unions) to avoid costly lawsuits by using the racial, ethnic, and gender employment data they are required to keep[44] to engage in self-analysis so as to determine whether protected groups are underutilized. (The EEOC *Affirmative Action Guidelines* and its *Uniform Guidelines on Employee Selection* are excerpted in appendixes 1 and 2 of this chapter.) The employee-selection guidelines note that where an employer or other user "has not maintained data on adverse [disparate] impact, . . . Federal enforcement agencies may draw an inference of adverse impact of the [employee] selection process from the failure of the user to maintain such data, if the user has an underutilization of a group in a job category, as compared to the group's representation in the relevant labor market, or, in the case of jobs filled from within, the applicable work force."[45] The same section of the guidelines contains the "four-fifths rule": "A selection rate for any race, sex, or ethnic group which is less than four-fifths (4/5) (or eighty percent) of the rate for the group with the highest rate will generally be regarded by Federal enforcement agencies as evidence of adverse impact." Adverse impacts are excusable if *validated* as being the result of job-related criteria. EEOC's guidelines relating to the validation of "selection procedures are intended to be consistent with generally accepted professional standards for evaluating standardized tests and other procedures,"[46] such as those prepared by professional societies in psychology and education, as well as those contained in standard texts and journals in the area of personnel selection.[47]

The Office of Contract Compliance Programs—as a condition of contract maintenance—requires larger federal contractors to engage in good faith efforts to remedy minority and female underutilization if required self-analysis exhibits deficiencies. OFCCP is subject to the *Uniform Guidelines on Employee Selection* that was just noted. Its affirmative action requirements for covered service and supply contractors are excerpted in appendix 3 of this chapter.

The employers' potential liability in connection with Title VII and its associated EEOC regulations prompted these words from Justice Scalia in his *Johnson v. Transportation Agency of Santa Clara County* (1987)[48] dissent:

> This Court's prior interpretations of Title VII, especially the decision in *Griggs v. Duke Power Co.,* subject employers to a potential Title VII suit whenever there is a noticeable imbalance in the representation of minorities or women in the employer's work force. Even the employer who is confident of ultimately prevailing in such a suit must contemplate the expense and adverse publicity of a trial, because the extent of the imbalance, and the "job relatedness" of his selection criteria, are questions of fact to be explored through rebuttal and counterrebuttal of a "prima facie case" consisting of no more than the showing that the employer's selection process "selects those from the protected class at a 'significantly' lesser rate than their counterparts." If, however, employers are free to discriminate through affirmative action, without fear of "reverse discrimination" suits by their non-minority or male victims, they are offered a threshold defense against Title VII liability premised on numerical disparities. Thus, after today's decision the failure to engage in reverse discrimination is economic folly, and arguably a breach of duty to shareholders or taxpayers, wherever the cost of anticipated Title VII litigation exceeds the cost of hiring less capable (though still minimally capable) workers. . . . A statute designed to establish a color-blind and gender-blind workplace has thus been converted into a powerful engine of racism and sexism, not merely permitting intentional race-and sex-based discrimination, but often making it, through operation of the legal system, practically compelled.

Office of Federal Contract Compliance Programs and Affirmative Action

Along with the EEOC, the Office of Federal Contract Compliance Programs (OFCCP) has been a leader in the development of employment affirmative action. Under OFCCP's administration in the late 1960s (under Executive

Order [EO] 11246), affirmative action became an authentic instrument of equal employment opportunity in the notoriously racist, federally funded construction industry for the first time since the term affirmative action was used in President Kennedy's 1961 federal contracting order. The prototype of the OFCCP's expansive affirmative action efforts was the famous "Philadelphia Plan," a project that the OFCCP undertook in connection with the construction industry in the Philadelphia area in 1969, but which did not receive final approval until the Nixon Administration in 1971. Basic elements of the Plan were the establishment by the OFCCP of "goals and timetables" for hiring specific percentages of "underutilized" minorities in each building trade, depending on their availability; and a required commitment by the covered contractors to use "good faith efforts" to achieve these goals.[49]

The Philadelphia Plan was upheld in a 1971 decision by the Third Circuit that still controls.[50] The Court held that the plan was constitutional, since it was based on an appropriate administrative determination that blacks were systematically excluded from the building trades on account of their race, and since inclusion of blacks in the building trades pursuant to the plan served the public interest by providing an adequate, integrated work force. The Court also held that the plan did not violate the "no preference" provisions of Title VII (see Section 703[j] above at page 42) since it did not arise under the statute, but rather was authorized by a presidential executive order (EO 11246).

Subsequently, the goals-and-timetables approach to equal employment opportunity was extended to all federal contracting and subsidized programs. The OFCCP undertaking is the most far-reaching governmentally initiated vehicle of affirmative action in the country[51]—an exemplar of "big government." On their face, the OFCCP goals and timetables requirement (and other requirements like it such as those encouraged by the EEOC), do not mandate preferences for minorities or women. They require only that employers make "good faith" efforts to find qualified members of underutilized protected groups. However, if such good faith efforts are not evident to federal scrutinizers, the result could be a loss of federal contracts or other severe penalties. According to an Appellate Court, by treating a Federal Communications Commission affirmative action goals requirement like the one imposed by OFCCP, there is the potential of federal sanctions pressuring employers to engage in preferential treatment. The Court presented the following view:

> Nor can it be said that the Commission's parity goals do not pressure license holders to engage in race-conscious hiring. . . . It cannot be seriously argued that this [good faith scrutiny] screening device does not create a strong incentive to meet the numerical goals. No rational firm— particularly one holding a government-issued license—welcomes a

government audit. Even DOJ [Department of Justice] argued . . . that they [the goals' guidelines] operated as "a *de facto* hiring quota," and that "broadcasters, in order to avoid the inconvenience and expense of being subjected to further review, will treat the guidelines as safe-harbors. . . ." [W]e do not think it matters whether a government hiring program imposes hard quotas, soft quotas, or goals. Any one of these techniques induces an employer to hire with an eye toward meeting the numerical target. As such, they can and surely will result in individuals being granted a preference because of their race.[52]

This view was disputed by OFCCP's senior trial attorney. She points out that the Agency's regulations mandate only "good faith" efforts to achieve numerical hiring goals, and explicitly forbid "preferences" and "quotas." In her view, "goals and timetables" are "benchmarks," rather than rigid legal requirements.[53]

Title VII and Sex Discrimination

The National Organization for Women (NOW) was created to prompt EEOC to take the ban against employment sex discrimination in Title VII of the 1964 Civil Rights Act as seriously as that Title's ban against race discrimination. But as the EEOC was pursuing the acceptance of disparate-impact affirmative action for African Americans, its initial regulations permitted state-protective legislation for women in the workplace (e.g., mandatory rest periods and exclusion from dangerous work), and even gender-specific job advertisements. Lobbied by the burgeoning corps of "second-wave" feminists, the Agency quickly shifted its regulatory gears, determining that the aforementioned gender bias ran afoul of Title VII.[54]

By the later 1960s, the feminist forces had resolved their old-time differences over "equal rights" versus "special protection," in favor of a sex-blind version of the former. Concurrently, however, the black movement was moving from an equal rights, color-blind posture to one which emphasized affirmative action's race consciousness in hiring, educational opportunities, and the like—all for the achievement of "equal results." Thus, feminists did not march in lockstep with the African-American civil rights movement.[55] But this soon changed. Women came to be classified as a protected group. In an early turnabout, feminist groups became vociferous advocates of affirmative action for women, and women soon gained a firm footing in the affirmative action mosaic.[56] Perhaps this reversal helps explain the defeat of the Equal Rights Amendment in 1982. As submitted to the states in 1972, its first section read: "Equality of rights under the law shall not be denied or abridged by the United States or by any State on account of sex."[57]

The Midcareer of Employment Affirmative Action

A Parting of the Ways

A case can be made that 1971 was about the time the war over employment affirmative action began, at least in the sense of providing the casus belli. Disparate-impact analysis was now an approved instrument of equal employment opportunity policy. Goals and timetables, to affirmative action's friends, seemed to be a way to promote aggressive hiring of females and other protected-group members without going against the American grain. The inner logic of both disparate impact and goals/timetables implied the need to use overt race-ethnic-gender-conscious devices to cure evils of the historical and societal oppression of minorities and women. In short, the seeds of affirmative action had begun to mature.

The champions of reform saw this development as an opportunity to move the country away from the ominous racial divide that had been revealed by the urban riots of the late 1960s.[58] Others, however, viewed it with profound alarm. In their eyes, the emergence of disparate-impact theory and goals/timetables signaled the beginning of an "inner transformation of the civil rights vision," from "nondiscrimination" as required by Title VII to "preferential treatment for minorities."[59] As the traditionalists saw it, the logic of preference was that

> employment discrimination should be defined and attacked statistically as a differential, rather than traditionally as an invidious and injurious act of prejudice. Its measure was simply the gap between white and minority employment rates. This presumptive new definition in turn rested on an implicit normative theory of proportional representation in the workforce.[60]

The upshot, so the old school concluded, was no less than that "by the early 1970s the legal majesty of the American state once again, as it had in the segregationist era between *Plessy* [*v. Ferguson* (1896)] and *Brown* [*v. Board of Education* (1954)], ordained that citizens who had wronged no one must be denied important rights and benefits because of genetic attributes like the color of their skin."[61]

Plainly, an ideological war over quotas and reverse discrimination was in the offing. The first skirmish took place in 1972 when the opponents of goals and timetables attempted—and failed—to amend the "no preference" clause in Title VII by inserting an explicit prohibition of *"discrimination in reverse"* through use of "fixed or variable numbers, proportions, percentages, quotas, goals, or ranges."[62] In addition to rejecting the proposed amendment, Congress extended Title VII's coverage to federal and state employees, and granted EEOC power to sue private employers.[63] From that point it was relatively clear sailing for affirmative action until the late 1980s.

There is little quarrel in the employment arena about remedies for disparate treatment (intentional discrimination affecting individuals), and these remedies have at times been dubbed "affirmative action." Thus, Section 706(g) of the 1964 Civil Rights Act reads: "If the court finds that the respondent has intentionally engaged in or is intentionally engaging in an unlawful employment practice . . . the court may enjoin . . . such unlawful employment practice, and order such *affirmative action* as may be appropriate."[64]

However, the battle over affirmative action largely concerns disparate-impact remedies. The principle of affirmative action as a remedy for disparate impact posits that, by its very nature, systemic bias against protected groups requires a cure that goes "beyond compensation to individuals for direct individual injury"[65]—which remedy is provided by disparate-treatment law. To the advocates of disparate-impact remediation, the injury that systemic bias produces is a congenital handicap that every member of the impacted group inherits at the moment of birth, namely, an inability to compete deriving solely from the immutable fact of minority/gender status. It is both necessary and desirable that race, national-origin, or gender-based disadvantage be redressed by a compensatory grant of race, ethnic, or gender-based advantage, irrespective of whether intentional wrongdoing can be proven in law. "Special help" to be sure, but only as a benign offset to unfair detriment, not as a substitute for qualification, or as a predeterminant of outcomes. Since, moreover, disparate impact is a function of group membership, the remedial compensation must be available to every group member, regardless of the harm suffered by that member.

In theory, then, affirmative action is not an end in itself, but a tool for ensuring equitable distribution of America's bounty. Disparate-impact thinking has given rise to court-ordered and voluntary public and private plans meant to remedy the socially undesirable, disparate conditions affecting protected groups. Since the enactment of the 1991 Civil Rights Act,[66] remediation of disparate impact by affirmative action has been authorized by statute. Let us now consider what the Supreme Court has said about affirmative action, recognizing that its constitutional rulings as of late have triggered a *nonremedial* approach to affirmative action referred to as *diversity* theory. Remedial affirmative action is meant to correct a legal wrong; nonremedial affirmative action seeks diversity. These functions are analytically distinct, although in practice they often merge. Take, for example, a hypothetical voluntary plan for preferentially admitting blacks to a university from which they have previously been excluded as a matter of policy. This plan would be denominated "remedial" affirmative action, since it deals with the effects of conduct which, in litigation, would likely be found illegal. On the other hand, if black "underrepresentation" in the student body is not attributable to racist policy or practice, the plan would fall under the heading of "nonremedial" affirmative action. In recent years, resort to nonremedial affirmative action has surged in the areas of employment and education, based on the claimed need to enrich society by greater inclusion of disadvantaged, and nondisadvantaged minorities.[67] This so-called *diversity* rationale has yet to gain popular approval or Supreme Court sanction.

Affirmative Action and the Supreme Court: The 1970s and 1980s

During the 1970s and 1980s, one main theater of operations in the "reverse-discrimination war" was the Supreme Court of the United States. Between 1978 and 1987, the Court decided a number of affirmative action cases. All were split decisions, often without majority support for the reasoning upholding the decisions, and with sharp differences among the justices. It is no wonder that this was so, given the novelty and difficulty of the issues, including: Is affirmative action a legitimate remedy? Should the burden of the remedy be imposed on innocent third parties? Is affirmative action compatible with the equal protection clause of the Fourteenth Amendment? Are quotas permissible under law? In terms of Title VII, key questions included how to interpret Sections 703(j) and 706(g). The former forbade *requiring* employers or labor unions to grant preferential treatment to any group for the purpose of correcting racial/sexual/ethnic imbalances. The latter concerned the nature of judicial power to correct intentional discrimination. (For the critical texts of Title VII, see above at pages 42–43.)

At the constitutional level, the critical constitutional dispute has been whether equal protection scrutiny of governmental action should be "midtier" (intermediate) or "strict." To survive midtier review, an affirmative action program must serve an *important* government interest, and employ means that are *substantially related* to that governmental end. On the other hand, strict scrutiny requires a *compelling* governmental interest, and means that are *narrowly tailored* to achieve that compelling interest. After years of inconclusive Supreme Court debate as to the merits of midtier versus strict judicial review, strict scrutiny was adopted by the High Court for racial/ethnic-governmental classifications, first for state government in *Richmond v. Croson* (1989),[68] and later for the federal government in *Adarand Contractors Inc. v. Peña* (1995).[69]

The following is a summary of the Court's decisions, during this period of the 1970s and 1980s, preceded by an italicized statement of key points made by them.

1.

Voluntary public affirmative action programs are not unconstitutional per se, but must undergo rigorous judicial review. State universities may consider race as a factor in admissions procedures, provided that no person may be excluded from consideration on grounds of racial or ethnic status.

Regents v. Bakke (1978)[70] was the Supreme Court's first attempt to define the standard of judicial review of voluntary public affirmative action. This case arose from a decision by a state university's medical school faculty to reserve sixteen of the one hundred entering class seats for qualified African, Hispanic, Asian, and Native-American applicants. Several black admittees scored lower on the standard Medical College Admission Test than some rejected whites, including Bakke, the plaintiff. Bakke claimed a violation of the equal protection clause and Title VI of the 1964 Civil Rights Act,[71] contending that he would have been admitted if not for the set-aside. This is the classic "reverse-discrimination" claim: illegal and unfair race-based exclusion of a qualified, innocent third party from an important benefit in favor of a less-qualified minority. The university contended that its admission policy was justified as a remedy for past "societal discrimination," and as an attempt to obtain the educational benefits that flow from an ethnically diverse student body.[72] By different 5–4 majorities, in each of which Justice Powell cast the controlling vote, the High Court affirmed the lower court's order directing that Bakke be admitted and invalidating the university's admission policy, but reversed its order enjoining the university from considering race as a factor in future admissions decisions.[73]

Four members (Stevens, joined by Burger, Stewart, and Rehnquist) held that whether race can ever be used as a factor in an admission decision, was not an issue before the Court;[74] Bakke's rejection on account of his race violated the "plain language" of Title VI;[75] and the lower court's judgment should be affirmed to the extent that it ordered Bakke's admission.[76]

Four other Justices (Brennan, Marshall, White, and Blackmun) held that the set-aside was constitutional, and therefore the lower court's judgment should be reversed in all respects:[77] Subject to the equal protection clause of the Fourteenth Amendment, Title VI does not bar preferential treatment of racial minorities as a means of remedying past societal discrimination;[78] racial classifications are not per se invalid under the Fourteenth Amendment;[79] this case is distinguishable from cases of invidious discrimination that are subject to strict scrutiny, since the set-aside does not stigmatize or disfavor any discrete group, but operates only for the purpose of helping disadvantaged minorities;[80] for such benign remedial racial classifications, the appropriate standard of review is intermediate scrutiny, which inquires whether the state has demonstrated an "important" purpose, and has used means that are "substantially" related to such purpose;[81] and the set-aside satisfied these requirements, since it reasonably addressed the important educational problem of correcting the societally discriminatory underrepresentation of minorities at the medical school.[82]

Justice Powell agreed with the Brennan plurality that the equal protection clause controlled and did not bar race-conscious remediation; therefore he voted with them to reverse the injunction of any future consideration of race for admissions.[83] However, he rejected their intermediate-scrutiny standard, opting instead for "the most exacting judicial examination." He concluded that the set-aside violated equal protection. Accordingly, he voted with the Stevens plurality to order Bakke admitted.[84]

Bakke decided only that a state university that receives federal funds may consider race as one factor, among others, in its admissions procedure, provided that it does not exclude any applicant from consideration on racial or ethnic grounds. Beyond that the decision sheds little light on the race-ethnic-gender-based preferences in employment, contracting, and voting that have engendered so much polarized controversy. Still, it remains a landmark case. It clearly enunciated the principle that the Constitution sanctions some forms of protected-group preference. And it previewed the main themes of the ensuing affirmative action controversy, in particular, the still-unresolved dispute over the concept of "quota" and its semantic cousin, "preference."[85]

Justice Powell's opinion for the Court is required reading. With no support from any other justice, he took positions on the twin issues of strict scrutiny and nonremedial affirmative action that today are the focus of affirmative action's most serious legal difficulties. (See pages 70–83 of this chapter; pages 143–158 of chapter 5; and pages 225–227 of chapter 8.)

The following is a topical summary of the Powell opinion:

Title VI does not require color-blindness, but "proscribe[s] only those racial classifications that would violate the equal protection clause [of the Fourteenth Amendment] or [its counterpart] in the Fifth Amendment:"[86]

[T]he voluminous legislative history of Title VI reveals a congressional intent to halt federal funding of entities that violate a prohibition of racial discrimination similar to that of the Constitution. Although isolated statements of various legislators, taken out of context, can be marshaled in support of the proposition that Sec. 601 enacted a purely colorblind scheme, without regard to the reach of the Equal Protection Clause, these comments must be read against the background of both the problem that Congress was addressing and the broader view of the statute that emerges from a full examination of the legislative debates.

The problem confronting Congress was discrimination against Negro citizens at the hands of recipients of federal moneys. . . . Over and over again, proponents of the bill detailed the plight of Negroes seeking equal treatment in [federally funded] programs. There simply was no reason for Congress to consider the validity of hypothetical preferences that might be accorded minority citizens; the legislators were dealing with the real and pressing problem of how to guarantee those citizens equal treatment.[87]

All racial or ethnic classifications are not per se invalid under the Fourteenth Amendment.[88] The Constitution does not mandate color-blindness. But it does mandate "the most exacting judicial examination" of such classifications, since they are "inherently suspect."[89] In order to justify the use of a "suspect classification," "a State must show that its purpose or interest is both constitutionally permissible and substantial, and that its use of the classification is 'necessary . . . to the accomplishment' of its purpose or the safeguarding of its interest."[90]

Countering the "effects of societal discrimination," absent "judicial, legislative, or administrative findings of constitutional or statutory violations," does not qualify as a compelling interest. "Title VII principles support the proposition that findings of identified discrimination must precede the fashioning of remedial measures embodying racial classifications."[91]

Attaining a diverse-student body is a clearly compelling interest. But ethnic diversity "is only one element in a range of factors a university properly may consider in attaining the goal of a heterogeneous student body," and must be "necessary to promote this interest."[92] The Davis set-aside in issue fails this test because it totally excludes nonminority applicants from a "specific percentage of seats. . . . [n]o matter how strong their qualifications, quantitative and extracurricular, including their own potential for contribution to educational diversity." Absent any past-discrimination findings, it violates their individual Fourteenth Amendment rights.[93]

In the evaluation of applications by disadvantaged minorities, race may properly be considered a positive factor in an admissions program flexible enough to consider "all pertinent elements" of educational diversity in light of the particular qualifications, and to place them on the same footing for consideration.[94]

2.

The federal Congress is not constitutionally barred from providing for "set-asides" of federal-construction funding for the benefit of minority business enterprises (MBEs), where such measures lie within its constitutional powers and are, in its judgment, reasonably necessary to counteract discriminatory denial of access to contracting opportunities.

In the historic case of *Fullilove v. Klutznick* (1980),[95] the Court, 6–3, held that the equal protection component of the Fifth Amendment's due process clause did not invalidate a 1977 federal law that required that at least 10 percent of the federal funds granted for local public works projects be used to procure supplies or services from firms owned by minority-group members. This was the first modern federal antidiscrimination statute to contain explicitly race/ethnic-based provisions. The lead opinion for the controlling Burger-White-Powell plurality deferred to Congress' judgment, since the set-asides derived from Congress' spending, commerce, and equal protection powers under the Constitution,[96] and, in Powell's view, were "a reasonably necessary means of furthering the compelling governmental interest in addressing the discrimination that affects minority contractors."[97]

Since 1980, *Fullilove* has fostered the creation of a host of federally funded MBE programs throughout the economy. Given that such programs are preeminent models[98] of federal affirmative action, it is fair to say that *Fullilove* and its progeny may have been its greatest entrepreneurial achievement.

Presently, however, the case seems to be in legal limbo. The Court has so far failed to rule on whether *Fullilove*'s outcome would meet the compelling-interest/narrow-tailoring requirement of the strict scrutiny standard that its 1995 *Adarand* decision imposed on federal affirmative action for the first time. (See pages 70–83 below.) In *Adarand,* the majority cast doubt on *Fullilove,* but said it was not necessary *today* to determine whether it would survive strict scrutiny.[99] At the time of this writing, that day has not arrived. This has left open such momentous questions as the scope of the Court's duty to defer to Congress, and whether the federal government is entitled to greater affirmative action leeway than the states and localities.

It is difficult to understand why the Court allows a cloud to linger over this trailblazing decision. No less an authority than Justice Powell—the "godfather" of strict scrutiny—acknowledged that the lead opinion in *Fullilove* incorporated the substance, if not the formal label, of strict scrutiny, and that the set-asides in issue effectively passed muster under that standard.[100] The *Adarand* equal protection claim (involving a federal, protected-group set-aside) is still unresolved. As of the present writing, the Supreme Court has declined to review the merits of the claim.[101] (On *Adarand,* see pages 54 above and 70–83 below.)

3.

Title VII of the 1964 Civil Rights Act permits voluntary adoption of race/ethnic-conscious affirmative action plans in the private-employment sector for the purpose of eliminating racial imbalance in segregated job categories. Such plans need not be predicated on proven past intentional discrimination, and are permissible if they do not unnecessarily trammel the legitimate interests or expectations of nonbeneficiary employees, and are designed to achieve a balanced work force but not to maintain a permanent balance.

United Steelworkers of America v. Weber (1979)[102]—the first Title VII "reverse discrimination" case to reach the High Court—arose from a collective bargaining agreement that reserved for black employees at a Louisiana aluminum plant 50% of the openings in a newly created, in-plant training program. The purpose of the program was to train unskilled production workers to fill craftwork openings. At the time, only 1.83% (5 out of 273) of the plant's skilled craftworkers were blacks, even though the local labor force was about 39% black. Under the agreement, at least 50% of the training slots were to be awarded to black applicants until the percentage of in-plant, skilled black craftworkers approximated the percentage of blacks in the local labor force. Selection for training was to be by seniority within each racial group. Since the plant's unskilled production force was 90% white, relatively few blacks were available to bid for selection. It thus transpired that, in the group initially selected, the senior black had less plant-wide seniority than some rejected white bidders, including Weber the plaintiff. Weber claimed that the affirmative action plan resulted in a race-based preference for junior blacks over senior whites, and therefore violated the ban on discrimination in Title VII.

Weber's claim was essentially that, even though he was junior to all of the successful white bidders, he was senior to all of the successful black bidders, and therefore, had he been black, his bid would have been accepted. This was the generic claim of reverse discrimination: race-based deprivation of a benefit due and owing to an innocent third party. The U.S. Fifth Circuit Court of Appeals upheld the claim, 2-1, holding that Title VII bars all race-based employment preferences, "including those preferences incidental to bona fide affirmative action plans."[103] In an opinion by Justice Brennan, the Supreme Court reversed, 5–2, saying that the provisions of Title VII do not prohibit all private, voluntary race-conscious affirmative action plans.[104] These provisions, as Brennan wrote, must be read against the background of legislative history and historical context:

> Congress' primary concern was with "the plight of the Negro in our economy.". . . . "[T]he relative position of the Negro worker [was] steadily worsening. . . ." Congress feared that the goals of the Civil Rights Act— the integration of blacks into the mainstream of American society— could not be achieved unless this trend was reversed. . . . "[T]he crux of the problem [was] to open employment opportunities for Negroes in occupations which have traditionally been closed to them." . . . [I]t was to this problem that Title VII's prohibition against racial discrimination in employment was primarily addressed.[105]

It follows that Congress could not have:

> intended to prohibit the private sector from taking effective steps to accomplish the goal that Congress designed Title VII to achieve. . . . It would be ironic indeed if a law triggered by a Nation's concern over centuries of racial injustice and intended to improve the lot of those who had "been excluded from the American dream for so long" . . . constituted the first legislative prohibition of all voluntary, private, race-conscious efforts to abolish traditional patterns of racial segregation and hierarchy."[106]

If, Brennan reasoned, Congress had intended to prohibit all race-conscious affirmative action, it could have provided that Title VII "would not require or *permit* racially preferential integration efforts."[107] However, the "no preference" clause in Section 703(j)[108] provides only that preferential treatment is not *required,* thus leaving the "natural inference that Congress chose not to forbid all voluntary race conscious efforts" to correct racial imbalances.[109]

In Brennan's view, the plan at issue fell on the "permissible side" of the affirmative action line, since like the 1964 Civil Rights Act, it was designed to break down old patterns of racial segregation and hierarchy; it did not "unnecessarily trammel" the interests of the white employees, as it did not require discharge of whites and their replacement with blacks, or absolutely bar their advancement; and it was a temporary measure, "not intended to maintain racial balance, but simply to eliminate a manifest racial imbalance."[110]

In articulating the "unduly trammeling" principle, the Court for the first time enunciated a standard for adjudicating the impact of affirmative action on nonminorities. Most of the Court's subsequent decisions in this period dealt with this issue.

The Rehnquist dissent in *Weber* was particularly vigorous, and it ended by saying:

> There is perhaps no device more destructive to the notion of equality than the *numerus clausus*—the quota. Whether described as a "benign discrimination" or "affirmative action," the racial quota is nonetheless a creator of castes, a two-edged sword that must demean one in order to prefer another. In passing Title VII, Congress outlawed *all* racial discrimination, recognizing that no discrimination based on race is benign, that no action disadvantaging a person because of his color is affirmative. With today's holding, the Court introduces into Title VII a tolerance for the very evil that the law was intended to eradicate, without offering even a clue as to what the limits on that tolerance may be. We are told simply that [the employer] Kaiser's racially discriminatory admission quota "falls on the permissible side of the line." By going not merely *beyond,* but directly *against* Title VII's language and legislative history, the Court has sown the wind. Later courts will face the impossible task of reaping the whirlwind.[111]

4.

The impact of race-conscious affirmative action by public employers on innocent third parties does not violate their equal protection rights if it is necessary to remedy past discrimination and does not unnecessarily trammel their legitimate interests or expectations. Race-conscious, out-of-seniority layoffs of nonminority employees by public employers violate the equal protection clause absent prior discrimination, and violate Title VII if they benefit nonvictims of discrimination. Court-ordered numerical union membership or promotion goals do not violate either the "no preference" clause of Title VII, or the equal protection clause if they are necessary to remedy past discrimination, are flexibly implemented, and do not seek to maintain permanent racial balance in the work force.

The Supreme Court has felt it necessary to reaffirm the *Weber* holding that race-conscious affirmative action is not reverse discrimination per se. Thus, in *Wygant v. Jackson Board of Education* (1986),[112] Justice Powell's plurality opinion reiterated the need for strict scrutiny of state-sponsored racial classifications, and then said:

> We have recognized, however, that in order to remedy the effects of prior discrimination, it may be necessary to take race into account. As part of this Nation's dedication to eradicating racial discrimination, innocent persons may be called upon to bear some of the burden of the remedy. "When effectuating a limited and properly tailored remedy to cure the effects of prior discrimination, such a 'sharing of the burden' by innocent parties is not impermissible."[113]

The problem is to determine how much of the burden the innocent party should be expected to bear—a process that necessarily works on a case-by-case basis. Still, some of the Court's decisions offer general guidelines. For example, in both of the layoff cases that came before the Court, the majority voted against affirmative action. In *Firefighters v. Stotts* (1984),[114] the Court held, 5–4, that a federal district court judge violated Title VII by modifying a consent decree so as to permit the layoff of senior white firefighters in order to retain junior blacks who had been hired pursuant to the decree. The asserted justification for this departure from the employer's long-standing seniority rules was the need to preserve the gains under the decree. The Court majority ruled that the district judge lacked authority under Section 706(g) of the Act[115] to disregard the seniority system, since there was no finding that any of the retained blacks had "actually been a victim of illegal discrimination."[116]

In *Wygant,* the Court reached a similar result, but on constitutional grounds. The case arose from a collective bargaining agreement that allowed out-of-seniority layoffs of public schoolteachers where necessary to retain current levels of minority employment. Without the benefit of a single majority opinion, the Court held, 5–4, that the layoff provision violated the equal protection rights of senior-white teachers who had been laid off in order to retain junior-black teachers.[117] A four-member plurality held that the provision failed both prongs of strict scrutiny:

1. The "compelling interest" prong was not satisfied by the asserted goal of remedying "societal discrimination" by providing "role models" for minority schoolchildren. There must be "convincing evidence" of prior discrimination by the governmental unit involved.[118]

2. The layoff provision was insufficiently narrowly tailored. Though hiring goals may burden some innocent individuals they simply do not impose the same kind of injury that layoffs impose. Denial of a future employment opportunity is not as intrusive as loss of an existing job. "While hiring goals impose a diffuse burden [within society generally], often foreclosing only one of several opportunities, layoffs impose the entire burden of achieving racial equality on particular individuals, often resulting in serious disruption of their lives. That burden is too intrusive. . . . Other, less intrusive means . . . such as the adoption of hiring goals—are available."[119]

The results in *Stotts* and *Wygant* were the crest of the antiaffirmative action sentiment in the Court at the time, and of the Reagan Administration's largely abortive attempt to limit affirmative action.[120] In later cases, during the 1980s, the Court's most redoubtable champion of affirmative action, Justice Brennan, was able to muster majority support for his views. In *Sheet Metal Workers v. EEOC* (1986),[121] the Court upheld a court order requiring a local union, which had ignored prior orders to admit blacks, to increase its black membership by 29.23%. The Court held, 6–3, that Section 706(g) of the Act[122] authorizes the district courts to order preferential relief benefiting individuals who may not be the actual victims of discrimination.[123] The main problem in the case was that the 29.23% African-American union membership requirement for blacks was arguably a quota-like, racial-balancing scheme prohibited by Section 703(j) of the 1964 Civil Rights Act.[124] Five members concluded that the goal did not violate either the equal protection clause or Title VII.[125] Of this five-member majority, a four-member plurality, including Justice Brennan, held the following:

> [R]ace-conscious affirmative measures [may not be invoked under Title VII] . . . simply to create a racially balanced work force.[126]

> . . . [A] court should consider whether affirmative action is necessary [under Title VII] to remedy past discrimination in a particular case before imposing such measures, and . . . should also take care to tailor its orders to fit the nature of the violation it seeks to correct.[127]

The Brennan plurality—in an opinion that supported the widespread affirmative action effort to establish goals and timetables—continued by saying that the 29.23% requirement was necessary "to assure the equal employment opportunities guaranteed by Title VII," because of the union's "long continued and egregious" exclusion of blacks, and in order to combat "the lingering effects of [this] pervasive discrimination."[128] The plurality concluded that the 29.23% figure was a goal (and not a firm quota) because the lower court had been flexible in applying its previous requirements, and was likely to do so in the future. In short, the aforementioned numerical requirement was "not being used simply to achieve and maintain racial balance, but rather as a benchmark [for] measur[ing the union's] compliance with [the court's] orders, rather than as a strict racial quota."[129] The goal was a temporary measure. It did not "unnecessarily trammel the interests of white employees": that is, no white union members were laid off, and there is no "absolute bar" to white applicants.[130]

To the plurality, the membership goal did not violate the equal protection clause. The Supreme Court has

> consistently recognized that government bodies constitutionally may adopt racial classifications as a remedy for past discrimination. . . .[131] We have not agreed, however, on the proper test to be applied in analyzing the constitutionality of race-conscious remedial measures. . . . We need not resolve this dispute here, since we conclude that the relief ordered in this case passes even the most rigorous test—it is narrowly tailored to further the Government's compelling interest in remedying past discrimination.[132]

In the Brennan plurality view, the Court is to consider several factors to determine whether the narrow-tailoring prong has been honored, including the necessity for the relief and the efficacy of alternative remedies; the flexibility and duration of the relief, including the availability of waiver provisions; the relationship of the numerical goals to the relevant labor market; and the impact of the relief on the rights of third parties.[133] The union's black membership goal passed this narrow-tailoring test, for much the same reasons given for the membership goal passage of the Title VII, 703(j) test, in particular because it had "only a marginal effect on the interests of white workers."[134]

Like union membership goals, race, ethnic, and gender-based hiring and promotion goals must pass muster under Section 703(j). *Firefighters v. Cleveland* (1986)[135] arose from a court order approving a consent decree under which the employer agreed to promote one black firefighter for every white promoted until a stipulated level of black employment was reached. This formula was clearly much closer to the quota line than the one sanctioned in the *Sheet Metal* case, but it too was approved, this time, 6–3. Justice Brennan's majority opinion concluded that the policy favoring voluntary compliance with the intent of the law overrode the arguable possibility that the evidence might not have justified a court order of such breadth.[136]

Precisely this possibility confronted the Court as a constitutional issue in *United States v. Paradise* (1987),[137] where a district judge had ordered the state of Alabama to promote one black state trooper for every white trooper promoted until 25 percent of promoted troopers was black. For decades, the State had engaged in open and pervasive racial discrimination in the hiring and promotion of troopers. The Court upheld the order, 5–4, ruling that the one-for-one requirement did not violate the Fourteenth Amendment's equal protection clause.[138] As in the *Sheet Metal* case, a four-member plurality, including Justice Brennan, concluded that this arguable quota amply met the strict scrutiny test.[139] Brennan's opinion stated that the Court has not

> in all situations "required remedial plans to be limited to the least restrictive means of implementation. We have recognized that the choice of remedies to redress racial discrimination is a 'balancing process left, within appropriate constitutional or statutory limits, to the sound discretion of the trial court judge.'" . . . There is no universal answer to the complex problems of desegregation; there is obviously no one plan that will do the job in every case. . . .
>
> The remedy imposed here is an effective, temporary, and flexible measure. It applies only if qualified blacks are available, only if the [State] . . . has an objective need to make promotions, and only if the [State] . . . fails to implement a promotion procedure that does not have an adverse impact on blacks. The one-for-one requirement is the product of the considered judgment of the District Court which, with its knowledge of the parties and their resources, properly determined that strong measures were required in light of the [State's] . . . long and shameful record of delay and resistance.[140]

5.

Title VII permits voluntary adoption of sex-conscious affirmative action plans by public employers for the purpose of eliminating statistically demonstrated, manifest (disparate-impact) imbalances in traditionally segregated job categories. Such plans need not be predicated on past discrimination by the employers who undertake them, and are permissible if they do not unnecessarily trammel the legitimate interests or expectations of male employees, and are designed to achieve a balanced work force but not to maintain a permanent balance.

The peak of Justice Brennan's influence came in *Johnson v. Transportation Agency of Santa Clara County* (1987),[141] where, for the first time, the Court was confronted with the issue of gender-conscious affirmative action. The Court held, 6–3, that a public employer's decision to promote a female to a skilled-craft job over a male applicant did not violate Title VII's prohibition of sex discrimination. The promotion was made pursuant to a voluntary affirmative action plan that was designed to move women into higher-ranking, traditionally male positions, and permitted consideration of the qualified applicants' sex as one factor in promotional decisions. The rejected male had scored two points higher than the promoted female in a qualifying interview, and claimed that he had been denied promotion solely for the reason of sex.

In rejecting this claim, Justice Brennan's majority opinion ruled that the principle of *United Steelworkers of America v. Weber* (1979)[142] applied to voluntary sex-conscious affirmative action designed to eliminate "a manifest imbalance that reflected under-representation of women in 'traditionally segregated job categories.' "[143] The majority concluded that the affirmative action plan at issue was valid under this principle, and that it was accordingly appropriate to give some weight to the promoted-female's sex.

The majority held that pursuant to the rule in *Weber*, voluntary affirmative action plans are permissible under Title VII if designed to correct a "manifest imbalance" in a "traditionally segregated job category." In determining whether such an imbalance exists in a job which requires special training, it is appropriate to compare the percentage of minorities or women in the employer's work force with those in the area work force who possess the relevant qualifications:[144]

> The requirement that the "manifest imbalance" relate to a "traditionally segregated job category" provides assurance both that sex or race will be taken into account in a manner consistent with Title VII's purpose of eliminating the effects of employment discrimination, and that the interests of those employees not benefiting from the plan will not be unduly infringed.[145]

In the majority's view, the only justification which Title VII requires of a voluntary affirmative action plan is conspicuous statistical imbalance,[146] demonstrative of a disparate societal/historical impact. Unlike the equal protection clause, the 1964 Civil Rights Act does not require that a voluntary affirmative action plan, even one adopted by a public employer, *be predicated on the employer's prior discrimination*. Such a requirement "could inappropriately create a significant disincentive for employers to adopt an affirmative action plan," thereby running counter to Title VII's underlying purpose of encouraging "employer efforts to eliminate vestiges of discrimination."[147] Importantly, public employers when fulfilling the objectives of Title VII are not restricted by the equal protection requirements of the Constitution. Answering Justice Scalia's insistence that these equal protection requirements were applicable (and consequently restricted affirmative action to curing the public employer's own unlawful discrimination),[148] the Court argued that Congress meant to free the states and their subdivisions from the constraints of the equal protection clause. Title VII "was enacted pursuant to the commerce power . . . and was not intended to incorporate . . . the commands of the Fifth and Fourteenth Amendments. . . . Even when that Title was extended to public employers in 1972, 'Congress expressly indicated the intent that the same Title VII principles be applied to governmental and private employers alike.' "[149]

According to the majority, the Santa Clara plan at issue complied fully with the *Weber* standard: The employer's female employees were traditionally employed in "women's" work, like office and clerical positions, and were "most egregiously underrepresented" in skilled-craft work (*zero* percent of 228 positions).[150] The plan did not set aside a specific number of jobs for women, but established hiring and promotional goals as guidelines for "statistically measurable" improvement.[151] The plan did not authorize "blind hiring" by the numbers to fulfill the goals, but required consideration of numerous factors, including the qualifications of female applicants for particular jobs.[152] Given the obvious imbalance in the skilled craft category, and the employer's commitment to eliminate such imbalances, "it was plainly not unreasonable for the . . . [employer] to determine that it was appropriate to consider . . . [sex] as one factor . . . in making its decision."[153] Furthermore, the plan did not unnecessarily trammel the interests of male employees, or create an "absolute bar" to their advancement. No person is excluded from consideration. Sex may be taken into account, but only as one of a number of factors. Women must compete with all other qualified applicants. Since the plaintiff was only one of seven qualified applicants, any one of whom could have been chosen, he was not absolutely entitled to the promotion, and cannot claim the unsettling of any legitimate expectation.[154] Finally, the plan was a temporary measure designed to achieve a balanced work force, not to maintain a permanent sexual or racial balance.[155]

The High Point of Affirmative Action's Career

The *Johnson* case was employment affirmative action's high watermark. It was the first time that a clear majority of the Supreme Court construed Title VII as a license for *public employers* to use "goals and timetables" in order to remedy the effects of societal/historical-employment discrimination, and without being concerned about the equal protection criteria in the Fourteenth Amendment of the Constitution. It represented the triumph of the view originally propounded by Justice Brennan in *Weber*—that Title VII legitimates voluntary resort by employers to numerically based remediation in order to correct statistical imbalances without "unnecessarily" injuring nonminorities. Thus, the *Johnson* majority opinion should be taken as a signal victory for disparate-impact theory.

The ascendancy of the disparate-impact school of antidiscrimination law in the employment arena was also apparent in the country at large. As noted, in 1979 and 1980, the EEOC had promulgated affirmative action and employee-selection guidelines which effectively embodied the *Weber* principle.[156] The OFCCP went further by requiring goals and timetables for federal contractors when they underutilized protected groups. By the late 1980s, affirmative action through employee-selection guidelines had taken root throughout the economy either voluntarily, or by court action, administrative regulation, or legislative dictate. The federal government's procurement policies extended substantial special considerations to minority and female entrepreneurs. Employment affirmative action was institutionalized in corporate

America, in the apparatus of the government, including the military, and the educational establishment.[157] Affirmative action had a powerful lobby in Congress. All told, it seemed to be winning the war.

But in fact it had achieved only a temporary truce. In the High Court, after 1987, Justice Brennan was on his way to becoming a spent force. The dominant voices now were becoming Chief Justice Rehnquist and Justice Scalia, both archenemies of affirmative action. In their respective dissents in *Weber*,[158] and *Johnson*,[159] these Justices contended that *all* race, ethnic, and sex-conscious employment remediation of the affirmative action variety constituted "discrimination" within the "plain meaning" of Title VII, and that *Weber* and its progeny were perversions of the law. The vehemence of their views virtually ensured that hostilities would resume.[160] And this is indeed what came to pass.

Hostilities Resume

The Turnaround

In 1989, the fortunes of war turned abruptly against affirmative action. The Supreme Court handed down no less than six decisions that set off all the alarms in the civil rights camp.[161] For our purposes, the two most important were the *Wards Cove v. Antonio* (1989) and *Richmond v. Croson* (1989) cases.

In *Wards Cove*,[162] a new antiaffirmative action majority on the Court undertook to reconsider the "proper application of Title VII's disparate-impact theory of liability."[163] The decision rattled so many cages that, as will be seen, Congress passed a law to overturn it. While now no longer part of case law, *Wards Cove* was symptomatic of a mind-set that undoubtedly has lingered in the Court to this day.

The case involved Title VII claims by nonwhite salmon cannery workers. These plaintiffs held low-paying, unskilled "cannery" jobs, and claimed that they had been excluded for racial reasons from higher-paying, skilled "noncannery" work assigned to white employees. The basis for the claim was alleged "subjective" bias in the employer's hiring practices, as evidenced "solely . . . [by] statistics showing a high percentage of nonwhite workers in the cannery jobs and a low percentage of such workers in the noncannery positions."[164] The Court, 5-4, reversed judgment for the plaintiffs. The majority opinion affirmed that subjective hiring practices may be analyzed under a disparate-impact model,[165] but held that the comparison between the racial composition of the cannery and noncannery work forces failed to make a prima facie case of disparate impact.[166]

According to the majority opinion by Justice White, the proper basis for the initial inquiry in a disparate-impact case is a comparison between the racial composition of the qualified persons in the labor market and the persons holding at-issue jobs. . . . [W]here such . . . statistics . . . [are] difficult if not impossible to ascertain . . . certain other statistics—such as measures indicating the racial composition of "otherwise qualified applicants" for at-issue jobs . . . are equally probative for [disparate-impact purposes].[167]

The main flaw in the comparison at issue was that the cannery work force did not reflect any pool of nonwhite applicants who were qualified for skilled noncannery positions: "If the absence of minorities holding such skilled positions is due to a dearth of qualified nonwhite applicants (for reasons that are not . . . [the employers'] fault), the . . . [employers'] selection methods or employment practices cannot be said to have had disparate impact on nonwhites."[168]

The majority acknowledged that the result would be different if the employers "deterred" nonwhites from applying for noncannery jobs.[169] In any case, the majority's concerns ranged far beyond the outcome of this particular litigation. In their view, to permit disparate-impact suits to go forward solely on the basis of simple statistical disparity,

at the very least, would mean that any employer who had a segment of his work force that was—for some reason—racially imbalanced, could be haled into court and forced to engage in the expensive and time-consuming task of defending the "business necessity" of the methods used to select the other members of his work force. The only practicable option for many employers would be to adopt racial quotas, insuring that no portion of their work forces deviated in racial composition from the other portions thereof; this is a result that Congress expressly rejected in drafting Title VII.[170]

In order to insulate employers from liability for " 'the myriad of innocent causes that may lead to statistical imbalances in the composition of their work forces,' "[171] the majority restated the legal standards that govern order, burden, and quantum of proof in Title VII disparate-impact litigation: As part of his prima facie burden, the plaintiff must show that "the application of a specific or particular employment practice" created the alleged disparate impact.[172] If a prima facie case has been made, the employer has the burden of "producing evidence of a business justification" for the challenged employment practice. This evidence must show that the practice significantly serves the employer's "legitimate employment goals," but need not show that it is " 'essential' " or " 'indispensable' " to the employer's business. This is a burden of production only. The burden of persuasion, namely, that of proving that discrimination has occurred, is on the plaintiff.[173] If the plaintiff identifies alternate hiring practices that reduce disparate impact, while equally serving the employer's legitimate employment goals, and the employer refuses to adopt them, this would refute any claim that the existing practices are not discriminatory.[174]

It is to be recalled that *Griggs* held that employers could defend themselves against disparate-impact claims by establishing that the employment practice excluding minorities was required by business necessity—that is, related to job performance. Case law subsequent to *Griggs* fashioned the business-necessity standard into one which was quite plaintiff-friendly. *Wards Cove* eased the judicial interpretation of what constitutes business necessity. Business necessity need not be something that was "indispensable" or "essential," but only a practice that promoted an employer's legitimate goals. In short, employer capacity to establish the business-necessity defense and to defeat disparate-impact suits was greatly facilitated.[175] The civil rights lobby construed *Wards Cove* and its companion cases as a direct frontal assault on *Griggs*,[176] and, acting under the umbrella of the Leadership Conference on Civil Rights (LCCR), mobilized its supporters in Congress for a counterattack. In 1990, the LCCR proposed a bill meant to overturn *Wards Cove*, and added compensatory and punitive damages and jury trials to the "make whole" remedies available for intentional violations under the 1964 Civil Rights Act. With the cooperation of the Senate and House labor committee staffs, the LCCR pushed its bill through Congress and produced the Civil Rights Act of 1990. However, the first President Bush vetoed the law, on the ground that the addition of punitive damages to the panoply of disparate-impact remedies unacceptably increased the risk of coerced quota-hiring. The veto stood, and so did *Wards Cove*—until the next session of Congress. In 1991, a softened version of the 1990 Act passed in Congress and was signed by President Bush.[177] The Civil Rights Act of 1991[178] is now the law of the land.

The 1991 Civil Rights Act

Many disciples of *Griggs* believed that the enactment of this law was a great, perhaps even a conclusive, victory for their cause.[179] Their rejoicing may have been premature. True, the Act repudiated *Wards Cove,* and its companion decisions;[180] formally incorporated disparate impact into Title VII (Sections 3[3], 116); and purported to adopt the principle of *Griggs*, and other pre-*Wards Cove* Supreme Court decisions, with respect to "business necessity" and "job related," burden of proof in disparate-impact cases, and affirmative action.[181] But the Act does not define key Title VII operative terms like "discrimination" and "disparate impact," or provide any fresh clues as to its intended meaning; indeed it compounds the numerous unsettled questions that already exist on that score. It is a virtual certainty that the legal controversy over affirmative action as an instrument of equal employment opportunity will continue as long as the statute remains on the books in its present form. Unless, that is, disparate impact and affirmative action are declared unconstitutional under strict scrutiny—a prospect that cannot be summarily discounted.

The Triumph of Strict Scrutiny: Croson, Adarand, and the Constitutionality of Affirmative Action Conducted by Government

Before 1989, the Supreme Court failed to produce a majority on the question of what kind of judicial review was constitutionally mandated in affirmative action cases. Its first encounter with this all-important issue was the 1978 *Bakke* case, which only five justices saw fit to decide on constitutional grounds, and in which Justice Powell alone espoused the strict scrutiny test in Fourteenth Amendment cases. In the 1986 *Wygant* case, Justice Powell garnered only plurality support for his restatement of this test, coupled with the "strong basis in evidence" standard for proof of the requisite past discrimination by the governmental unit involved. It was in the 1989 *Richmond v. Croson* case that, for the first time, a clear majority adopted Powell's reading of the Fourteenth Amendment's impact on state-sponsored affirmative action involving racial/ethnic classifications.[182]

The case involved a municipal "set aside," namely, the earmarking of public funds for the benefit of disadvantaged minority entrepreneurs.[183] The specific question was whether the city of Richmond, Virginia, violated the Fourteenth Amendment's equal protection clause by adopting a plan that required its prime contractors to subcontract at least 30 percent of their contracts to Minority Business Enterprises.[184] The stated purpose of the plan was to promote wider MBE participation in public construction.[185] The *Croson* majority of five members found that Richmond failed to survive strict scrutiny because it failed to demonstrate that its "set aside" served a "compelling government interest," and that it was "narrowly tailored" to meet that purpose.

Notwithstanding *Croson,* the Court initially declined to apply strict scrutiny to an affirmative action program sponsored by the national government. In *Metro Broadcasting Inc. v. FCC* (1990),[186] only a year after *Croson*, a 5–4 majority—on intermediate scrutiny grounds—upheld Federal Communications Commission (FCC) policies of awarding "enhancements" for minority ownership and management in radio and television broadcast licensing. The FCC policies were nonremedial attempts to comply with a statutory mandate to promote "diversification" in broadcast programming. The majority held that these policies did not violate the equal protection component of the Fifth Amendment.[187] In his opinion for the majority, Justice Brennan wrote:

> We hold that benign race-conscious measures mandated by Congress—
> even if those measures are not "remedial" in the sense of being designed
> to compensate victims of past governmental or societal discrimination—

are constitutionally permissible to the extent that they serve important governmental objectives within the powers of Congress [e.g., the commerce, and general welfare powers] and are substantially related to achievement of those objectives. . . . Our decision . . . [in *Croson*] concerning a [municipal] minority set-aside program . . . does not prescribe the level of scrutiny to be applied to a benign racial classification employed by Congress. . . .

We hold that the FCC minority ownership policies . . . serve the important governmental objective of broadcast diversity . . . [and] that they are substantially related to the achievement of that objective.[188]

After *Metro Broadcasting* the membership of the Court—and its balance of power—changed. In *Adarand Constructors, Inc. v. Peña* (1995),[189] a 5–4 majority of the current members (Rehnquist, O'Connor, Scalia, Kennedy, and Thomas) held that all racial classifications—federal, state, or local—are subject to strict judicial scrutiny. The majority rejected the "intermediate scrutiny" that *Metro Broadcasting* had adopted for federal affirmative action, and overruled it on that point.

The *Adarand* case arose from the rejection of a white contractor's low bid for a construction job that was awarded to a minority contractor under a federal set-aside program. The decision was confined to what should be the standard of constitutional review. As in *Croson,* Justice O'Connor delivered the majority opinion:

[It is a] . . . basic principle that the Fifth and Fourteenth Amendments to the Constitution protect *persons*, not *groups*. It follows from that principle that all governmental action based on race—a *group* classification long recognized as "in most circumstances irrelevant and therefore prohibited"—should be subjected to detailed judicial inquiry to ensure that the *personal* right to equal protection of the laws has not been infringed. . . . [W]e hold today that all racial classifications, imposed by whatever federal, state, or local governmental actor, must be analyzed by a reviewing court under strict scrutiny. In other words, such classifications are constitutional only if they are narrowly tailored measures that further compelling governmental interests. To the extent that *Metro Broadcasting* is inconsistent with that holding, it is overruled.[190]

In Justice O'Connor's circumspect words, the *Adarand* decision "alter[ed] the playing field in some important respects."[191] In fact, many questions remain unresolved. In the wake of the decision, President Clinton ordered a review of the entire federal affirmative action program. Based on the report of the review team,[192] the President announced on July 19, 1995 that he intended to continue the affirmative action program, modified so as to comply with the requirements of strict scrutiny.[193] Plainly he was relying on the Justice Department's view that the *Adarand* Court had not declared federal affirmative action unconstitutional.[194] While this is true, there is every reason to believe that, insofar as remedial affirmative action is based on disparate impact, *Adarand* has placed its constitutionality at risk. Granted that, in her opinion, Justice O'Connor wrote:

> [W]e wish to dispel the notion that strict scrutiny is "strict in theory, but fatal in fact." The unhappy persistence of both the practice and the lingering effects of racial discrimination against minority groups in this country is an unfortunate reality, and government is not disqualified from acting in response to it. . . . When race-based action is necessary to further a compelling interest, such action is within constitutional constraints if it satisfies the "narrow tailoring" test.[195]

However, this disclaimer should not cloud the fact that it is as plain as plain can be that, like every other member of the *Adarand* majority, Justice O'Connor harbors grave, deep-rooted doubts about the constitutionality of race/ethnic-based remediation for *group* discrimination.[196] As just seen, in the majority opinion, she explicitly derived the need for strict scrutiny from the principle that the constitution protects *persons,* not *groups,* and that *all* race/ethnic-based government action is a "group classification" that is prohibited "in most circumstances."[197] Further, affirmative action, as we have defined it, and as it is generally understood, is indeed a group remedy. Consequently, it would appear that the function of strict scrutiny under *Adarand* is to determine whether there are any circumstances in which affirmative action is *not* prohibited. It would be naive to pretend that the odds on an affirmative answer are overwhelmingly high. In the words of an eminent authority:

> [A] Supreme Court comprised of its current members may set the bar against affirmative action so high that virtually no firm, university, or contract-letting agency can surmount it. After all, many members of the current Court (and, plausibly, new members over the next decade) are characterologically, if not ideologically, conservative. Affirmative action is, in the eyes of almost all who think hard about it, an anomaly, sitting uncomfortably between the 1964 Civil Rights Act, which ostensibly barred its use, and Americans' desire for real, not merely nominal, racial equality. Even proponents agree that it is a stop-gap temporary measure—although essential, in their eyes. It is not difficult to envision a cautious, centrist Court deciding that enough is enough, except in rare circumstances.[198]

The threat to affirmative action posed by strict scrutiny helped cultivate diversity theory as a vehicle for its support. Diversity theory asks for no remedy for past racism, sexism, and the like; it focuses on proportional representation (and preferential treatment to achieve such) for groups now under the protective affirmative action umbrella because of the value associated with a better presentation of different viewpoints.[199] Remedial affirmative action has a theoretical end point (when remedies are achieved). Not so for diversity affirmative action, as the value of diversity never ceases. The *Adarand* decision would obviously govern review of *Metro Broadcasting*'s non-remedial "diversity" holdings, but like *Croson, Adarand* involved "remedial" affirmative action, and did not explicitly address the issue of "whether and in what settings non-remedial objectives can constitute a compelling interest."[200]

In any case, affirmative action's survival, if dependent on the current Supreme Court membership, is obviously at issue. The *Adarand* majority may simply be waiting for the right time to drop the other shoe. However, the threat to group affirmative action—to President Clinton's constitutional analyst, Professor Walter Dellinger—was not "life threatening." He argued that *Adarand* did not define the elements of what constitutes a compelling governmental interest. For this, we must look to *Croson* where Justice O'Connor, speaking for the Court, said that "[t]here is no doubt that where gross statistical disparities can be shown, they alone in a proper case may constitute prima facie proof of a pattern or practice of discrimination."[201] Dellinger continued by saying that while claims of general, historical, and societal discrimination will not be enough to support group affirmative action, significant statistical deviations between the number of qualified minorities and those given opportunities could suffice.[202]

Croson is routinely cited as the breakthrough decision on the standard of judicial review in affirmative action cases. What is less commonly remarked, but is made clear by the following excerpts from Justice O'Connor's opinion, is that the majority's ruling on the strict scrutiny standard was actually quite narrow. Thus, on the decisive "compelling interest" issue, the majority held only that reliance on societal discrimination was insufficient. But this decision did not, among other matters, explicitly address the critical question of whether an affirmative action defendant can ever survive strict scrutiny without a showing of specific past discrimination. (As we show at pages 225–227 in this volume, this question, together with its twin, the constitutionality of non-remedial affirmative action, has been pending ever since Justice Powell raised it in *Bakke,* and is now ripe for review by the High Court.) Further, if societal discrimination is not a proper basis for affirmative action, what kind of discrimination is? Surely, government discrimination is an appropriate candidate, but may one unit of government (e.g., a public university) take it upon itself to cure the sins of other units through affirmative action? How far back may we go in finding government discrimination? A decade? Twenty-five years? More? Further, while the majority made a number of elaborate "observations" about the "narrow-tailoring" issue in the case, it did not indicate how the observations might apply in another case.[203] A *Croson* excerpt from the O'Connor majority opinion follows:

Richmond v. Croson, 488 U.S. 469 (1989)

... [498] We think it clear that the factual predicate offered in support of the Richmond Plan suffers from the same two defects identified as fatal in *Wygant*. The District Court found the city council's "findings sufficient to ensure that, in adopting the Plan, it was remedying the present effects of past discrimination in the *construction industry.*" ... Like the "role model" theory employed in *Wygant*, a generalized assertion that there has been past discrimination in an entire industry provides no guidance for a legislative body to determine the precise scope of the injury it seeks to remedy. It "has no logical stopping point." "Relief" for such an ill-defined wrong could extend until the percentage of public contracts awarded to MBE's [minority business enterprises] in Richmond mirrored the percentage of minorities in the population as a whole.

Appellant argues that it is attempting to remedy various forms of past discrimination that are alleged to be responsible for the small number of minority businesses in the local contracting industry. Among these the city cites the exclusion of blacks from skilled construction trade unions and training programs. This past discrimination has prevented them "from following the traditional path from laborer to entrepreneur." The city also lists a host of nonracial factors which would seem to face a member of any racial group attempting to establish a new business enterprise, such as deficiencies in working capital, inability to meet bonding requirements, unfamiliarity with bidding procedures, [499] and disability caused by an inadequate track record.

While there is no doubt that the sorry history of both private and public discrimination in this country has contributed to a lack of opportunities for black entrepreneurs, this observation, standing alone, cannot justify a rigid racial quota in the awarding of public contracts in Richmond, Virginia. Like the claim that discrimination in primary and secondary schooling justifies a rigid racial preference in medical school admissions, an amorphous claim that there has been past discrimination in a particular industry cannot justify the use of an unyielding racial quota.

It is sheer speculation how many minority firms there would be in Richmond absent past societal discrimination, just as it was sheer speculation how many minority medical students would have been admitted to the medical school at Davis absent past discrimination in educational opportunities. Defining these sorts of injuries as "identified discrimination" would give local governments license to create a patchwork of racial preferences based on statistical generalizations about any particular field of endeavor.

These defects are readily apparent in this case. The 30% quota cannot in any realistic sense be tied to any injury suffered by anyone. The District Court relied upon five predicate "facts" in reaching its conclusion that there was an adequate basis for the 30% quota: (1) the ordinance declares itself to be remedial; (2) several proponents of the measure stated their views that there had been past discrimination in the construction industry; (3) minority businesses received 0.67% of prime contracts from the city while minorities constituted 50% of the city's population; (4) there were very few minority contractors in local and state contractors' associations; and (5) in 1977, Congress made a determination that the effects of past discrimination had stifled minority participation in the construction industry nationally.

[500] None of these "findings," singly or together, provide the city of Richmond with a "strong basis in evidence for its conclusion that remedial action was necessary." *Wygant,* 476 U.S., at 277 (plurality opinion). There is nothing approaching a prima facie case of a constitutional or statutory violation by *anyone* in the Richmond construction industry. *Id.,* at 274–275.

The District Court accorded great weight to the fact that the city council designated the Plan as "remedial." But the mere recitation of a "benign" or legitimate purpose for a racial classification is entitled to little or no weight. . . . Racial classifications are suspect, and that means that simple legislative assurances of good intention cannot suffice.

The District Court also relied on the highly conclusionary statement of a proponent of the Plan that there was racial discrimination in the construction industry "in this area, and the State, and around the nation." It also noted that the city manager had related his view that racial discrimination still plagued the construction industry in his home city of Pittsburgh. These statements are of little probative value in establishing identified discrimination in the Richmond construction industry. The fact-finding process of legislative bodies is generally entitled to a presumption of regularity and deferential review by the judiciary. But when a legislative body chooses to employ a suspect classification, it cannot rest upon a generalized assertion as to the classification's relevance to its goals. A [501] governmental actor cannot render race a legitimate proxy for a particular condition merely by declaring that the condition exists. The history of racial classifications in this country suggests that blind judicial deference to legislative or executive pronouncements of necessity has no place in equal protection analysis.

Reliance on the disparity between the number of prime contracts awarded to minority firms and the minority population of the city of Richmond is similarly misplaced. There is no doubt that "[w]here gross statistical disparities can be shown, they alone in a proper case may constitute prima facie proof of a pattern or practice of discrimination" under Title VII. *Hazelwood School Dist. v. United States,* 433 U.S. 299, 307-308 (1977). But it is equally clear that "[w]hen special qualifications are required to fill particular jobs, comparisons to the general population (rather than to the smaller group of individuals who possess the necessary qualifications) may have little probative value." *Id.,* at 308, n. 13. . . .

[502] In this case, the city does not even know how many MBE's in the relevant market are qualified to undertake prime or sub-contracting work in public construction projects. . . . Nor does the city know what percentage of total city construction dollars minority firms now receive as subcontractors on prime contracts let by the city. . . . Without any information [503] on minority participation in subcontracting, it is quite simply impossible to evaluate overall minority representation in the city's construction expenditures. . . .

[505] In sum, none of the evidence presented by the city points to any identified discrimination in the Richmond construction industry. We, therefore, hold that the city has failed to demonstrate a compelling interest in apportioning public contracting opportunities on the basis of race. To accept Richmond's claim that past societal discrimination alone can serve as the basis for rigid racial preferences would be to open the door to competing claims for "remedial relief" for every disadvantaged group. The dream of a Nation of equal citizens in a society where race is irrelevant to personal opportunity [506] and achievement would be lost in a mosaic of shifting preferences based on inherently unmeasurable claims of past wrongs. . . . We think such a result would be contrary to both the letter and spirit of a constitutional provision whose central command is equality.

The foregoing analysis applies only to the inclusion of blacks within the Richmond set-aside program. There is *absolutely no evidence* of past discrimination against Spanish-speaking, Oriental, Indian, Eskimo, or Aleut persons [those from the Aleutian Islands and its environs] in any aspect of the Richmond construction industry. The District Court took judicial notice of the fact that the vast majority of "minority" persons in Richmond were black. It may well be that Richmond has never had an

Aleut or Eskimo citizen. The random inclusion of racial groups that, as a practical matter, may never have suffered from discrimination in the construction industry in Richmond suggests that perhaps the city's purpose was not in fact to remedy past discrimination.

If a 30% set-aside was "narrowly tailored" to compensate black contractors for past discrimination, one may legitimately ask why they are forced to share this "remedial relief" with an Aleut citizen who moves to Richmond tomorrow? The gross overinclusiveness of Richmond's racial preference strongly impugns the city's claim of remedial motivation. . . .

[507] As noted by the court below, it is almost impossible to assess whether the Richmond Plan is narrowly tailored to remedy prior discrimination since it is not linked to identified discrimination in any way. We limit ourselves to two observations in this regard.

First, there does not appear to have been any consideration of the use of race-neutral means to increase minority business participation in city contracting. . . .

Second, the 30% quota cannot be said to be narrowly tailored to any goal, except perhaps outright racial balancing. It rests upon the "completely unrealistic" assumption that minorities will choose a particular trade in lockstep proportion to their representation in the local population. . . .

[508] [Further], . . . [u]nder Richmond's scheme, a successful black, Hispanic, or Oriental entrepreneur from anywhere in the country enjoys an absolute preference over other citizens based solely on their race. We think it obvious that such a program is not narrowly tailored to remedy the effects of prior discrimination. . . .

The Threat of Adarand

How *Croson* and *Adarand* are interpreted is important; it would be difficult to overstate the stakes. Recall that *Adarand*'s strict scrutiny net catches "all racial classifications, imposed by whatever federal, state, or local governmental actor."[204] The official position of the Department of Justice is that this language mandates strict scrutiny only for programs that use racial and ethnic criteria as "a basis for decision making."[205] Even under this questionable limitation,[206] strict scrutiny would clearly apply to every aspect of the federal government's large inventory of race and ethnic-based affirmative action programs in employment, procurement, education, health, research, grants-in-aid, and other areas,[207] where decisions were meant to be made on the basis of race or ethnicity. (For examples, see the appendix in chapter 1 above under the titles of "Military Recruiting," "Grants and Other Assistance," and "Federal Procurement Policies and Practices.")

Gender-oriented affirmative action presents another problem. In *Craig v. Boren* (1976),[208] the High Court settled on a "midtier" (intermediate) equal protection test for sex-discrimination claims: whether the disputed classification serves "important" government objectives and is substantially related to achieving them. Arguably, this rule has now been broadened. In *United States v. Virginia Military Institute* (1996),[209] the Supreme Court held, 7–1, that Virginia's maintenance of an exclusively male admissions policy at its storied military academy violated the equal protection clause. The Court indicated that, in order to prevail, a midtier defendant must demonstrate a justification that is not only *extremely persuasive,* but also *genuine, not hypothesized,* and untainted by sexual stereotypes.[210] There is a learned dispute over whether the "extremely persuasive" midtier rule in gender-discrimination law differs from the strict scrutiny rule, which is supposed to govern race, and national origin discrimination cases. (See chapter 5 at pages 165–167, and 168–171 below.)

Aside from gender discrimination, at the employment level alone, the federal government must—as a consequence of the strict scrutiny requirement—be prepared to defend every race and national origin-oriented measure which it voluntarily adopts "through legislation, regulation, internal agency procedures, or even individual employment decisions."[211] Thus, *Adarand* would apply to all of the following race-based federal employment and other decisions: (1) "situations where race is one of several factors as well as those in which race is the only factor"; (2) where race is involved in "the final judgment as to a particular decision, as well as to the various steps leading to that judgment"; (3) in the creation and implementation of formal and informal affirmative action programs, and in decisions of individual supervisors; and (4) in hiring, promotion, training, scholarships, transfers, and layoffs.[212] Even "[o]utreach and recruitment efforts conceivably could be viewed as race/ethnic-based decision making . . . subject to *Adarand* if . . . [they] work to create a 'minorities only' pool of applicants or bidders, or . . . are so focused on minorities that nonminorities are placed at a significant competitive disadvantage with respect to access to contracts, grants, or jobs."[213]

The foregoing are by no means the outside limits of possible federal exposure under *Adarand.* The Department of Justice holds that strict scrutiny is not applicable to the affirmative action plans which are mandated for federal contractors by the Office of Federal Contract Compliance Programs. This contention is based on the premise that "race-based decision making is not used to achieve" minority hiring goals under such plans, inasmuch as these goals are not quotas, preferences, or set-asides.[214] This must be considered an open question at this time. However, there is a small body of lower court strict scrutiny case law involving comparable "goals" affirmative action programs, and the courts are split on the applicability of *Adarand's* requirement of strict scrutiny.[215] If the government's position on Executive Order 11246 is ultimately disapproved, then all of the OFCCP's federal-contracting affirmative action programs involving at least one-third of the national workforce,[216] will fall under *Adarand's* sway. Certainly this would be appropriate to those who regard the "goals and timetables" requirements of the OFCCP as forceful inducements for race and ethnic-based preferences.

Adarand threatens to outlaw the public use of antidiscriminatory racial/ethnic preference. Any public body—be it the U.S. Government or a local library board—which attacks systemic bias through preferences in employment or contracting, runs the risk of potentially successful constitutional challenge. And, while the Court has yet to review the constitutionality of nonremedial affirmative action, some lower federal courts have, as will be seen, already condemned it on the authority of *Adarand*.

It appears that affirmative action's moment of truth is finally at hand. Should this nation seek a different road to equal opportunity?

The Unresolved Issues of Affirmative Action in Employment

Clarifying the Law

There is much about affirmative action law that needs clarification. Neither Title VII, nor the Civil Rights Act of 1991 define key terms like "discrimination," "preferential treatment," and "equal opportunity." The question of why Congress has not seen fit to shed light on these matters invites theorizing about congressional behavior. One view has it that legislators will commit themselves to popular measures while delegating problems to the administrators and the judges who then can be blamed when constituents complain.[217] This mode of legislative behavior opens the question of responsibility in a democratic society. How are the administrators and judges to be held accountable by a public that only dimly understands their activities and that cannot easily remove them?

The Supreme Court has delegated much affirmative action decision making to the subordinate courts, the legislatures, and the executives by requiring them to decipher the Court's puzzling affirmative action declarations. With respect to strict scrutiny alone, numerous questions abound, including: What kind of affirmative action programs are subject to strict scrutiny? Are "goals and timetable" undertakings exempt as the Justice Department insists? Are "outreach" efforts to be excluded on the grounds that they, like goals and timetables, do not involve decisions on racial or ethnic grounds? On this point, as we show at page 226, a split has developed among the federal courts of appeal, framing an issue about the scope of strict scrutiny which will have to be resolved by the Supreme Court.

Law professor Michelle Adams argues that outreach/exhortation is nonpreferential, and as such should not be evaluated under the lens of strict scrutiny. In her view, other affirmative action devices do not involve preferences: the keeping and the analysis of protected-group statistical portraits by employers, school administrators, etc.; and the evaluation of whether affirmative action hiring and admission goals have been achieved.[218] Surely, though, the use of the aforementioned techniques will potentially induce considerable preferential treatment. Given the potentiality of preferential treatment, should not strict scrutiny apply? Adams stresses that strict scrutiny might interfere with outreach activities, and this could "uneven the playing field" by denying the transmission of "opportunity" information to disadvantaged minorities.[219] One must inquire whether outreach is restricted to the truly disadvantaged? Should it be?

Aside from what affirmative action strict scrutiny covers, the prongs of that type of analysis are yet to be clarified by the Court. Government's own discrimination and its passive acquiescence in private discrimination have been cited at the highest federal levels as compelling reasons for affirmative action.[220] How should discrimination and passive acquiescence be defined?

What does the narrow-tailoring prong of strict scrutiny involve? In this connection, the Clinton Administration's Associate Attorney General instructed the government's top lawyers as follows:

> In determining whether race-based employment action is narrowly tailored to serve a compelling interest, the courts have usually considered the following factors: 1) whether the government considered race-neutral alternatives before using the racial or ethnic criteria, 2) the manner in which race or ethnicity is used in making decisions—*e.g.,* is it one of many factors to be considered, or is it the sole or dominant factor, 3) the comparison of any numerical target to the number of qualified minorities in the labor pool, 4) the scope of the program, 5) the duration of the program, and 6) the impact of the program on nonminorities.[221]

This instruction raises numerous questions: What neutral methods can adequately replace race and ethnic consciousness? Is socioeconomic disadvantage an appropriate substitute? To the Department of Justice, race and ethnicity, where employed as criteria, should be but one of many factors to be considered. But how is one to determine whether such multidimensionalism guided decision making? Also, the Justice Department noted that narrow tailoring prohibits burdens on nonminority employees that are too "oner-ous,"[222] leaving the problem of how to define onerousness.

Assuming disparate-impact theory is still constitutionally acceptable, it raises difficult comparative-analytical problems. In disparate-impact theory, employment practices do not necessarily pass muster simply because they may be "facially neutral" and not discriminatorily motivated. If "in fact [they] fall *more harshly* on one group than another and cannot be justified by busi-ness necessity," they are illegal. (See *Teamsters v. United States* [1977].)[223] The ultimate issue in disparate-impact analysis is thus not the mere *fact* of disparity, but its comparative *extent* or *degree*. It follows that proof of dispar-ate impact is primarily, if not entirely, a process of statistical measurement and inference.

This is, in any event, the view of professional statisticians versed in Title VII litigation. Indeed, *Griggs* came to the High Court because black appli-cants for hire and promotion by the defendant employer were failing its standard IQ tests "at a *substantially* higher rate than white applicants."[224] The Court attributed this disparity to the "inferior education" which African Americans as a class had long received in the state's traditionally segregated public schools. Notwithstanding the absence of any discriminatory intent on the employer's part, the Court concluded that the disparity created by use of the tests was "directly traceable to race," and would therefore violate Title VII's ban on discrimination unless justified by business necessity.[225] Three leading academic statisticians analyze *Griggs* in the following way:

> The present use of statistical evidence in employment discrimination cases stems in large part from *Griggs* . . . where the Supreme Court es-tablished "disparate impact" as a basis for challenging employment se-lection procedures under Title VII. . . . Under *Griggs,* use of a qualifications test for which the pass rate for black applicants is "sub-stantially" less than that of whites is illegal unless the employer can show that the use of the test is a business necessity. The burden of demonstrating business necessity being onerous . . . and proof of dis-criminatory intent being unnecessary, the prima facie showing of dispar-ate (or "adverse") impact may often be sufficient for the plaintiff to prevail. *Disparate impact cases are thus uniquely statistical, with much depending on the interpretation given to the word "substantial" and on how large a disparity must be to be judged substantial.*[226]

In this light, it is quite remarkable that the High Court has never defined "substantial," nor has it squarely adopted a statistical formula for quantifying it. In the *Griggs* opinion, the Court characterized, but did not specifically identify, the disparity; nor did it cite any record evidence in support of its finding that the black applicants' failure rate was "substantially higher," or (the related finding) that it was "markedly disproportionate."[227] Moreover, the Court has not attempted to fill this conceptual hole in any subsequent disparate-impact decisions, or, for that matter, in any of its disparate-treatment cases concerned with the intentional discrimination against individuals, where the meaning of "substantial" is no less decisive.

The closest that the Supreme Court has come to statistical precision in this connection was in *Hazelwood School District v. United States* (1977)[228]— a case involving the low number of blacks on the appellant's teaching staff. There, the Court said, with reference to the disparity, that "a fluctuation of two or three standard deviations [from random hiring rates] would undercut the hypothesis that decisions were being made randomly with respect to race."[229] While "standard deviation" and "random sampling" are well-established mechanisms of statistical inference, the Court did not identify a disparity of "two or three standard deviations" as "substantial." On this crucial point, it said only that "where gross statistical disparities can be shown, they alone may in a proper case constitute prima facie proof of . . . discrimination."[230]

Given the absence of an explicit Supreme Court statistical standard in disparate-impact and treatment theory, "a flood of statistical tests (since *Griggs*) [has] . . . thundered forth from the lower courts" in Title VII litigation, but members of the statistical fraternity insist that the need for a "*quantitative criterion of substantiality [is undiminished].*"[231]

Absent such a criterion, the law of employment discrimination remains a statistical enigma. This fact leaves us on the horns of a dilemma. As seen above, disparate impact is a creature of measurement by numbers. If, as some suggest,[232] we forego inferential statistics altogether, enforcement of the law becomes a game of chance. On the other hand, statistics by themselves are clearly not a panacea. A number of leading statisticians feel that "statistical analysis of employment patterns is highly questionable and of limited utility."[233] For example, reliance on "random sampling" procedures in hiring-discrimination cases may be illusory, because it overlooks the fact that "the employment process is necessarily highly non-random,"[234] and because random-sampling procedure is based "on the implicit . . . and highly questionable assumption that, in the absence of discrimination, the percentage of (alleged discriminatees) hired would not differ substantially from the percentage of . . . (such persons) in . . . (the relevant occupational) population."[235] Harvard's constitutional law expert, Professor Lawrence Tribe, has gone further insisting that the use of statistical inference hides unstated assumptions, and often focuses on those areas of legal controversy that are quantifiable but not necessarily the most important. Indeed, to Tribe, quantification efforts make manifest the vagueness of legal analysis, and thus weakens the edifice of the law by lessening respect for it.[236]

The statistical standard dilemma has been unresolved—hanging fire if you will—since the day that *Griggs* was handed down in 1971. If affirmative action is to have any claim to conceptual integrity, its proponents must, once and for all, demonstrate whether a meaningful quantitative criterion of "disparity" can be worked out;[237] and, if not, whether, like other legal coins of the realm (such as "reasonable"), *substantial* is a term that can never be defined in the abstract, but is nonetheless indispensable.

The Theoretical Impasse over Affirmative Action's Economic Impact

During the 1970s and 1980s, race, ethnic, and gender-conscious affirmative action programs became a fixture in public and private employment and contracting. What impact have these initiatives had? Surveys indicate that protected-group affirmative action programs were widely adopted by America's large corporations, whose executives cultivated them, numerical goals and all. Of the 128 chief executives of America's largest (by net income) industrial corporations who were interviewed about their affirmative action plans, 95 percent insisted that they would continue using numerical goals and guidelines for the promotion of minority and female-occupational progress. Affirmative action has become part of big business's organizational culture, nurtured by an entrenched affirmative action bureaucracy.[238] On the whole, small business apparently finds affirmative action economically unattractive. A spokesperson for the National Federation of Independent Businesses (an advocacy group representing some 60,000 small businesses) reported that affirmative action is low on the list of priorities for small business.

For all that blacks and women have begun to climb the job ladder, they are still underrepresented in senior executive and managerial positions, the professions, and academe. And while their comparative income shares are considerably higher than in 1964, they are still predominantly stuck in the low-paying levels of public and private employment. Moreover, black unemployment has never fallen below twice the rate of white joblessness, even during the historic explosion of economic growth and job creation of the 1990s.[239]

As the frame of reference widens, it becomes even more obvious that upward mobility is an equivocal phenomenon. The minority community exhibits the same extremes as the general population. By conventional standards of income, occupation, educational achievement, and home ownership in integrated neighborhoods, at least one-third of the black citizenry must be considered "middle class."[240] This counts as a major achievement by numerous African Americans who, in the face of endemic racial discrimination, have made economic progress that matches, or even surpasses, that of similarly situated whites.[241]

On the other hand, our urban slums are inhabited by a chronically unemployed or underemployed underclass, mostly black, mired in poverty, substandard housing, education, and health care, dysfunctional families, welfare dependency, drug addiction, and inadequate public services.[242]

By many measures, the last two decades have witnessed impressive gains by women in education, salaries, and participation in traditionally male occupations such as business, medicine, and law. Between 1960 and 1980, females earned some 60% of male income;[243] by 1985, full-time female workers earned 68% of full-time male median income; and—by 1997, 74%. Impressively, between 1985 and 1997, female, full-time median income rose by a faster rate (56%) than did that of males (43%).[244]

Without doubt, there has been an extraordinary growth of paid-female and young-mother employees. Thirty percent of married mothers with preschool children were in the labor force in 1965; by 1995, it was 64%. Contributing to this movement—and to the enhanced status of women in the workplace—were such factors as improved education; birthrate decline; the rise in divorce; the reduction in housework burdens because of modern appliances; the reduction in male-dominated heavy-industry and manufacturing jobs; and the concomitant rise in "service-job" opportunities;[245] and, of course, second-wave feminism itself. Affirmative action could very well have been involved, but how much and with what impact remain open questions.

The increased movement of women to the workplace has not been an unmixed blessing. Helping to generate its momentum was the large army of "deadbeat" former husbands who have not met their alimony and child-support responsibilities.[246] Moreover, analysts insist that the nation is suffering from a child care crisis. In 1995, some 60% of children between ages one and five were in nonparental child care or in early-education programs, and—allegedly—most nonparental child care is mediocre or worse. Attendants at care centers are paid salaries that hover around the minimum wage level; and about one-third leave their jobs annually creating much instability. Providers who care for children in their own homes earn less that those who are center-based.[247]

Initially, second-wave feminism was a strong proponent of governmental augmentation of group child-care facilities. But this advocacy has been muted, as women of higher-economic status and power often choose "nannies" to care for their young. Nannies work for little, and have no job security. All of which replicates the oppressive foreign-land environments they characteristically come from. Arguably, the nanny industry reinforces these long-standing inequalities in order to "liberate" more-fortunate women.[248] The solution to the child care "crisis" is, to many, a kind of "reverse feminism": encourage females to stay at home, caring for their young there.

Others insist on urging greater governmental, nonparental child care subsidization and regulation.[249]

Some commentators maintain that racial/ethnic/gender disparities have largely been overcome;[250] others insist that, in many important respects, they have not only widened, but are "demonstrably intractable."[251] What is plainly lacking is a standard of judgment that will enable us to evaluate these claims. At present, it is an open question whether equal employment opportunity is at hand.

This brings us up against an overriding question: assuming that we have made significant progress toward equal employment opportunity, does affirmative action deserve any credit? From the start, our macroeconomic theorists have been embroiled in doctrinal warfare. One school vehemently maintains that enforcement of Title VII impairs efficiency, and negates the market's inherent antidiscrimination mechanisms.[252] But, contrary to this "neoclassical" free-market dogma, a different camp insists that Title VII enhances the market's efficiency and its ability to end discrimination.[253] There is no basis for resolving this conflict. Indeed, the latest economic review has concluded that "the theoretical literature from labor economics generates ambiguous results on whether or not affirmative action programs result in efficiency gains or losses."[254]

Some prominent scholars insist that affirmative action has been critical to the recent expansion of the black middle class.[255] Indeed, the increase in the percentage of black families earning between $50,000 and $75,000 annually is noteworthy, rising from 11.7% in 1975 to 14.4% in 1996. During the same time frame, Hispanic families experienced an increase from 11.2 % to 13%.[256] On the other hand, Stephan and Abigail Thernstrom emphasize that middle-class African America was growing rapidly prior to affirmative action's inaugural. It does not follow, then, that affirmative action was the sine qua non of black middle-class growth.[257] What then was responsible? Those who have performed the most careful of statistical surveys disagree with each other. Thus, James P. Smith and Finis R. Welch claim that equal employment opportunity law produced a sharp increase in black-male income starting in 1967. But subsequent to 1972, this was followed by a downturn to more traditional levels when compared to whites. To them, equal employment opportunity laws had little long-term effect;[258] the driving force behind the rapid economic advance experienced by blacks between 1940 and 1970 was improved education.[259] John J. Donohue and James Heckman, however, suggest that the governmental changes brought by the civil rights movement of the 1960s constituted the major contributor to black progress between 1965 and 1975.[260] But even they feel that EEO laws have not had a detectable impact since 1975.[261]

Another straddle is plainly visible even in the most up-to-date research. The article published in the September, 2000, issue of the *Journal of Economic*

Literature by Harry Holzer and David Neumark is an exhaustive technical survey of the economic literature, focused primarily, though not exclusively, on whether race/ethnic/gender-based affirmative action "improves or impedes efficiency or performance." Its arcane methodology may be largely unintelligible to nonpractitioners of the dismal science. But that said, the following "empirical" "inferences"[262] are instructive: 1. "significant" labor market discrimination and "societal disadvantage" persist;[263] 2. to an extent that "may not be large," affirmative action "redistributes" jobs and government business from white males to minorities and women, thereby definitely increasing employment and contracting opportunity;[264] 3. "redistribution" has resulted in a reduction of about 10 to 15 percent in white male employment in "affirmative action establishments,"[265] and may have achieved "near proportional representation" for minority-owned businesses in public procurement and contracting awards;[266] 4. wages for minorities and women are about 10 percent higher in affirmative action establishments;[267] and 5. affirmative action does not materially impair efficiency or performance.[268] But these are *inferences*. The authors stress that "it is impossible to assess the overall efficiency or welfare effects of affirmative action from [available] evidence."[269] Moreover, "it seems very unlikely" that such evidence will ever be unearthed![270]

Conclusion: Equal Employment Opportunity and Affirmative Action

In the late 1960s, we set out on the road to mandated equality of employment opportunity. Clearly we are not at journey's end. Discrimination is still among us, and we cannot agree on how far we have come. We believe that many have benefited, but we are not sure of how much, or at what cost to others. We are particularly unclear on whether affirmative action has helped or hurt. When its most ardent advocates equivocate,[271] one must wonder if their cause may have been oversold.

It remains to be seen whether we will ever reach our destination.

Appendixes to Chapter Three

Appendix One

—⚬⚬⚬—

Uniform Guidelines on Employee Selection Procedures (1978)

29 CFR 1607 (2000)

§ 1607.1 Statement of purpose. . . .

B. *Purpose of guidelines.* These guidelines incorporate a single set of principles which are designed to assist employers, labor organizations, employment agencies, and licensing and certification boards to comply with requirements of Federal law prohibiting employment practices which discriminate on grounds of race, color, religion, sex, and national origin. They are designed to provide a framework for determining the proper use of tests and other selection procedures. These guidelines do not require a user to conduct validity studies of selection procedures where no adverse impact results. However, all users are encouraged to use selection procedures which are valid, especially users operating under merit principles. . . .

§ 1607.2 Scope. . . .

C. *Selection procedures.* These guidelines apply only to selection procedures which are used as a basis for making employment decisions. For example, the use of recruiting procedures designed to attract members of a particular race, sex, or ethnic group, which were previously denied employment opportunities or which are currently underutilized, may be necessary to bring an employer into compliance with Federal law, and is frequently an essential element of any effective affirmative action program; but recruitment practices are not considered by these guidelines to be selection procedures. . . .

§ 1607. 3 Discrimination defined: Relationship between use of selection procedures and discrimination.

A. *Procedure having adverse impact constitutes discrimination unless justified.* The use of any selection procedure which has an adverse impact on the hiring, promotion, or other employment or membership opportunities of members of any race, sex, or ethnic group will be considered to be discriminatory and inconsistent with these guidelines, unless the procedure has been validated in accordance with these guidelines, or the provisions of section [1607.]6 below are satisfied.

B. *Consideration of suitable alternative selection procedures.* Where two or more selection procedures are available which serve the user's legitimate interest in efficient and trustworthy workmanship, and which are substantially equally valid for a given purpose, the user should use the procedure which has been demonstrated to have the lesser adverse impact. . . .

§ 1607.4 Information on impact.

A. *Records concerning impact.* Each user should maintain and have available for inspection records or other information which will disclose the impact which its tests and other selection procedures have upon employment opportunities of persons by identifiable race, sex, or ethnic group as set forth in paragraph B of this section, in order to determine compliance with these guidelines. Where there are large numbers of applicants and procedures are administered frequently, such information may be retained on a sample basis, provided that the sample is appropriate in terms of the applicant population and adequate in size.

B. *Applicable race, sex, and ethnic groups for record keeping.* The records called for by this section are to be maintained by sex, and the following races and ethnic groups: Blacks (Negroes), American Indians (including Alaskan Natives), Asians (including Pacific Islanders), Hispanic (including persons of Mexican, Puerto Rican, Cuban, Central or South American, or other Spanish origin or culture regardless of race), whites (Caucasians) other than Hispanic. . . .

C. *Evaluation of selection rates.* The *"bottom line."* If the information called for by sections [1607.]4 A and B [of these guidelines] shows that the total selection process for a job has an adverse impact, the individual components of the selection process should be evaluated for adverse impact. If this information shows that the total selection process does not have an adverse impact, the Federal enforcement agencies, in the exercise of their administrative and prosecutorial discretion, in usual circumstances, will not expect a user to evaluate the individual components for adverse impact, or to validate such individual components, and will not take enforcement action based upon adverse impact of any component of that process, including the separate parts of a multipart selection procedure or any separate procedure that is used as an alternative method of election. However, in the following circumstances the Federal enforcement agencies will expect a user to evaluate the individual components for adverse impact and may, where appropriate, take enforcement action with respect to the individual components:

(1) Where the selection procedure is a significant factor in the continuation of patterns of assignments of incumbent employees caused by prior discriminatory employment practices, (2) where the weight of court decisions or administrative interpretations hold that a specific procedure (such as height or weight requirements or no-arrest records) is not job related in the same or similar circumstances. In unusual circumstances, other than those listed in (1) and (2) of this paragraph, the Federal enforcement agencies may request a user to evaluate the individual components for adverse impact and may, where appropriate, take enforcement action with respect to the individual component.

D. *Adverse impact and the "four-fifths rule."* A selection rate for any race, sex, or ethnic group which is less than four-fifths (4/5) (or eighty percent) of the rate for the group with the highest rate will generally be regarded by the Federal enforcement agencies as evidence of adverse impact, while a greater than four-fifths rate will generally not be regarded by Federal enforcement agencies as evidence of adverse impact. Smaller differences in selection rate may nevertheless constitute adverse impact, where they are significant in both statistical and practical terms or where a user's actions have discouraged applicants disproportionately on grounds of race, sex, or ethnic group. Greater differences in selection rate may not constitute adverse impact where the differences are based on small numbers and are not statistically significant, or where special recruiting or other programs cause the pool of minority or female candidates to be atypical of the normal pool of applicants from that group. Where the user's evidence concerning the impact of a selection procedure indicates adverse impact but is based upon numbers which are too small to be reliable, evidence concerning the impact of the procedure over a longer period of time and/or evidence concerning the impact which the selection procedure had when used in the same manner in similar circumstances elsewhere may be considered in determining adverse impact. Where the user has not maintained data on adverse impact as required, . . . the Federal enforcement agencies may draw an inference of adverse impact of the selection process from the failure of the user to maintain such data, if the user has an underutilization of a group in the job category, as compared to the group's representation in the relevant labor market or, in the case of jobs filled from within, the applicable work force.

E. *Consideration of user's equal employment opportunity posture.* In carrying out their obligations, the Federal enforcement agencies will consider the general posture of the user with respect to equal employment opportunity for the job or group of jobs in question. Where a user has adopted an affirmative action program, the Federal enforcement agencies will consider the provisions of that program, including the goals and timetables which the user has adopted and the progress which the user has made in carrying out that program and in meeting the goals and timetables. While such affirmative action programs may in design and execution be race, color, sex, or ethnic conscious, selection procedures under such programs should be based upon the ability or relative ability to do the work.

§ 1607.5 General standards for validity studies.

A. *Acceptable types of validity studies.* For the purposes of satisfying these guidelines, users may rely upon criterion-related validity studies, content validity studies or construct validity studies. . . .

B. *Criterion-related, content, and construct validity.* Evidence of the validity of a test or other selection procedure by a criterion-related validity study should consist of empirical data demonstrating that the selection procedure is predictive of or significantly correlated with important elements of job performance. . . . Evidence of the validity of a test or other selection procedure by a content validity study should consist of data showing that the content of the selection procedure is representative of important aspects of performance on the job for which the candidates are to be evaluated. . . . Evidence of the validity of a test or other selection procedure through a construct validity study should consist of data showing that the procedure measures the degree to which candidates have identifiable characteristics which have been determined to be important in successful performance in the job for which the candidates are to be evaluated. . . .

C. *Guidelines are consistent with professional standards.* The provisions of these guidelines relating to validation of selection procedures are intended to be consistent with generally accepted professional standards for evaluating standardized tests and other selection procedures, such as those described in the Standards for Educational and Psychological Tests prepared by a joint committee of the American Psychological Association, the American Educational Research Association, and the National Council on Measurement in Education (American Psychological Association, Washington, DC, 1974) (hereinafter "A.P.A. Standards") and standard textbooks and journals in the field of personnel selection. . . .

§ 1607.6 Use of selection procedures which have not been validated.

A. *Use of alternative selection procedures to eliminate adverse impact.* A user may choose to utilize alternative selection procedures in order to eliminate adverse impact or as part of an affirmative action program. . . . Such alternative procedures should eliminate the adverse impact in the total selection process, should be lawful and should be as job related as possible.

B. *Where validity studies cannot or need not be performed.* There are circumstances in which a user cannot or need not utilize the validation techniques contemplated by these guidelines. In such circumstances, the user should utilize selection procedures which are as job related as possible and which will minimize or eliminate adverse impact as set forth below.

(1) *Where informal or unscored procedures are used.* When an informal or unscored selection procedure which has an adverse impact is utilized, the user should eliminate the adverse impact, or modify the procedure to one which is a formal, scored or quantified measure or combination of measures and then validate the procedure in accord with these guidelines, or otherwise justify continued use of the procedure in accord with Federal law.

(2) *Where formal and scored procedures are used.* When a formal and scored selection procedure is used which has an adverse impact, the validation techniques contemplated by these guidelines usually should

be followed if technically feasible. Where the user cannot or need not follow the validation techniques anticipated by these guidelines, the user should either modify the procedure to eliminate adverse impact or otherwise justify continued use of the procedure in accord with Federal law.

§ 1607.7 Use of other validity studies.

A. *Validity studies not conducted by the user.* Users may, under certain circumstances, support the use of selection procedures by validity studies conducted by other users or conducted by test publishers or distributors and described in test manuals. While publishers of selection procedures have a professional obligation to provide evidence of validity which meets generally accepted professional standards (see section [1607.]5C [of these guidelines]), users are cautioned that they are responsible for compliance with these guidelines. Accordingly, users seeking to obtain selection procedures from publishers and distributors should be careful to determine that, in the event the user becomes subject to the validity requirements of these guidelines, the necessary information to support validity has been determined and will be made available to the user. . . .

Appendix Two

—⟨ϕϕϕ⟩—

Affirmative Action Guidelines of the Equal Employment Opportunity Commission

29 CFR 1608 (2001)

§ 1608.1 Statement of purpose

(a) *Need for Guidelines.* Since the passage of title VII in 1964, many employers, labor organizations, and other persons subject to title VII have changed their employment practices and systems to improve employment opportunities for minorities and women, and this must continue. These changes have been undertaken either on the initiative of the employer, labor organization, or other person subject to title VII, or as a result of conciliation efforts under title VII, action under Executive Order 11246, as amended, or under other Federal, State, or local laws, or litigation. Many decisions taken pursuant to affirmative action plans or programs have been race, sex, or national origin conscious in order to achieve the Congressional purpose of providing equal employment opportunity. Occasionally, these actions have been challenged as inconsistent with title VII, because they took into account race, sex, or national origin. This is the so-called "reverse discrimination" claim. . . . The Commission believes that by the enactment of title VII Congress did not intend to expose those who comply with the Act to charges that they are violating the very statute they are seeking to implement. Such a result would immobilize or reduce the efforts of many who would otherwise take action to improve the opportunities of minorities and women without litigation, thus frustrating the Congressional intent to encourage voluntary action and increasing the prospect of title VII litigation. The Commission believes that it is now necessary to clarify and harmonize the principles of title VII in order to achieve these Congressional objectives and protect those employers, labor organizations, and other persons who comply with the principles of title VII. . . .

(d) . . . These Guidelines describe the circumstances in which persons subject to title VII may take or agree upon action to improve employment opportunities of minorities and women, and describe the kinds of actions they may take which are consistent with title VII. . . .

§ 1608. 2 Written interpretation and opinion.

These Guidelines constitute "a written interpretation and opinion" of the Equal Employment Opportunity Commission as that term is used in section 713(b)(1) of title VII of the Civil Rights Act of 1964, as amended, 42 U.S.C. 2000e-12(b)(1), and §1601.33 of the Procedural Regulations of the Equal Employment Opportunity Commission, 29 CFR 1601.30; 42 FR 55,394 (October 14, 1977). Section 713(b)(1) provides:

"In any action or proceeding based on any alleged unlawful employment practice, no person shall be subject to any liability or punishment for or on account of (1) the commission by such person of an unlawful employment practice if he pleads and proves that the act or omission complained of was in good faith, in conformity with, and in reliance on any written interpretation or opinion of the Commission. . . . Such a defense, if established, shall be a bar to the action or proceeding, notwithstanding that . . . after such act or omission, such interpretation or opinion is modified or rescinded or is determined by judicial authority to be invalid or of no legal effect. . . ."

§ 1608. 3 Circumstances under which voluntary affirmative action is appropriate.

(a) *Adverse effect.* [Disparate Impact] Title VII prohibits practices, procedures, or policies which have an adverse impact unless they are justified by business necessity. In addition, title VII proscribes practices which "tend to deprive" persons of equal employment opportunities. Employers, labor organizations and other persons subject to title VII may take affirmative action based on an analysis which reveals facts constituting actual or potential adverse impact, if such adverse impact is likely to result from existing or contemplated practices.

(b) *Effects of prior discriminatory practices.* Employers, labor organizations, or other persons subject to title VII may also take affirmative action to correct the effects of prior discriminatory practices. The effects of prior discriminatory practices can be initially identified by a comparison between the employer's work force, or a part thereof, and an appropriate segment of the labor force.

(c) *Limited labor pool.* Because of historic restrictions by employers, labor organizations, and others, there are circumstances in which the available pool, particularly of qualified minorities and women, for employment or promotional opportunities is artificially limited. Employers, labor organizations, and other persons subject to title VII may, and are encouraged to take affirmative action in such circumstances, including, but not limited to, the following:

(1) Training plans and programs, including on-the-job training, which emphasize providing minorities and women with the opportunity, skill, and experience necessary to perform the functions of skilled trades, crafts, or professions;

(2) Extensive and focused recruiting activity;

(3) Elimination of the adverse impact caused by unvalidated selection criteria (see sections 3 and 6, Uniform Guidelines on Employee Selection Procedures (1978), 43 FR 30290; 38297; 38299 (August 25, 1978));

(4) Modification through collective bargaining where a labor organization represents employees, or unilaterally where one does not, of promotion and layoff procedures.

§ 1608.4 Establishing affirmative action plans.

An affirmative action plan or program under this section shall contain three elements: a reasonable self analysis; a reasonable basis for concluding action is appropriate; and reasonable action.

(a) *Reasonable self analysis.* The objective of a self analysis is to determine whether employment practices do, or tend to, exclude, disadvantage, restrict, or result in adverse impact or disparate treatment of previously excluded or restricted groups or leave uncorrected the effects of prior discrimination, and if so, to attempt to determine why. There is no mandatory method of conducting a self analysis. The employer may utilize techniques used in order to comply with Executive Order 11246, as amended, and its implementing regulations, including 41 CFR part 60-2 (known as Revised Order 4),[272] or related orders issued by the Office of Federal Contract Compliance Programs or its authorized agencies, or may use an analysis similar to that required under other Federal, State, or local laws or regulations prohibiting employment discrimination. In conducting a self analysis, the employer, labor organization, or other person subject to title VII should be concerned with the effect on its employment practices of circumstances which may be the result of discrimination by other persons or institutions. See *Griggs v. Duke Power Co.*, 401 U.S. 424 (1971).

(b) *Reasonable basis.* If the self analysis shows that one or more employment practices:

(1) Have or tend to have an adverse effect on employment opportunities of members of previously excluded groups, or groups whose employment or promotional opportunities have been artificially limited,

(2) Leave uncorrected the effects of prior discrimination, or

(3) Result in disparate treatment, the person making the self analysis has a reasonable basis for concluding that action is appropriate.

It is not necessary that the self analysis establish a violation of title VII. This reasonable basis exists without any admission or formal finding that the person has violated title VII, and without regard to whether there exists arguable defenses to a title VII action.

(c) *Reasonable action.* The action taken pursuant to an affirmative action plan or program must be reasonable in relation to the problems disclosed by the self analysis. Such reasonable action may include goals and timetables or other appropriate employment tools which recognize the race, sex, or national origin of applicants or employees. It may include the adoption of practices which will eliminate the actual or potential adverse impact, disparate treatment, or effect [of] past discrimination by providing opportunities for members of groups which have been excluded, regardless of whether the persons benefited were themselves the victims of prior policies or procedures which produced the adverse impact or disparate treatment or which perpetuated past discrimination.

(1) *Illustrations of appropriate affirmative action.* Affirmative action plans or programs may include, but are not limited to, those described in the Equal Employment Opportunity Coordinating Council "Policy Statement on Affirmative Action Programs for State and Local Government Agencies," 41 FR 38814 (September 13, 1976), reaffirmed and

extended to all persons subject to Federal equal employment opportunity laws and orders, in the Uniform Guidelines on Employee Selection Procedures (1978) 43 FR 38290; 38300 (Aug. 25, 1978). That statement reads, in relevant part:

When an employer has reason to believe that its selection procedures have . . . exclusionary effect . . . , it should initiate affirmative steps to remedy the situation. Such steps, which in design and execution may be race, color, sex or ethnic "conscious," include, but are not limited to, the following:

The establishment of a long term goal and short range, interim goals and timetables for the specific job classifications, all of which should take into account the availability of basically qualified persons in the relevant job market;

A recruitment program designed to attract qualified members of the group in question;

A systematic effort to organize work and re-design jobs in ways that provide opportunities for persons lacking "journeyman" level knowledge or skills to enter and, with appropriate training, to progress in a career field;

Revamping selection instruments or procedures which have not yet been validated in order to reduce or eliminate exclusionary effects on particular groups in particular job classifications;

The initiation of measures designed to assure that members of the affected group who are qualified to perform the job are included within the pool of persons from which the selecting official makes the selection;

A systematic effort to provide career advancement training, both classroom and on-the-job, to employees locked into dead end jobs; and

The establishment of a system for regularly monitoring the effectiveness of the particular affirmative action program, and procedures for making timely adjustments in this program where effectiveness is not demonstrated.

(2) *Standards of reasonable action.* In considering the reasonableness of a particular affirmative action plan or program, the Commission will generally apply the following standards:

(i) The plan should be tailored to solve the problems which were identified in the self analysis, see Sec. 1608.4 (a), supra, and to ensure that employment systems operate fairly in the future, while avoiding unnecessary restrictions on opportunities for the workforce as a whole. The race, sex, and national origin conscious provisions of the plan or program should be maintained only so long as is necessary to achieve these objectives.

(ii) Goals and timetables should be reasonably related to such considerations as the effects of past discrimination, the need for prompt elimination of adverse impact or disparate treatment, the availability of basically qualified or qualifiable applicants, and the number of employment opportunities expected to be available. . . .

Appendix Three

===~@/@/@~===

Office of Federal Contract Compliance Programs: Affirmative Action Programs

41 CFR 60 (2001)[273]

. . . § 60-2.10 General purpose and contents of affirmative action programs.

Purpose. (1) An affirmative action program is a management tool designed to ensure equal employment opportunity. A central premise underlying affirmative action is that, absent discrimination, over time a contractor's workforce, generally, will reflect the gender, racial and ethnic profile of the labor pools from which the contractor recruits and selects.

. . . (3) OFCCP has found that when an affirmative action program is approached from this perspective, as a powerful management tool, there is a positive correlation between the presence of affirmative action and the absence of discrimination.

(b) *Contents of affirmative action programs.* (1) An affirmative action program must include the following quantitative analyses:

(i) Organizational profile—Sec. 60-2.11;

(ii) Job group analysis—Sec. 60-2.12;

(iii) Placement of incumbents in job groups—Sec. 60-2.13;

(iv) Determining availability—Sec. 60-2.14;

(v) Comparing incumbency to availability—Sec. 60-2.15; and

(vi) Placement goals—Sec. 60-2.16.

(2) In addition, an affirmative action program must include the following components specified in the Sec. 60-2.17 of this part:

(i) Designation of responsibility for implementation;

(ii) Identification of problem areas;

(iii) Action-oriented programs; and

(iv) Periodic internal audits.

(c) *Documentation.* Contractors must maintain and make available to OFCCP documentation of their compliance with Secs. 60-2.11 through 60-2.17.

§ 60-2.11 Organizational profile.

(a) *Purpose.* An organizational profile is a depiction of the staffing pattern within an establishment. It is one method contractors use to determine whether barriers to equal employment opportunity exist in their organizations. The profile provides an overview of the workforce at the establishment that may assist in identifying organizational units where women or minorities are underrepresented or concentrated. The contractor must use either the organizational display or the workforce analysis as its organizational profile:

(b) *Organizational display.* (1) An organizational display is a detailed graphical or tabular chart, text, spreadsheet or similar presentation of the contractor's organizational structure. The organizational display must identify each organizational unit in the establishment, and show the relationship of each organizational unit to the other organizational units in the establishment.

(2) An organizational unit is any component that is part of the contractor's corporate structure. In a more traditional organization, an organizational unit might be a department, division, section, branch, group or similar component. In a less traditional organization, an organizational unit might be a project team, job family, or similar component. The term includes an umbrella unit (such as a department) that contains a number of subordinate units, and it separately includes each of the subordinate units (such as sections or branches).

(3) For each organizational unit, the organizational display must indicate the following:

(i) The name of the unit;

(ii) The job title, gender, race, and ethnicity of the unit supervisor (if the unit has a supervisor);

(iii) The total number of male and female incumbents; and (iv) the total number of male and female incumbents in each of the following groups: Blacks, Hispanics, Asians/Pacific Islanders, and American Indians/Alaskan Natives.

(c) *Workforce analysis.* (1) A workforce analysis is a listing of each job title as appears in applicable collective bargaining agreements or payroll records ranked from the lowest paid to the highest paid within each department or other similar organizational unit including departmental or unit supervision.

(2) If there are separate work units or lines of progression within a department, a separate list must be provided for each such work unit, or line, including unit supervisors. For lines of progression there must be indicated the order of jobs in the line through which an employee could move to the top of the line.

(3) Where there are no formal progression lines or usual promotional sequences, job titles should be listed by department, job families, or disciplines, in order of wage rates or salary ranges.

(4) For each job title, the total number of incumbents, the total number of male and female incumbents, and the total number of male and female incumbents in each of the following groups must be given: Blacks, Hispanics, Asians/Pacific Islanders, and American Indians/ Alaskan Natives. The wage rate or salary range for each job title must be given. All job titles, including all managerial job titles, must be listed.

§ 60-2.12 Job group analysis.

(a) Purpose: A job group analysis is a method of combining job titles within the contractor's establishment. This is the first step in the contractor's comparison of the representation of minorities and women in its workforce with the estimated availability of minorities and women qualified to be employed.

(b) In the job group analysis, jobs at the establishment with similar content, wage rates, and opportunities, must be combined to form job groups. Similarity of content refers to the duties and responsibilities of the job titles which make up the job group. Similarity of opportunities refers to training, transfers, promotions, pay, mobility, and other career enhancement opportunities offered by the jobs within the job group.

(c) The job group analysis must include a list of the job titles that comprise each job group. If, pursuant to Secs. 60-2.1(d) and (e) the job group analysis contains jobs that are located at another establishment, the job group analysis must be annotated to identify the actual location of those jobs. If the establishment at which the jobs actually are located maintains an affirmative action program, the job group analysis of that program must be annotated to identify the program in which the jobs are included.

(d) Except as provided in Sec. 60-2.1(d), all jobs located at an establishment must be reported in the job group analysis of that establishment.

(e) Smaller employers: If a contractor has a total workforce of fewer than 150 employees, the contractor may prepare a job group analysis that utilizes [Equal Employment Opportunity] EEO-1 categories as job groups. EEO-1 categories refers to the nine occupational groups used in the Standard Form 100, the Employer Information EEO-1 Survey: Officials and managers, professionals, technicians, sales, office and clerical, craft workers (skilled), operatives (semiskilled), laborers (unskilled), and service workers.

§ 60-2.13 Placement of incumbents in job groups.

The contractor must separately state the percentage of minorities and the percentage of women it employs in each job group established pursuant to Sec. 60-2.12.

§ 60-2.14 Determining availability.

(a) Purpose: Availability is an estimate of the number of qualified minorities or women available for employment in a given job group, expressed as a percentage of all qualified persons available for employment in the job group. The purpose of the availability determination is to establish a benchmark against which the demographic composition of the contractor's incumbent workforce can be compared in order to determine whether barriers to equal employment opportunity may exist within particular job groups.

(b) The contractor must separately determine the availability of minorities and women for each job group.

(c) In determining availability, the contractor must consider at least the following factors:

(1) The percentage of minorities or women with requisite skills in the reasonable recruitment area. The reasonable recruitment area is defined as the geographical area from which the contractor usually seeks or reasonably could seek workers to fill the positions in question.

(2) The percentage of minorities or women among those promotable, transferable, and trainable within the contractor's organization. Trainable refers to those employees within the contractor's organization who could, with appropriate training which the contractor is reasonably able to provide, become promotable or transferable during the AAP [affirmative action] program year.

(d) The contractor must use the most current and discrete statistical information available to derive availability figures. Examples of such information include census data, data from local job service offices, and data from colleges or other training institutions.

(e) The contractor may not draw its reasonable recruitment area in such a way as to have the effect of excluding minorities or women. For each job group, the reasonable recruitment area must be identified, with a brief explanation of the rationale for selection of that recruitment area.

(f) The contractor may not define the pool of promotable, transferable, and trainable employees in such a way as to have the effect of excluding minorities or women. For each job group, the pool of promotable, transferable, and trainable employees must be identified with a brief explanation of the rationale for the selection of that pool.

(g) Where a job group is composed of job titles with different availability rates, a composite availability figure for the job group must be calculated. The contractor must separately determine the availability for each job title within the job group and must determine the proportion of job group incumbents employed in each job title. The contractor must weight the availability for each job title by the proportion of job group incumbents employed in that job group. The sum of the weighted availability estimates for all job titles in the job group must be the composite availability for the job group.

§ 60-2.15 Comparing incumbency to availability.

(a) The contractor must compare the percentage of minorities and women in each job group determined pursuant to Sec. 60-2.13 with the availability for those job groups determined pursuant to Sec. 60-2.14.

(b) When the percentage of minorities or women employed in a particular job group is less than would reasonably be expected given their availability percentage in that particular job group, the contractor must establish a placement goal in accordance with Sec. 60-2.16.

§ 60-2.16 Placement goals.

(a) *Purpose:* Placement goals serve as objectives or targets reasonably attainable by means of applying every good faith effort to make all aspects of the entire affirmative action program work. Placement goals also are used to measure progress toward achieving equal employment opportunity.

(b) A contractor's determination under Sec. 60-2.15 that a placement goal is required constitutes neither a finding nor an admission of discrimination.

(c) Where, pursuant to Sec. 60–2.15, a contractor is required to establish a placement goal for a particular job group, the contractor must establish a percentage annual placement goal at least equal to the availability figure derived for women or minorities, as appropriate, for that job group.

(d) The placement goal-setting process [just] described . . . contemplates that contractors will, where required, establish a single goal for all minorities. In the event of a substantial disparity in the utilization of a particular minority group or in the utilization of men or women of a particular minority group, a contractor may be required to establish separate goals for those groups.

(e) In establishing placement goals, the following principles also apply:

(1) Placement goals may not be rigid and inflexible quotas, which must be met, nor are they to be considered as either a ceiling or a floor for the employment of particular groups. Quotas are expressly forbidden.

(2) In all employment decisions, the contractor must make selections in a nondiscriminatory manner. Placement goals do not provide the contractor with a justification to extend a preference to any individual, select an individual, or adversely affect an individual's employment status, on the basis of that person's race, color, religion, sex, or national origin.

(3) Placement goals do not create set-asides for specific groups, nor are they intended to achieve proportional representation or equal results.

(4) Placement goals may not be used to supersede merit selection principles. Affirmative action programs prescribed by the regulations in this part do not require a contractor to hire a person who lacks qualifications

to perform the job successfully, or hire a less qualified person in preference to a more qualified one.

(f) A contractor extending a publicly announced preference for American Indians as is authorized in 41 CFR 60-1.5(a)(6) may reflect in its placement goals the permissive employment preference for American Indians living on or near an Indian reservation.

§ 60-2.17 Additional required elements of affirmative action programs.

In addition to the elements required by Sec. 60-2.10 through Sec. 60-2.16, an acceptable affirmative action program must include the following:

(a) *Designation of responsibility.* The contractor must provide for the implementation of equal employment opportunity and the affirmative action program by assigning responsibility and accountability to an official of the organization. Depending upon the size of the contractor, this may be the official's sole responsibility. He or she must have the authority, resources, support of and access to top management to ensure the effective implementation of the affirmative action program.

(b) *Identification of problem areas.* The contractor must perform in-depth analyses of its total employment process to determine whether and where impediments to equal employment opportunity exist. At a minimum the contractor must evaluate:

(1) The workforce by organizational unit and job group to determine whether there are problems of minority or female utilization (*i.e.,* employment in the unit or group), or of minority or female distribution (*i.e.,* placement in the different jobs within the unit or group);

(2) personnel activity (applicant flow, hires, terminations, promotions, and other personnel actions) to determine whether there are selection disparities;

(3) compensation system(s) to determine whether there are gender, race, or ethnicity-based disparities;

(4) selection, recruitment, referral, and other personnel procedures to determine whether they result in disparities in the employment or advancement of minorities or women; and

(5) any other areas that might impact the success of the affirmative action program.

(c) *Action-oriented programs.* The contractor must develop and execute action-oriented programs designed to correct any problem areas identified pursuant to Sec. 60-2.17(b) and to attain established goals and objectives. In order for these action-oriented programs to be effective, the contractor must ensure that they consist of more than following the same procedures which have previously produced inadequate results. Furthermore, a contractor must demonstrate that it has made good faith efforts to remove identified barriers, expand employment opportunities, and produce measurable results.

(d) *Internal audit and reporting system.* The contractor must develop and implement an auditing system that periodically measures the effectiveness of its total affirmative action program. The [following] actions . . . are key to a successful affirmative action program:

(1) Monitor records of all personnel activity, including referrals, placements, transfers, promotions, terminations, and compensation, at all levels to ensure the nondiscriminatory policy is carried out;

(2) Require internal reporting on a scheduled basis as to the degree to which equal employment opportunity and organizational objectives are attained;

(3) Review report results with all levels of management; and

(4) Advise top management of program effectiveness and submit recommendations to improve unsatisfactory performance.

§ 60-2.18 Equal Opportunity Survey.

(a) *Survey requirement.* Each year, OFCCP will designate a substantial portion of all nonconstruction contractor establishments to prepare and file an Equal Opportunity Survey. OFCCP will notify those establishments required to prepare and file the Equal Opportunity Survey. The Survey will provide OFCCP compliance data early in the compliance evaluation process, thus allowing the agency to more effectively identify contractor establishments for further evaluation. The Survey will also provide contractors with a useful tool for self-evaluation.

(b) *Survey format.* The Equal Opportunity Survey must be prepared in accordance with the format specified by the Deputy Assistant Secretary [of Labor]. The Equal Opportunity Survey will include information that will allow for an accurate assessment of contractor personnel activities, pay practices, and affirmative action performance. At a minimum, this will include such data elements as applicants, hires, promotions, terminations, compensation, and tenure by race and gender. As use of the EO Survey develops and evolves, the Department may at some time determine that one or more of the data elements currently included in the EO Survey should be altered or deleted. . . .

§ 60-2.31 Program summary.

The affirmative action program must be summarized and updated annually. The program summary must be prepared in a format which will be prescribed by the Deputy Assistant Secretary [of Labor] and published in the FEDERAL REGISTER as a notice before becoming effective. Contractors and subcontractors must submit the program summary to OFCCP each year on the anniversary date of the affirmative action program.

§ 60-2.32 Affirmative action records.

The contractor must make available to the Office of Federal Contract Compliance Programs, upon request, records maintained pursuant to Sec. 60-1.12 of this chapter and written or otherwise documented portions of AAPs [affirmative action programs] maintained pursuant to Sec. 60-2.10 for such purposes as may be appropriate to the fulfillment of the agency's responsibilities under Executive Order 11246. . . .

§ 60-2.35 Compliance status.

No contractor's compliance status will be judged alone by whether it reaches its goals. The composition of the contractor's workforce (*i.e.,* the employment of minorities or women at a percentage rate below, or above, the goal level) does not, by itself, serve as a basis to impose any of the sanctions authorized by Executive Order 11246 and the regulations in this chapter. Each contractor's compliance with its affirmative action obligations will be determined by reviewing the nature and extent of the contractor's good faith affirmative action activities as required under Sec. 60-2.17, and the appropriateness of those activities to identified equal employment opportunity problems. Each contractor's compliance with its nondiscrimination obligations will be determined by analysis of statistical data and other non-statistical information which would indicate whether employees and applicants are being treated without regard to their race, color, religion, sex, or national origin.

Chapter Four

———〰———

Affirmative Action and the Primary and Secondary Schools

Prologue

In this chapter, we deal with affirmative action's troubled role in countering racial discrimination in the nation's elementary and secondary schools. Segregation has afflicted public classrooms throughout the country since long before the Civil War. At the turn of the last century, although grossly unjust, it gained a measure of constitutional respectability under the "separate but equal" umbrella of *Plessy v. Ferguson* (1896).[1] Thereafter, it continued to flourish, de jure (by law) in the South; de facto (in actuality though not imposed by law) in the North and West as a by-product of segregated housing.

Plessy's separate but equal formula was the constitutional linchpin for Jim Crow segregationism in America.[2] The formula was applied in order to legitimate black/white segregation in public parks, schools, prisons, courtrooms, and swimming areas.[3] Jim Crow was not restricted to the South where its practice was most pervasive. The separate but equal doctrine itself emerged from an 1850 Massachusetts high court opinion (*Roberts v. City of Boston*[4]) which upheld a law requiring school segregation in the city of Boston—the very citadel of abolitionism. In that case, Chief Justice Lemuel Shaw opined that the segregation requirement was aligned with sociological conditions and attitudes; would help maintain peace and calm; and was not violative of equal protection so long as blacks had a right to attend public schools.[5] Blacks in the North and West, moreover, were either excluded from public accommodations (hotels, theaters, and the like), or restricted to particular areas. Some states even barred the immigration of African Americans to their jurisdictions.[6]

109

Segregation reflected a racist belief in the inferiority of African Americans. They were regarded as a lesser people, incapable of participating in civic affairs as full citizens. In the South, they were disenfranchised, prohibited from jury service, and were the recipients of inferior public services.[7] Sadly, during the late nineteenth and early twentieth centuries, the U.S. Supreme Court was an important bulwark of black "lesser citizenship." *Plessy v. Ferguson* (1896) is illustrative. Moreover, in the *Civil Rights Cases* (1883),[8] the Court determined that the Fourteenth Amendment only applied to state and not private action, thus frustrating Congress' Reconstruction effort at abolishing segregation in public accommodations. Yet, even at this time the Supreme Court did provide some victories, limited as they were, for black civil rights. Legally imposed racial zoning in housing was nullified.[9] Here the Court determined that property rights were superior to the segregation rights afforded by *Plessy.* Further, the Court took some steps to enforce the Fifteenth Amendment by barring an Oklahoma literacy test for voting (which exempted most whites from testing, but included most blacks),[10] and a Texas ban on black participation in the Democratic primaries.[11] And from the depression years of the 1930s, the Court increased its support for the African-American freedoms embedded in Reconstruction's principles.

In the epochal *Brown v. Board of Education* (1954),[12] the Court struck down public school segregation imposed by government. The opinion (excerpted below) was a critical event in the abolition of Jim Crow. Soon after *Brown,* and relying entirely on *Brown* precedents, the Court abolished all state-sponsored segregation.[13] To constitutional scholar Kenneth L. Karst, *Brown* was both a culmination of an effort to eliminate segregation, and "the catalyst for a political movement that . . . encouraged challenges to other systems of domination and dependency: systems affecting women, aliens, illegitimate children, the handicapped, homosexuals."[14]

For all its merit, *Brown* was evasive. It mandated the remedy of "desegregation," but left unclear the question of whether this meant merely the abolition of racial bars, or required, in addition, active mixing of the races. *Brown*'s implementation was left to unguided case-by-case rulings by the federal district courts. [See *Brown v. Board of Education* (*Brown II*) (1955).[15]] In Title VI of the 1964 Civil Rights Act, Congress banned racial discrimination in federally subsidized education (and in other programs), and provided that violators be denied federal funds.[16] But it was not until the late 1960s and early 1970s that the High Court established "integration" as the legal standard of desegregation in constitutional litigation: "dual" systems of governmentally segregated schools were to be totally and rapidly dismantled and permanently replaced by "unitary" systems of racially balanced classrooms, facilities, faculties, curriculums, and support services.[17] The irony of *Brown* is that while it helped to dismember Jim Crow in public accommodations, student populations in the metropolitan areas of the North and West remain dramatically segregated.

Brown has been read by many (but not all) as resting on the theory that segregation psychologically and academically burdened black children by cultivating intellectually hobbling inferiority complexes. Social scientists, at the time of *Brown* were considerably unified in the belief that only integrated schools could smother that inferiority and improve African-American education.[18] In this chapter, we review more recent considerations regarding the value of school integration—opinions by Justices Marshall and Thomas; and books by Gary Orfield, Stephen C. Halpern, and David F. Armor. Marshall's dissent in *Board of Education of Oklahoma City v. Dowell* (1991)[19] reflects the previously mentioned "social scientist" point of view, and argues that the *Brown* opinion was based on it. A latter-day version of it is preached by Gary Orfield in his *Dismantling Desegregation* where he argues that the psychic and academic disadvantages of segregated schools are produced by their impoverished-student bodies and disillusioned-teaching staffs. Justice Thomas' concurrence in *Missouri v. Jenkins* (1995)[20] insists that *Brown*'s prohibition of segregation was strictly a product of constitutional interpretation of the equal protection clause, and was not rooted in the psychic-damage theory.[21] This view is compatible with the ethnocentrism that arose concurrently with the inferiority-complex school of school integration. Briefly, blacks could not constitutionally be barred from attending "white schools" on the basis of their race, but black schools could be just as educationally sound as those that were integrated. Stephen Halpern's work accepts this view, but he calls for adequate and compensatory funding for minority schools. Some even insist that African-American children have been retarded by white domination at school, and that they would do better in single-race environments led by members of their own race who could help purge feelings of dependency and inadequacy cultivated by past and present racism.[22] Ethnocentrism is also on display in the affirmative action battle over bilingualism, another topic of the review herein. Finally, this chapter analyzes David Armor's *Forced Justice,* a book that challenges the view that integrated schools improve minority academic performance.

In fact, if not in name, public school integration conceptually overlaps affirmative action thinking in employment, voting rights, and housing. Both apply racial/ethnic-consciousness and attempt group remedies for minorities. Both use proportional-representation guideposts to remedy past group discrimination, eradicate its lingering effects, and prevent its recurrence. There is a technical, legal distinction—though much watered-down in school desegregation cases outside of the South—which has served as a barrier to big city/suburban integration. *Brown*'s requirements only apply to *de jure/intentional* segregation perpetrated by government, and not *de facto* segregation caused by such factors as residential patterns. If followed to its logical conclusion, de jure theory does not permit the presumption, in law, of discrimination, as in the employment and political representation areas of disparate-impact law. Of course, de jure theory was not a barrier to the abolition of segregation in the South where government required it. Furthermore, the de jure limit was softened for northern and western schools in *Keyes v. School District # 1, Denver* (1973)[23] where it was ruled that if de jure segregation is found in one portion of a school district, the entire district is presumed de jure segregated. Many northern and western districts have been subject to comprehensive desegregation through this presumption doctrine.[24] The Supreme Court rejected Denver's argument that the concentration of races in the schools was the function not of racism, but of the School District's neighborhood student-placement policy. To education specialist Diane Ravitch:

> Denver's experience showed . . . [that] sufficient evidence could be assembled to prove that almost any de facto segregated school system was actually an unconstitutional de jure segregated school system. While school officials claimed that racial concentrations reflected residential patterns, over which the schools had no control, civil rights lawyers contended that school policies and other state actions were responsible for creating and maintaining segregated schools.[25]

Nonetheless, the de jure/de facto distinction did have an important impact on the integration of urban and suburban schools. After finding de jure segregation in the Detroit public schools, the District Court ordered a remedy, which required the transport of students from a number of suburban Detroit areas to Detroit proper. In opposition, the Supreme Court ruled in *Milliken v. Bradley* (1974)[26] that school districts could be ordered to participate in curing de jure segregation elsewhere only if they helped cause that segregation, or were guilty of segregating their own districts. The expense and time-consuming nature of meeting the *Milliken* challenge resulted in the attenuation of cross-district remedies. In large consequence, the pattern that is evident today is one where minority schools are concentrated in the core cities of metropolitan areas surrounded by predominantly white schools in the suburbs.

Some school districts have undertaken integration efforts on a voluntary, nonremedial basis—that is, without a determination that intentional segregation has occurred. The need for student diversity has been used to support such voluntarism, but this thesis has met with considerable constitutional difficulty. Key appellate cases concern the Boston Latin School as well as magnet programs in Virginia. The courts in these cases concluded that the involved schools were operating racial-balancing/diversity programs in opposition to the equal protection clause. In the Boston case, it was determined that racial/ethnic-balancing was not shown to be "either a legitimate or necessary means of advancing" diversity, assuming that diversity was a compelling state interest.[27] Virginia's racial balancing was found in violation of the narrow-tailoring prong of strict scrutiny. There, the precedent-setting case was *Tuttle v. Arlington County School Board* (1999)[28] where the Court determined that narrow tailoring was frustrated because innocent, third-party children were excessively burdened by the racial-balancing program. The Court said, "The innocent third parties in this case are young kindergarten-age children, like the Applicants who do not meet any of the [racial-balancing] Policy's diversity criteria. We find it ironic that a Policy that seeks to teach young children to view people as individuals rather than members of certain racial and ethnic groups classifies those same children as members of certain racial and ethnic groups."[29]

The school integration movement is now "sputtering" along in "troubled waters." In 1995, the Supreme Court ruled that a primary goal in desegregation cases is restoration of local control, irrespective of whether integration goals have been fulfilled.[30] Several large districts have resegregated, in part, after going to court and winning a declaration that they have achieved "unitary" (i.e., integrated) status, thus freeing them from court-ordered integration plans.[31] Additionally, the advocacy for racial/ethnic-balancing in the schools has become much muted (where voiced at all); smothered, in part, because of other educational reform crusades such as the charter-school and voucher movements. The former are public schools that have been granted a state charter to operate independently of the regular school system. Charter seekers hope to produce an alternate and improved-teaching environment that is supposedly not realized in the existing public school system.[32] Vouchers are cash grants to parents, permitting them to send children to private schools that would compete with public schools for governmental dollars. Both charters and vouchers could be vehicles for integration, but, combined, they now educate only some 226,000 out of the 52 million schoolchildren in America.[33] Their growth may be much limited by the public school establishment, which insists that vouchers and charter schools are academically unsound because they drain funds and good students from the regular schools. Moreover, critics charge, voucher undertakings could be found to violate the constitutionally mandated separation between church and state since the private schools involved are often parochial. Vouchers are also challenged on the grounds that state constitutions require that the allocation of public monies be restricted to public schools.

Passionate defenders of racial balancing in the public schools remain, but even to some of these, that symmetrization objective has become increasingly irrelevant,[34] for it is widely agreed that major progress toward that balance rests on the doubtful realization of housing integration.

The Epochal *Brown* Ruling

Affirmative action has not been confined to the workplace. During the same year as *Griggs v. Duke Power Co.* (1971), the Supreme Court—in *Swann v. Charlotte-Mecklenburg*—sanctioned racial-balancing integration as an appropriate remedy for the evils of segregated public education.[35] During the ensuing generation, in tandem with equal employment opportunity, court-ordered classroom integration and busing swept through our society. This process can be seen as a variant of affirmative action, disparate-impact remediation that calls for cures designed to overcome societal discrimination affecting minorities irrespective of whether nefarious intent can be proven. In legal theory, K-12 educational integration is mandated only in intentional (de jure) discrimination. This "intent" requirement, however, has been much softened. As noted above, if a portion of a district was found to have been intentionally segregated, the remainder of the district is *presumed* to have suffered the same fate.[36] Beyond that, the rationale for school desegregation is generically the same as that offered for the remediation of disparate impact by affirmative action in employment, voting rights, and housing: racial segregation and other abuses have imprinted generations of minority children with deep-rooted feelings of inferiority, apart from robbing them of the intellectual benefits of adequate schooling. Merely to condemn segregation, and order that it cease, as was done in *Brown* (1954), does not begin to repair the damage. Only if proportionately sized groups of African-American and/or Hispanic children are placed in the same classrooms as their white peers, through busing and other devices as necessary, can the scourge of educational inequality be expunged. In short, a theory of compensatory group relief for discrimination imposed on groups.[37]

Let us first turn to the legendary *Brown* opinion:

Brown v. Board of Education, 347 U.S. 483 (1954)

MR. CHIEF JUSTICE WARREN delivered the opinion of the Court.

[486] These cases come to us from the States of Kansas, South Carolina, Virginia, and Delaware. . . .

[487] In each of the cases, minors of the Negro race, through their legal representatives, seek the aid of the courts in obtaining admission to the public schools of their community on a nonsegregated basis. In each instance, [488] they had been denied admission to schools attended by white children under laws requiring or permitting segregation according to race. This segregation was alleged to deprive the plaintiffs of the equal protection of the laws under the Fourteenth Amendment. In each of the cases other than the Delaware case, a three-judge federal district court denied relief to the plaintiffs on the so-called "separate but equal"

doctrine announced by this Court in *Plessy v. Ferguson,* 163 U.S. 537 [1896]. Under that doctrine, equality of treatment is accorded when the races are provided substantially equal facilities, even though these facilities be separate. In the Delaware case, the Supreme Court of Delaware adhered to that doctrine, but ordered that the plaintiffs be admitted to the white schools because of their superiority to the Negro schools.

The plaintiffs contend that segregated public schools are not "equal" and cannot be made "equal," and that hence they are deprived of the equal protection of the laws. . . .

[489] Reargument was largely devoted to the circumstances surrounding the adoption of the Fourteenth Amendment in 1868. It covered exhaustively consideration of the Amendment in Congress, ratification by the states, then existing practices in racial segregation, and the views of proponents and opponents of the Amendment. This discussion and our own investigation convince us that, although these sources cast some light, it is not enough to resolve the problem with which we are faced. At best, they are inconclusive. The most avid proponents of the post-War Amendments undoubtedly intended them to remove all legal distinctions among "all persons born or naturalized in the United States." Their opponents, just as certainly, were antagonistic to both the letter and the spirit of the Amendments and wished them to have the most limited effect. What others in Congress and the state legislatures had in mind cannot be determined with any degree of certainty. . . .

[490] In the first cases in this Court construing the Fourteenth Amendment, decided shortly after its adoption, the Court interpreted it as proscribing all state-imposed discriminations against the Negro race. The doctrine of [491] "separate but equal" did not make its appearance in this Court until 1896 in the case of *Plessy v. Ferguson,* supra, involving not education but transportation. American courts have since labored with the doctrine for over half a century. In this Court, there have been six cases involving the "separate but equal" doctrine in the field of public education. In *Cumming v. County Board of Education,* 175 U.S. 528 [1899], and *Gong Lum v. Rice,* 275 U.S. 78 [1927], the validity of the doctrine itself was not challenged. In more recent cases, all on the graduate school [492] level, inequality was found in that specific benefits enjoyed by white students were denied to Negro students of the same educational qualifications. *Missouri ex rel. Gaines v. Canada,* 305 U.S. 337 [1938]; *Sipuel v. Oklahoma,* 332 U.S. 631 [1948]; *Sweatt v. Painter,* 339 U.S. 629 [1950]; *McLaurin v. Oklahoma State Regents,* 339 U.S. 637 [1950]. In none of these cases was it necessary to re-examine the

doctrine to grant relief to the Negro plaintiff. And in *Sweatt v. Painter,* supra, the Court expressly reserved decision on the question whether *Plessy v. Ferguson* should be held inapplicable to public education.

In the instant cases, that question is directly presented. Here, unlike *Sweatt v. Painter,* there are findings . . . that the Negro and white schools involved have been equalized, or are being equalized, with respect to buildings, curricula, qualifications and salaries of teachers, and other "tangible" factors. Our decision, therefore, cannot turn on merely a comparison of these tangible factors in the Negro and white schools involved in each of the cases. We must look instead to the effect of segregation itself on public education. . . .

[493] Today, education is perhaps the most important function of state and local governments. Compulsory school attendance laws and the great expenditures for education both demonstrate our recognition of the importance of education to our democratic society. It is required in the performance of our most basic public responsibilities, even service in the armed forces. It is the very foundation of good citizenship. Today it is a principal instrument in awakening the child to cultural values, in preparing him for later professional training, and in helping him to adjust normally to his environment. In these days, it is doubtful that any child may reasonably be expected to succeed in life if he is denied the opportunity of an education. Such an opportunity, where the state has undertaken to provide it, is a right which must be made available to all on equal terms.

We come then to the question presented: Does segregation of children in public schools solely on the basis of race, even though the physical facilities and other "tangible" factors may be equal, deprive the children of the minority group of equal educational opportunities? We believe that it does.

In *Sweatt v. Painter,* supra, in finding that a segregated law school for Negroes could not provide them equal educational opportunities, this Court relied in large part on "those qualities which are incapable of objective measurement but which make for greatness in a law school." In *McLaurin v. Oklahoma State Regents,* supra, the Court, in requiring that a Negro admitted to a white graduate school be treated like all other students, again resorted to intangible considerations: ". . . his ability to study, to engage in discussions and exchange views with other students, and, in general, to learn his profession." [494] Such considerations apply with added force to children in grade and high schools. To separate them from others of similar age and qualifications solely because of their race generates a feeling of inferiority as to their status in the community that may affect their hearts and minds in a way unlikely ever to be undone. The effect of this separation on their educational opportunities was well stated by a finding in the Kansas case by a court which nevertheless felt compelled to rule against the Negro plaintiffs:

"Segregation of white and colored children in public schools has a detrimental effect upon the colored children. The impact is greater when it has the sanction of the law; for the policy of separating the races is usually interpreted as denoting the inferiority of the negro group. A sense of inferiority affects the motivation of a child to learn. Segregation with the sanction of law, therefore, has a tendency to [retard] the educational and mental development of negro children and to deprive them of some of the benefits they would receive in a racial[ly] integrated school system."

Whatever may have been the extent of psychological knowledge at the time of *Plessy v. Ferguson,* this finding is amply supported by modern authority.[38] Any language [495] in *Plessy v. Ferguson* contrary to this finding is rejected.

We conclude that in the field of public education the doctrine of "separate but equal" has no place. Separate educational facilities are inherently unequal. Therefore, we hold that the plaintiffs and others similarly situated for whom the actions have been brought are, by reason of the segregation complained of, deprived of the equal protection of the laws guaranteed by the Fourteenth Amendment. This disposition makes unnecessary any discussion whether such segregation also violates the Due Process Clause of the Fourteenth Amendment. . . .

Brown's Progeny

The above 1954 opinion—often called *Brown I*—was followed by *Brown II* (1955)[39] where the High Court allocated the initial primary responsibility for fulfilling the requirements of *Brown I* to the federal district courts so as to encourage sensitivity to local conditions. In doing so, the district courts were directed to proceed "with all deliberate speed," and to use their very expansive equity powers to advance justice.[40]

Whether *Brown I* required the states to go beyond the abolition of de jure segregation was left unclear. In any event, southern states (the initial focus of concern) widely resisted integration efforts. The latter were pursued by the Office for Civil Rights (OCR), now in the Department of Education. OCR threatened the cutoff of federal education funds where integration was not actively pursued on the theory that such failure violated *Brown I*, as well as Title VI[41] of the 1964 Civil Rights Act that prohibits racial and national-origin discrimination in educational programs subsidized with federal funds.

Initially, federal education officials allowed jurisdictions with de jure-segregative histories to use "freedom of choice" plans, enabling parents to choose the schools their children were to attend. This scheme proved unsatisfactorily slow to federal officials who then sought more rapid integration. This quest prompted *Green v. County School Board* (1968)[42] in which the Supreme Court decided (fourteen years after *Brown I*!) that school districts which had practiced de jure segregation were required by *Brown I* to adopt plans which realistically promised to promptly convert school systems into ones "without a 'white' school and a 'Negro' school, but just schools."[43] A year later, the Court reaffirmed its *Green* doctrine:

> The question presented is one of paramount importance, involving as it does the denial of fundamental rights to many thousands of school children, who are presently attending Mississippi schools under segregated conditions contrary to the applicable decisions of this Court. Against this background the Court of Appeals should have denied all motions for additional time because continued operation of segregated schools under a standard of allowing "all deliberate speed" for desegregation is no longer constitutionally permissible. . . . [T]he obligation of every school district is to terminate dual school systems at once and to operate now and hereafter only unitary schools.[44]

The Court in 1971 continued its *Green* activist stance in *Swann v. Charlotte-Mecklenburg* by recognizing judicial enforcement of "racial-balancing" formulas and busing as among the equity powers granted the lower courts in *Brown II* to combat segregation. The *Swann* ruling directed school authorities to "make every effort to achieve actual desegregation."[45] This command was generally interpreted by the lower courts to require racial-balancing/proportional-representation programs.[46] The impact of this new requirement in the "Old South" was quite dramatic. Although that area had fought bitterly to maintain segregation, federal education officials threatening fund cutoffs under Title VI had prompted a considerable degree of race-conscious student assignment. By *Swann*'s date of 1971, most southern blacks went to school with whites. Although many all or predominantly black schools remained, later racial balancing in the South reduced that considerably.[47]

The causes of northern and western de jure segregation were more subtle and obscure than the open and blatant racism of the South. We have already emphasized that the Supreme Court facilitated the process of finding actionable discrimination in those areas by presuming the existence of de jure discrimination in an entire district where it was found to exist in any part of it.[48] Further, artful (but very expensive, and time-consuming) lawyering could produce the needed de jure evidence. In the words of Diane Ravitch:

> A permissive transfer policy was one such . . . piece of evidence. School officials claimed that they adopted it to minimize white flight, but civil rights lawyers argued that white students used such policies to escape schools that were growing blacker; conversely, a nonpermissive transfer policy could be characterized as evidence of intent to lock blacks into their neighborhood schools. A school board's decision to build a school in a minority community could be construed as a tacit effort to contain blacks; conversely, refusal to build in a minority community caused black students to attend antiquated and inferior schools.[49]

In the 1974 case of *Milliken v. Bradley*,[50] the Court overruled a district court order requiring numerous Detroit suburbs to engage in cross-district busing to help desegregate Detroit's predominantly minority schools. School districts, the Supreme Court ruled, could be required to participate in remedying another district's segregation only if they helped create it or were guilty of their own de jure segregation. *Milliken* dealt a severe blow to metropolitan integration. In the words of desegregation-scholar, Gary Orfield: "No longer was the most severe segregation found among schools within the same community; the starkest racial separations occurred between urban and suburban school districts within a metropolitan area."[51]

Recent Scholarship on School Integration

To throw more light on the question of school integration, this section reviews three recent volumes on school integration: those by Stephen Halpern, Gary Orfield and his colleagues, and David Armor.[52]

Stephen Halpern's volume, *On the Limits of the Law* argues that racial-ethnic balancing and its associated legalistic efforts to move children from school to school have concentrated civil rights concern on a matter of lesser importance, to the neglect of improving educational opportunities for black children.[53] This improvement requires not the physical shifting of bodies that the "legal rights" strategy of school integration involves (although that strategy may be of some help), but a disproportionate allocation of educational resources to poor children so that they might be given the same advantages as wealthier students. The enriched backgrounds of the latter enable them to do better in school.[54] Remarkably enough, Halpern paid no attention to government's long-standing inventory of social welfare, compensatory education, and economic improvement programs. Likewise, while warning of the threat that integration poses for our historically black colleges and universities,[55] he passed over the question of whether African Americans might fare as well in an integrated-collegiate milieu as on largely black campuses.

The bulk of Halpern's book deals with Title VI of the 1964 Civil Rights Act[56] that prohibits racial, national origin, and color discrimination in the conduct of any federally subsidized educational program. Administrative enforcement was in large measure the province of the Office for Civil Rights now in the Department of Education. OCR's ultimate statutory sanction is the withholding of funds.

Halpern claims that OCR was originally the vanguard for advancing the educational opportunities of African Americans through Title VI, but it surrendered this role to the courts during the Nixon Administration. He claims further, as noted, that the courts have compromised the mission of aiding African-American education by concentrating on physical integration, and not on educational and fiscal resources. Halpern supplements his integration-questioning brief with an unsparing critique of the OCR and the Justice Department. In this Halpern scenario, Nixon decides to emasculate the vigorous enforcement program that began under LBJ. His motives were crassly political: to shore up his southern support by ensuring that OCR would not withhold funds on a broad scale. To advance this scheme, he transferred the initiative in integration policy from OCR to the courts, where the hapless bureaucrats are overwhelmed by the lawyers of the civil rights lobby. Oddly, the latter are less committed to the substance of civil rights than one might expect; they use the courts as arenas for purely procedural wrangles over time-limits and similar lawyers' games. In any case, during the post-Nixon presidency (at least to the end of the first Bush Administration), OCR and the Department of Justice have been "paper tigers," habitually declining to commit their substantial resources to advance minority education through Title VI.[57] One advocacy group (Citizens' Commission on Civil Rights) emphasized that the Clinton OCR was particularly vigorous, not in the realm of interschool integration, but in the effort to reduce racial and ethnic bias in intraschool student placement and ability grouping.[58]

There is no passion for racially balanced school integration in Halpern's book; the opposite is the case for the 1996 volume by Orfield and his colleagues, *Dismantling Desegregation*.[59] "Research shows," Orfield writes,

> that desegregation opens richer opportunity networks for minority children, but without any loss for whites. Part of the benefit for minority students comes from learning how to function in white middle-class settings, since most of the society's best opportunities are in these settings. . . . [T]he theory is not one of white racial superiority but a theory about the opportunity networks that historic discrimination has

attached to white middle-class schools and about the advantages that come from breaking into those mobility networks.[60]

Orfield notes that studies of four school districts undertaken by the Harvard Project on School Desegregation found no evidence that compensatory-education efforts (e.g., extra funds) undertaken in segregated settings cured educational deficiencies,[61] and while better-designed compensatory programs may work, they cannot replace integration as the means for improving minority education.[62] Moreover, rather than find fault with school integration's complicated legalistic forays as Halpern does, Orfield calls for even more sophisticated lawyering to stem what he sees as a clear trend by the Supreme Court to remove districts found guilty of de jure segregation from judicial supervision.[63]

Dismantling Desegregation is a compilation of case studies, framed by a legal and political history of *Brown v. Board*'s "quiet reversal" (to quote from the book's subtitle) in the years since 1954. To Orfield, the reversal is a veritable counterrevolution. Simply put, the Supreme Court, he argues, has gradually, if not formally, disavowed *Brown* and *Charlotte-Mecklenburg*. This sorry process began in *Milliken I* (1974)[64] where the Court forbade interdistrict, urban-suburban integration as a remedy for urban segregation, save for those districts guilty of intentionally fostering segregation. With this decision, as Orfield puts it, "the impetus of *Brown* and the civil rights movement for desegregating American schools hit a stone wall,"[65] since mandatory suburban/inner city integration was much hobbled as a consequence. Seemingly to compensate for the damage done by *Milliken I,* the High Court in *Milliken II* (1977)[66] permitted lower courts in heavily minority and segregated areas (subject to *Milliken I* restraints) to allow the allocation of disproportionate benefits to schools there as a way of equalizing integrated and nonintegrated education. But even here the Court, in Orfield's view, is dismantling desegregation. He points to *Missouri v. Jenkins* (1995),[67] holding that programs for equalizing segregated and integrated education must be limited in time and scope, *and that the sponsoring school districts cannot even be required to show that any improvement in the segregated children's educational status has actually been achieved.* In Orfield's words, "[the] rapid restoration of local control [is now] the primary [Supreme Court] goal in desegregation cases."[68] And local control, to Orfield, invites resegregation.[69] If this is so, and if the studies assembled by Orfield reflect the national attitude, then integration may be truly doomed, since, as these studies suggest, most of the local communities—all over the country—have never been reconciled to the integration vision of *Brown* found in *Green* and *Swann*. Orfield bitterly laments this state of affairs, and he prays that *Brown* be revived through (among other ways) the extraordinarily contentious policy of cross-town and metropolitan busing. Orfield argues that

GOP presidents have been primary villains in the gutting of *Brown,* particularly through their choice of conservative judges.[70]

Orfield correctly notes that the greatest advances in school integration have come in the South.[71] What he does not assess are reports that Nixon—after he failed to slow southern integration in the courts—personally encouraged southern school officials to integrate their schools, participating in what became the largest school integration experienced in the nation.[72] Orfield also neglects to note the marked decline in the zeal for public school integration in the liberal camp. Even the NAACP (traditionally stationed at the forefront of school-integration proponents) has recently experienced a strong movement from within calling for that organization's nonsupport of K-12 desegregation. African Americans are increasingly frustrated by white resistance, the busing burden placed on black children, and the notion that good education requires schooling with whites. Consequently, there is growing black emphasis on equalization in such matters as funding, and a dampening of integration advocacy.[73]

Armor's *Forced Justice,* complements the Halpern and Orfield volumes in that it incisively details what the judiciary came to mean by school desegregation; the techniques used to achieve these judicial standards; and some of the results of these efforts.[74] The author is a seasoned court expert, with an impressive command of the specialized school integration literature. He clearly supports the goal of desegregation, but feels that the system now in place is failing to achieve that goal, and ought to be reconsidered. He offers a concrete alternative.

The book contains an exceptionally clear, concise, and comprehensive review of the judicial requirements regarding school integration. This is no mean accomplishment, considering that the Supreme Court never promulgated any uniform standards for implementing its mandates in *Charlotte-Mecklenburg.* For this dicey job, the states and localities were given broad discretion (subject to judicial guidance), with the result that a bewildering variety of proportional-representation schemes have sprung up. Commonly, they perform matches, by grade level and with prescribed deviations, between the racial/ethnic composition of a given student body and the corresponding composition of the school district as a whole. For example, Boston allowed a deviation of plus or minus 10%; Denver, 15%; and even greater deviations have emerged recently as many communities struggle with the problem. Where minority students comprise a large majority of the student population, the courts customarily impose an absolute numerical standard: for example, in St. Louis and Detroit, where the school populations are 75% African American, the desegregation goals are a 50/50 racial split.[75] Here, Professor Christine H. Rossell's scholarship adds an important point. During the 1970s, judges imposed *mandatory* reassignment plans to achieve racial-balancing goals. By 1981, new judicially spawned, racial-balance integration plans focused on *voluntary* student reassignment induced at most by enticing "magnet" schools. We have, in short, returned "full-circle" to "freedom of choice" (a 1965 emphasis[76]) because the courts—faced with "white flight" and other rejections of mandatory mechanisms—have come to view voluntarism as a more effective integration tool.[77]

Armor argues that involuntary desegregation has not brought about significant educational improvement. In his view, the stress on impairment of minority self-esteem, as per *Brown v. Board*, is exaggerated. Further, the socioeconomic condition of the African-American family, and federal compensatory undertakings, seem to be considerably more important to African-American educational achievement than is desegregation. Armor is also alarmed by the urban population shift that headline writers are wont to call "white flight." He notes that white flight is related to desegregation, but argues that it occurs to a lesser degree in communities that adopt voluntary plans.[78]

As a measure of educational pathology, Armor relies on a so-called index of exposure. This is said to express the degree to which minority students are "exposed" to whites in school settings. By his account, in his base year of 1968, the "typical" African-American student attended schools that averaged 43% white in the country's large school districts. In 1972, the exposure rose to 54%, only to fall by 1989 to 47%, a mere 4% above the base. For the "average" Hispanic student the index stood at 70% in 1968, but fell dramatically to 51% in 1989. Armor contends that the decline in these numbers reflects white flight.[79]

What to do? Armor proposes to replace existing policy with a decentralized program of voluntary integration based on magnet schools and a voucher system. This will significantly reduce white flight and ensure freedom of parental choice. Public subsidies will be provided, as necessary, to give poor parents meaningful options. Armor opines that freedom of choice will bring about a deeper understanding of minority concerns and a greater willingness to strive for educational equality.[80]

Some parts of this disturbing book are open to question. Is the index of exposure conceptually valid? If "exposure" means mere physical proximity, what exactly is the educational significance of Armor's numbers? If it is also supposed to measure intellectual and social interchange, how can such intangibles be quantified? Is Armor's negative appraisal of integration as even-handed as it might be? Is he too quick to write off the issue of self-esteem? Has he given adequate weight to Orfield's claim[81] that there has been a rise in minority test scores, and a decrease in minority drop out rates in integrated systems? Would his proposed voucher system unjustifiably deprive less favored public schools of active, concerned parents and promising students?

Be all that as it may, there can be no question that Armor has made a powerful case for reexamining affirmative action in the schools, and this reexamination should take into account the strong feelings that quality education can occur in non-integrated settings.

The Meaning of *Brown I*

The concept of psychic stigma arising from segregation was a central construct in *Brown I*. Further, social scientists were once nearly unanimous in agreement that single-race schools would continue cultivating inferiority complexes among black youngsters interfering with their learning. It followed that racially balanced schools were essential both to the elimination of such stigma, and in the achievement of black intellectual progress.[82] None of the books reviewed above accepts the psychic-damage thesis. Orfield's zealous integration advocacy is positioned on a different theory of psychological and sociological malaise: minority schools are much inhabited by the poverty-stricken, and poverty environments frustrate both learning and the acquisition of beneficial contacts. Armor's research helped reduce the psychic-stigma consensus among scholars by presenting material challenging the notion that racial balance would improve minority performance, heighten self-esteem, and better race relations.[83] Halpern, moreover, is a strong advocate of adequately funded, *single-race* schools.

Justice Marshall's 1991 dissent in *Board of Education of Oklahoma City v. Dowell* (1991) fully accepts the view that *Brown I* should be interpreted as requiring integration to alleviate the psychic damage of segregation. Justice Thomas' 1995 concurrence in *Missouri v. Jenkins* maintains that *Brown I* only mandated the end of state segregation, and permitted the extensive continuation of single-race schools. The opinions leave open the question of how *Brown I* should be interpreted.

Missouri v. Jenkins, **515 U.S. 70 (1995)**

Justice Thomas, concurring.

[114] It never ceases to amaze me that the courts are so willing to assume that anything that is predominantly black must be inferior. Instead of focusing on remedying the harm done to those black schoolchildren injured by segregation, the District Court here sought to convert the Kansas City, Missouri, School District (KCMSD) into a "magnet district" that would reverse the "white flight" caused by *de*segregation. . . .

[T]he [district] court has read our cases to support the theory that black students suffer an unspecified psychological harm from segregation that retards their mental and educational development. This approach not only relies upon questionable social science research rather than constitutional principle, but it also rests on an assumption of black inferiority. . . .

[115] The mere fact that a school is black does not mean that it is the product of a constitutional violation. . . . Instead, in order to find unconstitutional segregation, we require that plaintiffs "prove all of the essential elements of *de jure* segregation—that is, stated simply, a current condition of segregation resulting from *intentional state action directed specifically* to the [allegedly segregated] schools." . . . "[T]he differentiating factor between *de jure* segregation and so-called *de facto* segregation . . . is *purpose* or *intent* to segregate." . . .

[116] It should by now be clear that the existence of one-race schools is not by itself an indication that the State is practicing segregation. The continuing "racial isolation" of schools after *de jure* segregation has ended may well reflect voluntary housing choices or other private decisions. Here, for instance, the demography of the entire KCMSD has changed considerably since 1954. Though blacks accounted for only 18.9% of KCMSD's enrollment in 1954, by 1983-1984 the school district was 67.7% black. That certain schools are overwhelmingly black in a district that is now more than two-thirds black is hardly a sure sign of intentional state action . . . .

[118] When a district court holds the State liable for discrimination almost 30 years after the last official state action [as it did in this case], it must do more than show that there are schools with high black populations or low test scores. Here, the District Judge did not make clear how the high black enrollments in certain schools were fairly traceable to the State of Missouri's actions. I do not doubt that Missouri maintained the despicable system of segregation until 1954. But I question the District Court's conclusion that because the State had enforced segregation until 1954, its actions, or lack thereof, proximately caused the "racial isolation" of the predominantly black schools in 1984. In fact, where, as here, the finding of liability comes so late in the day, I would think it incumbent upon the District Court to explain how more recent social or demographic phenomena did not cause the "vestiges." This the District Court did not do.

Without a basis in any real finding of intentional government action, the District Court's imposition of liability upon the State of Missouri improperly rests upon a theory that racial imbalances are unconstitutional. . . . [119] This position appears to rest upon the idea that any school that is black is inferior, and that blacks cannot succeed without the benefit of the company of whites.

The District Court's willingness to adopt such stereotypes stemmed from a misreading of our earliest school desegregation case. In *Brown v. Board of Education*, 347 U.S. 483 (1954) *(Brown I)*, the Court noted several psychological and sociological studies purporting to show that *de jure* segregation harmed black students by generating "a feeling of inferiority" in them. Seizing upon this passage in *Brown I*, the District Court asserted that "forced segregation ruins attitudes and is inherently unequal." . . .

Thus, the District Court seemed to believe that black students in the KCMSD would continue to receive an "inferior education" despite the end of *de jure* segregation, as long as *de facto* segregation persisted. As the District Court later concluded, compensatory educational programs were necessary "as a means of remedying many of the educational problems which go hand in hand with racially isolated minority student populations." Such assumptions and any social science research upon which they rely [120] certainly cannot form the basis upon which we decide matters of constitutional principle.[84]

It is clear that the District Court misunderstood the meaning of *Brown I*. *Brown I* did not say that "racially isolated" schools were inherently inferior; the harm that it identified was tied purely to *de jure* segregation, not *de facto* segregation. Indeed, *Brown I* itself did not need to rely upon any psychological or social-science research in order to announce the simple, yet fundamental, truth that the government cannot discriminate among its citizens on the basis of race. See McConnell, Originalism and the Desegregation Decisions, 81 Va. L. Rev. 947 (1995). As the Court's unanimous opinion indicated: "[I]n the field of public education the doctrine of 'separate but equal' has no place. Separate educational facilities are inherently unequal." At the heart of this interpretation of the Equal Protection Clause lies the principle that the government must treat [121] citizens as individuals, and not as members of racial, ethnic, or religious groups. It is for this reason that we must subject all racial classifications to the strictest of scrutiny, which (aside from two decisions rendered in the midst of wartime, see *Hirabayashi v. United States*, 320 U.S. 81, (1943), *Korematsu v. United States*, 323 U.S. 214 (1944)) has proven automatically fatal.

Segregation was not unconstitutional because it might have caused psychological feelings of inferiority. Public school systems that separated blacks and provided them with superior educational resources— making blacks "feel" superior to whites sent to lesser schools— would violate the Fourteenth Amendment, whether or not the white students felt stigmatized, just as do school systems in which the positions of the races are reversed. Psychological injury or benefit is irrelevant to the question whether state actors have engaged in intentional discrimination—the critical inquiry for ascertaining violations of the Equal Protection Clause. The judiciary is fully competent to make independent determinations concerning the existence of state action without the unnecessary and misleading assistance of the social sciences. . . .

Given that desegregation has not produced the predicted leaps forward in black educational achievement, there is no [122] reason to think that black students cannot learn as well when surrounded by members of their own race as when they are in an integrated environment. Indeed, it may very well be that what has been true for historically black colleges is true for black middle and high schools. Despite their origins in "the shameful history of state-enforced segregation," these institutions can be " 'both a source of pride to blacks who have attended them and a source of hope to black families who want the benefits of . . . learning for their children.'". . . Because of their "distinctive histories and traditions," . . . black schools can function as the center and symbol of black communities, and provide examples of independent black leadership, success, and achievement.

Board of Education of Oklahoma City v. Dowell, 498 U.S. 237 (1991)

Justice Marshall, with whom Justice Blackmun and Justice Stevens join dissenting.

[251] Oklahoma gained statehood in 1907. For the next 65 years, the Oklahoma City School Board (Board) maintained segregated schools— initially relying on laws requiring dual school systems; thereafter, by exploiting residential segregation that had been created by legally enforced restrictive covenants. In 1972—18 years after this Court first found segregated schools unconstitutional—a federal court finally interrupted this cycle, enjoining the Board to implement a specific plan for achieving actual desegregation of its schools.

The practical question now before us is whether, 13 years after that injunction was imposed, the same Board should have been allowed to return many of its elementary schools to their former one-race status. The majority today suggests that 13 years of desegregation was enough. . . .

In my view, the standard for dissolution of a school desegregation decree must reflect the central aim of our school desegregation precedents. In *Brown v. Board of Education,* (1954), a unanimous Court declared that racially "[s]eparate educational facilities are inherently [252] unequal."

This holding rested on the Court's recognition that state-sponsored segregation conveys a message of "inferiority as to th[e] status [of Afro-American school children] in the community that may affect their hearts and minds in a way unlikely ever to be undone." Remedying this evil and preventing its recurrence were the motivations animating our requirement that formerly *de jure* segregated school districts take all feasible steps to *eliminate* racially identifiable schools.

I believe a desegregation decree cannot be lifted so long as conditions likely to inflict the stigmatic injury condemned in *Brown I* persist and there remain feasible methods of eliminating such conditions. Because the record here shows, and the Court of Appeals found, that feasible steps could be taken to avoid one-race schools, it is clear that the purposes of the decree have not yet been achieved, and the Court of Appeals' reinstatement of the decree should be affirmed. I therefore dissent . . . .

[257] Our pointed focus in *Brown I* upon the stigmatic injury caused by segregated schools explains our unflagging insistence that formerly *de jure* segregated school districts extinguish all vestiges of school segregation. The concept of stigma also gives us guidance as to what conditions must be eliminated before a decree can be deemed to have served its purpose. . . .

[258] Remedying and avoiding the recurrence of this stigmatizing injury have been the guiding objectives of this Court's desegregation jurisprudence ever since. These concerns inform the standard by which the Court determines the effectiveness of a proposed desegregation remedy. See *Green v. New Kent County School Bd.*, 391 U.S. 430 (1968). In *Green*, a school board sought to implement the mandate of *Brown I* and *Brown II* by adopting a "freedom of choice" plan under which individual students could specify which of two local schools they would attend. The Court held that this plan was inadequate because it failed to redress the effect of segregation upon "every facet of school operations—faculty, staff, transportation, extracurricular activities and facilities." 391 U.S. at 435. By so construing the extent of a school board's obligations, the Court made clear that the Equal Protection Clause demands elimination of every indicium of a "[r]acial[ly] identifi[able]" school system that will inflict the stigmatizing injury that *Brown I* sought to cure. *Ibid.* . . .

[259] Similarly, avoiding reemergence of the harm condemned in *Brown I* accounts for the Court's insistence on remedies that ensure lasting integration of formerly segregated systems. Such school districts are required to "make every effort to achieve the *greatest possible degree of*

actual desegregation and [to] be concerned with the elimination of one-race schools." *Swann [v. Charlotte-Mecklenburg*, 402 U.S. 1], 26. . . .

Ethnocentrism, Affirmative Action, and Bilingual Education

The modern civil rights movement for integration was supplemented in the later 1960s decade with ethnocentric themes of black, brown, and red power, and with the value of nurturing distinct forms of cultural expression. One dimension of ethnocentrism was the insistence that the training of "limited English proficient" (LEP) students in their native language and culture was important to their development. Denial of "native" learning was portrayed as damaging. This quest for ethnicity legitimization was an important force behind the congressional subsidization of bilingual education starting in 1968. Members of Congress, however, viewed bilingualism as a way of facilitating the learning of English. Not so—critics maintain—for many bilingual advocates allegedly support that approach in order to preserve the native language and culture of LEP students.[85] All sides, nonetheless, accepted bilingualism as a necessary affirmative action measure—as a form of remedial group compensation for the societal discrimination suffered by those with limited English skills.

As guardians of Title VI, The Department of Education's Office for Civil Rights (OCR) assumed the role of promoting appropriate language training for LEPs. The criticism of OCR's language-training role by those who question bilingualism sharply contrasts with Stephen Halpern's critique of that Agency's role in school integration. OCR is faulted not for laggardness as it is in Halpern's brief regarding public school racial integration, but for aggressively pursuing the *segregation* of students with limited English skills.[86]

Linda Chavez's indictment of the OCR in this regard is particularly severe. As President of the Center for Equal Opportunity, an organization devoted to the abolition of bilingual education, she wrote in 1998 that:

> OCR has repeatedly made clear its bias in favor of bilingual education in meetings and conversations with numerous school districts. OCR has been staffed with ideologues more interested in the politics of bilingual education than its effectiveness. Using the threat of a cut-off of funding, a dozen states and hundreds of school districts have been blackmailed into instituting bilingual programs. Bilingual education . . . is now harming over a million Hispanic children in American public schools.[87]

Bilingual education, as most widely understood, teaches academic subjects to LEPs in their native tongues. Gradually, training in English is provided so that students can transfer to mainstream classes where the language of instruction is English.[88] Chavez argued that bilingual education is largely restricted to Hispanics who are segregated from other students, even in their English instruction. In the Chavez scenario, some other language minorities are taken from the regular classes for only part of the day to get special "English as a Second Language" instruction in classrooms which have students from a variety of nationality backgrounds. Still other LEPs with different ancestries are gathered together for all or most of the day in sheltered/structured English "immersion" programs. Consequently, non-Hispanic minorities have a far more integrated-educational experience. In the Chavez view, OCR's promotion of bilingualism is discriminatory and prohibited by Title VI.[89] She argued further that bilingualism is nourished by Hispanic organizations to thwart the assimilative process so that their constituencies and power are preserved. Assimilation is frustrated because bilingual training typically lasts five to seven years, is restricted almost entirely to Spanish-language instruction, and often is associated with an Hispanic "cultural maintenance" emphasis.[90]

Some ten states mandate bilingual education, and most others permit its use. Congress, since 1968, has helped finance its operations.[91] To its backers, bilingualism is the appropriate vehicle in that students—while learning English—are not denied an education in the arts and sciences accessible to them in their native languages. The executive director of the League of Latin American Citizens (LULAC) insisted that bilingualism did not nurture separatism. "Our purpose," he said, "in supporting these [bilingual] programs is precisely that of helping students be better contributors to mainstream American society. Those who insist on relegating minority-language students to an inferior status by placing them in situations where they are doomed to lag behind or fail are those who are actually promoting a continued separation due to lack of communication and achievement."[92]

This was nonsense to former Congressperson Robert Livingston who claimed that the United States was the only nation in the world which cultivated the view that a national language is best taught if it is withheld and parceled out in small doses. The less time you spend in teaching English, the longer it takes to learn it. Teachers, he continued, are forced to watch multitudes of Hispanic children denied meaningful English instruction when they could learn English within a year. This must end, he demanded. The denial of English relegates Hispanic children to jobs as busboys when they could be doctors. There are 3.2 million LEPs (up from 1.5 million in 1985), and the number is growing. The problem goes beyond economics; there is a threat of national disunity, as English bonds us. What is more, the vast majority of valid studies demonstrate that bilingual education is worse than doing nothing for the growing LEP population.[93]

The discussion over the supposed segregative impact of bilingualism has added fuel to the already furious—and unresolved—combat over how best to teach LEPs. One widely discussed 1977 study (financed by the U.S. Government) reviewed 38 bilingual projects and studied 286 bilingual classrooms. It concluded that most bilingual students were Hispanic, but that only one-third were English deficient. In short, bilingualism barred those proficient in English from participating in integrated, mainstream classrooms.[94]

This report prompted Gary Orfield, a former friend of bilingual education and consistent champion of school integration, to say: "As now operated, I believe that the grants (for bilingualism from the national government) often provide for expensive, highly segregated programs of no proven educational value to children."[95] However, the studies on the matter vary. Indeed, a later Government Accounting Office study determined that bilingualism was indeed effective in English-language training.[96]

The Office for Civil Rights fashioned Title VI of the 1964 Civil Rights Act into an affirmative action vehicle for language minorities in a 1970 memorandum to school officials. This directive declared that "where inability to speak and understand the English language excludes national origin-minority group children from effective participation in the educational program offered by a school district, the district must take affirmative steps to rectify the language deficiency in order to open its instructional program to these students."[97]

The OCR memorandum, while requiring affirmative action, did not insist on any particular approach to curing language deficiencies. The Supreme Court assumed the same latitudinarian standard when it upheld OCR's interpretation of Title VI's requirements in *Lau v. Nichols* (1974).[98] That case involved a class-action suit brought under Title VI for the purpose of requiring that the San Francisco school system increase its efforts to help LEP students of Chinese ancestry overcome their English-language shortcomings. To the Court of Appeals, which assumed a "sink or swim" attitude, the students did not have a cause of action, as "[e]very student brings to the starting line of his education career different advantages and disadvantages caused in part by social, economic and cultural background, created and continued completely apart from any contribution by the school system."[99] The class-action students did not claim intentional mistreatment by the school system. Rather, they relied on Department of Health, Education, and Welfare guidelines that barred disparate-impact discrimination (be it intentional or not) in educational institutions receiving federal monies. In finding for the students, the Supreme Court approved these guidelines as appropriate for implementing Title VI of the 1964 Civil Rights Act. In so doing, the Court quoted from the administrative regulations as follows:

[The] [d]iscrimination among students on account of race or national origin that is prohibited includes "discrimination . . . in the availability or use of any academic . . . or other facilities of the grantee [educational institution]. . . ."

Discrimination is barred which has that *effect* [of restricting students in the use of educational resources] even though no purposeful design is present: a recipient [of federal money] "may not . . . utilize criteria or methods of administration which have the effect of subjecting individuals to discrimination" or [have] "the effect of defeating or substantially impairing accomplishment of the objectives of the program as respect individuals of a particular race, color, or national origin."[100]

In *Lau,* the Court offered no specific regimen for treating language deficiency. "Teaching English to the students of Chinese ancestry . . . is one choice. Giving instructions to this group in Chinese is another. There may be others. Petitioners ask only that the Board of Education be directed to apply its expertise to the problem and rectify the situation."[101]

Subsequent to *Lau,* OCR, in 1975, published what came to be called the *Lau* Guidelines, implementing the Court's ruling. But the latitudinarianism of that ruling vanished in that these new Guidelines construed as acceptable only LEP-training, which emphasized native-language instruction. The *Lau* Guidelines resulted in some five hundred consent agreements devised by OCR with the school districts.[102] To one former senior OCR official, "These plans were in a very real sense coerced agreements, since OCR threatened to cut off federal funds if a school did not implement a bilingual education program."[103]

The *Lau* Guidelines were not formulated in accord with the formal administrative law requirement that regulations from the bureaucracy be subject to public comment prior to implementation. When challenged on this ground in court, the Guidelines were withdrawn. In 1985, the Reagan Administration OCR notified the school districts with *Lau* Guidelines approved plans, that bilingualism was no longer required. Schools were to conform with the standards of the widely cited Fifth Circuit Court of Appeals opinion in *Castaneda v. Pickard* (1989).[104] That opinion ruled that the *Lau* assistance requirement could be met by using any technique judged educationally sound by at least *some* expert educators, so long as that technique was periodically evaluated and changed if found wanting. Reportedly, however, the *Casteneda* flexibility did not impede the Clinton Administration OCR from strongly reemphasizing bilingualism.[105]

A language-policy student has written that bilingualism advocacy involved an Hispanic ethnocentric-status quest—one that generated a "status backlash" by English only/English first movements. These latter movements find bilingual education threatening to their notion of the American way of life. The backlash has mobilized public opinion sufficiently to have English declared as the official language in at least eight states and numerous localities. Both bilingual and English first/only advocates view language as critical to cultural identity and allegiance. Consequently, the debate has been acrimonious, involving fevered charges and denials of racism, immigrant-bashing, and anti-Americanism.[106]

Doubtless, this status conflict fueled the furious debate over California's Proposition 227 (1998) which legalized a requirement that the English-deficient student be subject to sheltered English immersion in their schooling "not normally intended to exceed one year." Under this referendum initiative, once English-learners have acquired a good working knowledge of English, they are to be transferred to mainstream English classrooms. "Sheltered English immersion . . . means an English language acquisition process for young children in which nearly all classroom instruction is in English but with curriculum and presentation designed for children who are learning the language." Waivers, good for one year, from English immersion, and permitting the continuation of bilingualism can be obtained by parents for one of the following reasons: where children demonstrate good English skills by standardized tests; where children are ten or older, and the school educators feel that an alternative to immersion is appropriate; and where there are children under ten with special needs, that is, those who educators feel would do better with an alternative to English immersion. Written descriptions of these special needs are required to support these waivers, and these descriptions are subject to review and approval by local school superintendents who are to operate under guidelines created by local and state boards of education.[107]

Proposition 227 was ratified by a 61% majority, with fewer than 4 out of 10 Hispanics supporting it.[108] Claims of prejudice, racism, and discrimination were passionately voiced in post-referendum interviews, despite the efforts made by leading proponents of 227 to portray the measure as necessary for Hispanic upward mobility.[109] The Clinton Administration attacked 227 as too rigid, impeding the flexibility needed for English training.[110] In fact, however, the proposition allowed for a flexible waiver policy outlined above. At the onset of 227's implementation, the granting of waivers varied from jurisdiction to jurisdiction. Some 40% of Oakland and Hayward's LEPs were given waivers. In Berkeley, 14% were; but in Oceanside, only 5 of the 150 requests were allowed.[111]

At least initially, some school administrators fashioned "flexible" approaches in connection with the "nearly all in English" requirement in 227's immersion scheme. Many LEPs have experienced much Spanish instruction in their "English immersion."[112] Some districts used a 60%–40% English-foreign language formula in their "immersion" programs; other formulas included 80–20, and 70–30 distributions.[113]

A referendum modeled after 227 was ratified in Arizona,[114] but as California voted to limit bilingualism, school administrators in New York, New Jersey, and Connecticut remained committed to their extensive bilingual practices. But in those states, there was an increased emphasis on facilitating English acquisition. The *New York Times* report on the subject maintained that the difference between the East and West Coasts grew out of absence in the East of a popular referendum process capable of changing school policy. Consequently, to end bilingualism, state legislators would face a fierce battle with the teachers' unions and ethnic groups. And this they are most reluctant to do.[115] One bilingual opponent noted that "the only time you're going to see serious change in the Northeast is when you see big grassroots efforts that will serve as cover for legislators who want change."[116]

Sheltered immersion and bilingualism are affirmative action programs. Both involve group remedies for the purpose of helping protected minorities achieve full-measured participation in American life by avoiding the negative impact imposed on LEPs by an English-language society. And overcoming this societal/systemic disparate impact is a committed objective of the language activists on all sides. Their bickering and cries of conspiracy indeed reflect the intensity of that commitment. Despite the race and ethnic-consciousness associated with LEP affirmative action, it has escaped strict judicial scrutiny. In light of *Richmond v. Croson* (1989) and *Adarand Constructors Inc. v. Peña* (1995), should this exemption continue? Can a compelling case be made for any approach to the training of LEPs?

The Twilight of Public School Racial/Ethnic Balancing, and the Continuing Quest for Reform

Racial/ethnic balancing in the schools as a vehicle for improving minority performance has lost much of its vitality. It has been overshadowed by other quests to improve the supposedly flawed primary and secondary school system for all students. In the last half-century, the nation has been agitated by numerous education-reform proposals and policies. After the Soviet Union launched its space missile (Sputnik) in 1957, many were "up-in-arms" over the need to improve science and technology training. This concern led to such developments as the "new math," now largely abandoned to the relief of many parents and teachers. During the post-Sputnik Era, there was a particular focus on "open education" with its emphasis on increasing "self-directed" child learning. Teachers were to act more as facilitators, rather than as transmitters of book learning through formal lecturing, memorization, and the like.[117] At the opening of this "New Millennium," voucher subsidization and charter schools are very much in vogue.

Most whites report satisfaction with public schools, but only a minority of African Americans and Hispanics find theirs satisfactory. Both of these minority groups strongly support vouchers.[118] Existing voucher programs are meant to incorporate the minority poor and their children, but the criteria are economic, or (in the case of Florida) academic performance, and not race or ethnicity.[119]

Recent reform efforts have not been restricted to those discussed above. Few areas have been spared. A more comprehensive list of reform policies would include early childhood undertakings meant to overcome cultural deprivations (e.g., Head Start); higher graduation standards; curricular reform in every subject; and the redesign of teacher preparation.[120] Nonetheless—in the view of student-performance experts—"only a portion of the achievement gap between advantaged and disadvantaged students—and between minority and majority students" has been closed. "Moreover, most of the documented achievement gains have been in the form of fewer students achieving at very low levels." Societal forces largely uncontrollable by educators hinder reform: poverty; unstable communities, and the schools therein; and high mobility rates among disadvantaged students which are "often mirrored by the high turnover of principals and teachers. . . . Even if reforms are successfully implemented in a school, highly mobile students will not be able to attend long enough for the school to make a difference to them." It may be that school reform is of secondary importance for the disadvantaged young. "[I]ncreasing the supply of adequately paying jobs for their low-skilled parents may be more pressing than school improvement. . . . All this suggests that a much more broadly conceived educational and social reform agenda may be required to respond effectively to the needs of our increasingly diverse student population, and its most disadvantaged segments."[121]

Chapter Five

—~/*/*/*~—

Affirmative Action in Higher Education

Prologue

Access to higher learning is one of the most esteemed prizes in our society. In this chapter, we survey the intense legal and scholarly controversy over remedial and nonremedial (diversity) affirmative action as a vehicle of eligibility for this benefit.

Does the equal protection clause countenance race, ethnicity, or sex as criteria of admission to our colleges and universities? Does this depend entirely on proof of past discrimination; or may the need for more "diverse" student bodies also justify a resort to affirmative action? What is the capacity of state government and its referendum process to limit affirmative action in education and elsewhere? Manifestly, these are bedrock issues, but the Supreme Court has declined to answer them.

On the nonlegal front, we confront a bedlam of conflicting opinions about the value of affirmative action and the quest for student-body diversification in admissions policy; the substitution of "class preference" for race/ethnic preference; and the value of a testing meritocracy—that is, the benefit of standardized testing like the SAT versus grades and other indicia of competence.

Other major concerns surveyed in this chapter include the application of racial-balancing formulas to the formerly de jure-segregated Historically Black Colleges and Universities (HBCUs) and their white counterparts, the Traditionally White Institutions (TWIs); the constitutional status of single-sex schools; and requirements related to the prohibition of sex discrimination in Title IX of the Education Act of 1972.[1]

Affirmative Action and Student Admissions:
Bakke and the Scholarly Debate

Our universities and graduate schools are a separate battleground in the war against discrimination. In the past, they too often restricted or excluded minorities. Nevertheless, resistance to affirmative action conducted through preferential admissions policies is now clearly on the rise. For those seeking reasonable certainty in the law, the scenario is regrettable and saddening. To escape loss of federal funding under Title VI of the Civil Rights Act of 1964,[2] and prodded by the civil rights upheaval of the 1960s and the attendant desire "to develop interracial leadership for the future good of society,"[3] state-sponsored institutions devise preferential policies for admitting, and/or awarding scholarships to, assertedly deserving minority applicants. The devices have ranged from fixed quotas to weighted considerations of race, ethnicity, gender, and the like. These devices are supported either as group remedies for past discrimination, in accordance with orthodox affirmative action compensatory theory, and/or as attempts to ensure the diversity of the student body. Particularly since *Richmond v. Croson* (1989)/*Adarand Constructors Inc. v. Peña* (1995) and their strict scrutiny requirement, the dominant theme has come to be diversity. Application of the preferential formulas results in rejection of some non-minority applicants in favor of arguably less-qualified minorities. Suits claiming violation of constitutional guarantees and charging reverse discrimination follow. The issues reach the Supreme Court in 1974, but still await final resolution!

The Supreme Court's first encounter with reverse discrimination in university admissions ended in a 5–4 refusal to decide the merits of the case, on the disingenuous grounds that the issue had become moot! (See *DeFunis v. Odegard* [1974]).[4] The second time around was the watershed case of *Regents v. Bakke* (1978),[5] the High Court's first attempt to define the standard of judicial review for voluntary public affirmative action. (See the discussion of *Bakke* at pages 55–57 above.) The decision came to stand for the proposition that state-supported universities may apply race/ethnicity/gender as a criterion, among others, of admission.[6] Some viewed *Bakke* as representing the Court's first nonremedial application of strict scrutiny in that it was widely taken to mean that preferential admissions for diversity purposes could conform to the dictates of compelling government interest and narrow tailoring. In 1996, however, that view was rejected by the Fifth Circuit in *Hopwood v. Texas*.[7] Whether diversity concerns can support preferential admissions under strict scrutiny has since become one of the most controversial issues in civil rights law. *Hopwood* held that diversity can *never* be a "compelling interest" for strict scrutiny purposes, and that the University of Texas Law School violated the equal protection clause by lowering Law School Aptitude Test (LSAT) and grade requirements for minority applicants.[8]

The impact of *Bakke* on medical and law schools was the concern of Susan Welch and John Gruhl's volume *Affirmative Action and Minority Enrollments in Medical and Law Schools.*[9] To this end, the authors studied minority enrollment trends over the twenty-year periods before and after *Bakke.* Additionally, the volume relies on a survey of medical and law school admissions officers conducted in 1989.

Welch and Gruhl conclude that most medical and law schools practiced preferential minority admissions before and after *Bakke,* and that *Bakke* prompted an even greater emphasis on racial considerations in the admissions process. They cite Professor Bernard Schwartz's *Behind Bakke*[10] in their conclusion:

> "Virtually all universities and professional schools (after *Bakke*) have maintained their program for minority admissions and have operated them to secure roughly the same percentage of minority students each year." (B. Schwartz 1988, 155) An admissions official responding to our survey was only slightly more circumspect. ". . . *Bakke* taught me that I should be careful not to think or express myself in terms of quotas. I think too that it vindicated what most law schools had been doing for a long time, i.e., bending over backwards to give minorities a chance."[11]

Welch and Gruhl argue that by legitimating affirmative action, *Bakke* set the stage for dramatic increases in the number of blacks and Hispanics at the undergraduate level and in professional schools. Black college enrollment increased by 30% between 1986 and 1994. In that time, African-American acquisition of undergraduate degrees rose by 34%; master's by 40%. For the same period, Hispanic enrollment and the earning of bachelor's degrees surged by 50%. And Hispanics experienced almost the same increase in the winning of master's diplomas. Minority progress in medical and law schools has been equally impressive.

Welch and Gruhl's coupling of *Bakke* with the rise in minority undergraduate enrollment is not indisputable. Stephan Thernstrom—the noted historian—maintains that "[t]he vast majority of blacks and Hispanics [like other college students] then and now attend basically nonselective schools at which there are no racial double standards in admissions; there are hardly any standards at all." Thernstrom also takes Welch and Gruhl to task for failing to "even mention the academic difficulties of preferentially admitted medical students and the huge and shocking racial differential in rates of passing Part I of the Medical Boards and in qualifying as board-certified physicians in their specialty."[12] Thernstrom also accentuates the failure rate among minority law students in his critique of Linda Wightman's influential New York University Law Review article, *Threat to Diversity in Legal Education*.[13] There—relying on a formidable data base which included the 1990-1991 applicants and admittees to the American Bar Association (ABA)-approved law schools— she concluded that preferential admissions played a very significant role in minority admissions. So much so that if admission relied on LSAT scores and grades the result would have been "a law school student body that mirrored the ethnic makeup of law schools of thirty years ago."[14] Furthermore, the data suggested that there are *"no significant differences"* between preferential admittees and those accepted on grades and LSAT scores in terms of bar exam passage.[15] Thernstrom used Wightman's data to underscore black fail- ure in law school. He wrote that "washout" (by failing to graduate or pass the bar) for blacks "who entered law school as a result of racial preference—the vast majority of them . . . —was a horrendous 43.2 percent."[16] Thus, some four out of ten African Americans who entered ABA-approved law schools never became attorneys.[17] Of course, this Thernstrom challenge leaves impor- tant issues: Were the "washouts" really "washouts"? Did they not gain much from the law school experience? Has America benefited from their experience?

In the polemics of the debate over minority admissions, the proponents of class-based preference are particularly vociferous. For instance, Richard D. Kahlenberg, in *The Remedy*,[18] maintains that the substantial black-white gap in SAT scores is essentially a function of differences in economic status, rather than race, and therefore that race should be supplanted by consider- ation of class status as a criterion of admission. Contrary to this view, K. Anthony Appiah and Amy Gutmann contend that the SAT-gap statistics tend to support both race and class as admission criteria.[19] In other words, the statistics warrant an inference of both race disadvantage and class disadvan- tage, and class advocates have not adduced any independent basis for differ- entiating between the two. Therefore, it is inconsistent and unfair to exclude racial preference from the remedial picture. If this analysis has merit, it argues for retention of race-based affirmative action in higher education, in order to ensure the inclusion of meritorious blacks.[20]

An impassioned case for continuing race-based affirmative action in higher learning has been made by Ronald Dworkin in a New York Review of Books essay, *Affirming Affirmative Action*.[21] Dworkin reviews William Bowen and Derek Bok's *The Shape of the River: Long-Term Consequences Of Considering Race In College and University Admissions*,[22] and uses that review as a spring- board for a moral and practical defense of preferential affirmative action at the university level, and for antidiscrimination policy generally.

According to Dworkin, the Bowen and Bok book, written by two scions of the Ivy League, is the first comprehensive and statistically sophisticated study of the impact of affirmative action in higher education. It analyzes the undergraduate and postuniversity careers of over eighty thousand matriculants at the twenty-eight "most selective" universities that used preferential affirmative action.[23] It attempts to chart affirmative action's consequences for the individual students and graduates, their universities, and race relations in the country as a whole.[24] Bowen and Bok conclude that:

> [T]he most selective colleges and universities have succeeded in educating sizable numbers of minority students who have already achieved considerable success and seem likely in time to occupy positions of leadership throughout society . . . [and] that academically selective colleges and universities have been highly successful in using race-sensitive admission policies to advance educational goals important to everyone.[25]

Dworkin maintains that Bowen and Bok's underlying findings are the best evidence yet available that affirmative action "seems impressively successful . . . violates no individual rights and compromises no moral principles."[26] In defending this position, he surveys the affirmative action controversy in university admissions. This survey would strike liberals as a tour de force of succinct substantive exposition. Dworkin's contentions follow in summary form:

Affirmative action does not accept unqualified blacks.[27]

Blacks do not waste the opportunities offered by affirmative action.[28]

Affirmative action has produced, as hoped, more African-American businesspeople, professionals, and community leaders. According to Bowen and Bok, black elite-school graduates earn considerably greater incomes than the typical black with a bachelor's degree, and are "strikingly" more likely to participate in black community activities.[29]

Racial diversity in a university student body helps to break down stereotypes and hostility among students; the benefit endures in post-university life.[29a]

Affirmative action does not stigmatize blacks.[30]

Replacement of affirmative action by race-neutral standards would greatly reduce the proportion of blacks in prestigious institutions. Dworkin cites Bowen and Bok's estimate of a 50% to 75% drop in elite schools, and a calamitous drop in law and medical schools. Dworkin rejects the contention that these drops would not take place if preferences were confined to low-income applicants, given that so many African-American applicants are poor. Dworkin considers it a fallacy, because poor applicants are still predominantly white, so that even race-neutral tests aimed at economic diversity would greatly reduce the numbers of blacks.[31]

Affirmative action does not unfairly violate the rights of rejected white applicants.[32]

It is not the case that race-sensitive admissions policies judge applicants only as members of large groups, not as individuals.[33]

It is not the case that racial classifications are always wrong in principle.[34]

Race has a special psychological character as racial discrimination expresses contempt and completely destroys the victims' lives. Racial classifications can inflict a special form of injury, but "it would . . . be perverse to disallow . . . [their use] to help combat the racism that is the true and continuing cause of that injury."[35]

Dworkin castigates Stephan and Abigail Thernstrom for their allegedly misleading and shoddy material[36] which emphasizes that the high rate of black university dropouts is evidence of affirmative action's "disappointing, even counterproductive, results."[37] The Thernstroms argued that African Americans would not have so high a failure rate, and thus would have experienced a better growth experience, if more had attended less selective and competitive schools.[38] In Dworkin's view, Bowen and Bok's book was far more scholarly, and it demonstrated that the black dropout rate at the very elite schools was small "by national standards," although it was 11 percent higher than the white rate.[39]

However, the Thernstroms did note that in the very elite schools (the subjects of Bok and Bowen's book) pretty much all students graduate, given the high caliber of the admittees. But even here (save for Harvard and Princeton) blacks were at least twice as likely to drop out.[40]

At this juncture, we return to the survey by Harry Holzer and David Neumark[41] discussed previously at pages 85–86 . That omnibus survey of affirmative action literature deals with the impact of affirmative action on university admissions as well as employment. The "theoretical literature" is declared "ambiguous,"[42] but the following "empirical" findings are offered: affirmative action programs have played a "major role" in bringing about the "striking increase" in African-American and Hispanic undergraduate and graduate enrollments since the 1970s;[43] lower average minority SAT scores are not reliable indicators of preferential treatment or poor predictors of college success;[44] minority college students on average perform less well, but not more so at the most selective schools;[45] both black and white students benefit from attending selective schools;[46] there is some evidence that under performing-minority medical school students are ultimately more likely than nonminority MDs to treat minority or low-income patients;[47] there is only a little evidence that minority and female beneficiaries act as role models or mentors;[48] and although a diverse student body can improve "interracial or intercultural relations," "there is as yet *no* evidence that" "diversity results in better education *overall.*"[49]

What comfort will affirmative action disputants derive from these findings? The Holzer-Neumark article dismisses or questions some of the standard criticisms, for example, that affirmative action at selective schools presents minority students with challenges which they are not equipped to handle,[50] or that low SAT or grade scores predict poor academic performance.[51] On the other hand, proponents will obviously be dismayed by the unqualified rejection of diversity's asserted educational benefits. All told, it would appear that the authors consider affirmative action a mixed blessing at the university level. It should be noted that they do not address the problems of the Historically Black Colleges and Universities, and that they make no effort, at least in this survey, to study our troubled primary and secondary schools.

Strict Scrutiny and University Admissions: The *Hopwood* Case

Both remedial and nonremedial (diversity) arguments are advanced to support affirmative action in college and university admissions. But supporting remedial affirmative action—that is, affirmative action needed to remedy past or present discrimination—has become particularly difficult for select universities where the affirmative action issue is prominent. Most select universities and colleges compete very vigorously to attract qualified minorities and have not had a history of official segregation. In some cases, where universities had historically engaged in de jure segregation, arguments for remedial affirmative action to cure the lingering effects of such discrimination were rejected by some courts at the federal appellate level. See *Podberesky v. Kirwan* (1994)[52] where race-exclusive scholarships were rejected; and *Hopwood v. Texas* (1996),[53] where a preferential admissions program at the University of Texas Law School was outlawed. However, on other formerly de jure campuses, affirmative action is judicially and/or administratively required to help remedy the past. (See pages 158–163 in this volume.)

The Supreme Court has steadfastly declined a number of opportunities to rule on whether nonremedial affirmative action in university admissions is permitted by strict scrutiny. (See pages 152–154, 225–228 below.) The result is a festering controversy rooted in Justice Powell's holding in the 1974 *Bakke* case that student-body diversification, if properly practiced, would conform to the requirements of strict scrutiny. (See pages 56–57 above.) The controversy was inaugurated by the Fifth Circuit's 1996 *Hopwood* decision rejecting the Powell doctrine when it was posited by the University of Texas Law School in support of its preferential minority admissions policies. The

Law School's remedial claim—the need to thwart the vestiges of past discrimination—was also rejected in an opinion, excerpted below, that examines
a broad range of issues connected with the "compelling government interest"
prong of strict scrutiny.

Hopwood v. Texas, 78 F3d 932 (5th Cir 1996)

Jerry E. Smith, Circuit Judge delivered the opinion of the panel:

... [940] Under the strict scrutiny analysis, we ask ... : Does the racial
classification serve a compelling government interest? ... [941] [W]e
turn to the specific issue of whether the law school's consideration of
race as a factor in admissions violates the Equal Protection Clause. The
district court found both a compelling remedial and a non-remedial
justification for the practice.

First, the court approved of the non-remedial goal of having a diverse
student body, reasoning that "obtaining the educational benefits that flow
from a racially and ethnically diverse student body remains a sufficiently
compelling interest to support the use of racial classifications." Second,
the [district] court determined that the use of racial classifications could
be justified as a remedy for the "present effects at the law school of past
discrimination in both the University of Texas system and the Texas
educational system as a whole." ...

Justice Powell's separate opinion in *Bakke* provided the original
impetus for recognizing diversity as a compelling state interest in
higher education. ...

[944] Here, the plaintiffs argue that diversity is not a compelling governmental interest under superseding Supreme Court precedent. ... The
law school maintains, on the other hand, that Justice Powell's formulation in *Bakke* is law and must be followed—at least in the context of
higher education.

We agree with the plaintiffs that any consideration of race or ethnicity
by the law school for the purpose of achieving a diverse student body
is not a compelling interest under the Fourteenth Amendment. Justice Powell's
argument in *Bakke* garnered only his own vote and has never represented
the view of a majority of the Court in *Bakke* or any other case. ...

Justice Powell's view in *Bakke* is not binding precedent on this issue.
While he announced the judgment, no other Justice joined in that part of
the opinion discussing the diversity rationale. In *Bakke,* the word "diversity" is mentioned nowhere except in Justice Powell's single-Justice
opinion. In fact, the four-Justice opinion, which would have upheld the

special admissions program under intermediate scrutiny, implicitly rejected Justice Powell's position. . . .

Since *Bakke,* the [Supreme] Court has accepted the diversity rationale only once in its cases dealing with race. Significantly, however, in that case, *Metro Broadcasting, Inc. v. Federal Communications Comm'n,* 497 U.S. 547, 564-65 (1990), the five-Justice majority relied upon an intermediate scrutiny standard of review to uphold the federal program seeking diversity in the ownership of broadcasting facilities. In *Adarand,* the Court squarely rejected intermediate scrutiny as the standard of review for racial classifications, and *Metro Broadcasting* is now specifically overruled to the extent that it was in conflict with this holding. No case since *Bakke* has accepted diversity as a compelling state interest under a strict scrutiny analysis. . . .

[945] Within the general principles of the Fourteenth Amendment, the use of race in admissions for diversity in higher education contradicts, rather than furthers, the aims of equal protection. Diversity fosters, rather than minimizes, the use of race. It treats minorities as a group, rather than as individuals. It may further remedial purposes but, just as likely, may promote improper racial stereotypes, thus fueling racial hostility.

The use of race, in and of itself, to choose students simply achieves a student body that looks different. Such a criterion is no more rational on its own terms than would be choices based upon the physical size or blood type of applicants. . . .

[946] While the use of race *per se* is proscribed, state-supported schools may reasonably consider a host of factors some of which may have some correlation with race in making admissions decisions. The federal courts have no warrant to intrude on those executive and legislative judgments unless the distinctions intrude on specific provisions of federal law or the Constitution.

A university may properly favor one applicant over another because of his ability to play the cello, make a downfield tackle, or understand chaos theory. An admissions process may also consider an applicant's home state or relationship to school alumni. Law schools specifically may look at things such as unusual or substantial extracurricular activities in college, which may be atypical factors affecting undergraduate grades. Schools may even consider factors such as whether an applicant's parents attended college or the applicant's economic and social background. . . .

To believe that a person's race controls his point of view is to stereo-type him. . . .

Instead, individuals, with their own conceptions of life, further diversity of viewpoint. Plaintiff Hopwood is a fair example of an applicant with a unique background. She is the now-thirty-two-year-old wife of a member of the Armed Forces stationed in San Antonio and, more significantly, is raising a severely handicapped child. Her circumstance would bring a different perspective to the law school. The school might consider this [947] an advantage to her in the application process, or it could decide that her family situation would be too much of a burden on her academic performance. . . .

Finally, the use of race to achieve diversity undercuts the ultimate goal of the Fourteenth Amendment: [948] the end of racially-moti-vated state action. . . .

We now turn to the district court's determination that "the remedial purpose of the law school's affirmative action program is a compelling government objective." The plaintiffs argue that the court erred by finding that the law school could employ racial criteria to remedy the present effects of past discrimination in Texas's primary and secondary schools. The plaintiffs contend that the proper unit for analysis is the law school, and the state has shown no recognizable present effects of the law school's past discrimination. The law school, in response, notes Texas's well-documented history of discrimination in education and argues that its effects continue today at the law school, both in the level of educational attainment of the average minority applicant and in the school's reputation.

In contrast to its approach to the diversity rationale, a majority of the Supreme Court has held that a state actor may racially classify where it has a "strong basis in the evidence for its conclusion that remedial action was necessary.". . .

[950] Applying the teachings of *Croson* and *Wygant,* we conclude that the district court erred in expanding the remedial justification to reach all public education within the State of Texas. The Supreme Court repeat-edly has warned that the use of racial remedies must be carefully lim-ited, and a remedy reaching all education within a state addresses a putative injury that is vague and amorphous. It has "no logical stopping point." *Wygant* [v. *Jackson Board of Education* (1986)], 476 U.S. [267] at 275 (plurality opinion). . . .

[952] In sum, for purposes of determining whether the law school's admissions system properly can act as a remedy for the present effects of past discrimination, we must identify the law school as the relevant alleged past discriminator. . . . Moreover, as part of showing that the alleged present effects of past discrimination in fact justify the racial preference program at issue, the law school must show that it adopted the program specifically to remedy the identified present effects of the past discrimination.

Here, according to the district court: "The evidence presented at trial indicates those effects include the law school's lingering reputation in the minority community, particularly with prospective students, as a "white" school; an underrepresentation of minorities in the student body; and some perception that the law school is a hostile environment for minorities." . . .

As a legal matter, the district court erred in concluding that the first and third effects it identified—bad reputation and hostile environment—were sufficient to sustain the use of race in the admissions process. The Fourth Circuit examined similar arguments in *Podberesky* [*v. Kirwan,* 38 F3d 147 (1994)], a recent case that struck down the use of race-based scholarships. The university in that case sought, in part, to justify a separate scholarship program based solely upon race because of the university's "poor reputation within the African-American community" and because "the atmosphere on campus [was] perceived as being hostile to African-American students."

The *Podberesky* court rejected the notion that either of these rationales could support the single-race scholarship program. The court reasoned that any poor reputation by the school "is tied solely to knowledge of the University's discrimination before it admitted African-American students." The court found that "mere knowledge of historical fact is not the kind of present effect that can justify a race-exclusive remedy. If it were otherwise, as long as there are people [953] who have access to history books, there will be programs such as this."

We concur in the Fourth Circuit's observation that knowledge of historical fact simply cannot justify current racial classifications. Even if, as the defendants argue, the law school may have a bad reputation in the minority community, "[t]he case against race-based preferences does not rest on the sterile assumption that American society is untouched or unaffected by the tragic oppression of its past." "Rather, it is the very enormity of that tragedy that lends resolve to the desire to never repeat it, and find a legal order in which distinctions based on race shall have no place." Moreover, we note that the law school's argument is even weaker than that of the university in *Podberesky*, as there is no dispute that the law school has never had an admissions policy that excluded Mexican Americans on the basis of race.

The *Podberesky* court rejected the hostile-environment claims by observing that the "effects"—that is, racial tensions—were the result of present societal discrimination. There was simply no showing of action by the university that contributed to any racial tension. Similarly, one cannot conclude that the law school's *past* discrimination has created any *current* hostile environment for minorities. While the school once did practice *de jure* discrimination in denying admission to blacks, the Court in *Sweatt v. Painter,* 339 U.S. 629 (1950), struck down the law school's program. Any other discrimination by the law school ended in the 1960s.

By the late 1960s, the school had implemented its first program designed to recruit minorities, and it now engages in an extensive minority-recruiting program that includes a significant amount of scholarship money. The vast majority of the faculty, staff, and students at the law school had absolutely nothing to do with any discrimination that the law school practiced in the past.

In such a case, one cannot conclude that a hostile environment is the present effect of past discrimination. Any racial tension at the law school is most certainly the result of present societal discrimination and, if anything, is contributed to, rather than alleviated by, the overt and prevalent consideration of race in admissions.

Even if the law school's alleged current lingering reputation in the minority community—and the perception that the school is a hostile environment for minorities—were considered to be the present effects of past discrimination, rather than the result of societal discrimination, they could not constitute compelling state interests justifying the use of racial classifications in admissions. A bad reputation within the minority community is alleviated not by the consideration of race in admissions, but by school action designed directly to enhance its reputation in that community.

Minority students who are aided by the law school's racial preferences have already made the decision to apply, despite the reputation. And, while prior knowledge that they will get a "plus" might make potential minorities more likely to apply, such an inducement does nothing, *per se,* to change any hostile environment. As we have noted, racial preferences, if anything, can compound the problem of a hostile environment.

The law school wisely concentrates only on the second effect the district court identified: underrepresentation of minorities because of past discrimination. The law school argues that we should consider the prior discrimination by the State of Texas and its educational system rather than of the law school. The school contends that this prior discrimination by the state had a direct effect on the educational attainment of the pool of minority applicants and that the discriminatory admissions program was implemented partially to discharge the school's duty of eliminating the vestiges of past segregation.

As we have noted, the district court accepted the law school's argument that past [954] discrimination on the part of the Texas school system (including primary and secondary schools), reaching back perhaps as far as the education of the parents of today's students, justifies the current use of racial classifications. No one disputes that Texas has a history of racial discrimination in education. We have already discussed, however, that the *Croson* Court unequivocally restricted the proper scope of the remedial interest to the state actor that had previously discriminated. The district court squarely found that "[i]n recent history, there is no evidence of overt officially sanctioned discrimination at the University of Texas." As a result, past discrimination in education, other than at the law school, cannot justify the present consideration of race in law school admissions. . . .

The district court also sought to find a remedial justification for the use of race and, at the same time, attempted to distinguish *Croson* using *United States v. Fordice,* 505 U.S. 717 (1992). The court held that the law school had a compelling interest to "desegregate" the school through affirmative action. [955] The reliance upon *Fordice* is misplaced, however. The district court held that *Fordice*'s mandate to schools "to eliminate every vestige of racial segregation and discrimination" made *Croson* inapplicable, 861 F Supp. at 571, and reasoned that this mandate includes the effects of such prior practices or policies.

Fordice does not overrule *Croson.* The central holding of *Fordice* is that a state or one of its subdivisions must act to repudiate the continuing "policies or practices" of discrimination. 505 U.S. at 731-32. In other words, a state has an affirmative duty to remove policies, tied to the past, by which it continues to discriminate. The *Fordice* Court did not address, in any way, a state actor's duty to counter the present effects of past discrimination that it did not cause.

In sum, the law school has failed to show a compelling state interest in remedying the present effects of past discrimination sufficient to maintain the use of race in its admissions system. . . .

The Unresolved Controversy
over Nonremedial Affirmative Action

In 1997, the Supreme Court was presented with the opportunity to rule on the constitutionality of nonremedial diversity policy when it accepted certiorari in *Piscataway v. Taxman,*[54] where the Third Circuit Court of Appeals ruled that Title VII of the 1964 Civil Rights Act prohibited the nonremedial layoff of a white public school teacher and the retention in the same job of a black teacher. Since the teachers were equal in seniority and qualification, and since the sole reason for the layoff was racial preference, the case seemed to furnish a definitive, long-overdue vehicle for adjudicating nonremedial affirmative action. But it was not to be. After certiorari was granted, the parties settled the litigation by agreement, thereby thwarting the Court's apparent desire to clarify the law. Nevertheless, the Clinton Administration's *Piscataway* brief should be studied and compared with the Fifth Circuit's position on diversity in *Hopwood.*

The brief argued that a public employer could constitutionally take race into account for nonremedial purposes if race-consciousness was narrowly tailored to meet a compelling governmental purpose.[55] This document went on to say:

> There are some circumstances . . . in which an employer should be permitted to demonstrate that taking race into account for non-remedial purposes is narrowly tailored to further a compelling interest. For example, if an undercover officer is needed to infiltrate a racially homogeneous gang, a law enforcement agency must have the flexibility to assign an officer of the same race to that task. Against the backdrop of racial unrest, a diverse police force may be essential to secure the public support and cooperation that is necessary for preventing and solving crime. Prison institutions may find it impossible to cope with racial tensions without an integrated work force. And school districts may responsibly conclude that a diverse faculty is essential to dispel students' stereotypes and promote mutual understanding and respect. The careful, tailored use of race to serve similarly compelling goals would satisfy the Constitution's strict scrutiny standard.[56]

The brief is surely correct in its stress on the need "to dispel students' stereotypes and promote mutual understanding and respect." Clearly, too, interracial/interethnic mixing as a goal of college admissions policy would seem an eminently wise policy. Dworkin (among others), as noted, argues that race-sensitive admissions at select universities promotes this goal. Nonetheless, self-generated segregation still crops up on campus. A New York Times essayist wrote this about the University of California at Riverside:

> Most of the white and Asian students I spoke to felt quite cut off from black and Latino students. Social life was largely balkanized by ethnic identity. Only a few classes were small enough for the kind of sustained discussion that would feature the black or Latino "view." And the number of minorities in such upper-level classes was very small. Most of the minority students I spoke to said the same thing. As Felicia Brown, a black junior, put it, "the color lines here are very distinct; it's very rare that there's any kind of crossing." What about the dorms? It turned out that Brown had decided to live in the all-black "theme" dorm.

Indeed, racial self-segregation is such a widespread phenomenon on campus that you can hardly say it is caused by affirmative action. But it wouldn't be surprising if the preoccupation with supposed racial or ethnic points of view, not to mention the very existence of a separate set of admissions standards, had the effect of reinforcing boundaries of identity.[57]

University administrators and faculty members talk endlessly about the value of student diversity, and efforts have been made to acquire supportive data. One study involving data from a longitudinal survey of 25,000 students at 159 colleges and universities found that white college students reported increased satisfaction with college when they participated in cross-cultural undertakings (e.g., taking ethnic studies courses, and socializing with members of other races). At the same time, the researchers found that increasing the number of minorities on campus led to a somewhat lessened sense of community on the part of white students.[58] A 1999 Gallup Poll survey of the law schools at Harvard and the University of Michigan (sponsored by the Harvard Civil Rights Project and covering 1,820 students or 81% of the law school enrollees at those campuses) reported that nearly 65% of the respondents said that the ethnic and racial diversity in their classes improved discussion, and 87% said they changed their civil rights attitudes because of contacts with students of varied backgrounds.[59] However, a 1997 poll of 530 Harvard undergraduates conducted by students at the Harvard Kennedy School of Government found that 58% of the respondents reported that a significant amount of racial segregation existed on that campus.[60]

In the post-*Hopwood* era, some lower federal courts have upheld the constitutionality of race/ethnic-conscious, preferential admissions based on nonremedial diversity grounds. Others have not. In *Smith v. University of Washington Law School* (2000),[61] the Ninth Circuit upheld the preferential admissions program of that school, holding that Powell's *Bakke* opinion accepting diversity objectives under strict scrutiny was *implicitly* accepted by four additional justices (the Brennan plurality).[62] This despite the fact that the Brennan plurality in *Bakke* explicitly relied on the *remedial* thesis that the Davis plan served the important governmental interest of remedying the present effects of past discrimination.[63]

The "implicit-majority" thesis of *Smith* was not accepted by the District Court charged with ruling on the diversity/preference admission scheme operative at the University of Michigan's College of Literature, Science, and Arts. (See *Gratz v. Bollinger* [2000].[64]) The District Judge noted that the Supreme Court in *Bakke* did not *prohibit* the diversity rationale as a basis for admission preferences. He found that preferential treatment for the purposes of diversification served a compelling governmental interest because there was "solid evidence" that educational benefits flow from racially and ethnically diverse student bodies, including intellectual growth, better understanding of multiple perspectives, and more creative solutions to problem solving.[65] The *Gratz* Court stressed that "over 360 institutions represented by the Association of American Law Schools assert that they have learned through their extensive experience . . . that the quality of education for all students is greatly enhanced when student bodies include persons of diverse backgrounds, interests, and experiences, including racial and ethnic makeups."[66] Furthermore, the Michigan undergraduate preference plan was narrowly tailored as it treated minority status as only one factor, among many, in the admission process.[67]

By sharp contrast, a different District Court—ruling on protected-group preference admissions at the University of Georgia—rejected the diversity argument as totally speculative and intellectually bankrupt. To that Court, there was no hard evidence that persons from a "homogeneous" background could not work well with members of other groups. (See *Johnson v. University of Georgia* [2000].[68])

Confusion about the constitutionality of preferential-diversity admissions was compounded by a District Court determination that the University of Michigan Law School race/ethnic-conscious program was unconstitutional. In that case, Judge Feinberg—directly contrary to the Michigan undergraduate case cited above—found that the Supreme Court in *Croson* and *Adarand* (among other cases) had concluded that race classifications were unconstitutional unless they were "intended to remedy carefully documented effects of past [governmental] discrimination." (See *Grutter v. Bollinger* [2001].[69]) It was clear to that Court that the Supreme Court has rejected broad-gauged benign defenses for race classification—defenses like providing minority-role models, societal discrimination, and diversity.[70] But even if diversity was a compelling interest—and the judge pointedly noted that the law on the matter was still murky[71]—the law school admissions system was, in effect, a quota system, which frustrated the narrow-tailoring prong of strict scrutiny.[72]

By refusing to review this welter of conflicting decisions, the Supreme Court has unfortunately perpetuated the controversy over minority admissions by selective/competitive colleges and universities. Some argue that "[m]ore selective schools rely on preferences to a greater degree, but even second and third-tier schools discriminate on the basis of race."[73] To others, race/ethnic-based admissions decisions do not seem to be factors in entrance policies at the bulk of the nation's colleges, given the relative ease of admission.[74] What is sure though, is that attendance at elite schools is regarded by minority advocates as an important avenue for individual and protected-group progress. Some scoff at this view. Thus, Martin Trow, emeritus professor at Berkeley, wrote: "The notion that you have to go to one of the most selective universities to fulfill your potential, or to become a leader in America, betrays an elitist conception of American life."[75] Abigail Thernstrom, in her critique of Bowen and Bok's *The Shape of the River*, wrote that the authors argue

> that affirmative action in the highly selective institutions created the black middle class. It's an [h]istorical point; blacks made impressive and rapid gains in the decades before preferences. Moreover, where did they get the notion that in our wonderfully open and fluid society, degrees from certain colleges are make-or-break? . . . In fact, as they surely know, the economically and professionally successful of all races started out in a wide variety of schools.[76]

Matriculation at elite schools often poses academic challenges to preferential admittees, a problem more extensively recognized than openly acknowledged. Meanwhile, academic support for remedial courses is waning.[77] Stanford Professor Claude Steele hypothesizes that the stereotype that underrepresented minorities are less academically competent works in their minds to undercut self-esteem and intellectual performance.[78] However, James Traub's survey of students at Berkeley, the University of California at Riverside, and elsewhere did not uncover minority expressions of low self-esteem,[79] save for one black student who said, "When you want to start a study group, it's hard, there's a stigma that you're not as capable."[80] Vociferous administrative support for university affirmative action, and the fog of professorial silence about it are not unique. It appears that many academics would at least silently concur with a Berkeley professor's assertion that there is an "unwritten compact" at selective schools not to discuss affirmative action.[81] But significant opposition to affirmative action in higher education does exist. The opinions in *Hopwood, Podberesky, Johnson,* and *Grutter* that were just reviewed are important legal pillars of that opposition. California's Proposition 209 is another pillar. A similar referendum was ratified by the people in the state of Washington.[82] What follows are excerpts from California's Proposition 209:[83]

California Proposition 209

The state shall not discriminate against, or grant preferential treatment to any individual or group on the basis of race, sex, color, ethnicity, or national origin in the operation of public employment, public education, or public contracting. . . .

Nothing in this section shall be interpreted as prohibiting bona fide qualifications based on sex which are reasonably necessary to the normal operations of public employment, public education, or public contracting.

Nothing in this section shall be interpreted as invalidating any court order or consent decree which is in force as of the effective date of this section.

Nothing in this section shall be interpreted as prohibiting action which must be taken to establish or maintain eligibility for any federal program where ineligibility would result in a loss of federal funds to the state. . . .

This section shall be self-executing. If any part or parts of this section are found to be in conflict with federal law or the United States Constitution, the section shall be implemented to the maximum extent that federal law and the United States Constitution permit. Any provision held invalid shall be separable from the remaining portions of the section.

Faced with the difficulties presented by *Hopwood,* Proposition 209, and similar views, diversity advocates have adopted mechanisms meant to facilitate the presence of underrepresented minorities without violating existing strictures on race or ethnic-consciousness. Thus, after *Hopwood,* the Texas Legislature mandated that those high school graduates who rank within the upper 10% of their classes be admitted to Texas public colleges.[84] In Florida, the Board of Regents endorsed the governor's proposal guaranteeing those who fall within the upper 20% of their high school classes a place within the ten public universities of that State.[85] The University of California Regents also adopted a high school class-standing plan guaranteeing the upper 4% of high school graduates a seat at one of the University of California (UC) campuses. Further (starting in 2003), those who graduate between the upper 4 and 12.5% of their high school classes—if not allowed to enter the University after high school—will be offered "dual admission status," and will be admitted to the University once successfully completing two years of junior college.[86] Left unclarified in these plans is the status issue of which students are to be restricted to the less-prestigious schools and what difference it makes. Also left hanging is whether these California outreach efforts (and those referenced below) will pass muster under Proposition 209.

Other measures were undertaken in the wake of Proposition 209. For example, when first confronted with the barrier against using race, ethnicity, and gender, UC Irvine developed an elaborate applicant review system involving (in addition to grades and SAT [Scholastic Aptitude Test] performance) considerations about leadership/initiative; honors/awards; personal challenges; geographic challenges (which incorporated the quality of the geographically available educational resources); self and civic awareness; and specialized knowledge.[87] These "expanded criteria" "resulted in significant admissions gains for underrepresented ethnic groups—particularly African Americans, American Indians, and Chicanos."[88] Admissions officers reported that "we learned . . . that it is possible for a selective university to admit an academically well-prepared and diverse freshman class without the use of race or ethnicity as a factor in the review process."[89] Reportedly, deft "fiddling" of this sort also enabled Berkeley, in 1999, to admit 305 more undergraduate minorities than it had a year before when 209 was effectuated. A similar increase occurred at Boalt Hall, the Berkeley law school.[90] Most undergraduate minorities who were denied admission to Berkeley in 1998 "cascaded" to the less-prestigious UC campuses.[91] According to one federal judge's extensive review, between 1995 and 2000 the numbers of minorities in the UC system as a whole declined only 1%. And there was an increased minority population at three campuses.[92] The most elite UC schools experienced significant declines in minority populations that would have been greater had not intense drives been undertaken to recruit qualified blacks and Hispanics. At UCLA, for example, more than 200 new, need/merit scholarships were created, and these helped to recruit minorities.[93]

We have noted that some observers view "cascading" as a severe loss of opportunity. To them, admissions reconfiguration (such as that undertaken at UC Irvine) is incapable of producing a sufficient degree of diversity at elite schools.[94] Some of these same critics urge that economic deprivation/class status is an inadequate proxy for race/ethnicity because using an income variable would primarily benefit poor whites. Consequently, to these elite school diversity advocates, there is no good substitute for old-style, race/ethnic-conscious admissions.[95]

Admissions reconfiguration could involve reducing the impact of standardized tests where blacks and Hispanics tend to underperform relative to whites and Asians.[96] The Educational Testing Service (ETS)—the creator of the Scholastic Aptitude Test (SAT)—itself reportedly had a plan to confront the minority-performance issue. ETS calculated expected SAT scores based on fourteen different categories including family income, parental education, and high school socioeconomic mix. It concluded that Hispanics and African Americans will, as groups, score lower than whites or Asians. However, blacks and Hispanics who score 200 or more points higher than expected were to be dubbed "strivers," and this status, so ETS suggested, could be used by admissions officers as a positive, equity promoting, race/ethnic-blind eligibility factor.[97] Obviously, the "striver" scheme is hardly race/ethnic blind. Additionally, and questionably enough, it fosters group stereotyping. Perhaps these dimensions helped ETS to shelve the plan.

A novel (Bial-Dale) "Adaptability" test was experimentally employed by a number of universities, and "could provide one answer if we lose affirmative action,"[98] opined Harvard's Gary Orfield, who helped oversee the test's implementation. The Bial-Dale analysis tests what its promoters call "noncognitive" skills such as the ability to participate in a group assemblage of "Lego" figurines. These "noncognitive" tests are to be supplemented with extensive interviews focusing on how students will approach problems, for example, how poor grades can be remedied. This pilot scheme was to be used in 700 New York public high schools where the majority (but not all) of students are African American or Hispanic.[99] One must wonder whether the Bial-Dale approach will be administered on a race/ethnic-blind basis. Also, is performance in a group an appropriate admissions measuring device?

The University of California system has downgraded the SAT I (the aptitude test) by putting greater weight on the SAT II which tests knowledge of particular subjects like history, mathematics, and foreign languages. For admission, in addition to the SAT I, students must take the SAT II in writing and mathematics, but are free to pick a third field from those covered by the SAT II. This flexibility has been particularly helpful to Hispanics who, by taking the Spanish exam, are assisted in gaining admission.[100] The president of the UC system has urged the abolition of the SAT I to be replaced by a more "holistic" approach, including greater emphasis on SAT II-type exams.[101]

While some public universities scamper to find alternatives to "old style" affirmative action, others continue to employ its mechanisms, not infrequently using them to entice minorities from states where admissions officers are formally forbidden to use them. Once *Hopwood* ended overt preferences by public universities in Texas, many universities from other states increased their efforts to recruit minorities in Texas. Some schools (Indiana University, the University of Iowa, Tulane, and Washington University) either opened recruiting offices in Texas, or sent representatives to reside in that State for extended periods. Financial aid has been a primary "raiding" tool. The University of Oklahoma awarded about $3 million in financial aid to Texas students in 1999, some 16% of its total student-aid budget. The average Oklahoma award for a Texas minority student was $4,052; that for Texas whites, $3,207. The University of Iowa offered $5,000 annual scholarships for meritorious minority students. Affirmative action opponents see their efforts dissipated by out-of-state raiders who practice what Texas officials are forbidden to do. Uniform rules are demanded.[102] "National law should be, in fact, national," argued one law professor from the University of Georgia, "the Constitution shouldn't mean one thing in Texas and another in Georgia. The solution to that is for the United States Supreme Court to clarify what national constitutional law is."[103]

In the intense quest for minority students, California and Texas schools have responded with new financial aid packages. Mention has already been made of the two hundred new merit/need scholarships at UCLA. The University of Texas at Austin, and Texas A&M have developed race/ethnic-blind Adversity Index scholarships that award aid to poorer students who come from low-achieving high schools. Blacks and Hispanics—only 11% of the total number admitted to these schools in 1999—were awarded 61% of the adversity scholarships.[104]

During the 1990s, the U.S. Education Department view as to the legitimacy of race/ethnic-exclusive financial aid had a frenzied history, and one that reflects the unsettled nature of affirmative action law. Late in 1990, that Department's head of the Office for Civil Rights (OCR) insisted that the Department viewed race/ethnic exclusivity in financial aid as generally illegal. Stormy outcries followed, as did a departmental directive allowing public colleges to use private or state funds for minority-only financial aid so long as they did not use university-targeted, public appropriations for that purpose. However, when a new secretary was installed in March, 1991, a new policy was announced: the 1990 directives could be ignored, and—pending a review of the issue—universities could revert to their traditional affirmative action ways in the distribution of fiscal assistance. The first Bush Administration ended before final regulations were issued on the matter. New rules were issued by Secretary Richard W. Riley of the Clinton Administration in February, 1994. These guidelines permitted public-university aid reserved for minorities in order to either remedy past discrimination, or promote diversity. Shortly thereafter, the Fourth Circuit in *Podberesky v. Kirwan* (1994),[105] declared unconstitutional the University of Maryland's Banaker scholarships available only for blacks.[106]

OCR's chief explained why the Department did not change its guidelines after *Podberesky*. She argued that OCR and the Fourth Circuit agreed that minority-aid targeting was permissible to remedy the present effects of past discrimination; the difference was over what kind of "present effects" are to be cured, and who is responsible—an issue discussed in the preceding *Hopwood* excerpt above. In any event, the Department would not challenge aid-exclusivity, leaving that burden to private plaintiffs.[107] The former (Bush Administration) OCR head regarded this nonchallenge posture as "irresponsible." "It's allowing," he said, "discrimination to take place unless a private individual sues."[108] To him, the OCR's duty was to enforce the law, not ignore it.[109]

The Formerly De Jure Segregated Universities: The Historically Black Colleges and the Traditionally White Institutions

At one time, nineteen states racially segregated higher-educational institutions, thereby creating the "Historically Black Colleges and Universities (HBCUs)," and the "Traditionally White Institutions (TWIs)." HBCU expansion was facilitated by Congress in 1890 when it authorized the creation of separate black institutions under the land-grant college program.[110] Discrimination against African Americans by land-grant institutions was prohibited by that statute. But that law—antedating the comparable *Plessy v. Ferguson* (1896) doctrine—stipulated that "the establishment of such colleges separately for white and colored students will be held in compliance with the provisions of this Act if the funds received be equitably divided."[111]

De jure racial separateness was declared unconstitutional in *Brown v. Board of Education* (1954), but the federal government did not promote university integration in the formerly de jure-segregation states until the late 1960s.[112] The initial effort was regarded as so weak that private civil rights advocacy groups sued to spur greater OCR-integration efforts.[113] By 1977, this private-plaintiff suit resulted in the creation of the following OCR "dismantling segregation" regulations applicable to the former de jure-segregated states.[114] As in the case of public school desegregation, the regulations were meant to alleviate group wrongs through proportionality remedies:

• The mission of the TWIs and HBCUs was to be defined in nonracial terms.

• The HBCUs were to be academically strengthened so as to become attractive to nonblacks. But, importantly, the HBCUs were not subject to numerical goals for the increase in white students.

• Each of the states was to establish the goal of achieving in its public higher education system that proportion of black high school graduates which would at least be equal to the proportion of white high school graduates.

• The states were to adopt as a goal the reduction of the disparity between the proportion of white and black high school graduates entering TWIs.

• Each state was to take all reasonable steps to reduce any disparity between black and white higher education graduation rates.

• The states were to adopt as a goal—for positions requiring the doctorate—the employment of that proportion of blacks that would be coequal with the proportion of blacks in the relevant labor market who held the doctorate.

• The states were to adopt as a goal—for college/university positions not requiring the doctoral degree—the hiring of that proportion of blacks for those positions that would at least equal (1) the proportion of blacks with M.A.'s in the appropriate discipline from schools in the state system; or (2) the proportion of blacks in the relevant labor market with the necessary training, whichever was the greater.

Bedeviling the integration question in the formerly de jure states was the question of whether *Green v. New Kent County* (1968)[115] was applicable to higher education. That ruling for the K-12 level interpreted the equal protection clause as requiring school integration ("just schools") as contrasted with the mere abolition of racial attendance barriers. To the OCR, *Green* was surely applicable to higher education. That Agency's rules, as noted, established numerical goals for black attendance at TWIs, and HBCUs were to be made more attractive to white students. For two students of the subject, this was a profoundly mistaken policy.[116] To them, colleges are clearly different from grade schools. In the latter, the state commands attendance; college students choose whether to participate in higher education. The efforts to enhance HBCUs to attract whites has largely failed, and the pressure on TWIs to enroll more African Americans has siphoned needed intellectual talent from the HBCUs. HBCU enhancement encouraged more blacks to attend them, rather than attracting whites. Besides, there are African-American educational leaders who insist on maintaining HBCUs as essentially black institutions because such an environment is more conducive for African-American educational advancement. One leader maintained that the "historically white colleges are not capable of addressing the needs of black students because whites are socially and culturally deprived of understanding the needs, desires, abilities, and mores of black students."[117] Moreover, the HBCUs have such strong political support that the effort to convert them to "just schools" is not politically feasible.[118]

In the capstone case of *U.S. v. Fordice* (1992),[119] the overriding issue was the scope of Mississippi's constitutional duty to dismantle its dual system of publicly funded higher education: five "traditionally white institutions" and three historically black colleges and universities, all at one time *totally* segregated by law. The Court set aside a decision by the Fifth Circuit that the State had indeed complied with its duty by implementing race-neutral admissions standards at all of its campuses. The High Court held that the dispositive question was "whether Mississippi ha[d] left in place certain aspects of its prior dual system that perpetuate[d] the racially segregated higher education system."[120] The majority opinion framed the applicable standard as follows:

> If the State perpetuates policies and practices traceable to its prior de jure system that continue to have segregative effects—whether by influencing student enrollment decisions or by fostering segregation in other facets of the university system—and such policies are without sound educational justification and can be practicably eliminated, the State has not satisfied its burden of proving that it has dismantled its prior system. Such policies run afoul of the Equal Protection Clause, even though the State has abolished the legal requirement that whites and blacks be educated separately and has established racially neutral policies not animated by a discriminatory purpose.[121]

The Court held that the lower courts had applied the wrong standard, and, in so doing, had ignored the "readily apparent" evidence that "certain remnants" of the prior system were, or might be, unconstitutional under the standard that should have been applied. Accordingly, the Court remanded the entire matter for a full-scale examination of such remnants, including, but not limited to, four continuing practices which the Court itself chose to identify for "highlighting" purposes: (1) requiring "significantly higher" test scores for admission to TWIs than to HBCUs; (2) duplication of BA and MA programs at both TWIs and HBCUs; (3) classifying the eight schools by rank-ordered educational "mission" for funding purposes; and (4) operating all eight schools without consideration of waste or inefficiency. The Court held that these vestiges of the old regime tended to compromise students' freedom of choice and perpetuate segregation, and directed the remand courts to determine whether it would be "practicable and consistent with sound education practices" to eliminate or modify them.[122]

The *Fordice* decision initiated a remand process, which may run for years before the case comes back to the Supreme Court. Moreover, while it did not absolutely foreclose separate funding for the Mississippi HBCUs, it did refuse to approve such funding pending completion of the remand. Obviously, this relegates the Mississippi HBCUs, and by extension their counterparts in other states, to an indefinite limbo. Champions of HBCUs have indignantly denounced this straddle; but it is possible to forgive. More perhaps than any other type of desegregation case, the *Fordice* model requires the courts to craft a reconciliation of the seemingly irreconcilable. To order that publicly funded HBCUs be allowed to continue both as racially separate and as equally endowed would fly in the teeth of *Brown* and *Green*, and rouse the ghost of *Plessy*. But is there a tenable alternative? HBCUs have traditionally been—and may still be—the African American's only effective means of countering racist exclusion from mainstream learning; if they represent educational apartheid, the onus is on the segregators. To let them die in the name of desegregation would work the ultimate in cruel irony—the sacrifice of the resisting victim in order to punish his oppressor. In this light, it is perhaps understandable that the *Fordice* Court resorted to quasi-Solomonic finesse.

Eventually, the issue will have to be sorted out. What will be the way out of the dilemma? Will the day be carried by the anguished pleas of the HBCU advocates? Will the Supreme Court determine that the integrationist impulse of *Brown* and *Green* should be replaced, in our public institutions of higher learning, by some variant form of the "separate but equal" heresy? Will the Court try to preserve integration by redefining "racial identifiability" so that black institutions will have to admit more white students in order to preserve a substantial measure of separate identity? Will the black colleges die out because the conditions which created them no longer prevail? And when will we know?

The last question should be underscored given the refusal of the Supreme Court to review the post-*Fordice* District and Appellate Court decisions (*Ayers v. Fordice* [1995]) which mandated the establishment of equal admission standards for Mississippi's system of higher education, despite the claim that these would decimate the State's HBCUs.[123]

Admission to the HBCUs has been less difficult than acceptance at the TWIs, and the apparent objective of the Courts in *Ayers* was to reduce the stigma of lesser competence associated with the HBCUs—making them more attractive to white students. Likewise, the application of *Fordice* in Alabama focused on improving HBCU reputation. There, the State was ordered by the Court to both provide at least $100 million over the next fifteen years for the improvement of HBCU academic quality, and to finance scholarships reserved for nonblacks who attended HBCUs.[124] Both of these requirements became the subject of new suits; one brought by an African American who challenged the scholarship plan as unconstitutional discrimination against blacks.[125] In Mississippi, state authorities agreed to spend $500 million (over the next 17 years) to improve HBCUs in that State. To acquire full control of some $105 million, the Mississippi black colleges are required to achieve a 10% nonblack student population in the upcoming years.[126] Will the Mississippi plan promote segregation, particularly in light of the fact that the "nonblack" requirement incorporates such nonwhites as Asians?

Researchers at the Southern Education Foundation report that *Fordice* has yet to prompt an acceptable level of desegregation. HBCUs remain overwhelmingly black; TWIs remain the preserve of whites. To be sure, TWIs have adopted race-conscious affirmative action admission programs as a result of either negotiation with OCR, or court action. And (except for Texas) these programs are operative throughout the "Old South"—even in Mississippi and Louisiana that are covered by the Fifth Circuit's *Hopwood* opinion. Still, in 1996, only 8.6% of first-year students at the TWI "flagship" southern campuses were black, while about 20% of the population between 18 and 24 years of age in the South was black. A major objective for the Southern Education Foundation was to obtain an African-American population at the flagship campuses that much more closely approximated the percentage of young blacks in the population covered by these campuses. In short, an emphasis on proportional-representation integration, and to this end, the Foundation urged that state colleges expand their outreach efforts in the minority communities, helping the young there prepare for college.[127]

Justice Thomas' concurrence in *Fordice* described how the rule in *Fordice* is quite different from that of *Green*. The latter required thoroughgoing integration, and assumed that integration was educationally advantageous; the former requires integration only when it would be educationally sound, and Justice Thomas feels that there is much to be said for the educational soundness of the HBCUs as they currently exist. An excerpt of his *Fordice* concurrence follows:

United States v. Fordice, 505 U.S. 717 (1992)

. . . [748] In particular, we do not foreclose the possibility that there exists "sound educational justification" for maintaining historically black colleges as such. Despite the shameful history of state-enforced segregation, these institutions have survived and flourished. Indeed, they have expanded as opportunities for blacks to enter historically white institutions have expanded. Between 1954 and 1980, for example, enrollment at historically black colleges increased from 70,000 to 200,000 students, while degrees awarded increased from 13,000 to 32,000. See S. Hill, National Center for Education Statistics, The Traditionally Black Institutions of Higher Education 1860 to 1982, pp. xiv-xv (1985). These accomplishments have not gone unnoticed:

"The colleges founded for Negroes are both a source of pride to blacks who have attended them and a source of hope to black families who want the benefits of higher learning for their children. They have exercised leadership in developing educational opportunities for young blacks at all levels of instruction, and, especially in the South, they are still regarded as key institutions for enhancing the general quality of the lives of black Americans." Carnegie Commission on Higher Education, From Isolation to Mainstream: Problems of the Colleges Founded for Negroes 11 (1971).

I think it undisputable that these institutions have succeeded in part because of their distinctive histories and traditions; for many, historically black colleges have become "a symbol of the highest attainments of black culture." J. Preer, *Lawyers v. Educators: Black Colleges and Desegregation in Public Higher Education* 2 (1982). Obviously, a State cannot maintain such traditions by closing particular institutions, historically white or historically black, to particular racial groups. Nonetheless, it hardly follows that a [749] State cannot operate a diverse assortment of institutions—including historically black institutions—open to all on a race-neutral basis, but with established traditions and programs that might disproportionately appeal to one race or another. No one, I imagine, would argue that such institutional *diversity* is without "sound educational justification," or that it is even remotely akin to program *duplication,* which is designed to separate the races for the sake of separating the races. . . . It would be ironic, to say the least, if the institutions that sustained blacks during segregation were themselves destroyed in an effort to combat its vestiges.[128]

Scalia's concurrence in *Fordice* reminded the reader that *Brown I* barred de jure segregation because of its capacity to impose psychic harm on blacks. To him, however, "[l]egacies of the dual system"—that is, the HBCU and TWI state institutions—"that permit (or even incidentally facilitate) free choice of racially identifiable schools—while still assuring each individual student the right to attend *whatever* school he wishes" are not associated with these negative psychic consequences.[129] Is the Justice correct? Recall that to the typical social scientist at the time of *Brown v. Board* (1954), school integration was needed to alleviate segregation's stigmatic affliction hobbling African Americans.[130]

Gender Discrimination and Education

We are here concerned with Title IX of the Education Act of 1972,[131] which prohibits sex-based discrimination in the administration of any educational undertaking financially assisted by the federal government. The bar against governmental sex discrimination in the Constitution's equal protection guarantees is also a focus. Both the statute, which has been interpreted as requiring remedies for disparate-impact gender discrimination, and the Constitution are primary tools in combating sex discrimination in our educational institutions. Our initial focus is on equal protection doctrine.

Constitutional Sanctions and Single-Sex Schools

Sexual classification has long been the subject of equal protection litigation. Over the last few decades, the U.S. Supreme Court gradually assimilated changing societal attitudes about the role of women in social and domestic relations, employment, and personal conduct. In the modern era, the High Court has been active in using the Fifth and Fourteenth Amendments to emancipate women from age-old sexist stereotyping and harassment.

The statutory universe of the early 1960s contained much in the way of gender classification and discrimination. Work-protection legislation limited the number of hours women could work, the weight they could lift, and even the type of work (such as night work) they could undertake. Such protectionism—regarded as running afoul of Title VII of the 1964 Civil Rights Act—has been invalidated.[132] Title VII is not applicable, though, to the broad spectrum of sex-specific legislation which, among many other things, mandates that mothers in divorce situations be given preference in issues related to child custody; that fathers bear the primary burden for child support after divorce; that female prostitutes be subject to criminal punishment that was not imposed on their male customers; and that in statutory-rape cases only men be subject to punishment.[133] To what extent do the aforementioned and other existing sex-specific classifications, conform with the equal protection guarantees of the Constitution?

Before 1971, prevailing constitutional doctrine had it that state gender discrimination did not violate equal protection if such discrimination met the requirement of "mere rationality"—that is, if there was *any* basis in reason to support it. Given this lowest tier of equal protection judicial scrutiny, the Supreme Court did not invalidate a sex-discrimination statute until 1971.[134] Even as late as 1948, the Court accepted Michigan's statute denying bartender licenses to females unless they were the wives or daughters of male (not female) tavern owners.[135]

The High Court began to change its gender-discrimination, equal protection tack in *Reed v. Reed* (1971),[136] when it declared unconstitutional an Idaho statute providing that males be preferred as administrators of decedents' estates. The preferential treatment afforded males was deemed arbitrary, and thus not rational. Before her elevation to the Supreme Court, Ruth Bader Ginsberg appeared in *Reed* as an attorney, and in that role she advocated the adoption of a strict-scrutiny standard for sex-discrimination statutes.[137] Strict scrutiny was not adopted by the Court in *Reed,* but in *Frontiero v. Richardson* (1973),[138] a four-member plurality did champion the highest of standards.

In *Craig v. Boren* (1976),[139] the High Court settled on a "midtier," equal protection test for sex-discrimination claims: whether the disputed classification serves "important" government objectives and is substantially related to achieving them. Arguably, this rule has now been broadened. In *United States v. Virginia Military Institute* (1996),[140] the Supreme Court held, 7–1, in an opinion written by the now Justice Ginsburg, that Virginia's commitment to an exclusively male admissions policy at its storied military academy violated the equal protection clause. This decision not only toppled a major citadel of state-supported male exclusivity, but also teaches a lesson in the dynamics of antidiscrimination law.

The Court held that, in order to prevail, a midtier defendant must demonstrate a justification that is not only "exceedingly persuasive," but also "genuine, not hypothesized," and untainted by sexual stereotypes.[141] In the Court's no-nonsense view, Virginia's defenses fell far short of clearing this bar. The contention that the Virginia Military Institute's (VMI) males-only program furthers educational "diversity" was caustically dismissed as a lawyer's concoction, and the argument that the program is too rigorous for females was found to be empty-headed.[142]

There is a learned dispute over whether the "exceedingly persuasive" concept expands, or merely restates, midtier law.[143] Also, it remains to be seen whether the seemingly broadened midtier rule in gender-discrimination law differs from the strict-scrutiny rule that governs public race/ethnic-discrimination, and whether strict scrutiny should not be applicable to gender discrimination. What is more, the *Virginia* majority left open the issue as to the equal protection legitimacy of "separate but equal" single-sex schools. That majority insisted that it was not addressing the question; however it noted that

> [s]everal *amici* have urged that diversity in educational opportunities is an altogether appropriate governmental pursuit and that single-sex schools can contribute importantly to such diversity. Indeed, it is the mission of some single-sex schools "to dissipate, rather than perpetuate, traditional gender classifications." We do not question the Commonwealth's prerogative evenhandedly to support diverse educational opportunities.[144]

Later, the Court went to great lengths to insist that Virginia had not—as it claimed it did—remedied its equal protection violation by establishing the Virginia Women's Institute of Leadership (VWIL) at Mary Baldwin College, a private women's college geographically close to VMI. The majority concluded its exhaustive review of the VWIL's shortcomings relative to VMI with the following written by Justice Ginsburg:[145]

United States v. Virginia Military Institute, 518 U.S. 515 (1996)

... [553] Virginia's VWIL solution is reminiscent of the remedy Texas proposed 50 years ago, in response to a state trial court's 1946 ruling that, given the equal protection guarantee, African Americans could not be denied a legal education at a state facility. See *Sweatt v. Painter,* 339 U.S. 629 (1950). Reluctant to admit African-Americans to its flagship University of Texas Law School, the State set up a separate school for He[r]man Sweatt and other black law students. *Id.,* at 632. As originally opened, the new school had no independent faculty or library, and it lacked accreditation. Nevertheless, the state trial and appellate courts were satisfied that the new school offered Sweatt opportunities for the study of law "substantially equivalent to those offered by the State to white students at the University of Texas." . . .

Before this Court considered the case, the new school had gained "a faculty of five full-time professors; a student body of 23; a library of some 16,500 volumes serviced by a full-time staff; a practice court and legal aid association; and one alumnus who ha[d] become a member of the Texas Bar." This Court contrasted resources at the new school with those at the school from which Sweatt had been excluded. The University of Texas Law School had a full-time faculty of 16, a student body of 850, a library containing over [554] 65,000 volumes, scholarship funds, a law review, and moot court facilities.

More important than the tangible features, the Court emphasized, are "those qualities which are incapable of objective measurement but which make for greatness" in a school, including "reputation of the faculty, experience of the administration, position and influence of the alumni, standing in the community, traditions and prestige." Facing the marked differences reported in the *Sweatt* opinion, the Court unanimously ruled that Texas had not shown "substantial equality in the [separate] educational opportunities" the State offered. Accordingly, the Court held, the Equal Protection Clause required Texas to admit African Americans to the University of Texas Law School. In line with *Sweatt,* we rule here that Virginia has not shown substantial equality in the separate educational opportunities the State supports at VWIL and VMI. . . .

[556] A generation ago, "the authorities controlling Virginia higher education," despite long established tradition, agreed "to innovate and favorably entertain[ed] the [then] relatively new idea that there must be no discrimination by sex in offering educational opportunity." Commencing in 1970, Virginia opened to women "educational opportunities at the Charlottesville campus that [were] not afforded in other [state-operated] institutions." A federal court approved the Commonwealth's innovation, emphasizing that the University of Virginia "offer[ed] courses of instruction . . . not available elsewhere." The court further noted: "[T]here exists at Charlottesville a 'prestige' factor [557] [not paralleled in] other Virginia educational institutions."

VMI, too, offers an educational opportunity no other Virginia institution provides, and the school's "prestige"—associated with its success in developing "citizen-soldiers"—is unequaled. Virginia has closed this facility to its daughters and, instead, has devised for them a "parallel program," with a faculty less impressively credentialed and less well paid, more limited course offerings, fewer opportunities for military training and for scientific specialization. VMI, beyond question, "possesses to a far greater degree" than the VWIL program "those qualities which are incapable of objective measurement but which make for greatness in a . . . school," including "position and influence of the alumni, standing in the community, traditions and prestige." Women seeking and fit for a VMI-quality education cannot be offered anything less, under the Commonwealth's obligation to afford them genuinely equal protection. . . .

The decade of the 1990s witnessed a considerable interest in the expansion of single-gender schools, particularly for females and urban-minority males. All-male minority academies would, it was maintained, improve academic performance by eliminating female distractions, and by improving self-esteem through an emphasis on minority role models like Martin Luther King Jr., Marcus Garvey, and Paul Robeson. There are some studies indicating that minority males in single-gender school environments do have higher test scores than their coeducational counterparts. But the single-sex schools emphasize discipline and parental involvement, and it may be that the latter two variables operate without sexual segregation to improve scholarship.[146]

Nurturing all-female schools rests on such notions as that girls tend to be overawed and unreasonably stifled in the presence of males, particularly in the areas of science and mathematics; that they are both more harshly treated and ignored more by teachers than boys are; and that exams are too often "gender biased." Graduates of women's colleges, moreover, are far better represented in high-status positions than females who went to coeducational institutions.[147] A study that was often cited to support all-female schools was published in 1992 by the American Association of University Women (AAUW) and was titled, *How Schools Shortchange Girls*. But the Educational Foundation of that same organization published a later study in 1998, *Separated by Sex: A Critical Look at Single-Sex Education for Girls*. This report grew out of an extensive review of the empirical literature on the subject. Key points in that 1998 report concluded that there is no evidence that single-sex education is superior to coeducation; that some students prospered in a single-sex setting, but it was unclear whether coeducation could not produce the same results; that the long-term effect of single-gender learning was unknown; and that more scholarly attention had to be devoted to determining the components of a good education.[148]

Given the question-laden nature of single-sex education, how can public schools make an "exceedingly persuasive" case for them as is required by *U.S. v. Virginia*? California has begun an extensive experiment in single-gender education. When inaugurated in 1998, the key to legal conformity with the equal protection clause was thought to be strict equality between the boys' and girls' schools "down to the number of pencils in the classroom."[149] Is "separate but equal" an exceedingly persuasive educational technique?

Title IX and Education

Title IX of the Education Act of 1972 reads in part, "No person . . . shall, on the basis of sex, be excluded from participating in, be denied benefits of, or be subjected to discrimination under any education program or activity receiving Federal financial assistance."[150] In education, Title IX has been prominent as a tool for curbing sexual harassment, and for increasing female opportunities in college athletics.

Intercollegiate Athletics

Title IX's ban on educational gender discrimination helped engender a sizable enlargement in female athletic programs: the number of women participating in collegiate athletics has grown from 30,000 in 1971 to some 135,000 in the mid-1990s.[151] Feminist thinkers regard Title IX as a mechanism for eliminating restrictions on female participation in areas dominated by males, and as a vehicle for females to emphasize their talents and perspectives. To the more radical among feminist thinkers, Title IX, helps reduce the omnipresent male domination in our society.[152]

The dispute at Brown University over the meaning of Title IX in connection with female athletics has been important to the law affecting intercollegiate athletics. At a congressional committee hearing, Brown's then President Gregorian expressed his frustration with Title IX's administrative regulations: "These [administrative] rules and guidelines are so ambiguous, so inconsistent, and so imprecise that they leave judges with total discretion."[153] He concluded by saying that "proportionality . . . is the (judiciary's) paramount test."[154] Here, Gregorian was correct. The courts have widely imposed a proportionality test at the collegiate level for intercollegiate athletics financing. That is, either that the proportion of males and females participating in sports conforms with their proportions in the student body; or that the interests of the proportionately underrepresented sex are fully and effectively accommodated so that proportional interest representation is achieved. Should that test be extended to the other areas of university life?

Gender segregation is the accepted norm in intercollegiate sport. Title IX athletics discrimination claims accordingly pose unique analytical problems. In *Cohen v. Brown* (1996),[155] (the illustrative opinion in this area and one which involved the dispute President Gregorian was discussing above), a 2–1 majority of a First Circuit review panel reaffirmed the lower court's conclusion that the defendant Brown University, which maintained a significant numerical disparity between female participation in its sports program and its female student enrollment, violated Title IX by cutting off funding for certain female teams. Given the statistical disparity, the majority held that the cutoff demonstrated the University's failure to comply with its duty, under applicable federal administrative regulations, "effectively to accommodate" its female students. Thus, the disparity finding was critical in the analytical process.[156] In short, disparate-impact analysis and the need for proportional affirmative action relief is the keystone of *Cohen,* and of the four other circuit court decisions on which the majority relied.

The *Cohen* majority's rationale is open to question. It held that the lower court's female/male-proportionality ruling did not create an impermissible gender "preference" barred by Title IX. This was so, the majority said, because the remedial "gender-conscious" reallocation of funds mandated by the ruling would affect only resources for athletic programs that were *already* gender segregated. Accordingly, the appropriate way to correct disproportionalities in an existing gender-segregated milieu was to impose gender quotas! But this reasoning arguably runs contrary to a segment of Title IX requiring that the prohibition against educational sexual discrimination in that statute shall not

> be interpreted to require any educational institution to grant preferential treatment or disparate treatment to the members of one sex on account of an imbalance which may exist with respect to the total number or percentage of persons of that sex participating in or receiving the benefits of any federally supported program or activity, in comparison with the total number or percentage of persons of that sex in any community, State, section or other area.[157]

The *Cohen* majority grappled with the above-cited Title IX prohibition by arguing that, since colleges allocate moneys for male and female programs separately, gender-discrimination claims *must* compare the participation opportunities provided for both in order to follow Title IX's requirement that allocations for athletics disadvantage neither sex.[158]

The *Cohen* majority placed great weight on its understanding of the Office for Civil Rights' (OCR) *Policy Interpretation* of Title IX's administrative regulations. According to the *Policy Interpretation*, college athletics programs conformed with Title IX if

(1) intercollegiate level participation opportunities for male and female students are provided in numbers substantially proportionate to their respective enrollments; or (2) where the members of one sex have been and are underrepresented among intercollegiate athletes, whether the institution can show a history and continuing practice of program expansion which is demonstrably responsive to the developing interest and abilities of the members of that sex; or (3) where the members of one sex are underrepresented among intercollegiate athletes, and the institution cannot show a continuing practice of program expansion, . . . whether it can be demonstrated that the interests and abilities of the members of that sex have been fully and effectively accommodated by the present program.[159]

The *Cohen* majority ruled that Brown University had failed to conform to these administrative regulations because the proportion of female athletes (13.1% of all athletes) was not substantially proportionate to the total school female population, and because Brown did not otherwise appropriately cater to female interests. The University insisted that it provided athletic opportunities consistent with levels relative to interest, and that, as its statistics attempted to demonstrate, females were less interested in sports.[160] To which the majority replied:

Thus, there exists the danger that, rather than providing a true measure of women's interest in sports, statistical evidence purporting to reflect women's interest instead provides only a measure of the very discrimination that is and has been the basis for women's lack of opportunity to participate in sports. . . . [T]o allow a numbers-based lack-of-interest defense to become the instrument of further discrimination against the underrepresented gender would pervert the remedial purpose of Title IX. We conclude that, even if it can be empirically demonstrated that, at a particular time, women have less interest in sports than do men, such evidence, standing alone, cannot justify providing fewer athletics opportunities for women than for men.[161]

Brown also argued that the proportional-representation scheme imposed upon it would not pass the strict scrutiny test required by *Adarand v. Peña* (1995),[162] and that, as a result, Brown's equal protection rights under the Fifth Amendment were violated. The Court accurately noted[163] that "[i]t is well settled that the reach of the equal protection guarantee of the Fifth Amendment Due Process Clause—the basis for Brown's equal protection claim—is coextensive with that of the Fourteenth Amendment Equal Protection Clause." However, the Court majority ruled that intermediate scrutiny (and not strict scrutiny) was the appropriate standard for gender discrimination, and that *U.S. v. Virginia* changed nothing.[164] While the *Cohen* court defined intermediate scrutiny as requiring an "exceedingly persuasive justification," it maintained that the Supreme Court had used that standard for intermediate scrutiny in cases other than *U.S v. Virginia*. It also insisted that the proportionality requirement required of Brown measured up to the dictates of intermediate review because such balancing was needed to implement a federal statute.[165]

The provocative dissent in *Cohen* argued that the majority, by rejecting Brown's effort to prove that females had a lesser interest in sports, paralyzed the University's capacity to prove that it complied with the third prong of the *Policy Interpretation* that was just cited. In the dissent's view, the dispositive issue in the case was effectively restricted to crude numerical proportionality, though the majority incongruously asserted that the determination of female "interests" rather than mere numbers was central to its resolution, and that statistical balancing was not mandated by its opinion.[166] This majority claim that its opinion did not mandate statistical balancing was scathingly rejected. To the dissent, the first prong of the *Policy Interpretation* surely requires statistical balancing. The second prong is "essentially a test that requires the school to show that it is moving in the direction of satisfying the first prong," and that can only be done by showing an improvement in statistical balancing.[167] Finally, the third prong, interpreted as the majority does, dispenses with statistical balancing only because it chose to accord zero weight to one side of the balance by adopting a severe form of proportional-interest recognition. Even a single person with a reasonable unmet interest defeats compliance.[168]

The dissent contended that the "exceedingly persuasive justification" requirement of *U.S. v. Virginia* elevated the test applicable to sex-discrimination cases, and that test was surely not met here. Congress expressly disavowed the kind of quota scheme accepted by the majority.[169] "In addition,"

> the majority has put the power to control athletics and the provision of athletic resources in the hands of the underrepresented gender. Virtually every other aspect of college life is entrusted to the institution, but athletics has now been carved out as an exception and the university is no longer in full control of its program. Unless the two genders participate equally in athletics, members of the underrepresented sex would have the ability to demand a varsity level team at any time if they can show sufficient interest. Apparently no weight is given to the sustainability of the interest, the cost of the sport, the university's view on the desirability of the sport, and so on.[170]

Sexual Harassment on Campus

The law of sexual harassment seeks to protect against the disparate treatment of individuals. Additionally, punishing the sexual maltreatment of females is viewed as a deterrent against predatory sexual behavior endemic in the male species; and as a way of reducing the disparate impact on females generated by ingrained-male lust. However, one authority, discussed below, sees sexual harassment regulations on American college campuses as having an unfair disparate impact on the *male* student body.

In the school setting, Title IX litigation closely tracks the sexual harassment law of Title VII. The lead appellate case of *Lipsett v. University of Puerto Rico* (1988)[171] expounds the substantive elements of the sexual harassment violation under Title IX: either "quid pro quo" harassment—a demand for sexual favors in return for workplace benefits, or punishment for refusing the demand; and/or "hostile environment" harassment—the continuing display of sexual hostility or verbal abuse so severe or pervasive as to poison the workplace for the targets. The threshold fact question is always whether the demands, gestures, or expressions involved are "unwelcome" or "poisonous"—a tricky eye-of-the-beholder riddle for the conscientious fact finder. Title VII of the 1964 Civil Rights Act has also been interpreted by the Supreme Court as prohibiting "hostile environment" sexual harassment (including that of the same-sex variety) for *all* work environments covered by the Act.[172]

The Supreme Court has additionally held that a school district would be liable for damages under Title IX for being deliberately indifferent to teacher-student and student-on-student sexual harassment. In the latter case, the successful plaintiff must prove that the harassment is so severe and pervasive as to undermine the victim's education. (See *Davis v. Monroe County Board of Education* [1999].)[173]

At our universities and colleges, gender-harassment regulations have been created, or advocated. They are often preferentially female in objective in that they are meant to protect women against the allegedly more sexually aggressive and sexually disrespectful males.[174] In her book *Heterophobia,* Daphne Patai argues that these rules are cudgels used by academic feminists to rid the universities of male domination and male oppressiveness. To Patai, the view of males as the oppressors is unsound. Females are just as oppressive and offensive, sexually and otherwise. But the harassment rules—particularly those emanating from the "hostile environment" mold—routinely sacrifice the rights of the accused male in favor of the alleged female victims. Patai, in effect, argues that males have become the victims of disparate-impact discrimination as a consequence of campus societal norms generated by radical feminists. As a result, male due process is sacrificed, male freedom of speech is chilled, and interpersonal paranoia is generated at the universities.[175]

A different view of sex-harassment regulation is found in Stephen Schulhofer's *Unwanted Sex.* To him, millions of women face sexual harassment on campus, in the workplace, and in professional relationships. Federal law is biased in favor of males in that females, in a federal harassment lawsuit, have to prove that sexual advances are unwelcome, and this requirement has proved to be notoriously ambiguous and subjective. Better law would require males to prove that their advances were welcome.[176]

Chapter Six

---〜〜〜---

Affirmative Action and the Political Representation of Minorities

Prologue

In this chapter we review affirmative action's record in securing fair representation for America's racial/ethnic minorities and women.

The initial object of the Voting Rights Act (VRA) of 1965[1] was the enfranchisement of protected groups who had been denied the ballot through the governmental use of literacy, educational, or character tests. The Act banned such tests according to a prescribed formula; it did not require a showing of intentional discrimination before the ban took effect. The test ban was triggered by low voting or low-voter registration figures in the states and their subdivisions. The assumption of the Act was that such data reflected the oppressive societal burdens (like poor schools) imposed on African Americans and other minorities—burdens that resulted in greatly limiting minority voting. The Act's objective was to remove or reduce these discriminatory voting restraints. In brief, the Voting Rights Act was an affirmative action measure initially focused on several southern states where impediments to black voting were particularly egregious. Not much later, literacy tests for voting were totally banished nationwide on the obviously correct assumption, that the South had no monopoly on the mistreatment of minorities.

Thus, affirmative action in voting-test abolition began its work contemporaneously with affirmative action in employment and education. From the beginning, enforcement of the Act has largely secured protected-minority access to the polls. Once that was accomplished, the Act's primary target became "dilution," the claimed weakening of minority-voting power through

173

state and local election laws and practices. The government's antidilution program has included strong support for the creation of "majority-minority" voting districts by state and local-redistricting authorities. These districts, in which protected minorities comprise effective voting majorities, are designed to further the election of minority-preferred candidates for office.

In the 1990s decade, racial/ethnic districting encountered serious legal difficulties. The Supreme Court invalidated a number of majority-minority districts on constitutional grounds, and disapproved the policy of maximizing the number of such districts. Affirmative action's future voting rights role is uncertain.

This chapter is also concerned with the rancorous dispute over electoral affirmative action in redistricting. Is the VRA intended only to prevent racial/ethnic disenfranchisement, or also to assist in the election of minority-preferred candidates? Does fair representation require proportionality in the election of minority officeholders? Are racial/ethnic minorities underrepresented? Is *partisan* gerrymandering entitled to greater deference than *racial/ethnic* districting? Is the VRA intended to provide remedies for vote-dilution? Does a numerical majority in districts actually help minorities to attain their electoral goals? If not, what are the alternative methods for safeguarding their interests? These questions are main themes in the ideological war over affirmative action as we experience the post-2000 redistricting round. Adding to the complexity are the revolutionary demographic shifts that are now under way throughout the country.

The 1965 Voting Rights Act and Its Amendments

The Central Portions of the Voting Rights Act

The right to vote epitomizes the paradox of our federal system. Federal law *protects* this right,[2] but does not *create* it. Instead of a single national suffrage law, we must contend with a bewildering multiplicity of state and local systems. On the one hand, federal law imposes extensive constraints on the states' electoral prerogatives. On the other, the states, in substantial measure, control voter eligibility, districting, and the rules and procedures for *all* elections, federal as well as state. At bottom, the history of suffrage reform is the record of a protracted federal-state battle for the upper hand in this tempestuous relationship.[3]

It is a twice-told tale that the VRA came into being only when Congress finally realized that drastic federal intervention would be needed to end the almost century-old disenfranchisement of southern blacks.[4] In *South Carolina v. Katzenbach* (1966), the Supreme Court, 8–1, upheld the constitutionality of the VRA's Sections 4 and 5 as appropriate enforcement of the Fifteenth Amendment.[5] In his opinion for the Court, Chief Justice Warren wrote:

> The Voting Rights Act was designed by Congress to banish the blight of racial discrimination in voting which has infected the electoral process in parts of our country for nearly a century. The Act creates stringent new remedies for voting discrimination where it persists on a pervasive scale, and . . . [it] strengthens existing remedies for pockets of voting discrimination elsewhere in the country. . . . Congress felt itself confronted by an insidious and pervasive evil which had been perpetrated in certain parts of our country through unremitting and ingenious defiance of the Constitution. . . . Congress concluded that the unsuccessful remedies which it had prescribed in the past would have to be replaced by sterner and more elaborate measures in order to satisfy the clear commands of the Fifteenth Amendment.[6]

Section 5 of the VRA mandates that political jurisdictions which—under VRA Section 4—were required to end their literacy tests, because of the paucity of voters or registrants, are prohibited from imposing new voting procedures unless the U.S. attorney general registers no objection to them, or a special three-judge District of Columbia District Court authorizes them as nondiscriminatory in their treatment of protected groups. A covered (so-called "preclearance") jurisdiction may petition the District Court for the District of Columbia for a ruling that its proposed change "does not have the *purpose* and will not have the *effect* of denying or abridging the right to vote on account of race or color."[7] Or a "preclearance" jurisdiction may first seek *administrative* preclearance from the attorney general under the previously cited, two-pronged purpose/effect test, and thereafter appeal to the Court if approval is refused. The Act also authorizes private lawsuits to compel preclearance.[8] As of the mid-1990s, 9 states, 54 counties, and 12 municipalities were subject to the aforementioned preclearance requirement.[9]

Section 2 of the original Act barred states and their subdivisions from denying or abridging the right to vote on the basis of race or color. When Section 2 was amended in 1982, it took on a decidedly disparate-impact and antidilutionist cast. (See pages 182–186 below.)

Section 4 and Disparate Impact

Section 4[10] created a major affirmative action program. Once an important weapon in preventing blacks from voting, literacy tests, by that Section, can no longer be employed to bar suffrage and to work a disproportionate impact on the voting patterns of racial and ethnic minorities as they have in the past. To its everlasting credit, the VRA has opened America's voting booths to blacks, Latinos, and other minorities. It has significantly improved their ability to participate in the affairs of government.

The results of Section 4's implementation are impressive: Across the entire South, including the seven states originally targeted by the Act, registration to vote increased among voting-age blacks from 43.3% to 63.7% between 1964 and 1988—a jump of close to 50%. During the same period, black registrations in the five Deep South states almost tripled, rising from 22.5% to an astonishing 65.2%.[11] When the Act was inaugurated in 1965, there were fewer than 100 elected black officeholders in the seven targeted states, and less than 200 nationwide. By 1990, these numbers had soared to 3,394 in the targeted jurisdictions, and 7,370 nationally.[12] In the six states with the greatest Hispanic populations—Arizona, California, Florida, New Mexico, New York, and Texas—the number of elected Latino officials rose from 1,280 in 1973 to 3,592 in 1990.[13] Nationwide, the number of such officials increased from 3,063 to nearly 5,000 between 1984 and 1990 alone.[14] In 1965, when the VRA was passed, there were 5 African Americans and 3 Hispanics in Congress. In 1996, there were 17 Hispanics and 38 blacks, a six and sevenfold increase.[15]

In a large sense, these remarkable increases in minority officeholding may be ascribed to the operation of the VRA as a whole: abolition of discriminatory voting tests; preclearance requirements; expanded minority registrations; and increased minority voter turnout. But it is abundantly clear that a critical factor in the entire mix has been the adoption of majority-minority congressional and other legislative districts by state redistricting authorities.[16] For example, when 14 blacks and 6 Latinos came to Congress in 1992—the greatest absolute increase in minority representation ever in a single year— almost all of them were elected from majority-minority districts drawn under Sections 2 and 5.[17] Hispanics and blacks rarely win in majority-white congressional districts. In 1996, of the 38 blacks in the House, 31 came from majority-black districts, and 5 of the remaining came from majority-minority districts where Hispanics made up most of the nonblack population. All the Hispanic House members were from majority-minority districts.[18]

Creation of Majority-Minority Districts: Before the 1982 Voting Rights Act Amendments

As Section 4's implementation produced an explosive jump in registration and voting by southern blacks,[19] many of the affected Jim Crow jurisdictions countered with a campaign of "massive resistance" that some authorities liken to their attempts to evade *Brown v. Board of Education's*[20] 1954 school desegregation requirement.[21] While not designed to *deny* the vote to the newly enfranchised blacks, these schemes ran the vote-*dilution* gamut, ranging from blatantly discriminatory shifts from single-member to at-large or multimember elections in which black voters would be submerged in a sea of their white brethren, to racial gerrymanders, changing offices from elective to appointive status, majority instead of plurality run offs, and so on.[22] Congress had enacted Section 5 for the specific purpose of dealing with such attempts to circumvent the new law,[23] but the preclearance provisions were not invoked to address dilution through redistricting until the aftermath of *Allen v. State Board of Elections* (1969).[24]

In *Allen*, the Supreme Court interpreted Section 5 (the preclearance section) to protect not only the right to vote, but also the right to an *effective* vote.[25] That case involved Mississippi's effort to change the mode of electing county supervisors from a ward (district) mechanism to an at-large system. Critics regarded this change as an effort to smother the potency of new black voters by submerging them in mainly white, at-large voting areas.[26] Mississippi contended that Section 5 was restricted to registration for voting, and had no bearing on voting as such. The Court rejected this claim, and held that the change was preclearable because of its potential dilutive effect on African-American voting power. In so ruling, the Court said:

> The right to vote can be affected by a dilution of voting power as well as by an absolute prohibition on casting a ballot. Voters who are members of a racial minority might well be in the majority in one district, but in a decided minority in [a larger voting unit]. . . . This type of change could therefore nullify their ability to elect the candidate of their choice just as would prohibiting some of them from voting.[27]

In holding that redistricting is preclearable, *Allen* applied the antidilution principle of *Reynolds v. Sims* (1964), which held that the equal protection clause mandates equalization of voting districts by population ("one man, one vote") in order to preclude dilution of voting power.[28] *Reynolds* was a victory for *majority* rights; *Allen*'s linkage of minority rights to *Reynolds* consequently wedded majoritarian and minority theories of vote dilution.

Allen's extremely broad ruling established beyond question that *all* arguable electoral changes must be submitted for preclearance. In administering the "effect" prong of Section 5's purpose/effect test, the Department of Justice (DOJ) acted on the affirmative action premise that the Voting Rights Act's ultimate objective was not merely to pry open the doors of the voting booth, but also to help minorities elect minority candidates, and that race/ethnic-based districting was the sine qua non of fair minority representation.[29] This premise was based, among other things, on the African-American historic inability to elect black officials from white-majority districts.[30] Early on, DOJ's preclearance policy was to withhold preclearance of potentially discriminatory redistricting plans unless the redistricters agreed to include some form of majority-minority districting.[31] By the mid-1970s, it was common practice to include one or more "super" majority-minority districts (65% or more) in new-districting plans in order to pass preclearance scrutiny.[32] Although this antidilution program was initiated under the preclearance provisions of VRA Section 5, since 1982 it has been conducted mainly under amended VRA Section 2 (see below at pages 182–186). From the beginning, race-based districting has applied to Latino groups as well as to African Americans.[33]

For the most part, the courts initially approved DOJ's activist preclearance policy for redistricting.[34] The main reason for racial-districting's ascendancy was the impetus the *Allen* decision lent to DOJ's activist reading of its Section 5 preclearance power. Subsequently, however, the Supreme Court drastically curtailed its support for majority-minority districting under Section 5. In 1976, the Supreme Court refused to sanction DOJ's policy of attempting to compel covered jurisdictions to maximize the number of majority-minority districts. The lead 1976 *Beer v. United States* case[35] arose from a plan for reapportioning New Orleans' five city-council districts in order to accommodate a population increase. The City's population ratio was 55% white, 45% black, and its registered voter ratio was 65% white, 35% black. The redistricting plan called for five new districts arranged in the existing north-to-south pattern, with black-*population* majorities in two districts, and a registered black-*voter* majority in a third.[36]

The U.S. Attorney General denied the City's Section 5 request for several reasons, including the claim that, since the black neighborhoods were generally located in an "east to west progression," using north-to-south districts "almost inevitably would have the *effect* of diluting the *maximum potential impact* of the Negro vote."[37]

On the City's appeal, the District Court concluded that, given the opportunity to elect councilmembers in proportion to their share of the City's registered voters, or of the City's population, the City's African Americans would have been able to elect at least two or three. However, under the disputed plan, given the long history of racial bloc voting in the City, "Negroes would probably be able to elect only one, . . . the candidate from the one . . . district in which a majority of the voters were Negroes."[38] Therefore, the plan would have the effect of abridging the right to vote on account of race or color, and was not entitled to preclearance.[39]

The Supreme Court reversed, declaring that

[T]he purpose of Section 5 has always been to insure that no voting-procedure changes would be made that would lead to a retrogression in the position of racial minorities with respect to their effective exercise of the electoral franchise. . . .

[A] legislative reapportionment that enhances the position of racial minorities with respect to their effective exercise of the electoral franchise can hardly have the "effect" of diluting or abridging the right to vote on account of race within the meaning of Section 5. . . . [S]uch an ameliorative new apportionment cannot violate Section 5 unless it so discriminates on the basis of race or color as to violate the Constitution.[40]

The Supreme Court majority found that, under the previous reapportionment, none of the five city-council districts had a black-voting majority, and no black was ever elected to the council. By contrast, under the disputed plan, in addition to the black-voter-majority district, two would have black-population majorities. Accordingly, the majority held that there was "every reason to predict, upon the . . . hypothesis of bloc voting, that at least one and perhaps two Negroes [might] . . . well be elected to the council under [the disputed plan]." Therefore the plan could not have a dilutive "effect" in the sense of Section 5.[41]

The *Beer* retrogression doctrine limits Section 5 preclearance review of proposed redistricting plans to the question of whether they would impermissibly reduce minority-voting strength. This notion suggests a seemingly simple, objective standard for resolving redistricting disputes: will affected minorities be better, or worse off, in terms of their ability to elect? Apart, however, from the fact that this "nonretrogression" standard is not as simple as it may seem,[42] it has not been widely adopted as a definitive criterion of minority representation. It is not available for measuring *unchanged* rules and procedures in jurisdictions covered by Section 5, dating in some cases back to the end of Reconstruction, or to rules and procedures of any kind in uncovered jurisdictions. Furthermore, in the mainstream-liberal view, by mandating preclearance in nonretrogression cases, the *Beer* ruling precludes consideration of whether more "might be accomplished in terms of increasing minority representation."[43] In effect, the status quo has become a ceiling rather than a floor, and Section 5's function has been reduced to preventing erosion rather than sustaining the momentum of civil rights reform.[44] Thus, even though majority-minority districts first emerged as antidilution remedies from Section 5, preclearance law offers little help in defining dilution or evaluating race/ethnic-based districting.[45]

Beer confirmed that the Court's post-*Allen* view of antidilution and race-based districting was not invariably supportive. Shortly after the VRA's enactment, while refusing to rule that multimember districts inherently diluted minority-voting power, the Court allowed that they *might* be unconstitutional if operated "*designedly or otherwise* . . . to minimize or cancel out the voting strength of racial or political elements of the voting population."[46] In *Whitcomb v. Chavis* (1971), the Court, 5–4, rejected an equal protection claim based on the chronic inability of black ghetto residents in a multimember legislative district to elect proportionate numbers of their preferred candidates.[47] Since the Constitution does not mandate proportional representation, and since there was no evidence that the claimants had been discriminatorily denied an equal opportunity to participate in the political process, their underrepresentation, in the majority's view, did not result from dilution.[48] However, in *White v. Regester* (1973),[49] involving a similar claim, the Court, 5–4, reached the opposite conclusion. The majority held that the minority claimants had been deprived of the requisite opportunity by the "totality of the circumstances," including discriminatory-voting rules and invidious maltreatment, and it upheld the District Court's order to create new single-member legislative districts as the remedy for the unconstitutional dilution.[50] *White*'s criteria did not include discriminatory intent.[51] Still, in *City of Mobile v. Bolden* (1980),[52] a plurality decided that "in order to establish a violation either of Section 2 or of the Fourteenth, or Fifteenth Amendments, a minority voter must prove that a contested electoral mechanism was *intentionally* adopted or maintained by a state official for a discriminatory purpose."[53] This ruling caused a furor in the voting rights lobby because it appeared to vitiate minority rights—such as the ability to formulate majority-minority districts—under existing case law.[54] In 1982, "Congress substantially revised Section 2 to make clear that a violation could be proved by showing discriminatory *effect* alone and to establish as the relevant legal standard the 'results test' applied by this Court in *White v. Regester* and by other federal courts before *Bolden*."[55]

Just two years before *Bolden*, the Court did provide constitutional support for the creation of majority-minority districts in *United Jewish Organizations [UJO] of Williamsburg, Inc. v. Carey* (1977).[56] The Supreme Court, in that case, upheld a redistricting plan which, based on preclearance negotiations with DOJ, created a 65% "nonwhite" (black and Puerto Rican) supermajority in one district, and assigned part of the district's 30,000-member Hasidic Jewish community to another district. The reason for the reassignment was to ensure that the population of the nonwhite district did not exceed the applicable limit of one person, one vote. The Hasidim claimed that the dispersal violated their Fourteenth and Fifteenth Amendment rights by diluting their power to elect one of their own members to office.

The Court rejected this claim, 7–1. Justice White announced the judgment. Writing for himself and Justices Brennan, Blackmun, and Stevens, he concluded that the plan's use of racial criteria in attempting to comply with Section 5 and to secure the attorney general's approval did not violate the Fourteenth or Fifteenth Amendments.

> [C]ompliance with the [VRA] Act in reapportionment cases, . . . often necessitate[s] the use of racial considerations in drawing district lines. . . . [T]he Constitution does not prevent a State subject to the . . . Act from deliberately creating or preserving black majorities in particular districts in order to ensure that its reapportionment plan complies with Sec-

tion 5.[57] The permissible use of racial criteria is not confined to eliminating the effects of past discriminatory districting or apportionment.[58]

> . . . [I]n the process of drawing black majority districts in order to comply with [Section] 5, the State must decide how substantial those majorities must be in order to satisfy the . . . Act. . . . But whatever the specific percentage [of majority], the State will inevitably arrive at it as a necessary means to ensure the opportunity for the election of a black representative and to obtain approval of its reapportionment plan. . . . [A] reapportionment plan cannot violate the Fourteenth or the Fifteenth Amendment merely because a State uses specific numerical quotas in establishing a certain number of black majority districts.[59]

In Part IV of his opinion, writing for himself, and Justices Stevens and Rehnquist, Justice White concluded that, entirely apart from the need to comply with Section 5 of the statute, the State's "deliberately . . . purposeful"[60] use of race did not violate the Constitution:

> [The] plan represented no racial slur or stigma with respect to whites or any other race, and [therefore] no discrimination violative of the Fourteenth Amendment. . . . [N]or [was there] any abridgment of the right to vote on account of race within the meaning of the Fifteenth Amendment. . . .

> . . . [Even though] New York deliberately increased the nonwhite majorities in certain districts in order to enhance the opportunity for the election of nonwhite representatives from those districts . . . there was no fencing out of the white population from participation in the political processes of the county, and the plan did not minimize or unfairly cancel out white voting strength.[61]

UJO stands for the proposition that the Constitution permits the use of racial criteria and numerical quotas in drawing district lines, absent proof of collateral damage. Chief Justice Burger filed a dissent, which foreshadowed the racial gerrymander decisions of the 1990s. (See pages 185–193 below.) He wrote:

> The result reached by the Court today in the name of the Voting Rights Act is ironic. The use of a mathematical formula tends to sustain the existence of ghettos by promoting the notion that political clout is to be gained or maintained by marshaling particular racial, ethnic, or religious groups in enclaves. It suggests to the voter that only a candidate of the same race, religion, or ethnic origin can properly represent that voter's interests, and that such candidate can be elected only from a district with a sufficient minority concentration. The device employed by the State of New York, and endorsed by the Court today, moves us one step farther

away from a truly homogeneous society. This retreat from the ideal of the American "melting pot" is curiously out of step with recent political history—and indeed with what the Court has said and done for more than a decade. The notion that Americans vote in firm blocs has been repudiated in the election of minority members as mayors and legislators in numerous American cities and districts overwhelmingly white. Since I cannot square the mechanical racial gerrymandering in this case with the mandate of the Constitution, I respectfully dissent.[62]

Antidilution under Amended Section 2

As amended in 1982, Section 2 prohibits the imposition of any voting rule or procedure "which *results* in denial or abridgement of the right to vote on account of race, color, or membership in a language minority."[63] A violation of the aforementioned occurs where the "totality of circumstances" discloses that:

> [T]he political processes leading to nomination or election . . . are not equally open to participation by members of a . . .[protected] class . . . in that its members have less opportunity than other members of the electorate to participate in the political process and to elect representatives of their choice. The extent to which members of a protected class have been elected to office . . . is one circumstance which may be considered: *Provided,* that nothing in this Section establishes a right to have members of a protected class elected in numbers equal to their proportion in the population.[64]

The statutory language and its history[65] underscore the primary features of the 1982 amendments:

• That the adoption of the "results" test in Section 2(a) "squarely decoupled" Section 2 from the Supreme Court's holding in *City of Mobile v. Bolden* (1980)[66] that statutory-dilution claims under the original Section 2 required proof of discriminatory purpose.[67]

• The "totality of circumstances" provisions of Section 2 incorporated the constitutional dilution test that the Court formulated in *White v. Regester* (see pages 179–180), and that did not include an intent requirement.[68]

• Section 2 is violated if "plaintiffs do not have an equal opportunity to participate in the political processes and to elect candidates of their choice." Proof of a violation could include a "variety of factors," depending on the rule, practice, or procedure called into question. There is no requirement that any particular number of factors be proved, or that a majority of them point one way or the other.[69]

The new Section 2 has displaced Section 5 as the primary, federal-statutory guardian of minority voting rights.[70] As the Supreme Court has explained:

[M]anipulation of district lines can dilute the voting strength of politically cohesive minority group members, [either] by *fragmenting* the minority voters among several districts where a bloc-voting majority can routinely outvote them, or by *packing* them into one or a small number of districts to minimize their influence in the districts next door. Section 2 prohibits either sort of line-drawing where its result, " ' interact[ing] with social and historical conditions,' impairs the ability of a protected class to elect its candidate of choice on an equal basis with other voters."[71]

Given that the rationale of the "results" test is the mirror image of the "effects" test that is enshrined in the law of equal employment opportunity and education reform as the basis of remedial affirmative action,[72] it is plain that Congress intended amended Section 2 to function as the affirmative action vehicle for remedying vote dilution.[73] In this respect, it is subject only to the disclaimer, which provides, in essence, that the statute does not *mandate* proportional representation. However, it is not clear whether the quest for such proportionality is constitutionally *permissible*. By design or otherwise, this circumstance has left open a most fundamental unresolved voting rights issue: is it a legitimate social goal to foster election of minority-preferred candidates in numbers which approximate the minorities' shares of the population?[74]

By far the most troubling question about Section 2 is whether the application of the results test, which it codified, has produced an acceptable standard of fair representation. On this point, the lead case is *Thornburg v. Gingles* (1986).[75]

Since 1982, the great bulk of affirmative action, racial/ethnic-dilution litigation has taken place under Section 2.[76] The contours of this litigation were defined in *Gingles*, where the Supreme Court for the first time construed the amended Section 2.

The black plaintiffs in this landmark case were residents of several multi-member districts in North Carolina that had been established under a legislative redistricting plan. They claimed that the State's choice of the multimember districts diluted their votes by "submerging them" in white majorities. Specifically, the plaintiffs contended that the multimember districts contained several contiguous concentrations of black citizens large enough to function as effective voting *majorities* in single-member districts. The Court upheld the dilution claim with respect to four of the disputed districts, but rejected it in a fifth, where the minority-preferred candidate had won in six successive elections.[77]

As the primary basis for its judgment, the Court majority employed two standards: the level of minority electoral success, and the extent of racial bloc voting.[78] These factors were embodied in the evidentiary test which Justice Brennan set out in his opinion for the majority:

The essence of a Section 2 claim is that a certain electoral law, practice or structure interacts with social and historical conditions to cause an inequality in the opportunities enjoyed by black and white voters to elect their preferred representatives. . . . [M]ultimember districts and at-large voting schemes may " 'operate to minimize or cancel out the voting strength of racial [minorities].' " . . . The theoretical basis for this type of impairment is that where minority and majority voters consistently prefer different candidates, the majority, by virtue of its numerical superiority, will regularly defeat the choices of minority voters. Multimember districts and at-large voting schemes, however, are not per se violative of minority voters' rights. . . . Minority voters who contend that the multimember form of districting violates Section 2 must prove that the use of a multimember electoral structure operates to minimize or cancel out their ability to elect their preferred candidates. . . .[79]

. . . *First*, the minority group must be able to demonstrate that it is sufficiently large and geographically compact to constitute a majority in a single-member district. . . . *Second*, the minority group must be able to show that it is politically cohesive. . . . *Third*, the minority must be able to demonstrate that the white majority votes sufficiently as a bloc as to enable it—in the absence of special circumstances, such as the minority candidate running unopposed—usually to defeat the minority's preferred candidate.[80]

Under *Gingles*, the results test was established as the expansive foundation of dilution law. In true disparate-impact fashion, what counted for Justice Brennan was whether—not why—racial bloc voting diluted minority votes.[81] *Gingles* established the rule that, regardless of the lawmakers' intent, a voting district that has the effect of impermissibly diluting the voting strength of an identifiable minority group violates Section 2 and warrants affirmative relief. The three-part test is not restricted to cases arising from the electoral impotence of minorities submerged in multimember systems, as in *Gingles* itself. It applies also in single-member cases where the plaintiffs have achieved some representation, but claim that their ability to gain the maximum has been diluted.[82]

Even though *Gingles* unequivocally embraced the results test, it left behind considerable confusion and uncertainty about its scope. The Court did not define the decision's basic terms, for example, *geographical compactness, cohesive, usually, or majority*. It failed to make clear whether the three-prong test supplants the nine factors enumerated in the Congressional description of "totality of the circumstances."[83] It did not address the extremely controversial issue of whether Section 2's reference to "representatives of their choice" impliedly contains a same-race limitation. Most significantly, the Court indicated that, in a dilution case, difficulty in electing minority-preferred candidates and the extent of racially polarized voting outweigh geographical compactness in importance.[84] During the post-1990 redistricting cycle, this ruling led many states to ignore compactness in creating new majority-minority districts, thus setting the stage for the racial-gerrymander litigation of the 1990s. In short, *Gingles* exemplifies the support/opposition syndrome in dilution case law; on the one hand, the Court enshrined the results test, but on the other hand, laid down the basis for the greatest challenge to its application.[85]

Justice Brennan's ruling that "the single-member district is generally the appropriate standard" of minority representation[86a] encouraged the lower courts and DOJ to promote creation of single-member, majority-minority districts in preclearance jurisdictions during the redistricting round of the 1990s. By triggering this explosion of new majority-minority districts, the ruling provided the raw material for the current constitutional controversy over racial gerrymandering.[86] Moreover, it provoked an ideological clash in the Court. In her concurrence, Justice O'Connor rejected the rationale of the ruling on the ground that it was tantamount to endorsement of "rough" proportionality, which while "not quite the same as a right to strict proportionality . . . [is] inconsistent with Section 2's disclaimer and with the results test that is codified in Section 2."[87] The racial-gerrymander cases of the 1990s make it clear that the rift over this crucial issue persists to this day.

The "Racial-Gerrymander" Cases of the 1990s and the Constitutional Requirements of the Equal Protection Clause

Background

In a line of decisions issued between 1993 and 1996, the Supreme Court established the rule that majority-minority districts drawn with race as the "predominant" factor are presumptively unconstitutional racial gerrymanders under the equal protection clause—a presumption which can be overcome only if the districting at issue survives strict judicial scrutiny.[88] In these decisions, the Court, 5–4, invalidated majority-black districts which had been created in North Carolina, Georgia, and Texas during the post-1990 census redistricting round.

With these actions the Court opened a new chapter in the controversy over the appropriate remedy for voting-discrimination, though its standards remain murky. Nonetheless, it is already abundantly clear that these decisions have called into question the government's race/ethnic-based antidilution program.

Strictly speaking, "gerrymandering" is synonymous with "dilution." Both terms connote drawing district lines in a way that arbitrarily limits the voting power of identifiable groups. In general usage, these terms imply distortion, political favoritism, or racial bias. In fact, both are forms of "districting," which "*always* involves choices among competing apportionment schemes that may favor one or another political party, incumbent official, regional interest, minority group, etc."[89] In this sense, " 'all *districting is gerrymandering.*'"[90]

Generically, "racial gerrymanders" result from " 'the deliberate and arbitrary distortion of [voting] district boundaries . . . for . . . [racial] purposes.'"[91] They were the stock-in-trade of racial segregation in the post-Civil War South.[92] They have "come in various shades": at-large configurations that submerge minority groups in nonminority-majority multimember districts; "cracking," dispersing minorities among various districts where they will always be in the minority; "stacking," a large minority concentration within a larger nonminority population; and concentrating minority voters into districts where they constitute supermajorities.[93]

The 1990's Decisions

Between 1990 and 1992, during the post-1990 redistricting cycle, 14 states created 15 new black-majority districts and 10 new Latino-majority districts. These dramatic changes were attributable to pressure by the Department of Justice in preclearance negotiations; fear of government and private "Section 2" suits in the wake of *Gingles*; and the agitation for increased minority representation. Through the use of enhanced computer technology, many of the new districts were drawn with convoluted lines that completely obliterated long-standing county and city boundaries.[94]

Shaw v. Reno (1993) and its progeny through the end of the millennium represent the cutting edge of a reignited antiaffirmative action counterrevolution that challenges the efficacy, the legality, and the morality of majority-minority districting.[95] These cases emerged from the crucible of preclearance negotiations. They were brought by white plaintiffs who did not claim dilution of their own voting rights. They were all decided, 5–4, by the same bloc: Justices Rehnquist, Scalia, O'Connor, Kennedy, and Thomas. It remains to be seen whether the "predominance-of-race" doctrine—which emerged from these decisions—is, in fact, a mechanism for declaring majority-minority districts unconstitutional in the future.

However this plays out, there is inflamed controversy over the Voting Rights Act's role, and this will not abate, whether affirmative action stays or goes. As we experience the onset of the new redistricting round following the year 2000 census, the time has come to reevaluate the Voting Rights Act. This evaluation should consider the thinking of the Court majority on racial gerrymandering as well as the views of the justices who have dissented from it.

Shaw v. Reno (1993)[96] was the Court's first brush with North Carolina's Twelfth Congressional District, a single-member majority-black district, that the State created in order to meet the Department of Justice's (DOJ) preclearance demand for a *second* new majority-black district in the State's post-1990 reapportionment plan.[97] The district consisted of a narrow, bizarrely-shaped band of linked black-population concentrations, traversing several counties and cities, plainly designed to elect a black congressperson.[98] The case held that the plaintiffs stated an equal protection claim for relief by alleging that the district was an unconstitutional racial gerrymander, since its shape showed that it *must* have been drawn solely to ensure election of black officeholders.[99] The following is an excerpt from Justice O'Connor's opinion for the Court, effectively expressing the "race-as-predominant-factor" principle:

> [The district] . . . is so extremely irregular on its face that it rationally can be viewed only as an effort to segregate the races for purposes of voting, without regard to traditional districting principles and without sufficiently compelling justification.[100] . . .

> When a district is obviously created solely to effectuate the perceived common interests of one racial group, elected officials are more likely to believe that their primary obligation is to represent only members of that group, rather than their constituency as a whole. This is altogether antithetical to our system of representative democracy.[101]

The dissenting justices contended that the equal protection clause bars racial districting only if it denies access to the polls or dilutes voting strength, citing *UJO v. Carey* (1977).[102] (See pages 180–182, where the Court in *UJO* rejected an equal protection attack on a majority-minority district, on the ground that the white plaintiffs had not been harmed. Consequently, in the dissents' view, *UJO* was indistinguishable from *Shaw*.[103])

Miller v. Johnson, 515 U.S. 900 (1995)

In this case the Court applied the rule of *Shaw v. Reno* in striking down a majority-black district in Georgia, which the State drew in order to comply with DOJ's preclearance demand for a *third* such district. Justice Kennedy's opinion for the Court is the definitive statement of the rule. His opinion was unguided by *UJO v. Carey*'s support of majority-minority districting. Following is an extended excerpt:

> Justice Kennedy delivered the opinion of the Court:

> [903] The constitutionality of Georgia's congressional redistricting plan is at issue here. In *Shaw v. Reno,* 509 U.S. 630 (1993), we held that a plaintiff states a claim under the Equal Protection Clause by alleging that a state redistricting plan, on its face, has no rational explanation

save as an effort to separate voters on the basis of race. The question we now decide is whether Georgia's new Eleventh District gives rise to a valid equal protection claim under the principles announced [904] in *Shaw*, and, if so, whether it can be sustained nonetheless as narrowly tailored to serve a compelling governmental interest.

The Equal Protection Clause of the Fourteenth Amendment provides that no State shall "deny to any person within its jurisdiction the equal protection of the laws." Its central mandate is racial neutrality in governmental decision making. . . .

[905] In 1965, the Attorney General designated Georgia a covered jurisdiction under [Section] 4(b) of the Voting Rights Act. In consequence, [Section] 5 of the Act requires Georgia to obtain either administrative preclearance by the Attorney General or approval by the United States District Court for the District of Columbia of any change in a "standard, practice, or procedure with respect to voting" made after November 1, 1964. The preclearance mechanism applies to [906] congressional redistricting plans, and requires that the proposed change "not have the purpose and will not have the effect of denying or abridging the right to vote on account of race or color." . . .

A special session opened in August 1991, and the General Assembly submitted a congressional redistricting plan to the Attorney General for preclearance on October 1, 1991. . . . [907] The Department's objection letter noted a concern that Georgia had created only two majority-minority districts. . . .

The General Assembly returned to the drawing board. A new plan was enacted and submitted for preclearance. This second attempt . . . increased the black populations in the Eleventh, Fifth and Second Districts. The Justice Department refused preclearance again, relying on alternative plans proposing three majority-minority districts. . . .

Twice spurned, the General Assembly set out to create three majority-minority districts to gain preclearance. Using the ACLU's [American Civil Liberties Union] "max-black" plan as its benchmark, the General Assembly enacted a plan that [included the newly-designed Eleventh District at issue in this case]. . . .

[909] The Almanac of American Politics has this to say about the Eleventh District: "Geographically, it is a monstrosity, stretching from Atlanta to Savannah. Its core is the plantation country in the center of the state, lightly populated, but heavily black. It links by narrow corridors the black neighborhoods in Augusta, Savannah and south-

ern DeKalb County." Georgia's plan included three majority-black districts, though, and received Justice Department preclearance on April 2, 1992.

. . . [The plaintiffs], five white voters from the Eleventh District, filed this action against various state officials . . . (Miller Appellants) in the United States District Court. . . . Their suit alleged that Georgia's Eleventh District was a racial gerrymander and so a violation of the Equal Protection Clause as interpreted in *Shaw v. Reno*. . . .

. . . [911] Just as the State may not, absent extraordinary justification, segregate citizens on the basis of race in its public parks, buses, golf courses, beaches, and schools, so did we recognize in *Shaw* that it may not separate its citizens into different voting districts on the basis of race. The idea is a simple one: "At the heart of the Constitution's guarantee of equal protection lies the simple command that the Government must treat citizens 'as individuals, not as simply components of a racial, religious, sexual or national class.' " . . . When the State assigns voters on the basis of race, it engages in [912] the offensive and demeaning assumption that voters of a particular race, because of their race, "think alike, share the same political interests, and will prefer the same candidates at the polls." Race-based assignments "embody stereotypes that treat individuals as the product of their race, evaluating their thoughts and efforts—their very worth as citizens—according to a criterion barred to the Government by history and the Constitution." . . . They also cause society serious harm. As we concluded in *Shaw:* "Racial classifications with respect to voting carry particular dangers. Racial gerrymandering, even for remedial purposes, may balkanize us into competing racial factions; it threatens to carry us further from the goal of a political system in which race no longer matters." . . .

[914] It is true that redistricting in most cases will implicate a political calculus in which various interests compete for recognition, but it does not follow from this that individuals of the same race share a single political interest. The view that they do is "based on the demeaning notion that members of the defined racial groups ascribe to certain 'minority views' that must be different from those of other citizens," the precise use of race as a proxy the Constitution prohibits. . . .

[916] Redistricting legislatures will, for example, almost always be aware of racial demographics; but it does not follow that race predominates in the redistricting process. . . . The distinction between being aware of racial considerations and being motivated by them may be difficult to make. This evidentiary difficulty, together with the sensitive nature of redistricting and

the presumption of good faith that must be accorded legislative enactments, requires courts to exercise extraordinary caution in adjudicating claims that a state has drawn district lines on the basis of race. The plaintiff's burden is to show, either through circumstantial evidence of a district's shape and demographics or more direct evidence going to legislative purpose, that race was the predominant factor motivating the legislature's decision to place a significant number of voters within or without a particular district. To make this showing, a plaintiff must prove that the legislature subordinated traditional race-neutral districting principles, including but not limited to compactness, contiguity, respect for political subdivisions or communities defined by actual shared interests, to racial considerations. Where these or other race-neutral considerations are the basis for redistricting legislation, and are not subordinated to race, a State can "defeat a claim that a district has been gerrymandered on racial lines.". . .

[917] In our view, the District Court applied the correct analysis, and its finding that race was the predominant factor motivating the drawing of the Eleventh District was not clearly erroneous. The court found it was "exceedingly obvious" from the shape of the Eleventh District, together with the relevant racial demographics, that the drawing of narrow land bridges to incorporate within the District outlying appendages containing nearly 80% of the district's total black population was a deliberate attempt to bring black populations into the district. . . .The court found that "it became obvious," both from the Justice Department's objection letters and the three preclearance rounds in general, "that [the Justice Department] would accept nothing less than abject surrender to its maximization agenda." . . . [918] It further found that the General Assembly acquiesced and as a consequence was driven by its overriding desire to comply with the Department's maximization demands. . . . And in its brief to this Court, the State concedes that "[i]t is undisputed that Georgia's eleventh is the product of a desire by the General Assembly to create a majority black district." Hence the trial court had little difficulty concluding that the Justice Department "spent months demanding purely race-based revisions to Georgia's redistricting plans, and that Georgia spent months attempting to comply." On this record, we fail to see how the District Court could have reached any conclusion other than that race was the predominant factor in drawing Georgia's Eleventh District; and in any event we conclude the court's finding is not clearly erroneous. . . .

[920] Race was, as the District Court found, the predominant, overriding factor explaining the General Assembly's decision to attach to the Eleventh District various appendages containing dense majority-black popu-

lations. As a result, Georgia's congressional redistricting plan cannot be upheld unless it satisfies strict scrutiny, our most rigorous and exacting standard of constitutional review.

To satisfy strict scrutiny, the State must demonstrate that its districting legislation is narrowly tailored to achieve a compelling interest. There is a "significant state interest in eradicating the effects of past racial discrimination." The State does not argue, however, that it created the Eleventh District to remedy past discrimination, and with good [921] reason: There is little doubt that the State's true interest in designing the Eleventh District was creating a third majority-black district to satisfy the Justice Department's preclearance demands. . . .

[924] Instead of grounding its objections on evidence of a discriminatory purpose, it would appear the Government was driven by its policy of maximizing majority-black districts. . . .

[925] In utilizing [Section] 5 to require States to create majority-minority districts wherever possible, the Department of Justice expanded its authority under the statute beyond what Congress intended and we have upheld. . . .

[926] Based on this historical understanding, we recognized in *Beer* that "the purpose of [Section] 5 has always been to insure that no voting-procedure changes would be made that would lead to a retrogression in the position of racial minorities with respect to their effective exercise of the electoral franchise." 425 U.S., at 141. The Justice Department's maximization policy seems quite far removed from this purpose. . . .

[927] The end [the eradication of invidious discrimination] is neither assured nor well served, however, by carving electorates into racial blocs. "If our society is to continue to progress as a multiracial democracy, it must recognize that the automatic invocation of race stereotypes retards that progress and causes continued hurt and injury." It takes a short-sighted and [928] unauthorized view of the Voting Rights Act to invoke that statute, which has played a decisive role in redressing some of our worst forms of discrimination, to demand the very racial stereotyping the Fourteenth Amendment forbids. . . .

Subsequent to *Miller,* in 1996, the Court ruled that a number of congressional districts were shaped predominantly by racial considerations and would not pass strict scrutiny. One of these was the redistricting plan involved in *Shaw v. Reno* (1993).[104] In *Shaw v. Hunt* (1996),[105] the Court invalidated

North Carolina's Twelfth Congressional District, maintaining that strict scrutiny was not satisfied despite the fact that the district was created to conform with the Section 5 preclearance requirements imposed by DOJ. DOJ's objective, to the Court, was to maximize the number of majority-minority districts. That Department was bluntly reminded by the Court that the national government was not authorized to require the states to maximize the number of majority-minority districts.

In *Bush v. Vera* (1996),[106] three Texas majority-minority districts were also struck down in 1996 as unconstitutional under the *Miller* rule. Reflecting extraordinary differences within the Court over representational standards, six separate opinions were filed, none joined by more than three justices. The principal opinion in support of the judgment was delivered by Justice O'Connor, writing for herself, Chief Justice Rehnquist, and Justice Kennedy. In restating the *Miller*[107] rule, Justice O'Connor said: [Strict scrutiny does not] "apply to all cases of intentional creation of majority-minority districts, . . . [but only upon a showing] . . . that other, legitimate districting principles were 'subordinated' to race."[108]

Justice Thomas, joined by Scalia, rejected O'Connor's disavowel of strict scrutiny with regard to some intentionally created majority-minority districts. In a caustic vein, he wrote that "Only last Term, in *Adarand Constructors Inc. v. Peña* [1995], we vigorously asserted that all government racial classifications must be strictly scrutinized."[109]

Shaw v. Reno and its progeny cases in the 1990s evoked a number of harsh dissents from Justices Stevens, Souter, Ginsburg, and Breyer. The dissenters expressed their commitment to enhancing minority voting power as a legal and moral imperative. In their view, the *Shaw* doctrine is constitutional heresy, impossible to apply, and should be repealed. A representative sample is the following excerpt from the *Bush v. Vera* dissent filed by Justice Souter, normally the Court's most dedicated guardian of stare decisis:

[The predominance test is inherently flawed because many] . . . traditional districting principles cannot be applied without taking race into account and are thus, as a practical matter, inseparable from the supposedly illegitimate racial considerations.[110]

[In continuing to adhere to this doctrine, the Court fails] . . . to provide a coherent concept of equal protection injury . . . [or a coherent test for determining its existence].[111] [It is impossible to comply with *Miller's*] . . . obligation to untangle racial considerations from so-called "race-neutral" objectives (such as according respect to community integrity and protecting the seats of incumbents) when the racial composition of a district and voter behavior bar any practical chance of separating them.[112]

[The Court's options for dealing with *Shaw*'s unworkability are] . . . to confine the cause of action by adopting a quantifiable shape test or to eliminate the cause of action entirely. . . . [T]here is presently no good reason that the Court's withdrawal from the presently untenable state of the law should not be complete.[113]

Redistricting in the Post-2000 Era

The *Shaw/Miller* cases of the 1990s pose extraordinary redistricting puzzles. Among other matters, how does one determine whether race/ethnicity predominates in legislative district construction? As a way of thwarting the "predominance" barrier, one analyst suggests that districts be constructed with sizable minority-voting populations, but not a majority. His thesis is that in such districts minorities, though politically strong, will have to cooperate with whites to achieve their legislative objectives, and that such districting will be regarded by the Court as promotive not of segregation but of integration. Consequently, that kind of racial/ethnic ("minority-interest") gerrymandering would likely be accepted by the Supreme Court.[114]

The Court may have been affected by such a "less-than-a-majority" thesis in the first major *Shaw/Miller* case of the new millennium—*Hunt v. Cromartie* (2001).[115] Once again, that high tribunal visited the Twelfth North Carolina Congressional District that it struck down in 1996 in *Shaw v. Hunt*.[116] Thereafter, the State redrew the District, reducing the number of split-counties and cities, and reducing its former black-voting majority to 47%, but essentially retaining its irregular shape. On a challenge that the new District violated the *Shaw/Miller* doctrine, the district court found that the State's motivation had been predominantly racial, and held the new District unconstitutional. However, in the *Cromartie* case, the Supreme Court, in yet another 5–4 ruling, reversed, holding that the plaintiffs had failed to sustain their burden of proving that racial considerations were "dominant and controlling," and that the District Court's findings were "clearly erroneous."[117] The decision turned on the undisputed evidence that the District's black voters registered and voted Democratic between 95% and 97% of the time.[118] In his opinion for the majority, joined by Justices O'Connor, Stevens, Souter, and Ginsburg, Justice Breyer held that this evidence warranted a finding that "race in this case correlates closely with political behavior."[119] In accordance with prior declarations by the High Court, this correlation sufficed to refute the District Court's conclusion.[120]

Cromartie, in effect, upheld the constitutionality of District 12, thereby marking the first time that the Court actually applied the "political-affiliation" (political-gerrymandering) defense in a racial-gerrymandering case. Moreover, the defense is available, under Justice Breyer's rationale, in any case "where majority-minority districts (or the *approximate* equivalent) are at issue and where racial identification correlates highly with political affiliation."[121] *Hunt v. Cromartie* thus legitimates creation of largely or mostly black, Hispanic, or Asian districts, if shown to be motivated by traditional political considerations.

However, the scope of the political-affiliation defense is not clear at this time. *Cromartie* applied, but did not clarify, the Court's prior decisions concerning strict scrutiny of the motivation for districting, and for the right to engage in "constitutional political gerrymandering."[122] It is unknown whether the requisite political motivation must be shown in accordance with stipulated substantive and evidentiary guidelines or whether the outcome in each case will depend entirely on its specific facts, as construed by individual justices.[123] Furthermore, the Court has yet to elucidate the difference between "constitutional" and "unconstitutional" *political* gerrymandering *or* the difference, if any, between racial and political gerrymanders. These overriding issues implicate complex policy considerations, but the Court has failed to promulgate standards of adjudication.[124]

In short, *Hunt v. Cromartie* notwithstanding, the controversy over racial districting is far from over. In the light of the currently ongoing demographic revolution (see pages 198–199 below), one may expect a large increase in Hispanic and Asian-controlled voting districts and a tidal wave of resultant equal protection litigation. In this connection, it must be borne in mind that *Cromartie* did not repeal the *Shaw/Miller* doctrine; on the contrary, all nine justices apparently agree that the doctrine of applying strict scrutiny to districting where racial/ethnic considerations are predominant is still the law of the land. Therefore, if a race/ethnic-conscious redistricting plan fails to give due weight to traditional districting principles, then it must either assert and substantiate a political-affiliation defense, or else withstand strict scrutiny. Given the continuing lack of guidelines, many redistricters may be unable to sustain these burdens.[125]

One must conclude, then, that, even as liberalized by *Hunt v. Cromartie*, *Shaw/Miller* has cast an ominous cloud over race/ethnic-conscious remedies for dilution. Whether the end is nigh depends on the nature of the changes in the Court's membership or orientation which may take place in the near term. Justices Scalia and Thomas, the Court's most militant opponents of affirmative action, have disavowed the concept of dilution in voting rights law.[126] If they should come to dominate the majority, the Court could be expected to dispense with the formality of strict scrutiny, and deal with racial gerrymanders as intrinsically unconstitutional. This would almost certainly bar any new majority-minority districts and bring that dimension of affirmative action's career in voting rights to a standstill. On the other hand, it is conceivable that the decisive role in determining whether there shall be any new race/ethnic districts will be assumed by Justice O'Connor. As the Court's swing vote in voting rights cases, she might succeed in persuading her colleagues to take a less drastic approach.[127] Either way, any redistricting agency that ignores the *Shaw/Miller* rule, acts at its peril.

Women and Electoral Politics

Freedom from gender discrimination is not an element of the Voting Rights Act as it is in Title VII of the 1964 Civil Rights Act and Title IX of the 1972 Education Act. The great struggle to abolish the "dilution" of female-voting power came in the suffrage struggle of the nineteenth and early twentieth centuries. A decade after the ratification of the Nineteenth Amendment (1920)— which barred the denial or abridgment of the right to vote on the grounds of sex—the vibrancy of the feminist movement evaporated politically, to be born again with the second-wave feminism of the 1960s and thereafter.[128] The dream of some suffragettes that female voting and political participation would end war and produce social harmony and justice was obviously not realized.[129] Even after suffrage was gained, the bias against females in elected positions was "strong enough to make female candidacies almost irrelevant."[130] But the feminist movement of recent vintage helped produce a remarkable turnabout. Prejudice against females running for office has collapsed in large measure. In the words of a respected analyst, David Lauter:

> With the exception of some regions of the deep South, where gender prejudice remains stronger than elsewhere, a female candidate who can overcome the structural barriers facing "outsider" candidacies—most notably fund-raising—can now run a viable race for any statewide or regional elective office. As the National Women's Political Caucus . . . discovered in a comprehensive survey covering more than fifty thousand individuals who had run for office between 1972 and 1992, women incumbents are as successful in gaining reelection as are men, and female candidates for open legislative seats now win at the same rate as male candidates. Indeed, pollsters and political consultants in both parties believe that in some parts of the country, gender alone actually now provides women a small but notable advantage. American history provides no comparable example of so rapid a decline of prejudice against a previously disfavored group.[131]

Lauter contradicts himself somewhat by noting that females have to spend more to prove that they are *credible* candidates.[132] Nevertheless, the increase in female elected-officeholding has been steadily (though slowly) rising since 1975 to the late 1990s: from 8% of the state legislators to 22%; from 10% of the state executive positions to 28%; and from 4% of Congress to 12%.[133] Why aren't the figures more in harmony with the fact that females constitute more than half of the population? Incumbency strength is part of the answer. Another factor is that women have less "access to the traditional business and professional networks that allow many men to raise funds."[134] Basic to the latter is our society's allocation of the primary child-rearing and home-maintenance roles to women.

Our electoral districts are not, of course, formally designed for the representation of men or women as distinct groupings, as are racial/ethnic majority-minority districts. However, party leaders have taken the goal of increasing female-political participation seriously, for they have come to aggressively seek out viable women candidates.[135] Specialized funds have been created to encourage female candidacies. For instance, EMILY's List (which, when operative, was reserved for women Democrats), and the WISH List (for Republicans).

What difference would getting more women in office make? As reported by Professor Beth Reingold, there is much in the scholarly literature asserting that women treat the issues concerned with females and children with greater sensitivity than do men. Some evidence suggests, too, that women office-holders were more responsive to their constituents' needs.[136] From her own studies including an in-depth survey of the California and Arizona Legislatures, Reingold concluded (admittedly in an "ambiguous, complicated, and conditional"[137] way) that: "In short, the behavior of public officials is by no means completely or even primarily a function of sex or sex ratios, even when it concerns the representation of women's policy and policymaking preferences."[138] Possible reasons for this "genderless" phenomenon include the more or less equal gender distributions in the governmental districts served; partisan/ideological affiliations that override gender orientation; and institutional norms of reciprocity, collegiality, and courtesy.[139] She finds little evidence to support the view that female/male similarities are a function of male dominance in the legislative process which has worked to generate servile female submission to the male agenda.[140]

Epilogue

Differing Schools of Thought on the Voting Rights Act

The VRA began America's long-delayed attempt to achieve full voting rights for minorities. Over the past thirty-five years, affirmative action has indisputably provided our racial, ethnic, and gender groups with a considerable measure of political opportunity. Yet, as we close the books on the old millennium, the nation is embroiled in harsh debate over minority voting rights.

What many see, overall, is incomplete voting rights reform. To them, despite the substantial progress, race remains at the fault line of American politics. Racially polarized voting remains the salient characteristic of our system; King's vision of multiracial coalitions is a utopian fantasy.[141] Relative to their share of the electorate, minorities are grossly underrepresented.[142] In terms of registration and voting rates, blacks and Latinos lag far behind whites; in no state do they hold elective office at levels equal to whites.[143] But even if proportional representation is reached, minorities numerically would be but a small grouping subject to white dominance in many state and local legislatures, and surely in Congress.[144] In short, minorities, according to this view, have a long way to go before they enter the Promised Land of political equality.

Nonetheless, another school of thought holds that the VRA has overprotected minorities. In this view, affirmative action has grafted racial preference onto a law that was designed to protect access—and nothing more.[145] "Equal treatment alone," that is, guaranteed access, so the argument goes, has been "deemed insufficient to compensate" for centuries of exclusion. Accordingly, just as in the case of employment discrimination,

> minority preference [has been] required to produce the proportionally equal results that would have been expected in the absence of discrimination. In voting rights law, affirmative action policy has taken the form of giving preference to selected minorities in electoral districting arrangements. The potential power of these minorities, most notably blacks and Hispanics, is protected from dilution, while all other groups and interests are denied such protection.[146]

Moreover, "the logic of affirmative action in voting rights . . . extend[s] beyond equal access to the ballot box and reach[es] toward minority representation in elective office that approximates the demographic profile of protected classes."[147]

To this school, application of the "results" test and the concept of "dilution" under amended Section 2 has conferred on protected minorities a privilege that no other citizens can claim: namely, the *legal right* to elect preferred candidates in numbers which are proportional to population-share. Racial proportionality is now the legal standard of fair minority representation.

Exhibit A in this brief are the numerous single-member, majority-minority districts that have come into being in Section 2 litigation, or in Section 5 preclearance negotiations. To the extent that such units have brought about "safe" minority seats, they prove that the VRA has been turned into a racial quota system. This is anathema. It breeds backlash and resegregation. Furthermore, as a growing segment of minority opinion now reflects, it is inimical to long-range minority interests. Political affirmative action stigmatizes and ghettoizes its supposed beneficiaries; it impedes the coalition-building without which we can never have true civil rights reform.

It follows that the Voting Rights Act must be purged. The sole statutory voting right should be the right to cast secret ballots and to have them fairly counted, and the statutory mechanisms limited to enforcement of that right. The "results" test and the doctrine of dilution should be abolished, the doctrine of intentional discrimination restored, and the range of the attorney general's discretionary preclearance authority sharply curtailed. If these changes should decrease the number of minority officeholders, or their influence on policy, so be it. No group should have the right to elect by the numbers. As long as they enjoy equal access and equal procedural rights, minorities should be content to take their chances in the political arena, just like everybody else.

Needless to say, these views have been scathingly denounced by pro-affirmative action elements of the civil rights community.[148] However, to one degree or another, they apparently resonate with the current Supreme Court majority, as well as with the growing segment of the public at large that opposes affirmative action in employment and education.

Reevaluating the Voting Rights Act

These warring schools of thought confirm that there is an urgent need to reevaluate the voting rights program. This is bound to be an extremely difficult undertaking. At present the politics of race and ethnicity are approaching a "boiling point" in this country; what with the near parity between Republicans and Democrats in the Congress and many state legislatures, redistricting promises to be a central political dispute in the years to come.[149] Further, the post-2000 census redistricting round was faced with a radical transformation in the country's racial and ethnic makeup. The states are much engaged with the usual redistricting problems of population growth:[150] one person, one vote; competition for federal dollars; conflicting political demands; and preclearance negotiations. In addition, they are confronted with the host of unfamiliar demographic phenomena that the 2000 census disclosed, including the explosive nationwide growth of the Hispanic minority and its incipient ascendancy over African Americans, and the displacement of non-Hispanic white majorities in many of our major cities.[151] It stands to reason that redistricting will be far more difficult than ever.

In our opinion, any attempt to grapple with minority districting concerns must begin with the following steps: concern with the redefinition of majority and minority-voting rights; and review of the objectives of civil rights reform. In our majoritarian system, it has long been an article of faith that political dominance and the power to control elections is the prerogative of the group with the *numerical majority* of the population. Has that principle been overtaken by events? The 2000 census has disclosed that entrenched "non-Hispanic white" majorities have been, or soon will be, dethroned by seismic population shifts in California, Texas, Florida, Hawaii, New Mexico, and the District of Columbia.[152] Obviously, the country's political map will have to be redrawn.

The question is whether numerical hegemony or some nonnumerical principle of political organization applies where no group has a numerical majority.

Take California, where the non-Hispanic white population has fallen from 56% of the state total a decade ago to less than half, while the Hispanic and Asian shares rose to nearly 33% and 12% respectively; and where the erosion of the white share continues steadily.[153] Among many other things, these changes mean that the voting strength of all three minorities must be recalculated, in order to determine whether any of them might be entitled to protection against dilution, and what type of districting and voting mechanisms would provide such protection. This could be accomplished either by applying numerical *plurality* requirements, or by devising voting procedures encouraging effective coalitions. California's wise men must decide.

It is expected that racial and ethnic diversification à la California will happen nationwide within the next half century; "[t]hen everyone will be a minority."[154] There is no way of predicting the ultimate impact on minority voting rights, but it seems plain that the days of the numerical majority model are numbered. We feel that a first priority of minority voting rights reform should be to develop the correct replacement.

Granted that fair legislative representation is a centerpiece of our democracy, to what extent does its efficacy depend on the racial/ethnic identity of legislators? A seemingly intractable controversy over "descriptive" (same race) versus "substantive" (influence on policy) representation has spawned a plethora of conflicting views. Some insist,[155] others deny,[156] that a minority influences the policy process only to the extent that it elects fellow group members to office. But in practice the two theories of representation often overlap. Descriptive representation normally can serve as a mechanism for gaining substantive representation, because, rightly or wrongly, the minority expects one of its own to be more responsive to its needs than a nonminority legislator. To be sure, such expectations are not always fulfilled; the incidence of such failures should be factored into any policy review. Moreover, a minority might not *need* descriptive representation if its bloc voting power is critical to the reelection of its nonminority representatives, for instance, southern white Democrats. All told, experience suggests that the desirability of descriptive or substantive representation must be assessed on a case-by-case basis.

There is considerable doubt that majority-minority districting has advanced fair minority representation very much.[157] This suggests a policy under which single-member districts with less than controlling racial majorities can provide minorities with equal opportunity to participate in the political process and to elect candidates of their choice. In such districts, minorities would require the assistance of crossover voting from other groups. In formulating this coalition-districting policy, the primary problem would be to prescribe the requisite level of minority voting strength.[158] Assuming that such a requisite level can be devised, the outcome of *Hunt v. Cromartie* (2001), which involved a 47% black district, suggests that the Court would find "minority-influence" districts constitutional. (See above at pages 193–194.)

Other minority-empowering electoral policies have been suggested:

Cumulative Voting: Each voter has as many votes as the at-large seats to be filled, and may distribute them as one sees fit. Theoretically, a cohesive minority can elect its candidate even in the face of a hostile majority by concentrating its votes.

Limited Voting: Each voter has fewer votes than the at-large seats to be filled. Theoretically, the majority cannot capture every seat even by voting a straight ticket, but a cohesive minority with enough votes may control at least one.

Lowering the 50% plus 1 margin of victory permitting plurality winners.

These are all modified at-large remedies. Proponents maintain that they can be implemented without recourse to controversial single-member districting while producing reasonably equivalent electoral outcomes.[159]

Advocates of minority power also urge the embrace of various legislative mechanisms including: Minority vetoes; supermajority requirements for certain legislative enactments; and cumulative voting by legislators by presenting legislative alternatives in multiples of three or more. These are forms of "proportionate interest representation." A leading advocate offers it as "[a] normative directive to reinvigorate the basic motivation for [the VRA]" by attempting to "move the process of governmental decision making away from a majoritarian model toward one of proportional power."[160]

Most of the controversy over minority voting rights would be mooted by amendment of VRA. For example, Congress could state in clear language whether the Act is intended only to provide access to the polls, or, in addition, to foster election of minority representatives. Similarly, it could tell us whether, and how, the Act is supposed to protect the right to vote against dilution. By taking such long overdue steps, Congress would put a welcome stop to all the quarrelsome speculation about its presumed intent.

Congress and/or the Supreme Court should elucidate the relationship between the VRA and the equipopulation rule in *Reynolds v. Sims* (1964),[161] which postulates that population is the "controlling criterion" of districting disputes. To what extent does the rule permit deviations for race/ethnic-based or partisan districting? To put it somewhat differently, if there is a conflict between one person, one vote, and a racial or partisan district, which prevails? What are the standards of constitutionality of political gerrymanders? If these differ from the standards for racial gerrymanders, why the difference? In *Davis v. Bandemer* (1986),[162] the Court ruled that disputes over the constitutionality of partisan gerrymanders are justiciable, but declined to set any standards for determining such disputes. Given the pivotal role of political gerrymanders under *Hunt v. Cromartie* (2001), it seems pertinent to inquire whether these standards differ from those that govern racial/ethnic majorities.

Surely too, the issue of proportional representation must be dealt with. As one commentator has astutely remarked: "The debate over voting rights is a . . . variant of a long-standing issue in political science—the relative merits of . . . proportional representational systems. . . .[P]roportionality is something of a dirty word in the Anglo-American tradition. Americans prefer to use terms such as *fairness* and *nondilution* . . . without explicitly defining them."[163]

The specific issue is the propriety of the long-standing ban on the maintenance of a ratio between racial minorities' population share and the number of their descriptive representatives. (See the disclaimer in VRA Section 2 on page 182 above.) In our view, the Supreme Court's muddled treatment of the problem indicates the need for reconsideration. As seen, in the 1971 *Whitcomb* case, and again in the 1980 *Bolden* case (see above at pages 179–180), the Court ruled that proportional representation is not a legitimate dilution remedy. But it seems to us that the Court's actions in other dilution cases are not consistent with that conclusion. For example, the Court's repeated failures to formulate broadly acceptable representational baselines bespeak a tacit refusal to acknowledge that rough proportionality is an obvious standard.[164] By the same token, majority-minority districting is analytically a form of proportionality.[165] By approving it in the 1986 *Gingles* case, the Court in effect created a right to that form. As matters stand, however, we have not created a specific basis for deciding whether minority voters in fact enjoy an equal opportunity to participate in the political process. The time has come to determine once and for all whether proportional representation should be recognized as the appropriate measure.

To conclude: In 1966, Chief Justice Warren said of the VRA, "Hopefully, millions of non-white Americans will now be able to participate for the first time on an equal basis in the government under which they live."[166] Has this hope been realized? If voting rights affirmative action should be declared off-limits, what will take its place fifty years from now when all Americans have become minorities?

Chapter Seven

─◦◦◦─

Affirmative Action
and Fair Housing

Prologue

Affirmative action meant to craft racially and ethnically balanced neighborhoods has received but little federal attention. Ironically, residential segregation is at the heart of educational segregation and has operated as a barrier to the elimination of inner-city poverty. Nevertheless, residential segregation has survived all attempts at public regulation, particularly the Fair Housing Act (FHA/Title VIII) of 1968.[1]

The FHA was the Great Society's last major civil rights initiative. It prohibits public and private discrimination in the sale or rental of residential housing on account of race, color, religion, sex, national origin, disability, or family status. FHA's implementation by the Department of Housing and Urban Development (HUD) has focused on mitigating forbidden, intentional discrimination in real estate matters. HUD's enforcement of the 1866 Civil Rights Act[2] has also been important in this connection. In implementing these statutes, HUD has largely ignored the force of societal/systemic discrimination as manifested in white flight to the suburbs and exclusionary zoning.[3]

At the birth of the FHA, civil libertarians believed that the dismemberment of intentionally discriminatory residential barriers would result in widespread black/white racial integration. HUD's reluctance to extend its enforcement of FHA beyond forbidden intentionalism (and proactively cultivate racial/ethnic balancing) is attributable to such diverse factors as the lack of controlling Supreme Court precedent regarding disparate impact in the housing area; antipathy to housing affirmative action within the civil rights community; and administrative foot-dragging. Whatever the correct explanation, HUD's residential-integration program has had, at best, only a marginal impact on the segregated pattern in the nation's housing.

Housing Segregation

Times change, it is said. But not, it seems, in our neighborhoods. The war for civil rights has been waged. Open housing advocates have had their say. "Fair housing" laws adorn national, state, and local statute books. Here and there, racial frontiers are even being crossed—at least temporarily. Yet, by and large, we remain a nation of segregated enclaves. Virtually every metropolitan area in the land includes ghettos of blacks (and increasingly Latinos), ringed by affluent white neighborhoods or suburbs. The central-city ghettos are studies in urban decay, mired in poor jobs, poor schools, and poor public services—breeders of an American underclass. The outlying neighborhoods and suburbs (though some of them have become extensions of the black city ghetto) remain bastions of white exclusivity, and racial exclusion. One wonders how long these explosive ingredients can be kept from erupting into destructive urban upheavals, as they did in the terrible Los Angeles race riot of 1992.

During the first-half century after the Civil War, African Americans remained primarily a rural people congregated in the South. Shortly before World War I, blacks began a major migration to urban America. (See page 31 above.) Today, they are predominantly urban.[4]

In the cities, African Americans have been concentrated in ghetto areas in large measure as a consequence of white racism abetted by governmental support. The latter included police acceptance of white harassment directed at blacks moving into nonghetto areas; judicially enforced, racially restrictive covenants; and local governments which were steadfast in the maintenance of apartheid through such devices as regulations governing where blacks could reside.[5] For some time, the federal government shamefully facilitated segregation. The Federal Housing Administration greatly assisted home purchasing by whites by guaranteeing mortgages requiring low down payments and long periods of amortization. But this aid was not (until the 1970s) available for older housing in the central cities where blacks were forced to live. It is not surprising, then, that blacks remain far behind whites in real-property wealth accumulation.[6] Further, the massive development of the "lily-white" suburban America immediately after World War II is partially attributable to restrictive-racial covenants required (until 1950) by the Federal Housing Administration for new suburban developments. Federally supported urban renewal and highway construction in postwar America also uprooted African-American communities, necessitating an even greater concentration of blacks in the ghettos that remained.[7]

The residential segregation nurtured in the first half of the twentieth century has continued. An analysis of the 1990 and 2000 Census data by the Mumford Center at the State University of New York at Albany[8] reported the following: The typical metropolitan-area white person lived in a neighborhood (defined as a census tract of 4,000–6,000 people) which was 86% white in 1990, and 80% white in 2000. The average metropolitan-area black person lived in a neighborhood that was 56% black in 1990, and 51% black in 2000. While some progress in black/white integration was evident in the 2000 Census,[9] Hispanics and Asians have become more "isolated" in the large majority of metropolitan areas.[10] Further, while blacks and whites are living in more integrated areas than in 1990, the children are not, particularly in the major metropolitan areas of the Midwest and Northeast. Typically, minority children are raised in an area where they are a majority.[11]

The negative disparate impact of racial segregation is forcefully emphasized. To Gary Orfield, "[I]n a white-dominated society, separate is inevitably unequal both in terms of resources that go into a community and in terms for the way in which society values that community, its institutions, and its people. . . . [T]he basic problem that integration addresses is the problem of white prejudice and the fact of institutional and individual discrimination in favor of whites and white communities."[12]

A National Advisory Commission on Civil Disorders (Kerner Commission) was presidentially created in 1967 to report on the reasons for and the cure of the racial disorders that convulsed the nation during the 1960s. In its report, the Commission highlighted urban residential segregation, arguing that its continuation would greatly limit black access to good jobs as these were rapidly becoming suburbanized. Continued exclusion of blacks from good jobs would have other disparate impacts of a catastrophic nature. Poverty would increase; families would be torn asunder because male breadwinners—overwhelmed with feelings of inadequacy—would abandon their family responsibilities; and social order would be threatened.[13]

Writing in the 1990s, Professor William Julius Wilson adopted a theme similar to that of the Kerner Commission when he argued that a "new urban poverty" has emerged in the nation's urban ghettos marked by a far more pervasive impoverishment than had existed there in the 1950s. The cause, primarily, has been the movement of jobs to the distant suburbs, and the "spatial mismatch" between the residencies of the very poor African Americans and employment availability.[14] (See pages 236–238 below.)

In its review of residential segregation, the Kerner Commission also warned that "[w]hen disadvantaged children are racially isolated in the schools, they are deprived of one of the significant ingredients of quality education: exposure to others with strong educational backgrounds. [Important studies] . . . establish that the predominant social/economic background in a school exerts a powerful impact on achievement."[15] This educational thesis is still emphasized in the current literature.[16]

One scholar summarized the impact of residential segregation in the following way:

> A complex, interlinked cycle of racial discrimination and economic disparity continues to keep many African Americans from experiencing equal opportunities in the suburbs, and the effects are likely to impede meaningful residential integration in the immediate future. Economic, educational, and social disparity has resulted from intractable patterns of segregation. As a result of this disparity, it is difficult for many blacks to afford suburban housing. This absence of African Americans from suburban locales feeds white prejudice, which in turn motivates continuing subtle discrimination. Core resistance to integration in the suburbs runs deep and is unlikely to be overcome by increased contact between whites and blacks when strong social and economic disincentives also exist, not the least of which is the lowering of status and property values that may be associated with integration. Faced with these impediments, many African Americans reasonably may choose to live in predominantly black areas in which a sense of community exists and a decent life is available.[17]

Integration proponents vociferously demand sweeping, affirmative action cures: broad-scale, race-conscious governmental mandates, and incentives that will racially diversify the segregated neighborhoods.[18] By contrast, champions of race neutrality maintain that the true causes of residential segregation are ingrained segregationist "attitudes" in *both* black and white households, and economic barriers. In other words, both blacks and whites either *prefer* segregated living or cannot afford anything else. In this view, emphasis on housing-integration affirmative action is pointless: it will not ameliorate the attitudinal and economic problems, but most likely will exacerbate them.[19] In its most radical formulation—so-called "critical race theory"—we are presented with a view which rejects racial integration as a current social goal.[20] Various minority politicians have also opposed prointegrative housing measures, fearing reductions in their power base.[21]

Federal Antidiscrimination Law Affecting Housing

The equal protection clause in the Fourteenth Amendment prohibits state or local land-use policies or practices designed to prevent minorities from buying or leasing affordable housing in areas they desire.[22] The Thirteenth Amendment, moreover, abolished slavery and authorized Congress to enforce that prohibition through appropriate legislation. Such legislation—the Supreme Court came to conclude in 1968—included statutory efforts to eradicate public and privately imposed "badges of slavery" like restrictions on property ownership once placed on slaves. (See pages 23–25 above.) The Court reached this conclusion in *Jones v. Mayer* (1968), a case involving the 1866 Civil Rights Act, and one that resurrected the Thirteenth Amendment for contemporary use.[23] Jones was barred from purchasing a home solely because he was African American. He asserted that the 1866 Act prohibited a sales ban of that nature.

Jones v. Mayer, 392 U.S. 409 (1968)

Mr. Justice Stewart delivered the opinion of the Court:

[412] In this case we are called upon to determine the scope and the constitutionality of an Act of Congress, 42 U.S.C. 1982 [the 1866 Civil Rights Act], which provides that:

"All citizens of the United States shall have the same right, in every State and Territory, as is enjoyed by white citizens thereof to inherit, purchase, lease, sell, hold, and convey real and personal property." . . .

[439] The constitutional question in this case, therefore, comes to this: Does the authority of Congress to enforce the Thirteenth Amendment "by appropriate legislation" include the power to eliminate all racial barriers to the acquisition of real and personal property? We think the answer to that question is plainly yes.

"By its own unaided force and effect," the Thirteenth Amendment "abolished slavery, and established universal freedom. . . ." [I]t is at least clear that the Enabling Clause of that Amendment empowered Congress to do much more. For that clause clothed "Congress with power to pass *all laws necessary and proper for abolishing all badges and incidents of slavery in the United States.*"

Those who opposed passage of the Civil Rights Act of 1866 argued in effect that the Thirteenth Amendment merely authorized Congress to dissolve the legal bond by which the Negro slave was held to his master. Yet many had earlier opposed the Thirteenth Amendment on the very ground that it would give Congress virtually unlimited power to enact laws for the protection of Negroes in every State. And the majority leaders in Congress—who were, after all, the authors of the Thirteenth Amendment—had no doubt that its Enabling Clause contemplated the sort of positive legislation that [440] was embodied in the 1866 Civil Rights Act. Their chief spokesman, Senator Trumbull of Illinois [said], . . .

". . . I have no doubt that under this provision [Section 2 of the Thirteenth Amendment—the enabling clause]. . . we may destroy all these discriminations in civil rights against the black man; and if we cannot, our constitutional amendment amounts to nothing. It was for that purpose that the second clause of that amendment was adopted, which says that Congress shall have authority, by appropriate legislation, to carry into effect the article prohibiting slavery. Who is to decide what that appropriate legislation is to be? The Congress of the United States; and it is for Congress to adopt such appropriate legislation as it may think proper, so that it be a means to accomplish the end."

Surely Senator Trumbull was right. Surely Congress has the power under the Thirteenth Amendment rationally to determine what are the badges and the incidents of slavery, and the authority to translate that determination into effective legislation. Nor can we say that the determination Congress has made is an irrational [441] one. For this Court recognized long ago that, whatever else they may have encompassed, the badges and incidents of slavery—its "burdens and disabilities"—included restraints upon "those fundamental rights which are the essence of civil freedom, namely, the same right . . . to inherit, purchase, lease, sell and convey property, as is enjoyed by white citizens." Just as the Black Codes, enacted after the Civil [442] War to restrict the free exercise of those rights, were substitutes for the slave system, so the exclusion of Negroes from white communities became a substitute for the Black Codes. And when racial discrimination herds men [443] into ghettos and makes their ability to buy property turn on the color of their skin, then it too is a relic of slavery.

Negro citizens, North and South, who saw in the Thirteenth Amendment a promise of freedom—freedom to "go and come at pleasure" and to "buy and sell when they please" would be left with "a mere paper guarantee" if Congress were powerless to assure that a dollar in the hands of a Negro will purchase the same thing as a dollar in the hands of a white man. At the very least, the freedom that Congress is empowered to secure under the Thirteenth Amendment includes the freedom to buy whatever a white man can buy, the right to live wherever a white man can live. If Congress cannot say that being a free man means at least this much, then the Thirteenth Amendment made a promise the Nation cannot keep. . . .

A centerpiece of modern housing reform is the Fair Housing Act. This Statute includes Title VIII of the Civil Rights Act of 1968, and its amendments. The Act targets discrimination in the ownership, sale, lease, and rental of residential dwellings, together with the cluster of related activities: advertising, brokerage, financing, and property insurance. The declared goal is "affirmatively" to provide national "fair housing."[24] A portion of the Act's central prohibitions follows:

United States Code, Title 42 (2000)

§ 3604-Discrimination in the sale or rental of housing and other prohibited practices

As made applicable by section 3603 of this title and except as exempted by sections 3603(b) and 3607 of this title, it shall be unlawful—

(a) To refuse to sell or rent after the making of a bona fide offer, or to refuse to negotiate for the sale or rental of, or otherwise make unavailable or deny, a dwelling to any person because of race, color, religion, sex, familial status, or national origin. (b) To discriminate against any person in the terms, conditions, or privileges of sale or rental of a dwelling, or in the provision of services or facilities in connection therewith, because of race, color, religion, sex, familial status, or national origin. (c) To make, print, or publish, or cause to be made, printed, or published any notice, statement, or advertisement, with respect to the sale or rental of a dwelling that indicates any preference, limitation, or discrimination based on race, color, religion, sex, handicap, familial status, or national origin, or an intention to make any such preference, limitation, or discrimination. (d) To represent to any person because of race, color, religion, sex, handicap, familial status, or national origin that any dwelling is not available for inspection, sale, or rental when such dwelling is in fact so available. (e) For profit, to induce or attempt to induce any person to sell or rent any dwelling by representations regarding the entry or prospective entry into the neighborhood of a person or persons of a particular race, color, religion, sex, handicap, familial status, or national origin.

The Fair Housing Act of 1968 (which a number of circuit courts of appeal concluded was rooted in the Thirteenth Amendment[25]) sought to eliminate the "badges of slavery" in residential transactions. But the 1968 Act not only goes beyond African Americans in its coverage; it also differs from the 1866 Civil Rights Act in other respects. Thus, the 1968 Act empowers the federal officials to assist aggrieved parties and prohibits specific practices like discriminatory advertising, financing, and brokerage services. The focus of the housing integrationists, in the 1968-era, was on removing those racially motivated government and real estate barriers which frustrated rentals and home purchases by blacks. These barriers, so the thinking had it at that time, imprisoned African Americans in the ghetto; their elimination promised substantial integration.[26] This assumption proved faulty despite the decline of these impediments, and the associated expansion of black-housing opportunities. To one commentator:

> Despite the hope that outlawing housing discrimination would result in desegregation, African Americans in metropolitan areas continue to live in neighborhoods that are composed predominantly of members of their own race. In particular, the replication of this segregation in the suburbs to which African Americans are moving in large numbers, seems to contradict the assumptions of 1968, at which time it was argued that blacks were trapped in central city ghettos due to discrimination by the housing industry, hostile white suburbs, and timid government.[27]

The 1968 Act does not explicitly limit its reach to *intentional* violations. Moreover, it directs the attorney general to combat discrimination by bringing "pattern or practice" suits that have "general public importance."[28] To some, this suggests that the Act was intended to encompass both the "effects" (irrespective of intent) that is, the disparate-impact standard of proof, as well as the "intent," standard, just as under Title VII of the 1964 Civil Rights Act. A number of federal circuit courts of appeal have so held. To these courts, a protected minority complainant can establish a prima facie case by presenting evidence that a facially race-neutral policy has had a disparate/adverse impact on his minority. For example, the grievant can offer statistical evidence that his minority has had a much greater rate of rental or purchase rejection than whites. The burden would then shift: In order to escape liability, the defendant would have to prove a "business necessity," namely, a legitimate, nondiscriminatory business reason for its conduct.[29] In short, to these courts, the 1968 Act incorporates disparate-impact theory, allowing its use to provide affirmative action group remedies as a cure for societal, historical discrimination affecting protected groups without the need to prove that the discrimination was intentional.

As recently as 1994, the Department of Justice and HUD solemnly pledged to apply disparate-impact theory under Title VIII where appropriate.[30] It would appear, then, that Title VIII tracks the equal employment opportunity modus operandi of Title VII of the 1964 Civil Rights Act, and Section 2 of the Voting Rights Act, with respect to disparate impact, and that the federal government is involved in achieving racially balanced communities, just as it has sought proportional representation in employment, and majority-minority legislative districts to enhance minority representation. But this is misleading. The Supreme Court has yet to address the question of disparate impact under FHA's Title VIII. In fact, even though the Act became law in 1968, the Court has not formally decided either its constitutionality or *any* of its standards of evidence. There is no *Griggs v. Duke Power Co.* (1971), *Thornburg v. Gingles* (1986), or *Swann v. Charlotte-Mecklenburg* (1971) in housing-discrimination law. This is remarkable, not to say extraordinary, given that housing discrimination is so intimately interwoven with discrimination in employment and public education that a Justice Department spokesperson recently considered it to be the "root" of the latter.[31] In any event, the classic fair-housing cases which the Supreme Court has so far decided on the merits are not related to Title VIII. *Buchanan v. Warley* (1917)[32] nullified intentional racial-residential zoning as contrary to equal protection. *Shelley v. Kraemer*[33] (1948) ruled that judicial enforcement of intentionally imposed, racially restrictive covenants constituted forbidden "state action" under the Fourteenth Amendment. As we have seen, in *Jones v. Mayer* (1968),[34] the issue was the constitutionality of 42 U.S.C. § 1982, the codification of a Reconstruction statute that provided that all citizens had the same rights as whites to buy, sell, and lease property. And in the more recent Title VIII case of *United States v. Starrett City Associates* (1988), the Court denied certiorari for a Second Circuit Court of Appeals holding that the management of a privately owned apartment building violated the Fair Housing Act by basing rental decisions on explicit racial quotas for the purpose of achieving racial integration.[35]

While the Supreme Court has pointedly refused to decide whether Title VIII incorporates disparate-impact theory,[36] it accepted the judicial ruling that a remedy for HUD's intentional segregation of public housing in Chicago was the requirement that HUD spread its subsidized housing around the Chicago metropolitan area.[37] Moreover, in its focus on Title VIII's prohibition of intentional real estate discrimination, the Court has been liberal, finding that the Act prohibited "blockbusting" and "redlining," and that the Act's "standing to sue" provision was sufficiently broad to permit whites to sue landlords on the grounds that they were denied the right to live in an integrated environment.[38]

The High Court's failure to rule on whether Title VIII incorporates disparate-impact theory has been only one bar to federal race-conscious, prointegrative efforts in housing. Major impediments have been federal administrative foot-dragging,[39] congressional ambiguity, and lack of enthusiasm—if not hostility—in the civil rights community.[40] We are then witness to a major exception in recent civil rights law and policy. Whereas, in the areas of voting, employment, and education, race-conscious, integrative/proportional-representation affirmative action has been very prominent in federal administrative action, this has not been the case in the housing realm. One close observer reported in 1998 that the national government has been so hesitant in applying disparate-impact theory in establishing Title VIII violations that it has never brought a housing disparate-impact claim in a lawsuit. He wrote further that it was not until 1980 that the federal government began using "testers" (minorities and whites who claim to have similar economic and social backgrounds when seeking housing) to determine whether landlords are intentionally discriminating in an unlawful way, though that device had proven to be effective for some time before.[41] Even in the administration of governmentally subsidized housing, there have not been "long-term, coordinated, adequately funded [federal] efforts targeted on desegregation."[42] Some pro-integrative state and local efforts have been undertaken, but these—like those at the federal level—have had but a marginal impact on America's residential "apartheid."[43]

Given the present-day absence of a broad *political* constituency for race-conscious housing affirmative action,[44] it is safe to assume that the eradication of forbidden race/ethnic-intentional discrimination will continue to be the mainstay of Title VIII enforcement.[45] The continuation of segregation; the phenomenon of resegregation; and the "expansion of the ghetto" to the suburbs underscore a primary dilemma: Is residential segregation compatible with the education, employment, and public-service needs of blacks? If not, what race-conscious, pro-integrative techniques can be used that will conform both to the mandates of Title VIII and the equal protection clause? These crucial questions bring us to policies aimed at achieving and maintaining residential integration.

Integration Achievement and Maintenance

Not all those who oppose housing discrimination are strong advocates of housing integration. Thus, Stokely Charmichael and Charles Hamilton, in their book *Black Power,* argued that integrationists assumed that housing decency required life in an essentially white neighborhood—an attitude that to them reflected notions of white superiority.[46] They are not alone. On the other hand, integration exponents argue that segregated-black communities are destined to remain subject to the disparate impact of separate and unequalness in terms of municipal services and societal respect.[47] Skepticism among blacks about pro-integrative measures (beyond the abolition of intentional discrimination) is nourished—among other reasons—because of their capacity to interfere with black housing choice.[48] The "resident-selection," "affirmative-marketing" techniques discussed below aim at racially balanced communities, with potentially strong restraints on black access to prevent "white flight." Nonetheless, the objective of these integration-achievement measures is to help African Americans by placing at least a portion of their communities in enriched, desegregated environments.[49] These measures include (1) site-selection strategies for governmentally assisted housing, (2) affirmative marketing ("special-mobility programs"), (3) resident-selection controls, and (4) "fair share" requirements.

Site Selection

Some lower federal courts have supported the Fair Housing Act (FHA) as an integration mechanism, and not as an Act restricted to requiring race neutrality in real estate transactions. As early as 1970, the Third Circuit Court of Appeals made this clear in *Shannon v. HUD* (1970).[50] There, HUD was accused of failing to take steps against the segregative impact of a publicly assisted, multi-unit complex which that Department had sponsored. The project would have supposedly increased the already high density of low-income African Americans in the area.[51] The Circuit Court ruled that the FHA required that HUD go beyond administering that Act in a color-neutral fashion. Because of that Act and Title VI of the 1964 Civil Rights Act, HUD could no longer

> remain blind to the very real effect that racial concentration has had in the development of urban blight. Today such color blindness is impermissible. Increase or maintenance of racial concentration is prima facie likely to lead to urban blight and is thus prima facie at variance with the national housing policy. . . . We hold . . . that the Agency [HUD] must utilize some institutionalized method whereby, in considering site selection or type selection, it has before it the relevant racial and socioeconomic information necessary for compliance with its duties under the 1964 and 1968 Civil Rights Acts.[52]

Affirmative Marketing

Critics report that HUD site selection has been largely ineffectual as an integration device,[53] partially because project location has been subordinated to demands that housing assistance be directed to minority areas.[54] Increasingly, desegregation advocates focus on "affirmative-marketing"/"special-mobility" techniques that counsel prospective tenants, or home buyers, to seek residences in areas they would not ordinarily consider. That is, African Americans are encouraged to consider white areas; whites are urged to look in minority-impacted, or integrated places.[55] Housing-search counseling has been supplemented with such aid as help with moving expenses, landlord outreach, and post-placement advising.[56] Counseling of this nature has been challenged as deflecting information away from blacks to prevent "white-flight" segregation.[57] Deflection, on the other hand, has been countenanced as serving the compelling need for integration.[58]

That HUD's affirmative marketing has been effective is adamantly denied by a prominent housing scholar, Florence Wagman Roisman. She claimed that "HUD's own studies show that a lot of the projects that are supposed to have affirmative fair-housing marketing plans don't have them and even when they have them, they're not followed and the people who work there don't know about them or laugh them off."[59] HUD's own 1995 affirmative-marketing/special-mobility analysis was more positive. That analysis surveyed 21,000 Section 8 (rent subsidy) minority and majority recipients in four metropolitan areas. These were serviced by programs where affirmative-marketing counseling and landlord outreach were coupled with the administration of HUD's rental voucher (and certificate) program. Voucher and certificate subsidies allow low-income recipients to rent modestly priced private housing anywhere it is available. The mobility study generated a report referred to by its authors as the "first limited, empirical comparison of locational outcomes generated by public housing [subsidized housing in fixed locales] and tenant-based [Section 8 voucher] rental assistance programs." The latter produced "significantly greater dispersion of assisted families . . . in areas less segregated and less poverty-stricken than public housing residents."[60] Additionally, integrative moves by assisted families were associated with improved educational and employment outcomes. Nevertheless, patterns of economic and racial segregation persist among Section 8 voucher recipients, particularly with African Americans[61]—a situation which must be frustrating to dispersion exponents who regard vouchers as a major vehicle for racial balancing.

A University of Minnesota Law School research report summarized HUD's special-mobility programs in the following way:

> Special mobility programs have been implemented on too small a scale and for too short a time-period to have had a significant impact on poverty and racial concentration at the national level. Between 1969 . . . and 1994, fewer than 12,000 low-income minority households have moved to new locations under all of the special mobility programs combined. This number is quite small in light of estimates that in 1990 there were 5.9 million black residents living in urban census tracts where the black poverty rate was at least forty percent.[62]

In *Walker v. City of Mesquite* (1999),[63] a panel of the Fifth Circuit Court of Appeals determined that a race-conscious, site-selection court order was subject to strict scrutiny; while the "helping hand" of race-conscious affirmative marketing was not. To remedy the past discrimination perpetrated by the Dallas Housing Authority (DHA), the district court ordered that new public housing acquired by the DHA be located in predominantly white areas.[64] The appellate tribunal viewed this order as a racial classification that had to conform with the narrow-tailoring component of strict scrutiny. Narrow tailoring would not be satisfied "until less sweeping alternatives—particularly race neutral ones—have been considered . . . tried" and found wanting.[65] One less sweeping alternative—affirmative marketing used with Section 8 vouchers—was also a part of the lower-court remedy. As explained by the Court of Appeals, this affirmative-marketing endeavor included the "helping hand" of signing bonuses for landlords accepting Section 8 tenants. The Appeals Court concluded that affirmative marketing was to be tried and evaluated as a total remedy for the DHA's past discrimination before the race-conscious, site-selection order could be judged as narrowly tailored.[66] Left precariously hanging is the question why affirmative marketing was not regarded as a racial classification and, thus, subject to strict scrutiny.

Resident Selection

Courts have authorized racially conscious, resident-selection processes though Title VIII, on its face, precludes such orders save, perhaps, as a cure for previous intentional discrimination. Thus, in *Otero v. New York City Housing Authority* (1973),[67] the Second Circuit applauded a housing authority racial-balancing policy limiting the number of black residents. The Court said:

> The [New York City Housing] Authority is obligated to take affirmative steps to promote racial integration even though this may in some instances not operate to the immediate advantage of some non-white persons. . . . Action must be taken to fulfill, as much as possible, the goal of open, integrated residential housing patterns and to prevent the increase of segregation, in ghettos, of racial groups whose lack of opportunities the [FHA] Act was designed to combat. Senator Mondale . . . pointed out that the proposed law [Title VIII] was designed to replace the ghettos "by truly integrated and balanced living patterns." . . . We hold . . . that the Authority may limit the number of apartments to be made available to persons of white or non-white races, including minority groups, where it can [be] show[n] that such action is essential to promote a racially balanced community and to avoid concentrated racial pockets that will result in a segregated community.[68]

The 1973 *Otero* Court ruled that the racial balancing involved in the case conformed with the Constitution's equal protection requirement as integration was an essential governmental interest.[69] However, a First Circuit panel (*Raso v. Lago* [1998][70]) held in 1998 that a racial-balancing plan adopted by HUD in Boston was not subject to the strict scrutiny applied in *Otero*. In Boston, a group of predominantly white residents (the "old West Enders") had been removed to make way for urban renewal. Pursuant to Massachusetts law, the developer of new assisted housing in the West End gave first-tenancy preference to that dislocated group. HUD—conforming both to a consent decree it had agreed to in connection with its alleged discriminatory practices

in Boston, and to its reading of the pro-integrative dictates of the FHA—
sought to reduce the scope of the preference granted to the old (predominantly white) West Enders. Under the new plan, half of the apartments were
to be made available by lottery with no preference to the former residents of
the area. The *Raso* Court agreed that HUD's effort was racially motivated in
that it sought to promote integration rather than allotting the apartments to the
predominantly white group. The Court ruled, however, that since the HUD
lottery plan was race-blind, there was no racial classification involved, and no
reason to invoke strict scrutiny. HUD's consent decree and the FHA were
sufficient to uphold the Department's program in this case.[71] The Court explained itself thus:

> The primary test is that any government action—regardless of benign
> intent—is suspect if it has been taken on the basis of a "racial
> classification"; in such cases, the classification must be justified by a
> compelling state interest and narrow tailoring. . . . The term [racial
> classification] normally refers to a governmental standard, preferentially
> favorable to one race or another, for the distribution of benefits. Yet
> under the plan adopted in this case, the apartments freed from statutory
> preference are made available to *all* applicants regardless of race. . . .[72]

In short, the Court maintained that the former West Enders were denied
nothing because of their race. Is this correct? Did not that group lose its 100
percent preference under Massachusetts law because it was predominantly
white, and because HUD wanted to advance integration?

In 1988, a Second Circuit panel ruled—in *United States v. Starrett
City*,[73]—against extending the *Otero v. New York City Housing Authority*
precedent to cover a long-term quota scheme at the Starrett City housing
complex. That complex is an enormous one, consisting of some 5,881 publicly subsidized apartments located in 46 high-rise buildings. The management of the complex sought—and generally maintained—a racial balance of
64% white; 22% black; and 8% Hispanic. The goal was to avoid "tipping,"
the jargon for white exodus.[74]

The *Starrett* Court found that race-conscious affirmative action did not
necessarily violate federal statutory and constitutional provisions. However,
a plan that involves racial distinctions must be temporary. White flight may
be taken into account in the integration equation. But "it cannot serve to
justify attempts to maintain integration at Starrett City through inflexible
racial quotas that are neither temporary nor used to remedy past racial discrimination or imbalance within the complex." Starrett City's reliance on
Otero was misplaced. In *Otero,* the creation of a ghetto and racial unbalance
seemed certain without the temporary, pro-white, tenant-placement plan.[75]
The Court concluded enigmatically by saying:

We do not intend to imply that race is always an inappropriate consideration under Title VIII in efforts to promote integrated housing. We hold only that Title VIII does not allow appellants to use rigid racial quotas of indefinite duration to maintain a fixed level of integration at Starrett City by restricting minority access to scarce and desirable rental accommodation otherwise available to them.[76]

Segregation in the nation's publicly assisted housing units has been extensive, and particularly severe, in the "public housing" projects, inaugurated during the New Deal. Some of the latter have become so physically and socially deficient that they were destroyed. In 2000, the Clinton Administration accepted a plan to demolish almost all of Chicago's high-rise public housing units, replacing them with low-density, mixed-income rentals scattered around the city.[77] In the waning days of the Administration, moreover, HUD proposed a public-housing integration plan—one designed to transform the existing demographic characteristics of those units. That proposal, as in the case of disparate-impact remediation, focused on providing group remedies for wrongs imposed on groups. Notably, it was to be a group-amelioration effort driven by economic standards in large measure. The final rule[78]—applicable in October, 2001—reportedly conformed to the following general proposal, but it allowed for considerable flexibility by local agencies administering family public housing units. It remains to be seen whether a significant degree of racial/ethnic/economic integration will be achieved.

Proposed Rule to Deconcentrate Poverty and Promote Integration in Public Housing—*Federal Register*, Vol 65, NO. 74, 20686 April 17, 2000

. . . [20686] Public housing is a form of subsidized housing development that is typically developed and managed by local public housing agencies (rather than private or nonprofit landlords), with funding from HUD.

For decades, many of the Nation's cities and towns sited public housing developments in predominantly low-income, minority neighborhoods. Discriminatory local political processes thus concentrated a large share of the locality's most affordable, subsidized rental units in geographic areas that tended to be . . . older, more dilapidated, higher in poverty, less politically powerful, and more poorly supported by public services than other areas. It was hardly the dream that our Nation's founding fathers, or the framers of Federal housing policy in the last century, envisioned. And the results of discrimination in the siting of public housing have been all too predictable: opportunity denied, racial and economic isolation perpetuated, and a mountain of civil rights litigation.

Unfortunately, the challenge is broader than where public housing developments have been sited. Over the years, compounding the frequent problem of discriminatory siting was a second local practice: discrimination in the lease-up processes that open particular public housing developments or provide Section 8 rental subsidies (vouchers) to households of particular racial and socioeconomic backgrounds. In some cases, relatively higher income families might have been directed to higher income, "better" buildings in better neighborhoods, or similar discrimination might have been practiced on the basis of racial or ethnic background. In others, local actions might not have been undertaken to counteract discriminatory siting over the years.

With the issuance of this revised rule, the Administration initiates another historic shift in the direction of housing policy and a significant strengthening of HUD's role as a promoter of opportunity and protector of civil rights. Fulfilling the aims and expectations outlined in the Quality Housing and Work Responsibility Act of 1998 (also known as the Public Housing Reform Act), this revised rule specifies what local public housing agencies must do, as part of the Public Housing Agency Plans they submit to HUD in order to receive funding, to deconcentrate poverty and affirmatively further fair housing in the public housing program and to affirmatively further fair housing in the Section 8 voucher program.

No longer will an agency, whether by intent or by default, be able to [20687] concentrate relatively low-income families in some buildings and higher income families in other buildings. Under this revised rule, a local public housing agency will meet the first requirement— deconcentration—by bringing higher income tenants into relatively lower income buildings and lower income tenants into relatively higher income buildings. This will be accomplished by classifying buildings and prospective tenants according to their income levels and then making lease-up decisions . . . that gradually improve the income mix of each building under a public housing agency's management. In order to achieve deconcentration, an agency must skip particular families on its waiting list, as necessary. In addition, an agency may apply local admission preferences created to serve special, high-need groups: homeless persons, victims of domestic violence, and families with severe rent burden (greater than fifty percent of household income).

In addition, a public housing agency must meet the revised rule's second principal requirement by preparing and carrying out its Plan in ways that protect the civil rights of families served. First, each agency must carry out its Plan in conformity with Federal civil rights laws, including provisions of the Civil Rights Act of 1964 and the Fair Housing Act of

1968. Beyond the basic requirement of nondiscrimination, however, an agency should affirmatively further fair housing to reduce racial and national origin concentrations. As this revised rule indicates, HUD will take action to challenge civil rights certifications where it appears that a [public housing agency] PHA Plan or its implementation does not reduce racial and ethnic concentrations and is perpetuating segregation or is, worse yet, creating new segregation. If HUD offers this challenge, the onus will be on the public housing agency to establish that it is providing the full range of housing opportunities to applicants and tenants or that it is implementing affirmative efforts. Affirmative efforts may include the marketing of geographic areas in which particular demographic groups typically do not reside, additional consultation and information for applicants, and provision of additional support services and amenities to a development. . . .

Regulating Real Estate Advertising and Financing

A number of communities have limited real estate solicitation and for-sale sign practices in order to frustrate "blockbusting." Also, public and private groups have offered below-market, mortgage-lending incentives to help solidify neighborhoods against "ghettoization." A survey of these mortgage incentives in the Cleveland area reports that most of that aid has benefited whites in order to prevent resegregation.[79]

The for-sale sign and solicitation regulation undertaken by several governments in the Chicago area was examined in *South Suburban Housing Center v. Greater South Suburban Board of Realtors* (1991).[80] The solicitation regulation barred realtor entreaties to homeowners who indicated (by putting their names on a list distributed by the municipalities involved) that they did not want salespeople calling. The realtors argued in *South Suburban* that the solicitation bans were meant to keep whites from selling, thus discriminating against black home seekers in a fashion contrary to Title VIII.[81] The Appellate Court rejected that argument, saying that there was no real evidence that the solicitation ban ordinances were intended to discriminate against African Americans. Nor would the bans have "a discernable discriminatory effect on the potential home-buying public, even if it is predominantly black, since those who opted to be placed on the solicitation ban list were least likely to offer their homes for sale in the first place."[82]

The solicitation bans and the restrictions on the size, placement, and number of "for sale" signs also came under First Amendment "free speech" scrutiny. Both sets of restraints were judged as limits on commercial speech, allowable if they served a substantial government interest, and were no more extensive than necessary to serve that interest. Using this form of intermediate scrutiny, the Court rejected the realtors' arguments, finding that the solicitation bans properly served the important interest of privacy, while the substantial municipal value of environmental aesthetics was accommodated by sign regulation. (See 935 F2d at 888–898.)

Fair Share/Inclusionary Zoning

To Charles M. Haar, in his book *Suburbs under Siege*,[83] the New Jersey Supreme Court offered a provocative new opportunity for suburban racial integration through its Mount Laurel "doctrine"—a doctrine much discussed by scholars.[84] By that doctrine, the New Jersey Supreme Court, in 1975, liberally read the State Constitution's general welfare and equal protection provisions as requiring the State's municipalities to affirmatively make provision for low and moderate-income housing. This constitutional reading was meant to ensure that those local governments would assume a "fair share" of the regional need for such dwellings.[85] The Mount Laurel "fair share" doctrine,[86] to Haar, was meant to provide minorities the possibility of real estate ownership in the white suburbs along with "the web of goals it furthers—independence, dignity, civil peace, and democracy."[87] This, to Haar, was the doctrine's "singular achievement."[88]

Haar noted that the Mount Laurel doctrine enabled thousands of people to live in attractive suburban communities, but it was unclear to him how many of these were minorities.[89] Other scholars reported that minorities were not often Mount Laurel beneficiaries.[90] Haar did make clear that many minorities were priced out of the low and moderate-cost units,[91] and that Mount Laurel remedies were not tied to other social welfare services. He also concluded that "[w]ithout a full panoply of social efforts—education, day care, job training—lower and upper income residents continue to feel estranged from one another, generating greater social distance even as geographical distance is reduced."[92]

The Institute on Race and Poverty at the University of Minnesota shares Haar's enthusiasm for "fair share" whose hallmark is legislation requiring municipalities to "take affirmative actions" to help low and moderate-income people obtain decent "affordable housing," usually through some form of voluntary or mandated "inclusionary" zoning. The primary advantage of fair share policy is that, unlike Title VIII (the Fair Housing Act of 1968), it targets the "systemic nature of segregation," rather than the culpability of identified exclusionary actors. Consequently, fair share provides a more systematic approach "to providing affordable housing" than does Title VIII.[93] The states have adopted a variety of fair share policies: New Hampshire requires its localities to provide reasonable opportunities for the siting of prefabricated homes that are popular with the nonrich. Every city in California is mandated to produce a long-term, housing-development program that is designed to meet pressing needs. Massachusetts fair share law takes the form of facilitating challenges to economically exclusionary zoning.[94] The Institute proposes "affirmative goals (including race-based criteria) and timetables for the creation of affordable housing in suburban areas."[95] For example, requiring earmarking of a certain percentage of new developments for affordable housing, and requiring the creation of affordable housing as condition for developing upscale units.[96] However, at the close of the year 2000 Minnesota report, the reader is informed that the Mount Laurel plan has had mixed results: "Since the mid-1980s close to 25,000 [low and moderate-income] units have been made available in New Jersey through constructed and rehabilitated housing. . . . Because Mount Laurel housing fails to take account of race, however, the new housing has mirrored segregated housing patterns."[97]

Epilogue

Residential-integration concerns continue to remain at the lower end of the affirmative action "totem pole." [98] There is sharp dispute among civil rights advocates over the merits of affirmative action for housing desegregation. Strenuous arguments can and have been made supportive of the ghetto's racial homogeneity: for example, it is argued that black political strength and talent is kept cohesive and strong, rather than dissipated through population dispersion.[99] Critics—like the late, eminent sociologist E. Franklin Frazier[100]—insist, however, that a mainstay of ghetto cohesiveness is the selfish commitment of black political leaders to self-protection and aggrandizement. But there is much more behind integration reluctance. Pro-integration affirmative action in housing has been shackled to the "tipping" variable, a notion that an area will tip to segregation once the black population reaches a certain point. The estimates as to when this point is reached oscillate widely, but they generally hover around 20 percent. Conformity with the tipping standard translates into limits on black housing choice, and this helps to explain the pro-integration reluctance of civil rights groups and government. One must wonder whether white attitudes should govern the integration process. If the "tipping" thesis is correct, and followed, the large majority of African Americans will be restricted to the ghetto for the foreseeable future. But is the tipping thesis correct? Are not white attitudes mellowing? Whites have come to at least accept freedom of choice for minorities in employment, schooling, and voting. Is there hope for housing?

Ardent civil libertarians have endorsed a variety of integration-achievement and maintenance schemes. A number of these have been touched upon.

All have been conducted on a relatively small scale with marginal impact. Consequently, we are unable to contradict the views of a leading student in the housing field:

> [F]ederal agencies, especially HUD, almost perfectly mirror the confusion, apathy, and shortsightedness of Congress, civil rights leaders, and the public. Ambiguity about the requirement or need to promote housing desegregation is echoed, and amplified, within the corridors of HUD, the Department of Justice, and the Office of Management and Budget. No federal agency is likely to develop a coherent, comprehensive desegregation strategy when it is whipsawed by congressional and budgetary pressures, and when its "natural" allies remain silent, confused, or antagonistic. Also, how does an agency begin systematic desegregation when there is judicial uncertainty about the legality of race-conscious tools needed to desegregate?[101]

We end by reemphasizing some of the key questions raised in this chapter: Is residential racial/ethnic integration a legitimate civil rights goal? Or should we insist only on freedom of access and egress? How much racial segregation is explained by economics; by personal preferences? To what extent is it necessary or appropriate to employ racial preferences, or even undisguised quotas, in making decisions about access, rents, and financing? To what extent can housing integration policy appropriately regulate zoning and land use restrictions; advertising and marketing, including even "for-sale" signs; mortgage lending and "redlining"; property insurance; and such real estate brokerage chicanery as "blockbusting"? How should the impact of residential segregation on school segregation be addressed by law? Should racial-balancing occupancy limits be outlawed, or sanctioned? To pose the policy questions in the broadest terms, should government undertake to persuade whites to remain when minorities move into "their" neighborhoods; or to move into neighborhoods with substantial minority populations; or to persuade blacks to move into predominantly or all-white neighborhoods; or to stabilize racially balanced neighborhoods in order to prevent resegregation?

Chapter Eight

━━∽*∿∽*━━

Facing Affirmative Action's Future

Prologue

Affirmative action's day of reckoning has dawned. Should protected-group preference be retained as antidiscrimination policy?

The federal affirmative action about which we quarrel today started mainly as an "outreach" program meant to attract minority candidates for jobs, contract grants, and college admission. Thereafter, it was transformed into a far-reaching policy of applying race, ethnic, and gender preferences and other considerations in decisions about employment, government procurement of services and supplies, legislative districting, K-12 student-attendance policies, English-language instruction, university admissions, and—in a limited fashion—housing. The transition was designed to improve the lot of historically disadvantaged minorities and women; but it came at the cost of widespread, often legitimate, popular resentment. The question that readers now must ask is whether affirmative action has struck a reasonable balance between competing equities. Are its costs outweighed by its benefits; and, if not, what should be done?

The judgment will be exceedingly difficult. Unlike Reconstruction's abortive "emancipation" program, affirmative action cannot be written off as a failure to address the problem of American racism. All of affirmative action's many race, ethnic, and gender-based plans target discrimination, but they vary considerably in design and outcome. While they have made undeniable remedial inroads, there is profound disagreement—learned and otherwise— over the extent and the social costs of their impact. Separating heat from light

223

in this controversy is at best a daunting task. To a great extent, moreover, affirmative action is still a work in progress.

In this closing chapter, we offer some comments and raise major issues about the materials, which have been assembled in the preceding pages. We hope that this will help our readers to draw their own conclusions.

Affirmative Action as an Instrument of Equal Opportunity: Genesis, Variety, and Uncertainty

Genesis

The friends of affirmative action would paraphrase Pascal and argue that if group race, ethnic, and gender-conscious programs did not exist, it would be necessary to invent them. To them, this is the simple lesson of the disparities existing in America's workplaces, its schoolhouses, voting booths, and neighborhoods. The civil rights revolution came into being because of intolerable inequities in jobs, education, housing, and civil rights affecting those we have come to protect under the affirmative action umbrella. The architects of affirmative action envisioned the end of discrimination as a stepping stone toward equalizing access to America's bounty. It was in the furtherance of this Rawlsian concept of social justice that they made fighting fire with fire— minority/female discrimination with minority/gender-based remedies—the cornerstone of antidiscrimination policy. We urge our readers to judge these remedies (with their abundance of preferences) in terms of success or failure as instruments of social policy—not as the workings of original sin, as some would have it.

The Varieties of Affirmative Action

An important dimension of affirmative action's aspects is the diversity of its applications. Some prominent critics reduce the entire enterprise to a single outcome,[1] but this is a woeful misrepresentation. At the federal level alone, the national government constructed an impressively large inventory of race, ethnic, and gender-based programs that differed widely in design and result.[2] These plans often contained explicitly preferential provisions, but are fundamentally distinguishable in at least the following respects:

Origin: executive order, court order, statute, or administrative regulation;

Nature: whether they mandate, or merely authorize consideration of race, ethnicity, or gender;

Tools: whether they contemplate application of outreach efforts, preferences, goals, timetables, set-asides, quotas, or other forms of assistance;

Constituencies: specifically defined minorities, and/or generalized references to minorities and females;

Benefits: recruitment, training, employment, educational access, contracts and grants (including procurement set-asides), participation in federally assisted education and housing programs, voting rights; and

Collateral Effect: degree of adverse impact, if any, on nonbeneficiaries.

The gist of remedial affirmative action is the versatile use of protected-group status to undo the lingering effects of past and present societal, historical discrimination—intentional or not—and to prevent its recurrence. In passing judgment, it is imperative to avoid confusion between its singularity of objective and multiplicity of application.

The Uncertainty of Affirmative Action

The federal affirmative action program necessarily reflects constant change in the society that it monitors and regulates. Changes in affirmative action policies are inevitable. Aside from the changes wrought by the Clinton "mending shop," affirmative action faces alterations from hostile or supportive judges and state legislators. Moreover, it must deal with a growing number of serious operating challenges such as the revolutionary transformation of the economy; intractable black and Hispanic unemployment; demands for adoption of a nonremedial (diversity) rationale; changes in constituencies due to demographic shifts such as the "majoritarianization" of minorities as in California;[3] and the persistent claim of racial bias in the administration of the criminal justice system.

Doubtless, affirmative action's future, like its past, will be a "stormy sea"—an uncertainty compounded by a constellation of unsettled legal questions and ideological claims. We now focus on central examples of these issues.

Central Legal Issues

The Constitutional Questions

Strict Scrutiny and Nonremedial Affirmative Action

As we saw in chapter 3, the standard of judicial review has been an overriding constitutional issue in affirmative action litigation. In the 1989 *Richmond v. Croson*[4] and 1995 *Adarand v. Peña*[5] minority "set-aside" decisions, and in the 1993 *Shaw v. Reno* majority-minority redistricting case, the Supreme Court's race-neutral majority seemed to lay this crucial question to eternal rest, holding, in opinions written by Justice O'Connor: *All* federal, state, and local racial/ethnic classifications, "benign" or otherwise, must be narrowly tailored to further a compelling interest;

and absent proof of "specifically identified" past discrimination, preferences flowing from such classifications violate the equal protection clause.

There is now reason to question whether this bedrock issue has been settled after all. An unmistakable split has emerged among the federal circuit courts of appeal over whether strict scrutiny applies to facially neutral outreach/recruitment plans. These cases involve "affirmative action" in the sense of the Office of Federal Contract Compliance Programs guidelines for administering the Executive Order (EO) 11246 program for government contractors—that is, the establishment of numerical goals and timetables for hiring and promoting minorities without resorting to preferential hiring or treatment. Some circuits hold that such plans are not subject to strict scrutiny under *Adarand* because they do not unduly burden nonbeneficiaries.[6] Other circuits hold, to the contrary, that *Adarand*'s mandate must be applied literally, and that plans based on numerical hiring goals necessarily encourage quotas, even if they do not explicitly require preferential hiring.[7]

When the Supreme Court reviews this conflict, as one assumes that eventually it must, is it a foregone conclusion that the 1995 O'Connor version of strict scrutiny will be reaffirmed? In a 1996 redistricting opinion, the author herself wrote that strict scrutiny does *not* apply to "*all* cases of intentional creation of majority-minority districts."[8] (See page 192 above.)

In chapter 6, we saw that antidilutive (majority-minority) voting districts are analytically indistinguishable from any of the other "benign" preferences which the Justice has viewed with such abhorrence in the past. Textually, then, O'Connor's dictum invites speculation. Has she changed her position? If yes, how would she vote in a review of the cited conflict among the circuits regarding affirmative action outreach efforts? In our view, it is not beyond the realm of possibility that she would favor reconsideration of *Adarand,* and that, as the Court's acknowledged swing vote on civil rights issues, she could persuade four other members to join her.

Reconsideration would provide the Court with a vehicle for specifically determining the constitutional status of disparate-impact theory. This theory is the central conceptual basis of remedial affirmative action, with its emphasis on group rights and nonvictim entitlements. However, as we saw in chapter 3, under the teaching of *Adarand*, strict scrutiny derives from the conviction that group rights are unconstitutional "in most circumstances."[9] (See pages 72–73 above.) Arguably, then, this decision *impliedly* holds that remedial affirmative action may inherently violate equal protection. Surely an issue of such keystone importance must not be left to implication. The Court must tell us whether strict scrutiny is a genuine test, as Justice O'Connor promised in *Adarand,*[10] and must answer the numerous questions that have arisen over its scope and application.

Reconsideration would also enable the Court to conduct a long-overdue review of the relationship between strict scrutiny and remediation. As we also saw in chapter 3 (pages 56–57), Justice Powell in his controlling *Regents v. Bakke* (1978) opinion applied strict scrutiny in two different ways. First in rejecting the societal discrimination defense, he held that remediation of specified past discrimination was a condition of the disputed set-aside's constitutionality under the strict scrutiny test.[11] Second, in ruling on the nonremedial "diversity" defense, he also applied strict scrutiny analysis: Student body diversity was a "compelling interest," but the Davis set-aside was not "necessary" to further it—*not* because it failed to remedy past discrimination, but because it violated nonminority applicants' present equal protection rights.[12]

By thus decoupling strict scrutiny and remediation, Justice Powell set the table for the advocates of nonremedial diversity. However, this was more than two decades ago, and Justice Powell wrote only for himself. Strange as it may seem, in all that time the Supreme Court never rendered a majority opinion dealing directly with the relationship between strict scrutiny and nonremedial preference. Today, it should no longer have the option of disengagement, since the Powell doctrine has now been called into question, and is the subject of another split in the Federal circuits. On the authority of *Croson* and *Adarand,* a panel of the Fifth Circuit has held in the *Hopwood* case, that consideration of race for the nonremedial purpose of achieving student-body diversity can never be a "compelling interest," and that Justice Powell's view is not "binding precedent."[13] (See pages 144–146 in this volume.) The First Circuit, on the other hand, specifically disagrees with the *Hopwood v. Texas* (1996) panel's pronouncement that the Powell doctrine is "dead." "[W]e assume . . . that *Bakke* remains good law and that some iterations of 'diversity' might be sufficiently compelling, in specific circumstances, to justify race-conscious action."[14] In *Smith v. University of Washington Law School* (2000),[15] the Ninth Circuit upheld the preferential-admissions program of that school, holding that the Powell opinion accepting diversity objectives under strict scrutiny was *implicitly* accepted by four additional justices.

Only the Supreme Court can tell us whether *Bakke* lives. But so far it has refused to review any of the pertinent cases. The upshot is that the legal status of "diversity" is completely up in the air. This at a time when its proponents' clamor grows louder by the day,[16] and in the face of the claim that there is substantial evidence that it has been successfully applied in a number of different contexts.[17]

School Integration and the Historically Black Colleges and Universities
Almost a half century has passed since *Brown v. Board of Education,* but, due in large part to vacillation by the Supreme Court, it is not clear whether its integration mandate will—or should—ever be fulfilled. As we saw in chapter 4 (at pages 119, 121–122), the Court has made a 180-degree turn

during its stewardship of *Brown*'s legacy—from uncompromising advocate of federally directed integration to proponent of local control. There may— or may not—be a causal relationship between this shift and the resurgence of segregation in our public schools. Whatever the case, the public interest demands that the High Court tell us whether segregation is still inherently unconstitutional, and, if yes, whether integration is still the indicated remedy for racial/ethnic segregation.

As soon as possible, the Court should determine the constitutional bearing of race, ethnicity, and gender on eligibility for university admissions and scholarships. By continuing to refuse review of the conflict over *Bakke*, the Court helps to magnify the serious crisis in the realm of higher learning. This issue first came before the Court a generation ago in the *DeFunis v. Odegard* (1974) matter; but today it is literally the case that no university administrator in the country can be sure of the legal rights and obligations in this connection.

The High Court must, once and for all, determine the constitutional status of publicly funded segregation in higher learning. In chapter 5, we learned that the future of our Historically Black Colleges and Universities is an open question after more than a generation of litigation. In our view, the Supreme Court should not allow the *United States v. Fordice* (1992) case to become like Dickens' "endless" lawsuit in *Bleak House, Jarndyce v. Jarndyce.*

Voting Rights

For majority-minority districts, as with any derivative of disparate-impact/remedial affirmative action, *Adarand* is the Sword of Damocles. Is strict scrutiny, as mandated by *Shaw v. Reno* (1993)[18] and *Miller v. Johnson* (1995),[19] the death warrant of race/ethnic-based redistricting? (See chapter 6.) One surmises that every redistricting agency in the country has grappled with this question, while pondering the results of the current decennial census. Which O'Connor will answer—the author of *Adarand* (1995), or of *Bush v. Vera* (1996)?

Fair Housing

In chapter 7, we noted that the Supreme Court has never passed on the constitutionality of the Fair Housing Act of 1968, or many of the standards that apply to its enforcement. It has even refused to decide the propriety of disparate-impact remediation under this law. Of all the instances of judicial inaction that we have encountered, this is the most unfathomable. It is generally agreed that housing discrimination is our worst, most intractable civil rights problem, both of itself and as a source of collateral discrimination. The federal government has been hesitant in the use of affirmative action techniques to root out systemic discrimination and promote integrated housing; and this is surely attributable, at least in part, to the lack of a clear signal from the Supreme Court. Under these circumstances, it is very difficult to understand why the Court would deliberately distance itself from the field of action.

Gender Issues

The time has also come for the High Court to resolve the question of whether intermediate scrutiny is to remain the standard of equal protection review for gender discrimination, and if so, how the formulation of mid-tier scrutiny in *United States v. Virginia Military Institute* (1996) is to be distinguished from strict scrutiny. (See above at pages 165, 170–171.) It is to be recalled that in that case the Court held that gender discrimination met equal protection mandates if an "exceedingly persuasive justification"[20] could be found for it. How an "exceedingly persuasive justification" differs from strict scrutiny is unclear, as is the rationale for not applying the same equal protection standards to race, ethnic, *and* gender discrimination.

We have noted (see above at pages 168–171) that the circuits have interpreted Title IX of the 1972 Education Act[21]—which bars sexual discrimination in education activities receiving federal financial aid—as requiring female/male proportionality in athletics funding. Is gender proportionality required by the Act? In areas outside of athletics? Can gender proportionality in education be constitutionally supported by an "exceedingly persuasive justification"?

Statutory Issues

Title VII case law—the core of equal-employment statutory jurisprudence—is a hodgepodge of irreconcilable interpretations, like the majority and dissenting opinions in the *United Steelworkers of America v. Weber* (1979)[22] case. (See pages 58–60 herein.) Even after a generation of judicial warfare, the battle still continues over whether the goal of antidiscrimination law is "equal treatment" or "equal results."

Congress helped foment this confusion by neglecting to establish the vocabulary of equal employment opportunity law. For example, neither Title VII of the 1964 Civil Rights Act, nor its 1991 amendments, offer a clue about what Congress meant by such key statutory terms as *equal opportunity, discrimination,* or *preferential treatment.* By design or otherwise, policy making initially was almost totally delegated to the administrative bureaucracies and the judiciary, resulting, for better or for worse, first in affirmative action's extensive capture of the economy and now in the looming possibility of its demise. In our view, Congress must reclaim responsibility for civil rights reform, by resolving all doubts about Title VII's meaning, and by formulating comprehensive guidelines for its enforcement.

At a minimum, the following are open questions:

1. Is it the purpose of "equal opportunity" to improve the socioeconomic status of minorities and women, or only to end invidious discrimination?

2. What is the meaning of "discriminate" in 42 USC § 2000e-2(a) (1) of Title VII?[23]

3. What is the meaning of "disparate impact" in Section 105 of the 1991 amendments [42 USC 2000e - 2(k) (1) (A)]?
• Does it relate to "discriminate" in 42 USC § 2000e - 2(a) (1)?
• Does it relate to "adversely affect . . . status" in 42 USC § 2000e - 2(a) (2)?
• Was the inclusion of the concept of disparate impact in the amended Title VII intended to ratify the holding in *Griggs v. Duke Power* Co. (1971),[24] that unjustified adverse group effects of facially neutral employment practices can violate Title VII?
• What is the meaning of "business necessity" and "job related" in Section 105 of the 1991 amendments [42 USC § 2000e - 2 (k) (1) (A)]?
• Which decisions of the Supreme Court govern the parties' burden of proof in the trial of disparate-impact cases?
4. Does the Equal Employment Opportunity Commission's 80 percent rule (29 CFR 1607.4. D. [2000]) apply to the sufficiency of statistical evidence in the trial of disparate-impact cases? (See appendix 1 of chapter 3 for excerpts from 29 CFR 1607.)
5. What is the meaning of "affirmative action" in Section 116 of the 1991 amendments? (105 Stat 1079.)
• How does it relate to "affirmative action" under 42 USC § 2000e - 5(g)?
• Which decisions of the Supreme Court govern the status of "affirmative action" under Section 116 of the 1991 amendments?
• Are the 1991 amendments intended to validate voluntary affirmative action through race, ethnic, and gender preferences in order to remedy the effects of societal discrimination and/or preclude its recurrence? (The 1991 statutory amendments are found in Pub L 102 -166, 105 Stat 1071.)
6. Does Title VII sanction affirmative action for nonremedial purposes?
7. What is the meaning of "preferential treatment" in 42 USC § 2000e-2(j) of Title VII? Does the Title permit preferential treatment?

The difficulty of the questions we have enumerated has warranted careful judicial deliberation. However, after a generation of legalistic disputation, we yearn for greater firmness in the legal rights and wrongs of affirmative action. It is sobering to consider how many fundamental legal questions await closure.

While the writers hope otherwise, the Supreme Court's affirmative action clarification will probably proceed at a slow and incremental rate. The analytical problems involved are formidable, and there are fierce opinions on the matter, both in and outside the Court. The decisive moral question is how far "equality" can be stretched? How does the state resolve the inherent conflict between the citizenry's freedom of choice and its own moral duty to eradicate bias? Has government the legal right and moral duty to impose limits on the expansion of minority and female rights? There is no explicit guidance for the solution of these issues in the words of the Constitution. Given the absence of such guidance, the eye-crossing analytic problems, and the enormous political controversy, it should be recognized that affirmative action is a labyrinth in which even the most-seasoned, legal travelers easily lose their way. Consequently, those seeking a near-term, energetic High Court initiative for the adoption of specific and comprehensive standards in this area are likely to be disappointed. For example, on November 27, 2001, in *Adarand Constructors, Inc. v. Mineta,* the Supreme Court decided, for purely procedural reasons, not to review the merits of the *Adarand* dispute, which as we saw at pages 70–74 in this volume, first came before the Court in 1995, and involves not merely the meaning of strict scrutiny but affirmative action's right to survive. The Court's breathtaking decision leaves these momentous issues up in the air. It is only the latest instance of the Court's reluctance to decide basic affirmative action issues. Those affected by the failure of the Court to provide guidance will doubtless view the Court's moral authority as considerably deficient. On the other hand, a major Court historian—Robert G. McCloskey—praised the caution, deliberateness, and incrementalism that the Court has historically exercised, theorizing that this operational mode was the Court's most efficient way to exercise its moral authority and promote justice and decency. He wrote:

> Surely the record teaches that no useful purpose is served when the judges seek all the hottest political caldrons of the moment and dive into the middle of them. . . . The Court's greatest successes have been achieved when it has operated near the margins rather that in the center of political controversy, when it has nudged and gently tugged the nation, instead of trying to rule. . . . [C]onsider the long campaign on behalf of laissez-faire from 1905 to 1934, with its pattern of concession to the principle of regulation, dotted here and there with a warning that the principle could be carried too far. . . . The Court ruled more in each case when it tried to rule less, and that paradox is one of the clearest morals to be drawn from its history.[25]

The congressional avoidance of statutory clarification is rooted in the difficult analytical and ideological problems that have limited the Court. Both the legislative and judicial schemes of problem avoidance have resulted in an enormous and very questionable allocation of rule-making power to the administrators. The elaborateness of the rules issued by the Equal Employment Opportunity Commission and the Office of Federal Contract Compliance Programs illustrates the problem. (See the appendixes in chapter 3.) As David Schoenbrod sees it, lawmaking delegation impedes democracy because the administrators are largely unremovable by the electoral process. Further, legislators exercise their power without responsibility by unfairly deflecting criticism onto administrators, thus immunizing themselves against removal.[26] Lawmaking delegation to administrators is defended with notions that elected representatives have neither the time, nor the expertise to treat the details of complicated problems. Surely though, the representatives are, on the whole, as competent as the bureaucrats. And it is expected of them to make the time to confront problems that are central to the nation's welfare.

In setting out an agenda for the Supreme Court and the Congress, we have avoided taking any position on the merits, but have sought only to provide the reader with a bridge over the legal terrain that should be traversed before venturing onto the battlefield. There is an ideological terrain also, and the major claims thereupon should also be highlighted.

The Ideological Clash

The unremitting dispute that envelops affirmative action stems from the clash between two theories of equal opportunity.

Affirmative action exemplifies the principle that "society should do what it can to 'level the playing field' among individuals who compete for positions . . . so that all those with relevant potential will eventually be admissible to pools of . . . [competing] candidates."[27] In this version, "leveling" is achieved by honoring race, ethnic, and gender preferences and other aids in various arenas of competition.[28] The most common justification is the claimed need to compensate disadvantaged individuals for the legacy of past discrimination.[29]

Arrayed against this is the principle that "in the competition for positions . . . all individuals who possess the attributes relevant for . . . the duties of [a] position [should] be included in the pool of eligible candidates, and that an individual's possible occupancy of the position [should] be judged only with respect to those relevant attributes."[30] The corollary is that race, ethnicity, or sex should not count for or against an individual's eligibility for a job, when they are not relevant for its duties.

Thus preference versus merit. The voluminously chronicled debate over affirmative action boils down to an exchange of claims and counterclaims, attacks and defenses, by the advocates of these polar opposites.

To assist the reader in weighing this exchange, the following is a synopsis of its main themes:

Affirmative action's proponents justify minority and gender-based measures as remedies for present effects of past discrimination; preventives of recurrence; and devices for securing crucially needed inclusion of diverse minorities in our highly competitive, demographically fluid economy. Color-blindness promotes exclusion; the merit principle is far more honored in the breach than in the observance. The claim of reverse discrimination is a myth.

The opposing camp maintains that affirmative action discriminates against innocent whites; compromises merit; benefits nondisadvantaged minorities; stigmatizes its beneficiaries; perpetuates racism; and promotes economic inefficiency.

Readers should evaluate these claims—as well as the legal/policy issues presented above, and throughout the volume—by consulting the earlier specialized chapters. To help the reader assemble expanded arguments on "both sides" (and thus build a bridge to judgment), we summarize in the next section the writings of a representative sample of distinguished disputants, believing it appropriate for readers to reference them as they develop their own conclusions. We leave to the readers the exacting task of attempting to resolve the fierce disputes they will encounter, and sorting out the broad areas of agreement.

A Prelude to Judgment:
A Sampler of Distinguished Disputants

Christopher Edley Jr.'s *Not All Black and White*[31] is a quixotic addition to the affirmative action literature. The book urges the necessity of race-conscious programs, but it is very much marked by queasy doubts about their validity. Truly, the issue is *not all black and white!*

Those who are committed to color-blind governmental policy are castigated by Edley as failing to grasp the immorality of their postures.[32] Edley maintains that a serious, widening "opportunity gap" exists between American whites and blacks, based on morally unacceptable racial disparities.[33] Race-conscious policies that go beyond color-blindness are morally justifiable as a critical element in a program for bringing about "morally equal opportunity," in the sense of a full and equal chance to develop and use one's talents.[34] While affirmative action has "moral costs" in terms of "consequences" for third parties, it may be justified by the benefits, provided that the need for race-based measures is minimized through consideration of race-neutral alternatives.[35] In Edley's view, this moral calculus is an integral element of the communal vision that Americans should share.[36]

Despite Edley's advocacy of race-consciousness, he stresses that "it is almost impossible, . . . to separate the effects of pure *antidiscrimination* norms from the effects of *additional* measures commonly thought of as 'affirmative action.' "[37] Another major problem with race consciousness is noted by Edley when he emphasizes that the proper administration of affirmative action requires great sensitivity (as in considering race-neutral alternatives), lest the moral cost be too high. He writes that "The value intensive choices . . . are tough ones, and . . . that there are more tough jobs than there are good people to fill them . . . and we have a poor understanding of the extent to which we can mitigate—by regulation, training, or enforcement—the damage done when character fails."[38] Moreover, affirmative action cost-benefit evaluations are, to him, impossible in this real world.[39]

Given these misgivings, one must wonder why Edley is so committed to race-conscious affirmative action. *Croson* and *Adarand*'s requirement of strict scrutiny poses additional problems for Edley. The proof of discrimination required by strict scrutiny is most difficult to come by, he tells us.[40] Many federal affirmative action programs were inaugurated without the detailed evidentiary findings strict scrutiny now requires.[41] Importantly, he continues, racial "exclusion is not solely—or, today, even primarily—the result of present discrimination and racial animus. A large factor is the 'birds of a feather' tendency to prefer people like oneself. In hundreds of subtle ways, this tendency pervades American social and economic life, and the aggregate effect is to divide us, starving ourselves and our institutions of the benefits that come from having more diverse and inclusive communities."[42] Through this route, Edley comes to embrace "diversity theory" as an integral part of affirmative action.[43] It is a theory free from the constraints of strict scrutiny, but—as we have seen—it is not a theory legitimated as yet by the Supreme Court.

Stephan and Abigail Thernstroms' *America in Black and White*[44] depicts the *Adarand* case as a necessary antidote for alleged corruption of Title VII[45] by disparate-impact theory but claims that, as treated by the Clinton Administration, "*Adarand* . . . had been a waste of the Supreme Court's breath."[46]

The Thernstroms not only present affirmative action in employment as legally perverse, but also as a fomenter of racial bitterness and conflict.[47] And all of this possibly for naught, because there are no grounds to believe that employment affirmative action improved the economic lot of blacks, save perhaps in increasing the number of black professionals like doctors and lawyers. But professionals are a small portion of African America. That society, as a whole, has been making very strong economic advances since the 1940s. It is terribly wrong, the Thernstroms maintain, to view black economic gains as a function of disparate-impact remediation.[48] "The best generalization to make . . . is that the trends visible in the first period [1940-1970] continued in the second [post-1970] without notable change."[49]

Doubtless, liberals will tend to dismiss the Thernstrom tome as merely acerbic conservative scolding. This would be a mistake. The first segment of this large book provides an extensive history of African America from "Jim Crow" times. It would be difficult for anyone who reads the Thernstrom account of Jim Crow monstrosities and their moving treatment of Martin Luther King Jr.'s undertaking, not to become a greater champion of black civil rights. The volume is an exhaustively researched, panoramic treatment of our race relations; while the tone is openly polemical, the authors offer statistical support to a degree which demands the respectful attention, if not the agreement, of every reader. Major positions taken by the Thernstroms include the following:

Affirmative action is rooted in the legal distortions of disparate-impact theory; is counterproductive, and perpetuates racism.[50]

The status of blacks has "improved dramatically" over the last half century "by just about every possible measure of social and economic achievement."[51] Much of the improvement antedated affirmative action.

"Hard-core" white racism is a thing of the past.[52] While racism has "obviously" not disappeared, "racial tolerance" is now the social "norm."[53]

Existing socioeconomic inequality "is less a function of white racism than of the racial gap in levels of educational achievement, the structure of the black family, and the rise in black crime."[54] The cure for this "serious" situation is adoption of "color-blind public policies," which embody "the sense that we are one nation—that we sink or swim together, that black poverty impoverishes us all, that black alienation eats at the nation's soul, and that black isolation simply cannot work."[55]

Continuation of disparate-impact and diversity affirmative action would necessarily heighten racial separation, and would "spell disaster in a nation with an ugly history of racial subordination and a continuing problem, albeit dramatically diminished, of racial intolerance."[56]

Inner-city black poverty—"the single most depressing fact about the state of black America today"[57]—has persisted since the 1970s notwithstanding affirmative action.[58]

While most black citizens are law-abiding, African Americans are "represented far out of proportion to their numbers"[59] in arrest, conviction, and incarceration for crime.[60] These disparities are not attributable to bias in the criminal justice system.[61] The evidence does not seem to support the charge that administration of the death penalty is racially biased.[62] The Thernstroms argue that "if the African-American crime rate suddenly dropped to the current level of the white crime rate, we would eliminate a major force that is driving blacks and whites apart and is destroying the fabric of black urban life."[63]

The evidence does not establish that the current level of racial discrimination in employment and contracting warrants continuation of affirmative action.[64] Notwithstanding the recent trend against affirmative action in the Supreme Court's rulings against employment/procurement, racial preferences face an uncertain future, since the Clinton Administration and the civil rights groups are attempting to nullify those rulings.[65]

There are those who would challenge the optimistic dimension of the Thernstrom account. One student argues that the "most glaring economic fact of the past-quarter century [has been] widening inequality."[66] To Congressperson Bernie Sanders, the "United States has, by far, the most unfair distribution of wealth and income of any major nation. The richest 1% of the population now owns as much wealth as the bottom 95% of all Americans combined."[67] Concurrent with the recent explosion in the number of billionaires, low-wage American workers work the longest hours and earn the lowest pay in the industrial world: for instance, the average hourly earnings of production and nonsupervisory employees, adjusted for inflation, fell from $14.00 in 1973 to $12.77 in 1998.[68] The notion that the exponentially widening income gap is mitigated by the opportunity to move up the scale is a "conceit." The "richest country in the history of the universe tolerates a poverty rate of about 20% among its children, and about 35% among its black children."[69]

To critics, the extraordinary economic boom of the 1990s has, if anything, magnified persistent racial, ethnic, and gender disparities in employment opportunities. Black unemployment, perennially at least twice that of white joblessness,[70] actually rose.[71] Despite highly publicized exceptions, minority representation in senior management and executive positions, the professions, and academe remains as marginal as when Congress took note of it in the 1991 Civil Rights Act.[72] Within our minority communities, the extremes of socioeconomic status replicate those of the general population.

Tom Wicker provides a dramatically different account from that of the Thernstroms in *Tragic Failure*.[73] America's white majority has for some time jettisoned the goal of an integrated America where blacks fully share in the nation's benefits. True, the African-American middle class has grown, but the underclass of that minority has burgeoned at a much faster rate. In 1970, the underclass numbered some 700,000—one half of 1% of the population. By 1980, there had been a virtual explosion, with the very poor numbering 2.5 million, or 1.37% of the entire population. The largest U.S. cities are now overwhelmed with a minority-underclass population packed into ghettos racked by crime, violence, family breakdown, school drop outs, drugs, and the like. The outlook is not a good one. Middle-class blacks and whites have fled the social turmoil of the inner city, and their absence augments the social disorientation of those areas.[74]

Professorial support for Wicker's journalistic account is to be found in William Julius Wilson's *When Work Disappears*,[75] a book that underscores the environmental forces shaping the new urban-poor ghettos: the extraordinary decline in well-paying jobs requiring lesser skills; the increased-educational requirements for better-paying jobs; racially restrictive mortgage practices that prevented middle-class blacks from purchasing homes in the ghetto areas, thus encouraging them to leave; the lowering of income levels required of those living in low-rent public housing, and converting those homes to havens of the dispossessed; and the refusal of suburban areas to accept more low-rent public housing.[76]

Wilson's book helpfully reviews other efforts to describe the roots of the new urban poor. George Gilder's *Wealth and Poverty*; and Charles Murray's *Losing Ground* argued that social-welfare programs undercut self-reliance and increased joblessness. Richard Herrnstein and Charles Murray's *Bell Shaped Curve* insists upon genetic inferiority as the cause. But Wilson notes that geneticists insist that there is no clear line between genetic and environmental influences.[77]

Wilson is among our leading academic authorities on race and poverty. *When Work Disappears* is an authoritative, recent portrait of America's urban crisis:

• There are in *every* major metropolitan area, festering center-city ghettos, populated by blacks, assorted-ethnic minorities, and low-income whites; mired in unemployment,[78] job displacement, declining real wages, family dysfunction, escalating-medical and housing costs, scarcity of affordable child-care facilities, sharp decline in quality of public education, crime and drug trafficking; gripped by explosive intergroup tensions based on racial, class, cultural, and linguistic differences;[79] and exacerbated by "the poisonous racial rhetoric of certain highly visible spokespersons."[80]

• A "clear racial divide" exists between the central cities and the suburbs.[81]

• This crisis calls the efficacy of disparate-impact affirmative action and its compensatory-remedy emphasis into serious question. The problems originating in historical racism, Wilson flatly asserts, "cannot be solved through race-based remedies alone."[82] Based on analysis of voluminous data on income, employment, and educational attainment, he finds that affirmative action policies "based solely on . . . racial group membership"[83] have disproportionately benefited "the more advantaged members of minority groups,"[84] in terms of college admissions and higher-paying jobs, but have not opened up "broad avenues of upward mobility for the masses of disadvantaged blacks."[85] Nevertheless, he argues that, as long as minorities are "underrepresented in higher-paying and desirable positions,"[86] affirmative action programs will be a necessity. These programs should recognize that the problems of the disadvantaged "are not always clearly related to previous racial discrimination,"[87] and should address the *environmental* factors that afflict the disadvantaged of all races, that is, those bearing on "economic class position or need."[88] At the same time, Wilson is keenly aware that affirmative action based solely on need would systematically exclude many middle-income blacks from desirable positions, since it would leave them at the mercy of "standard . . . measures of performance [which] are not sensitive to the cumulative effects of race."[89] Accordingly, he proposes "a comprehensive race-neutral initiative"[90] to address economic and social inequality, which would serve as "an extension of—not a replacement for—opportunity-enhancing programs that include race-based criteria to fight social inequality."[91] Such programs should employ flexible criteria of evaluation in college "admission, hiring, job promotion, and so on, and should be based on a broad definition of disadvantage that incorporates notions of both *need and race*."[92] Wilson's initiative would also include programs "that can be accurately described as purely race-neutral, such as national health care, school reform, and job training based on need rather than race, that would strongly and positively impact racial minority populations but would benefit large segments of the dominant white population as well."[93]

To flesh out his vision, Wilson has put forward wide-ranging, specific proposals for educational reform and job training;[94] city-suburban integration and cooperation;[95] increases in minimum wage and health insurance coverage;[96] measures for surmounting the "spatial mismatch" between residence and job location, including increased public transportation, and job referral facilities;[97] and last-resort public employment, and retraining of displaced low-skilled workers.[98]

Wilson concludes with a plea for a new, broad-based political coalition to press for economic and social reform, and to dissipate the "paralysis" which, in his view, has taken hold of national policy under both Republican and Democratic administrations.[99]

For reasons similar to those of Wilson, Wicker urges the maintenance of affirmative action, *along with* a major enlargement of race-neutral public works and educational programs. Wicker insists on the need for a new political party for these purposes. Only in this fashion can we counter the total disinterest by the major parties in the plight of the undererclass.[100]

In what may be affirmative action's eleventh hour, Richard D. Kahlenberg's *The Remedy*[101] proposes to install race-neutral, class-based preferences in order to ensure genuine equality of opportunity for the economically disadvantaged of all groups. The preferences would apply in entry-level employment, education, and contracting. In this regime, the 1964 and 1991 Civil Rights Acts would remain in effect for the purpose of dealing with ongoing and future race, ethnic, and gender discrimination; but such *preferences* would be implemented only in the "very rare instances"[102] that conform strictly to the *Croson* and *Adarand* rulings.[103]

Kahlenberg has proposed the shift, not because he believes race has been overemphasized—in his words, "there are plenty of times when race *is* the issue"[104]—but mainly to redress the marginalization of the moral basis of class-based disadvantage. Class-based programs, he vehemently insists, must *supplant* today's protected-group programs, rather than merely *supplement* them.[105]

Kahlenberg's point of departure is the asserted failure of protected-group preferences to provide genuine equal opportunity, long-term color-blindness, benefits of integration, or even compensation for past discrimination.[106] The net result, in his view, has been overinclusion of *advantaged* minorities and underinclusion of their *disadvantaged* brethren—a very bad social imbalance which class-based affirmative action will help correct.[107]

The Remedy as a policy proposal suffers from a number of shortcomings. Its attack on racial preferences is unaccountably limited. It bypasses voting rights completely, and touches on housing segregation only in passing. Since "equal opportunity" in this "new regime" would be confined to "starting places," it would appear that Kahlenberg does not advocate social regulation of discrimination in *post*-hire employment (e.g., refusal to promote) or *post*-admission higher education (e.g., refusal to grant tenure). Indeed, Kahlenberg says that class-based preferences "would not be employed for promotions, since the idea is to provide disadvantaged young people with a chance to prove themselves, not to promote preferences as a way of life."[108] In Kahlenberg's Darwinian world, discrimination ceases to concern society after hire on the job or admission to college. But this position ignores the real world of discrimination.

Even Kahlenberg's commitment to the abolition of protected-group preference is far from clear, as he would keep disparate-impact theory operative as insurance against current or future racial-ethnic-gender discrimination.[109] But the disparate-impact model of discrimination is central to racial, ethnic, and gender affirmative action remediation! [See, e.g., *Griggs v. Duke Power Co.* (1971),[110]—a decision that he specifically approved.[111]] To retain it would seem to guarantee the preservation of preferences, rather than moderate their effects, or their extinction.

Kahlenberg's calculus in the implementation of class-based preferences would grant disproportionate benefits to poor blacks since their backgrounds are even more disadvantaged than poor whites.[112] Doubtless, such a mechanism would be seen as "stealth" affirmative action and duplicitous, hardly the attitudes promotive of the racial harmony Kahlenberg espouses.[113]

Kahlenberg has not articulated a governing rationale for his *Remedy*. He steadfastly maintains that "the ultimate test of class-based affirmative action is whether it provides individual equality of *opportunity . . .* not equality of group *results*."[114] But, as he candidly acknowledges, this distinction is always lost in practice: "Inevitably, universities and employers do treat people as members of groups, for at some point the tradeoff between fairness and efficiency tips in favor of the latter."[115] Therefore, a policy oriented totally to class would be unenforceable,[116] and it is incumbent for Kahlenberg to formulate a more realistic "ultimate test."

Given these shortcomings, it is clear that if a case can be made for class-preference, *The Remedy* does not do the job.

Has then the black community progressed since the 1960s, or is the racial gap in socioeconomic status wider than ever? Is racial tolerance the social norm in today's America, or are our cities hotbeds of racial animosity? Should affirmative action's ethnic/racial/gender special considerations and preferences be banished forever from our country; or should they be cleaned up and kept in place? Do we need a third party, or must we limp along with the two major parties we already have?

Such key writers as the Thernstroms, William Julius Wilson, and Tom Wicker (grouping Wilson and Wicker for the moment), differ so radically that one wonders if they live in the same country. Still some broad areas of agreement are discernible:

Some Minorities have Progressed

But how far? And at what cost?

By the conventional econometric standards of income, occupation, educational achievement, and home ownership, at least one-third of our black population is "middle-class."[117] The Thernstroms claim that about one-third of all black families now live in "generally integrated" suburbs.[118] In Wicker's words: "Despite the difficulties and disappointments of desegregation, despite continuing prejudice and discrimination, numerous African-Americans [have] made economic progress that [compares] well with or [betters] that of whites moving up from poorer status into the middle class."[119] But the aftermath of this upward movement has been the "degradation of the ghetto, the communities . . . left behind."[120] As chronicled in Wilson's book, the last thirty-five years have witnessed the emergence of "a very poor, disproportionately African-American [underclass] living in drug-plagued, inner-city areas bereft of adequate job opportunities and hampered by inadequate public services."[121] The "lurid new visibility" of the ghetto underclass has largely obscured the growth of the black middle class.[122]

The Thernstroms are ambivalent. They note, and lament, the persistence of black poverty, yet hesitate to acknowledge its extent. According to Wilson, the disadvantaged African-American population, particularly the ghetto poor, has regressed steadily since the early 1970s in terms of joblessness, concentrated poverty, family breakup, and receipt of welfare. By 1993, "the average poor black family . . . slipped further below the poverty level than in any year since the Census Bureau started collecting such data in 1967."[123] In Wicker's terse formulation, "as the black middle class expanded, the urban underclass grew even faster."[124] It strains belief that this situation could prevail in such a wealthy country, especially during a period of unprecedented economic growth. The Thernstroms, however, point to the fact that "a majority of blacks are not poor, and a majority of poor Americans are not black."[125] It is difficult to see what bearing such statistical nostrums, even if valid, can have on the fact that inner-city poverty is intensely concentrated within all our major cities, and has an "overwhelmingly racial cast."[126]

Racial Tensions Persist

Beyond this, total disagreement prevails.

The Thernstroms contend that America has largely overcome its odious legacy of racism. The hard-core white variety is extinct. There have been "incidents" in recent years, but the level of racial animosity has been greatly exaggerated by politicians, including President Clinton, the "civil rights lobby," the academy, and most of the "mainstream media." In fact, racial tolerance is now the prevailing social norm. True, most African Americans do not believe this; but this is because they too often come in contact with the "wrong" kinds of whites, and have not yet developed an immunity to false racist innuendo ("psycho-facts"). In time, this too will pass. Racial attitudes are undergoing great change.[127] For instance, white opposition to affirmative action, fair housing, and "other racial questions," stems primarily from political ideology, unrelated to "gut feelings toward African Americans."[128] Also, white opposition to residential integration, once the norm, has declined rapidly in recent years;[129] "white attitudes would seem to allow for considerably more residential integration than is actually to be found in our cities today."[130]

The Thernstroms are simply not reading from the same page as Wilson, Wicker, and Edley. Wilson reports that racial antagonisms are rife in urban America. Relations among *all* our races, not just black and white, have soured. Ghetto joblessness, crime, and gang violence are perceived to spill over into other parts of our cities, resulting in "fierce class antagonisms" in the higher-income black communities located near the ghettos, and heightened anti-black racial animosity, among central-city and suburban whites, and especially among lower-income white ethnic and Latino groups who live near the black ghettos. In essence, a racial struggle for power and privilege is being waged by have-nots in the central cities, and has flowed over into the rest of the metropolitan areas.[131]

Wicker's findings speak for themselves: American cities are hotbeds of racial animosities. Racial "incidents" in school buildings and college campuses are commonplace. Old hate groups have reemerged and new ones have formed. Worse, evidences of animosity toward, or disdain for, the other race can be found even among educated middle-class whites and African Americans.[132]

Edley offers the bleakest vision of all. America's attitudes and behavior about race are akin to "a deep . . . neurosis, a mental disorder or illness."[133] Our nation suffers from "a virulent strain of resistant racism, gut-pure and simple as sin."[134] These racial tensions cannot be dissolved "by reason, by passion, or by experience."[135] The most we can hope for is an armistice, a "constructive peace."[136]

Orlando Patterson's *The Ordeal of Integration*[137] calls for an affirmative action compromise as to its length of operations. Patterson is a distinguished scholar of slavery and maverick polemicist. The book is a "jihad" against "the dogmatic ethnic advocates and extremists"[138] of the left and right who are polluting reasoned discourse with poisoned evaluations of black-America's condition, including the outrageous lie that the nation is wallowing in an intractable race crisis.[139]

In Patterson's opinion, our forty-year, antidiscrimination program has been a great success in that (with carefully noted exceptions) it has moved our country "toward greater integration. . . not merely in neighborhoods, but in the economic, social, cultural, political, and moral life of the nation. . . . Afro-Americans, from a status of semiliterate social outcasts as late as the early fifties, have now become an integral part of American civilization and are so recognized both within the nation and outside it."[140]

To Patterson, the "two nations" and "racism forever" views are criminally perpetrated by the mass media (which thrives on ghetto carrion); pundits; and race leaders (whose punditry and brokerage roles are exalted by the perpetual-racism thesis); and by timorous liberal academics who remain politically correct in order to avoid the "Tom" and "Oreo" and similar epithets.[141] Actually, black/white relations have never been better even though the races largely remain geographically separate.[142] Further, blacks are positive about their own situation. Survey research tells us that fewer than 40 percent of African Americans feel that they have been subject to discriminatory treatment, although most feel that blacks generally are mistreated.[143] For many, integration has been painful, if not traumatic, but African-American progress—though far from complete—has been nothing short of "astonishing"; indeed, in many respects, "unparalleled," "amazing," even "extraordinary."[144]

Patterson's sanguine appraisal of black-America's situation echoes the Thernstroms' optimistic view,[145] even going them one further in rhapsodizing on the lot of the "vast majority" of blacks.[146] Like them, he fully acknowledges the dreadful problems of the urban underclass, but intimates that this situation may be improving.[147] And like them he fiercely denounces the "out-of-touch" naysayers and "pessimists."[148]

However, Patterson and the Thernstroms are directly at odds over the *reasons* for Afro-American upward mobility. Without a whiff of supporting social science data, Patterson argues that affirmative action has been "the single most important factor accounting for the rise of a significant Afro-American middle class."[149] As noted, the Thernstroms find it impossible to attribute special significance to affirmative action in the upward economic advance experienced by blacks since the 1940s.[150] They also maintain that affirmative action is illegal, counterproductive, and perpetuates racism; therefore they demand its immediate abolition and restoration of traditional color-blindness, and other meritocratic values.[151] Patterson acknowledges that affirmative action is flawed, but he would nevertheless compromise and maintain it for the next fifteen years, phasing it out and ultimately replacing it with class-based preferences for the American-born poor.[152]

Patterson's position regarding affirmative action and integration is not an unqualified success. He has failed to define affirmative action. While it is reasonably clear that he equates affirmative action with preferences and dis-parate-impact remediation, such a matter should not be left to inference, particularly given Patterson's preoccupation with semantic rigor. Thus—to exorcise the demons misrepresenting the nature of America's social relation-ships—requires, Patterson insists, a change in our vocabulary. In his stern regime, terms like "race," "black," "white," "race-relations," and "racism" give way to "ethnic groups," "Afro-Americans," "Euro-Americans," and "eth-nocentrism or class prejudice."[153]

Patterson is of two minds with respect to the success of integration. On the one hand, he proclaims its success, telling us that black/white relations have never been better.[154] Later, he ruefully notes that there is a strong trend toward voluntary resegregation on and off campuses[155] that to him amounts to a "lamen-table betrayal and abandonment of the once cherished goal of integration."[156]

Patterson's presentation is marked by an arresting and sometimes breath-taking eclecticism. His basic posture is light years away from "pessimists" like Edley, Wilson, and Wicker. Yet his support[157] of a diversity rationale for affirmative action reads like Edley's brief[158] for the same; and his proposal for class-based affirmative action could have been written by Wilson or Wicker. He cannot abide by dogma, but is not above a little himself, as witness his bald claim that ultimately integration *must* mean intermarriage.[159] All told, his book is a compelling example of the rich diversity in the equal rights debate, and a clarion call for further scholarly study.

Public opinion research can help sort out the quarrel over race percep-tions. One of the most impressive recent works in this field is Donald R. Kinder and Lynn M. Sanders, *Divided by Color*.[160] The subject of this book is the basis of the views that white and black Americans hold on matters of race. Of the authors' voluminous findings,[161] the most relevant are:

1. The most striking feature of public opinion on race is how emphati-cally black and white Americans disagree with each other. Race has been, and remains, our most difficult subject. In this area, unlike most others concerned with public policy, American opinion is tenaciously firm, consistent, and more difficult to alter.

2. Many whites support racial equality in principle, but are considerably less enthusiastic about policies for bringing the principle to life.

3. The differences between blacks and whites over equal opportunity, social welfare assistance to blacks, and affirmative action are "extraordinary." Overwhelming white majorities oppose affirmative action; overwhelming black majorities support it. However, of all antidiscrimination policies, affirmative action is the least popular among blacks and whites alike.

4. The most important, though not the only, determinant of white public opinion on race policy is racial resentment based on the stereotypical notion that blacks are "unwilling to try and too willing to take what they have not earned."[162] "Most whites believe that their racial group is more industrious, smarter, more loyal, less violent, and more self-reliant than blacks."[163]

5. Most black Americans support remedial affirmative action in principle, but feel that it has not yet been implemented in education and employment. Blacks continue to believe that they face discrimination in schooling and employment, among other areas.

6. Racial differences are not a "mask for class differences." Race, not class, divides contemporary American society over social policy.

7. Racial differences in American politics are more dramatic now than ever before.

8. The racial divide is deep, widening, and persistent. There is no reason to believe that it is about to become obsolete.

At pages 269–272 of their text, Kinder and Sanders address the body of "notable and in many ways admirable"[164] opinion research that tends to support the Thernstroms' views, including Paul Sniderman and Thomas Piazza, *The Scar of Race,*[165] cited by the Thernstroms as an "important book."[166] Under the heading *Whitewashing Prejudice,* Kinder and Sanders squarely reject the central theme of these works, namely, that white racism is no longer (to cite Sniderman and Piazza) "the primary factor [in] the contemporary arguments over the politics of race."[167] Notwithstanding that "revolutionary changes" have taken place in white Americans' racial attitudes, they maintain that "resentments rooted in racial difference continue to shape American opinion powerfully."[168]

Readers skilled in reading scholarly tea leaves will draw their own conclusions. The Wilson-Wicker class-plus-race recipe seems to deserve serious consideration, but there are at least two drawbacks. First, as Kinder and Sanders have demonstrated, class is not an issue for most Americans. Second, there is little momentum for the creation of a new political coalition, or third party, dedicated to promoting class preferences for the poor.

Those who follow Kinder and Sanders will surely question the Thernstroms' position.[169] Moreover, in Randall Kennedy, *Race, Crime, and the Law,*[170] they will find ample grounds for skepticism about some of the Thernstroms' views on crime. This is a study of race discrimination in our criminal justice system. Kennedy's much needed, ably researched and written treatise concerns itself with the dimensions of the area: For example, the staggeringly disgraceful history of unequal application of the criminal law to African-Americans; the use of race as a proxy for criminality; and the bearing of racial bias on the administration of our criminal justice system, particularly the death penalty, drug law, and jury selection.

Indisputably, the issue of black crime, so-called, is the most incendiary aspect of race relations in this country. Many whites instinctively associate blackness and crime, despite the fact that the majority of blacks are law-abiding. On the other hand, many blacks are consumed by cynicism, mistrust, and outrage over the police and the courts. Professor Kennedy has been widely acclaimed for his evenhandedness. He has declared a deep reluctance "to use racial criteria in efforts to redress racial disadvantage."[171] He insists upon a Constitution that "looks beyond looks." Color-blind administration of the criminal law is his essential remedy. Accordingly, he disapproves of minority jury-seat guarantees and other proposed affirmative action remedies for discriminatory jury-selection procedures. To Kennedy, racial disparities do not necessarily reflect racial bias, and he condemns "activists" for automatically citing statistical disparities as proof of police bias.[172] (The Thernstroms make the same point at pages 272–274 of *America in Black and White*.) He acknowledges frequent racial maltreatment of black suspects, defendants, and criminals, but stresses that "more burdensome now in the day-to-day lives of African-Americans are private, violent criminals (typically black) who attack those most vulnerable without regard to racial identity"[173]— a judgment that earned him a commendation in the Thernstrom book.[174]

But there is another side to Kennedy, which the Thernstroms have not cited. While, as mentioned, he cautions against overplaying racial disparities, he is also fully aware that they often point directly to official racism. He demands an end to indiscriminate racial-profiling/stop-and-search police techniques.[175] Importantly, he scathingly denounces the courts for rejecting statistical evidence of bias in capital cases. (See the notorious *McCleskey v. Kemp* [1987] case.[176]) It is fair to say that Professor Kennedy would not second the Thernstroms' opinion that the argument that racism infects our policing is essentially meritless.[177]

Conclusion

In the federal regime of modern civil rights reform, race, ethnic, and gender-based affirmative action has had an extraordinary career of ups and downs. To its friends, affirmative action has been regarded as an important element in the battle against the oppressiveness visited upon minorities and females. Some of its advocates maintain that, as an antidiscrimination device, it should be supplemented by much greater public attention to factors beyond racism and sexism, such as family planning, trade practices with low-wage countries, antitrust law, monetary policy, and national full employment policy.[178]

Affirmative action reduces to the application of special assistance (including preferences) in order to achieve proportional representation of minorities and females in the workplace and in other spheres from which they have been discriminatorily excluded. While experiencing pendulum swings of approval and disapproval in the courts of law and public opinion, remedial preferences and other assistance have become embedded in our government apparatus as well as in the corporate and educational establishments. From the beginning, affirmative action has been a creature of racial, ethnic, and gender politics. Even though it cannot and does not claim that it has brought about equal opportunity, its abolition would undoubtedly exacerbate tensions. Presently, affirmative action appears to be in danger of possible extinction at the hands of a hostile judiciary and some state legislatures. In what may well be affirmative action's eleventh hour, its advocates seek, so far with only marginal prospects of success, judicial and popular approval of a nonremedial rationale of "diversity."

Nonetheless, there is no way of telling who will win the war we have tried to chronicle in these pages. It bears remembering that the leading voices which may have the final say—Congress and the judiciary—have not yet spoken clearly. Until they do, the outcome of the war will be unknown.

We end by referencing Steven Steinberg's *Turning Back*.[179] This volume is affirmative action's "Book of Lamentations." He gives credit to the "civil rights movement" and to the remedial legislation of the 1960s for liberating African-American citizens from "Jim Crow" official racism.[180] However, he passionately condemns society for not "following through" on these advances by creating the conditions of economic and social equality thus far thwarted by white racism.[181] This, he states, has been the mission of affirmative action. However, not only are there "persistent and even widening gaps between blacks and whites in incomes and living standards,"[182] but there is an "ominous new trend to *blame* blacks for the ills that afflict American society."[183]

The country, Steinberg maintains, is at a "crossroads, still uncertain whether to take the road back to the benighted past, or to forge a new path . . . to a historical reconciliation between black and white citizens."[184] What will it take to resolve this dilemma, perhaps to "move history forward again?"[185] Steinberg's answer: " 'the mounting pressure' that emanates from those segments of black society that have little reason to acquiesce in the racial status quo. It has yet to be seen exactly what form resistance and protest will take."[186]

One fervently hopes that this Cassandra is mistaken. But can one suppress the gnawing suspicion that this is not so? If one or more of affirmative action's group remedies are jettisoned in the near term, how will its successor, if any, come into being? And what will it be? We await the answers with apprehension.

Notes

―᷽᷽᷽᷽―

Chapter 1. Introduction

1. In this book "discrimination" means invidious (i.e., unfair or unjust) treatment of people. "Societal (systemic) discrimination" means societally rooted invidious treatment of people on account of group membership or affiliation. "Protected group" means the racial and ethnic (national origin/ancestral) and gender groups covered by antidiscrimination laws and regulations. "Minorities" are the racial and ethnic groups so covered. "Affirmative action" means the general policy for treating societal discrimination. There are many specific policies for implementing this general policy.

2. Disparate treatment of *individuals* remains a legitimate topic, but, in our view, a relatively noncontroversial antidiscrimination target, and we have accordingly paid little attention to it.

3. For analysis of compensation theory, see page 53.

4. Title VII of the 1964 Civil Rights Act, Pub L 88–352, 78 Stat 241, codified, as amended, at 42 USC § 2000e *et seq* (2000).

5. Congressional Research Service, The Library of Congress, American Law Division, *Compilation and Overview of Federal Laws and Regulations Establishing Affirmative Action Goals or Other Preferences Based on Race, Gender, or Ethnicity: A Report to Senator Robert Dole* at 5–32 (February 17, 1995). The material in this report has been rearranged, and the abbreviation U.S.C.S. therein has been changed to read USC.

6. *Affirmative Action Review: Report to the President* 40–42, 55–63 (July 19, 1995) submitted by George Stephanopoulos, Senior Adviser to the President and Christopher Edley Jr., Special Counsel to the President.

7. 42 USC § 2000e *et seq.*

8. 29 CFR Part 1608. The guidelines state the EEOC's position that when employers voluntarily undertake in good faith to remedy past discrimination by race or gender-conscious affirmative action means, the agency will not find them liable for reverse discrimination.

9. 42 USC § 2000e–16(b).

10. 42 USC § 2000e–16(b)(1).

11. 5 USC § 7201.

12. 5 CFR § 720.205(b) (1991).

13. 15 USC § 636(j)(15).

14. 10 USC [§] 2323.

15. See Surface Transportation Assistance Act of 1982, Pub. L. 97–424, 96 Stat. 2100 (*January* 6, 1983); superseded by Surface Transportation and Uniform Relocation Assistance Act of 1987, Pub L 100–17, 101 Stat 132 (STURAA); Intermodal Surface Transportation Efficiency Act of 1991.

16. 15 USC § 644(g); Federal Acquisition Regulation, 8 CFR § 52.219–8.

17. "Small" varies with the industry, but the maximum number of employees varies between 500 and 1,500. See Federal Acquisition Regulations (FAR) Part 19.102. The DOD wealth test is personal assets not more than $750,000, excluding business assets and personal residence.

18. 49 CFR part 23; 48 CFR § 52.219–8.

19. Sources for this section from The New York Times, natl ed are Steven Holmes, *Administration Cuts Affirmative Action While Defending It*, A17 (May 6, 1997); John M. Broder, *U.S. Readies Rules over Preferences Aiding Minorities*, A1, A13 (May 6, 1997); Steven Holmes, *Broadcasters Vow to Keep Affirmative Action*, A12 (July 30, 1998); Neil Lewis, *F.C.C. Revises Rule on Hiring of Women and Minorities*, A6 (January 21, 2000). Other sources are Jonathan Peterson, *Clinton to Unveil New Approach to Job Preferences*, The Los Angeles Times, A1, A15 (June 24, 1998); The White House, Office of the Press Secretary, *Procurement Reform: SDB Certification and the Price Evaluation Adjustment Program*, 1ff (June 24, 1998).

20. 515 U.S. 200.

21. Published Papers and Addresses of President William J. Clinton, *Remarks on Affirmative Action, July 19, 1995* at 1113 (U.S. Government Printing Office, 1995).

22. In 1994, two scholars reported that in the largest of the SDB programs— Section 8(a)—99% of the benefits went to businesses owned by people of color. George R. La Noue and John C. Sullivan, *Presumptions for Preferences,* 4 J of Policy History 439, 463 (1994).

Chapter Two. The Roots of Affirmative Action, the Women's Movement, and the Groups Covered by Affirmative Action

1. See chs 3, 4, 5, 6 in this volume.

2. See Herman Belz, *Equality Transformed* 12–13 (Transaction, 1991) to this effect.

3. Eric Foner, *Reconstruction* 67 (Perennial/Harper, 1988) (emphasis added).

4. During the final phase of the War, and for two years after it ended, federal policy for relations with the South was controlled by Johnson's so-called "Presidential Reconstruction" program. See Eric McKittrick, *Andrew Johnson and Reconstruction* (U of Chicago Press, 1960); Herman Belz, *A New Birth of Freedom* 35–50 (Greenwood, 1976). Congress' confrontation with the president over policy in 1865–1867, including the famous impeachment, is one of the most fascinating chapters in our national history. See Foner, *Reconstruction* at chs 6–8 (cited in note 3).

5. Rogers M. Smith, *Legitimating Reconstruction*, 108 Yale L J 2039, 2064 (1999); John Hope Franklin, *Slavery and the Constitution*, in Leonard W. Levy,

Kenneth L. Karst, and Dennis J. Mahoney, eds, *Civil Rights and Equality* 61 (Macmillan, 1989).

6. Eric Foner, *The Story of American Freedom* 75 (Norton, 1998).

7. Kenneth M. Stampp, *The Peculiar Institution* ch 2, 430 (Vintage /Random, 1989); John Hope Franklin and Alfred A. Moss Jr., *From Slavery to Freedom* ch 8 (Knopf, 8th ed, 2000).

8. *Dred Scott v. Sandford*, 19 How (60 U.S.) 393, 404–406 (1857).

9. Harold M. Hyman, *Thirteenth Amendment (Framing)* at 102; Kenneth L. Karst, *Thirteenth Amendment (Judicial Interpretation)* at 106; William I. Nelson, *Fourteenth Amendment (Framing)* at 118; Kenneth L. Karst, *Equal Protection of the Laws* at 30; Charles L. Black Jr., *State Action* at 44; William Gillette, *Fifteenth Amendment (Framing and Ratification)* at 125; Ward E. Y. Elliott, *Fifteenth Amendment (Judicial Interpretation)* at 129, in Levy, Karst, and Mahoney, eds, *Civil Rights* (cited in note 5).

10. See Harold M. Hyman, *Civil Rights Act of 1866 (Framing)* at 113; Theodore Eisenberg, *Civil Rights Act of 1866 (Judicial Interpretation)* at 115, in Levy, Karst, and Mahoney, eds, *Civil Rights* (cited in note 5).

11. 1866 Civil Rights Act ch 31, §1, 14 Stat 27, codified at 42 USC § 1982 (2000).

12. Ch 28, 15 Stat 14 (1867).

13. Foner, *Reconstruction* at 276–280 (cited in note 3).

14. Eric Foner, *The Strange Career of the Reconstruction Amendments*, 108 Yale L J 2003, 2006 (1999).

15. Id.

16. Alfred W. Blumrosen, *Modern Law* 17 (U Wisconsin Press, 1993).

17. Michael Les Benedict, *Reconstruction,* in Kermit L. Hall, et al, eds, *The Oxford Companion to the Supreme Court of the United States* 381, 382 (Oxford U Press, 1992).

18. Pub L 88–352, 78 Stat 241, codified, as amended, generally at 42 USC § 1971 *et seq* (2000).

19. Codified at 42 USC § 2000a *et seq* (2000).

20. Codified, as amended, at 42 USC § 2000d *et seq* (2000).

21. Codified, as amended, at 42 USC § 2000e *et seq* (2000).

22. Pub L 89–110, 79 Stat 437, codified, as amended, at 42 USC § 1973 *et seq* (2000).

23. Pub L 90–284, 82 Stat 81, codified, as amended, at 42 USC § 3601 *et seq* (2000).

24. Kenneth L. Karst, *Introduction,* in Levy, Karst, and Mahoney, eds, *Civil Rights* at xi (cited in note 5).

25. Eric Foner, *Reconstruction* 281–291, 602 (Perennial/Harper, 1988); Kenneth M. Stampp, *The Era of Reconstruction* 165–174 (Vintage/Random, 1965); John Hope Franklin, *Reconstruction after the Civil War* 109–112 (U Chicago Press, 1994); Franklin and Moss, *From Slavery to Freedom* at chs 12–13 (cited in note 7).

26. On the end of Reconstruction under the "compromise" of 1877, see Foner, *Reconstruction* at xxvii, 575–583 (cited in note 25); Stampp, *Reconstruction* at 210 (cited in note 25); C. Vann Woodward, *Compromise of 1877*, in Levy, Karst, and Mahoney, eds, *Civil Rights* at 161 (cited in note 5).

27. Stampp, *Reconstruction* at 214 (cited in note 25). See Foner, *Reconstruction* at 602–603 (cited in note 25); Franklin, *Reconstruction* at 169–219 (cited in note 25).

28. Foner, *Reconstruction* at 277 (cited in note 25).

29. Id.

30. For example, a proposed declaration that all persons are equal before the law failed. See Earl M. Maltz, *Civil Rights, The Constitution, and Congress, 1863–1869* at 21–28 (U Press of Kansas, 1990). So did a proposed federal guarantee of state-law voting rights. Id at 36–37, 46–47, 81, 141–145; Foner, *Reconstruction* at 257–261 (cited in note 25); Stampp, *Reconstruction* at 141–144 (cited in note 25).

31. Maltz, *Civil Rights and the Constitution* at 94 (cited in note 30).

32. The Fourteenth Amendment was adopted in order to shore up the constitutionality of the 1866 Civil Rights Act, but it did not replicate the statute's unprecedented enumeration of substantive rights. Nor did it specifically refer to universal manhood suffrage, even though, as seen, Congress later made this the centerpiece of reunion. The Amendment's deliberately broad language strongly suggests the belief that the principle of equal citizenship was compatible with states-rights dogma. See Karst, *Equal Protection of the Laws*, in Leonard W. Levy, Kenneth L. Karst, and Dennis J. Mahoney, eds, *Civil Rights* 33 (Macmillan, 1989). By the same token, the Fifteenth Amendment's reference to the "right to vote" was not necessarily a claim of national origin. Compare the earlier Act of 1867, under which the all-important black franchise was to come into being not pursuant to self-executing federal mandate, but through state constitutional amendments. See Maltz, *Civil Rights and the Constitution* at 37 (cited in note 30).

33. See Michael Les Benedict, *Constitutional History and Constitutional Theory*, 108 Yale L J 2011, 2026–2027 (1999).

34. Foner, *Reconstruction* at 258–259 (cited in note 25).

35. Benedict, *Constitutional History and Theory* at 2203 (cited in note 33).

36. Foner, *Reconstruction* at 277 (cited in note 25).

37. Id.

38. Eric Foner, *The Story of American Freedom* 65 (Norton, 1998).

39. See Stampp, *Reconstruction* at 122–123 (cited in note 25).

40. Maltz, *Civil Rights and the Constitution* at 37 (cited in note 30).

41. See Eric Foner, *Reconstruction* 119–123, 587–601 (Perenial/Harper, 1988); Franklin, *Reconstruction* 127–128, 169, 203, 211–213 (cited in note 25); Keith J. Bybee, *Mistaken Identity* 14–16 (Princeton U Press, 1998).

42. In 1870 and 1871, Congress enacted a series of "Force Acts" authorizing armed intervention by the occupation force in order to protect black voters, but these measures were too little, too late. See Foner, *Reconstruction* at 119–123, 342–343, 442–444, 458–459, 558–563, 580–583 (cited in note 41); Kenneth M. Stampp, *Reconstruction* 200–219 (Vintage/Random, 1965).

43. Foner, *Reconstruction* at 106 (cited in note 41).

44. Id at 103–104.

45. Stampp, *Reconstruction* at 125–133 (cited in note 42).

46. Foner, *Reconstruction* at 106 (cited in note 41).

47. Id at 3–6, 156–159; Stampp, *Reconstruction* at 188 (cited in note 42).

48. Jay R. Mandle, *Not Slave, Not Free* ch 1 (Duke U Press, 1992).

49. Stampp, *Reconstruction* at 120 (cited in note 42). For an encyclopedic account of the slaves' occupational skills, see Eugene D. Genovese, *Roll, Jordan, Roll* 285–398 (Vintage/Random, 1974). During Reconstruction, the great majority of skilled Southern craftsmen (former slaves) were routinely barred from off-plantation work in their trades on account of their race. See Mandle, *Not Slave, Not Free* at 21–24, 30–32 (cited in note 48).

50. Stampp, *Reconstruction* at 122 (cited in note 42).

51. Eric Foner, *Strange Career of the Reconstruction Amendments,* 108 Yale L J 2003, 2007 (1999).

52. Foner, *Story of Freedom* at 131–132 (cited in note 38).

53. Eric Foner, *Reconstruction* at 604 (cited in note 41).

54. See *Teamsters v. United States*, 431 U.S. 324, 349ff (1977) for the Supreme Court's analysis of disparate treatment and disparate impact.

55. See Herman Belz, *Equality Transformed* (Transaction, 1991).

56. See Alfred W. Blumrosen, *Modern Law* (U Wisconsin Press, 1993).

57. Foner, 108 Yale L J at 2003, 2007 (cited in note 51).

58. See Foner, *Story of Freedom* at 131 (cited in note 38).

59. 163 U.S. 537. See Foner, 108 Yale L J at 2007 (cited in note 51), and *Story of Freedom* at 133 (cited in note 38).

60. 163 U.S. 537, 544.

61. Id at 559.

62. 16 Wall (83 U.S.) 36.

63. 92 U.S. 542, 555.

64. 92 U.S. 563, 564.

65. 100 U.S. 313.

66. 100 U.S. 303.

67. 109 U.S. 3.

68. See further commentary on these cases in Leonard W. Levy, Kenneth L. Karst, and Dennis J. Mahoney, eds, *Civil Rights and Equality* 157, 163, 169, 173, 185 (Macmillan, 1989).

69. 347 U.S. 483. See Douglas Rae, *Equalities* 32–33, 41, 80, 103 (Harvard U Press, 1989).

70. Michael Les Benedict, *Constitutional History and Constitutional Theory,* 108 Yale L J 2011, 2033–2035 (1999).

71. Eric Foner, *Story of Freedom* at 131–132 (cited in note 38).

72. Id at 135.

73. Id at 185–193, 236–247.

74. Leon F. Litwack, *Trouble in Mind* 218–219 (Knopf, 1998).

75. *Gaston County v. United States*, 395 U.S. 285 (1969); *Griggs v. Duke Power Co.,* 401 U.S. 424 (1971).

76. John Hope Franklin and Alfred A. Moss, Jr., *From Slavery to Freedom* 515–521 (Knopf, 8th ed, 2000); Litwack, *Trouble in Mind* at 135, 314, 405, 430, 481–496 (cited in note 74). The modern phase of the Great Migration is described in Nicholas Lemann, *The Promised Land* (Knopf, 1991).

77. Jay R. Mandle, *Not Slave, Not Free* 72 (Duke U Press, 1992).

78. *Editor's Introduction,* in Paul Burstein, ed, *Equal Employment Opportunity* 1, 9–12 (Aldine De Gruyter, 1994); Herbert Hill, *Black Labor* at 9–12 in id; Franklin

and Moss, *From Slavery to Freedom* at 515–521 (cited in note 76); John Charles Boger, *Race and the American City,* in John Charles Boger and Judith Welch Wegner, eds, *Race, Poverty, and American Cities* 3, 9 and ns 44–47 (U North Carolina Press, 1996); Wegner, *Notes and Reflections* in id at 551. It should be noted that the same pattern of urban decay has come to pass in the major metropolitan areas of the South.

79. See *Affirmative Action Review: Report to the President,* 7–8, 40–42 (July 19, 1995), submitted by George Stephanopoulos, Senior Adviser to the President and Christopher Edley Jr., Special Counsel to the President.

80. Peter Dreier, *America's Urban Crisis,* in Boger and Wegner, eds, *Race, Poverty, and American Cities* at 79, 102 (cited in note 78); Wegner, *Notes and Reflections* in id at 551–552.

81. Mandle, *Not Slave, Not Free* at 32, 68 (cited in note 77).

82. Christina Hoff Sommers, *Who Stole Feminism?* 74–86 (Touchstone/Simon & Schuster, 1994).

83. Cited in Mary Becker, Cynthia Grant Bowman, and Morrison Torrey, *Cases and Materials on Feminist Jurisprudence* 6 (West, 1994).

84. Id.

85. William L. O'Neill, *feminism in America* 3–48 (Transaction, 2d rev ed, 1989); David Conway, *Free-Market Feminism,* in David Conway, ed, *Free-Market Feminism* 1, 6–9 (IEA [Institute of Economic Affairs] Health & Welfare Unit, 1998).

86. Eric Foner, *The Story of American Freedom* 112 (Norton, 1998).

87. O'Neill, *feminism in America* at 119–176 (cited in note 85).

88. Hugh Davis Graham, *Civil Rights and the Presidency* 48 (Oxford U Press, 1992).

89. O'Neill, *feminism in America* at 254–294 (cited in note 85).

90. Graham, *Civil Rights and the Presidency* at 48–50 (cited in note 88).

91. Id at 9.

92. Id.

93. Cited by Conway, ed, *Free-Market Feminism* at 10–11 (cited in note 85).

94. Editor's *Introduction,* in John David Skrentny, ed, *Affirmative Action,* 41 American Behavioral Scientist 877, 881–883 (1998).

95. George R. La Noue and John C. Sullivan, *Presumptions for Preferences,* 6 J of Policy History 439 (1994) *(L/S I); Deconstructing the Affirmative Action Categories,* 41 Am Behavioral Scientist 913 (1998) *(L/S II); Gross Presumptions,* 41 Santa Clara L Rev 103 (2000) *(L/S III).*

96. For a summary of the federal MBE programs, see L/S III at 103 n 1 (cited in note 95); Also see the appendix to chapter 1 at pages 17–22 in this volume.

97. Pub L 95–507, 92 Stat 1761, codified, as amended, at 15 USC 637(a) *et seq* (2000).

98. L/S I at 443 (cited in note 95). For a history of minority set-asides, see L/S III at 119–120 (cited in note 95); Herman Belz, *Equality Transformed* 195, 201, 296 n 46 (Transaction, 1991).

99. 13 CFR 124.103(b) (2000) (emphasis added).

100. L/S I at 442 and L/S III at 110 (cited in note 95).

101. L/S III at 122–123 (cited in note 95).

102. Id at 129–130, 138–139, 157–159.

103. L/S I at 449 (cited in note 95).

104. See 15 USC 637(a)(5) (racial or ethnic bias); 15 USC 637(a)(6)(A) (2000) (income limits).

105. L/S III at 123, quoting from an SBA policy manual (cited in note 95).

106. Id at 107–108.

107. L/S II at 920–923; L/S III at 129–131, 156 (cited in note 95).

108. L/S III at 122, 129–130 (cited in note 95).

109. Id at 138–139.

110. Id at 146–147.

111. Id at 122–124.

112. Id at 106, 147.

113. L/S I at 442–444, 445–446, 461; L/S III at 135–136 (cited in note 95).

114. Id at 441.

115. L/S III at 104, 112, 119, 136–139, 158–159 (cited in note 95).

116. Id at 159.

117. Id at 110.

118. Hugh Davis Graham, *Unintended Consequences,* 41 Am Behavioral Scientist 898, 898–912 (1998).

119. 29 CFR §1607.4 B (2000).

120. Christopher Edley Jr., *Not All Black and White* (Hill and Wang, 1996), 174.

121. Id.

122. Id at 176.

123. Id at 177.

124. Orlando Patterson, *The Ordeal of Integration* 192–193 (Civitas/Counterpoint, 1997).

125. Id at 193.

126. Id at 10.

127. Id at 9–10.

128. Id at 148.

129. Id at 9, 148–156, 163.

130. Id at 148, 158–166.

131. Id at 192.

132. Id at 193.

133. Id.

134. Id at 79–81.

Chapter Three. The Career of
Affirmative Action in Employment

1. On Booker T. Washington, see John Hope Franklin and Alfred A. Moss Jr., *From Slavery to Freedom* 299–306 (Knopf, 8th ed, 2000).

2. Id at 353–354, 452–454; Diane Ravitch, *Troubled Crusade* 120–128 (Basic, 1983). *Brown v. Board of Education* (1954) is located at 347 U.S. 483.

3. Hugh Davis Graham, *The Civil Rights Era* 10 (Oxford U Press, 1990).

4. Id at 14–15.

5. Id at 15, 19, 95.

6. Jay R. Mandle, *Not Slave, Not Free* 95–97 (Duke U Press, 1992); Ravitch, *Troubled Crusade* at 138–141 (cited in note 2); John Charles Boger, *Race and the American City,* in John Charles Boger and Judith Welch Wegner, eds, *Race, Poverty, and American Cities* at 6, 46 ns 19, 20 (U North Carolina Press, 1996); Graham, *Civil Rights Era* at 74–76, 104–106, 405 ns 3, 4 (cited in note 3). For graphic accounts of the "nonviolent" civil disobedience struggle, see Taylor Branch, *Parting The Waters* (Simon & Schuster, 1988), and *Pillar of Fire* (Simon & Schuster, 1998); Southern Poverty Law Center, *Free at Last* (Southern Education Foundation, 1989).

7. Executive Order (EO) 10925 (emphasis added). EO 10925 was superseded in 1965 by EO 11246, 3 CFR 1964–1965 Compilation at 339 n 2.

8. See Graham, *Civil Rights Era* at 95–99 (cited in note 3); Paul Burstein, *Discrimination, Jobs, and Politics* 9 (U Chicago Press, 1998).

9. Burstein, *Discrimination and Jobs* at 8 (cited in note 8).

10. Pub L 88–352, 78 Stat 241, codified, as amended, generally at 42 USC § 1971 *et seq* (2000).

11. 42 USC § 2000e *et seq* (2000).

12. See authorities collected at Leonard W. Levy, Kenneth L. Karst, and Dennis J. Mahoney, eds, *Civil Rights and Equality* 253, 262–263 (Macmillan, 1989).

13. Pub L 89–110, 79 Stat 437, codified, as amended, at 42 USC § 1973 *et seq* (2000).

14. Executive Order 11246 (cited in note 7).

15. John A. Andrew III, *Lyndon Johnson and the Great Society* 23 (Ivan R. Dee, 1998).

16. *Editor's Introduction,* in Paul Burstein, ed, *Equal Employment Opportunity* ix–x (Aldine De Gruyter, 1994); David L. Rose, *Twenty-Five Years Later: Where Do We Stand on Equal Employment Law Enforcement?* 42 Vand L Rev, 1121, 1132 (1989).

17. Theodore Eisenberg, *Civil Rights Act of 1964,* in Levy, Karst, and Mahoney, eds, *Civil Rights* at 235, 236 (cited in note 12).

18. Id at 235–236.

19. The statistical data presented to Congress on these inequities is summarized in Rose, *Equal Employment Law Enforcement* at 1129–1132 (cited in note 16); Alfred W. Blumrosen, *Modern Law* 292 (U Wisconsin Press, 1993).

20. Pub L 88–352, 78 Stat 241, § 703(a)(1)(2), codified at 42 USC § 2000e–2(a)(1)(2) (2000). Similar prohibitions apply to nonreferral for employment and exclusion from union membership. See Pub L 88–352, 74 Stat 241, § 703(b)(c), codified at 42 USC § 2000–2(b)(c) (2000).

21. Pub L 88–352, 78 Stat 241, § 703(j), codified, as amended, at 42 USC § 2000e–2(j) (2000).

22. Pub L 88–352, 78 Stat 241 § 706(g), codified at 42 USC § 2000e–5(g) (1) (2000).

23. See Blumrosen, *Modern Law* at 47–49 (cited in note 19) for analysis of the so-called "Dirksen-Mansfield Compromise" that led to this odd result.

24. Id at 176.

25. Id at 174.
26. Id at 176.
27. Id at 242.
28. Id at 55.
29. Id at 69–70, 101–102.
30. Id at 110, 255, 351 n 2.
31. Id at 80–85, 115–117.
32. Id at 73–75, 80–85, 112–171, 255.
33. Id at 74.
34. Rose, *Equal Employment Law Enforcement* at 1121, 1135 (cited in note 16).
35. Blumrosen, *Modern Law* at 73–75 (cited in note 19).
36. Id at 65–66, 74, 114–116, 292–294, 382 n 21; Rose, *Equal Employment Law Enforcement* at 1162–1166 (cited in note 16).
37. Id at 1136.
38. Hugh Davis Graham, *Civil Rights Era* 95, 189–204 (Oxford U Press, 1990).
39. 404 U.S. 424 (1971).
40. Graham, *Civil Rights Era* at 389 (cited in note 38).
41. The 1964 Civil Rights Act permitted employers "to give and act upon the results of any professionally developed ability test, provided that such test, its administration, or action upon the results is not designed, intended, or used to discriminate because of race." 42 USC § 2000e–2h (2000). The EEOC's 1966 testing guidelines interpreted a "professionally developed ability test" to mean "a test which fairly measures the knowledge or skills required by the particular job or class of jobs the applicant seeks, or which fairly affords the employer a chance to measure the applicant's ability to perform a particular job or class of jobs." See *Griggs v. Duke Power Co.,* 401 U.S. at 431 n 9; Rose, *Equal Employment Law Enforcement* at 1136 (cited in note 16). Appendix 1 to this chapter contains excerpts from the current guidelines designed to provide a uniform set of principles for the federal agencies regarding the use of employment tests and other selection procedures.
42. Blumrosen, *Modern Law* at 96 (cited in note 19).
43. Id at 121.
44. Rose, *Equal Employment Law Enforcement* at 1121, 1132 (cited in note 16).
45. 29 CFR § 1607.4 D (2000).
46. Id at 1607.5 C (2000).
47. Id.
48. 480 U.S. 616, 676–677.
49. Alfred W. Blumrosen, *Modern Law* 124–131 (U Wisconsin Press, 1993). See Debra A. Millenson, *Whither Affirmative Action: The Future of Executive Order 11,246,* 29 U Memphis L Rev 679, 687–691 (1999).
50. *Contractors Ass'n. of Eastern Pennsylvania v. Secretary of Labor,* 442 F2d 159 (3d Cir), cert denied 404 U.S. 854 (1971).
51. Hugh Davis Graham, *Voting Rights and the American Regulatory State,* in Bernard Grofman and Chandler Davidson, eds, *Controversies in Minority Voting* 177, 185 (Brookings, 1992).
52. *Lutheran Church-Missouri Synod v. FCC,* 141 F3d 344, 352–354 (D.C. Cir 1998).

53. Millenson, *Whither Affirmative Action* at 681–684 (cited in note 49).

54. Hugh Davis Graham, *Civil Rights and the Presidency* 9–10, 107–111 (Oxford U Press, 1992).

55. Id at 114–116, 204.

56. William Henry Chafe, *The Paradox of Change: American Women in the 20th Century* 203 (Oxford U Press, 1991).

57. Cited in Mary Becker, Cynthia Grant Bowman, and Morrison Torrey, *Cases and Materials on Feminist Jurisprudence* 24 (West, 1994). When first introduced to Congress in 1923, the first sentence of the proposed Equal Rights Amendment read: "Men and women shall have equal rights throughout the United States and in every place subject to its jurisdiction." Id at 22.

58. For a revealing account of the adoption of affirmative action as an instrument of crisis management, see John David Skrentny, *Ironies of Affirmative Action* ch 4 (U Chicago Press, 1996).

59. Graham, *The Civil Rights Era* 116–117, 456–457 (cited in note 38).

60. Id at 120.

61. Id at 460.

62. Blumrosen, *Modern Law* at 154 (cited in note 49).

63. Id at 153–155.

64. 42 USC § 2000e–(5)(g)(1) (2000) (emphasis added).

65. Ronald J. Fiscus, *The Constitutional Logic of Affirmative Action* xiii (Duke U Press, 1992).

66. Pub L 102–166, 105 Stat 1071, codified at 42 USC § 1981 (2000) and elsewhere in sections of 42 USC.

67. For an extended statement of the nonremedial rationale, see Christopher Edley Jr., *Not All Black and White* 9, 134, 121–141, 189–197 (Hill and Wang, 1996); Nicholas deB. Katzenbach and Burke Marshall, *Not Color Blind, Just Blind*, The New York Times Magazine 42ff (February 22, 1998); Orlando Patterson, *The Ordeal of Integration* 157 (Civitas/Counterpoint, 1997).

68. 488 U.S. 469.

69. 515 U.S. 200.

70. 438 U.S. 265.

71. 42 USC § 2000d *et seq* (2000).

72. 438 U.S. 265, 306.

73. Id at 271–272.

74. Id at 411.

75. Id at 412. In relevant part, Title VI provided that "No person . . . shall, on the ground of race . . . be excluded from participation in . . . any program . . . receiving Federal financial assistance." 42 USC § 2000d (2000).

76. 438 U.S. at 421.

77. Id at 325–326.

78. Id at 328–340.

79. Id at 355–356.

80. Id at 357–358, 373–375. According to the equal protection clause, no state shall "deny to any person within its jurisdiction the equal protection of the laws."

81. 438 U.S. 359. The "intermediate scrutiny " test was established by the Court in *Craig v. Boren* 429 U.S. 190 (1976) for adjudication of gender-discrimination claims. See chapter 5 at pages 164–168.

82. 438 U.S. 265, 362, 369–375.

83. Id at 272, 325–326.

84. Id at 271, 421.

85. For example, the decision serves as a primer on the meaning of "quota." The parties differed over whether the set-aside was a "racial quota" because white applicants could not compete for the reserved minority seats (id at 288 and n 26), or merely a "goal" of minority representation, with neither a "floor" nor a "ceiling" on the total number of minority admittees. Id.

For Justice Powell, it was dispositive that white applicants were limited to competition for only 84 seats rather than the 100 open to minority applicants. In his view, since the limitation was racial on its face, it violated equal protection whether described as a quota or as a goal. Id at 289–290 and n 27. Justice Powell also opined that an admissions program which gives appropriate individualized weight to "all pertinent elements of diversity," including race, in evaluating applications by disadvantaged minorities, would pass muster. Id at 317–318.

Justice Brennan held that although the set-aside excludes whites, it will not likely result in "harm comparable to that imposed on . . . minorities by racial segregation." The "purpose [of the set-asides] is to overcome the effects of segregation by bringing the races together, that is, by reducing the number of white admittees in order to make room for a reasonable percentage . . . of otherwise underrepresented qualified minority applicants." Id at 374 and n 58. The Davis plan does not discriminate against its purported beneficiaries: it does not establish a quota in the invidious sense of a ceiling on the number of minority admittees, or stigmatize them as inferior (id at 375–376); and there is no constitutional difference between setting aside a fixed number of seats for qualified minority applicants, and—as suggested by Justice Powell—using race as a "positive factor" in evaluating applications by disadvantaged minorities. In terms of result, these approaches are simply different ways of factoring racial preferences into the admission process. Exclusions of nonminority candidates under both are constitutionally equivalent. Id at 378–379, and see Justice Powell's rejoinder at 318–319.

86. Id at 287.

87. Id at 284–285.

88. Id at 287.

89. Id at 291.

90. Id at 305. On this point, Justice Powell wrote only for himself. However, his formulation provided the conceptual basis of the "strict scrutiny" test that the Court's current race-neutral majority espouses. See this chapter at pages 70–79.

91. Id at 306–310 and n 44.

92. Id at 311–315.

93. Id at 319–320.

94. Id at 316–318.

95. 448 U.S. 448.

96. Id at 475–480 (opinion of Burger, C.J.) In *Bolling v. Sharpe,* 347 U.S. 497 (1954), the Supreme Court held that the due process clause of the Fifth Amendment imposes an equal protection duty on the federal government. The Fifth Amendment requires that "No person shall be . . . deprived of life, liberty, or property without due process of law."

97. 448 U.S. at 515.

98. George R. La Noue and James C. Sullivan, *Presumptions for Preferences,* 4 J of Policy History 439, 441 (1994).

99. 515 U.S. 200, 235.

100. 448 U.S. at 495–496.

101. *Adarand Constructors, Inc. v. Mineta,* 151 L Ed 2d 489 (2001).

102. 443 U.S. 193.

103. Id at 200.

104. Id at 208.

105. Id at 202–203.

106. Id at 204.

107. Id at 205.

108. See above at page 42 for text.

109. 443 U.S. at 206.

110. Id at 208–209.

111. Id at 254–255.

112. 476 U.S. 267.

113. Id at 280–281.

114. 467 U.S. 561.

115. For text, see above at pages 42–43.

116. 467 U.S. at 581–583.

117. 476 U.S. 267, 284.

118. Id at 274–278.

119. Id at 283–284.

120. Candidate Reagan promised to abolish or drastically restrict race/ethnic/ gender-based equal employment opportunity policies and practices. Due, however, to internal differences in his Administration, and to the fact that affirmative action was so deeply entrenched in the economy, President Reagan failed to bring about any permanent EEO changes. His civil rights agenda was reduced to deliberate underenforcement by the EEOC, and to pursuit of victims only/prior discrimination court rulings. See Herman Belz, *Equality Transformed* 181–207 (Transaction, 1991); Alfred W. Blumrosen, *Modern Law* 267–269 (U Wisconsin Press, 1993); Robert Detlefsen, *Civil Rights Under Reagan* (Inst. for Contemporary Studies, 1991); Steven A. Shull, *A Kinder and Gentler Racism?* 154 (M. E. Sharpe, 1993).

121. 478 U.S. 421.

122. For text, see above at pages 42–43.

123. 478 U.S. at 482.

124. The text is at page 42 above. See Justice O'Connor's dissenting *Sheet Metal* opinion, 478 U.S. at 495–496, on the distinction between "goals" and "quotas" under Title VII. In this connection, see Ronald J. Fiscus, *The Constitutional Logic of Affirmative Action* (Duke U Press, 1992).

125. 478 U.S. at 483.
126. Id at 475.
127. Id at 476.
128. Id at 476–477.
129. Id at 477–478.
130. Id at 479.
131. Id at 480.
132. Id.
133. Id.
134. Id.
135. 478 U.S. 501.
136. Id at 508–509.
137. 480 U.S. 149.
138. Id at 185–186.
139. Id at 171–185.
140. Id at 184–185.
141. 480 U.S. 616.
142. 443 U.S. 193. See the discussion of *Weber* at pages 58–60 above.
143. 480 U.S. 616, 631.
144. Id at 632, citing *Hazelwood School District v. United States,* 433 U.S. 299 (1977).
145. 480 U.S. 616, 632.
146. Id at 630, 633.
147. Id at 632.
148. Id at 663.
149. Id at 628 n 6.
150. Id at 635–636.
151. Id at 621–622.
152. Id at 636–637.
153. Id at 637.
154. Id at 637–638.
155. Id at 639–640.
156. Blumrosen, *Modern Law* at 242–245, 261–262 (cited in note 120).
157. Herman Belz, *Equality Transformed* 196–200 (Transaction, 1991); John David Skrentny, *Ironies of Affirmative Action* 141, 232 (U Chicago Press, 1996); Melvin I. Urofsky, *Affirmative Action on Trial* 20–22 (U Press Kansas, 1997). Also see appendixes in chapters 1 and 3 of this volume.
158. 443 U.S. 193, 219.
159. 480 U.S. 616, 658.
160. In his *Johnson* dissent, Justice Scalia called on the Court to overrule *Weber.* Id at 673.
161. All of these decisions involved employment discrimination issues: *Wards Cove v. Atonio,* 490 U.S. 642 (1989); *Price Waterhouse v. Hopkins,* 490 U.S. 228 (1989); *Patterson v. McLean Credit Union,* 491 U.S. 164 (1989); *Lorance v. AT&T Technologies,* 490 U.S. 900 (1989); *Martin v. Wilks,* 490 U.S. 755 (1989). For summaries of these decisions, see David A. Cathcart and Mark Snyderman, *The Civil Rights*

Act of 1991, 8 Labor Law 849 (1992); Blumrosen, *Modern Law* at 424 n 6 (cited in note 176). The sixth decision was *City of Richmond v. Croson Co.,* 488 U.S. 469 (1989), involving the set-aside of municipal funds for the benefit of minority contractors.

162. 490 U.S. 642.

163. Id at 650.

164. Id.

165. Id at 648, citing *Watson v. Fort Worth Bank & Trust,* 487 U.S. 977 (1988).

166. 490 U.S. 642, 655.

167. Id at 650–651.

168. Id at 651–652.

169. Id at 651 n 7.

170. Id at 652.

171. Id at 657.

172. Id.

173. Id at 659.

174. Id at 660–661.

175. *The Civil Rights Act of 1991,* 106 Harv L Rev 1621, 1623–1624 (1993). See also *Developments in the Law,* 109 Harv L Rev 1568, 1579 (1996).

176. For a statement of this view, see Alfred W. Blumrosen, *Modern Law* at 279–282 (U Wisconsin Press, 1993).

177. For a legislative history and analysis of the Act, see J. B. Franke, *The Civil Rights Act of 1991,* 17 S Illinois U L Rev 267 (1993).

178. Pub L 102–166, 105 Stat 1071, codified in scattered sections of 2, 29, and 42 USC (1999).

179. See Blumrosen, *Modern Law* at 284–288 (cited in note 176).

180. 42 USC § 1981 note (2000).

181. Id.

182. 488 U.S. 469, 505, 507–508.

183. For a history of minority set-asides, beginning with their initiation by the Small Business Administration during the Great Society era, see Belz, *Equality Transformed* at 195, 201, 296 n 46 (cited in note 157); George R. La Noue and James C. Sullivan, *Presumptions for Preferences,* 4 J of Policy History 439 (1994); *Deconstructing the Affirmative Action Categories,* 41 Am Behavioral Scientist 913 (1998); *Gross Presumptions,* 41 Santa Clara L Rev 103 (2000); *Fullilove v. Klutznick,* 448 U.S. 448 (1980).

184. 488 U. S. 469, 477–478.

185. Id at 478.

186. 497 U.S. 547.

187. Id at 600–601.

188. Id at 564–566.

189. 515 U.S. 200.

190. Id at 227.

191. Id at 237.

192. *Affirmative Action Review: Report to the President* (July 19, 1995), submitted by George Stephanopoulos, Senior Adviser to the President and Christopher Edley Jr., Special Counsel to the President.

193. Published Papers and Addresses of President William J. Clinton, *Remarks on Affirmative Action*, July 19, 1995 at 1112–1113 (U.S. Government Printing Office, 1995).

194. Walter Dellinger, *Memorandum to General Counsels Re Adarand* 1(Office of Legal Counsel, U.S. Dept of Justice, June 28, 1995).

195. 515 U.S. 200, 237.

196. Dellinger, *Memorandum Re Adarand* at 5 (cited in note 194).

197. 515 U.S. at 227. The concurring opinions of Scalia, id at 239, and Thomas, id at 240ff, virtually demand a flat constitutional ban. Scalia believes that "government can never have a 'compelling interest' in discriminating on the basis of race in order to 'make up' for past racial discrimination." This is the view that he had previously expressed in *Croson* (488 U.S. at 524), thereby eliciting a declaration of support in principle by Justice Kennedy (see 488 U.S. at 734 ff), and which, in effect, tracks Rehnquist's dissent in the *Weber* case (see 443 U.S. at 219ff).

198. Jennifer L. Hochschild, *The Future of Affirmative Action*, 59 Ohio State L J 997, 1034 (1998).

199. Richard D. Kahlenberg, *The Remedy* 27–41 (Basic, 1996).

200. Dellinger, *Memorandum Re Adarand* at 14 (cited in note 194).

201. 488 U.S. at 501.

202. Dellinger, *Memorandum Re Adarand* at 10 (cited in note 194).

203. 488 U.S. at 492, 519.

204. 515 U.S. 200, 227.

205. John R. Schmidt, *Memorandum to General Counsels: Re Post-Adarand Guidance on Affirmative Action* 1 (U.S. Dept of Justice, Office of the Associate Attorney General, February 29, 1996).

206. The government's "basis for decision-making" theory was rejected in *Lutheran Church-Missouri Synod v. FCC*, 141 F3d 344, 351 (D.C. Cir 1998). But cf *Raso v. Lago*, 135 F3d 11 (1st Cir 1998).

207. See Dellinger, *Memorandum Re Adarand* at 1 (cited in note 194).

208. 429 U.S. 190.

209. 518 U.S. 515.

210. Id at 531–534.

211. Schmidt, *Re Post-Adarand Guidance* at 3 (cited in note 205).

212. Id.

213. Dellinger, *Memorandum Re Adarand* at 7 n 13 (cited in note 194).

214. Schmidt, *Re Post-Adarand Guidance* at 5 (cited in note 205). Also open at this time, in the Department of Justice's view, is *Adarand*'s applicability to court-ordered or approved remedial directives. Dellinger, *Memorandum Re Adarand* at 7 n 9 (cited in note 194).

215. Debra A. Millenson, *Whither Affirmative Action: The Future of Executive Order 11,246*, 29 U Memphis L Rev 679, 704 (1999).

216. Id at 696.

217. See authorities collected at Samuel Issacharoff, Pamela S. Karlan, and Richard H. Pildes, *The Law of Democracy* 435 (Foundation Press, 1998).

218. Michelle Adams, *The Last Wave of Affirmative Action*, 1998 Wisc L Rev, 1395, 1398–1399.

219. Id at 1398–1399.

220. For example, see Walter Dellinger, *Memorandum to General Counsels Re Adarand* 10 (Office of Legal Counsel, U.S. Dept of Justice, June 28, 1995).

221. Schmidt, *Re Post-Adarand Guidance* at 12 (cited in note 205).

222. Id at 16.

223. 431 U.S. 324, 335 n 15 (emphasis added).

224. 401 U.S. 424, 426 (1971) (emphasis added).

225. Id at 430–431.

226. Paul Meier, Jerome Sacks, and Sandy L. Zabell, *What Happened in Hazelwood*, in Morris DeGroot, Stephen E. Fienburg, and Joseph B. Kadane, eds, *Statistics and the Law* 2 (Wiley, 1986) (emphasis added).

227. 401 U.S. at 429.

228. 433 U.S. 299.

229. Id at 312 n 17.

230. Id at 307–308.

231. Meier, Sacks, and Zabell, *What Happened in Hazelwood*, in DeGroot, Fienberg, and Kadane, eds, *Statistics and the Law* at 3, 5 (emphasis added); Dolores A. Conway and Harry V. Roberts, *Regression Analysis in Employment Discrimination Cases* 107–165; Robert F. Coulam and Stephen Fienberg, *The Use of Court-Appointed Statistical Experts* 305–331, in DeGroot, Fienberg, and Kadane, eds, *Statistics and the Law* (cited in note 226).

232. See material in Meier, Sacks, and Zabell, *What Happened in Hazelwood*, in DeGroot, Fienberg, and Kadane, eds, *Statistics and the Law* at 24 (cited in note 226).

233. Id at 5.

234. Id at 4–5.

235. Id at 7.

236. Lawrence Tribe, *Trial by Mathematics: Precision and Ritual in the Legal Process*, 84 Harv L Rev 1329, 1329–1393 (1971).

237. "Expert" discussion on quantitative criteria can be found in Meier, Sacks, and Zabell, *What Happened in Hazelwood* at 1–39; Stephen E. Fienberg, *Comment* 41–46; Meier, Sacks, and Zabell, *Rejoinder* 47–48; Conway and Roberts, *Regression Analysis in Employment Discrimination Cases* at 305–331, in DeGroot, Fienberg, and Kadane, eds, *Statistics and the Law* (cited in note 226).

238. Anne B. Fisher, *Business Likes to Hire by the Numbers,* Fortune 26ff (September 16, 1985); Herman Belz, *Equality Transformed* 196–202 (Transaction, 1991).

239. Alfred Blumrosen, *Modern Law* 301–304 (U Wisconsin Press, 1993); In the month of January, 2000, while the national unemployment rate fell to a 30-year low of 4%, the black rate rose from 7.9% in December, 1999 to 8.2%. See Jeanine Aversa, *January Jobless Rate Falls to 30 Year Low of 4%*, Boston Globe C1 (February 5, 2000). Also see Debra A. Millenson, *Whither Affirmative Action*, 29 U Memphis L Rev 679, 731–737 (1999); *Affirmative Action Review: Report to the President* chs 3, 4 (July 19, 1995) submitted by George Stephanopoulos, Senior Adviser to the President and Christoper Edley Jr., Special Counsel to the President.

240. Stephan and Abigail Thernstrom, *America in Black and White* 183–184 (Simon & Schuster, 1997); U.S. Department of Commerce, *Statistical Abstract of the United States, 1998* (118th ed) 472 (Washington, D.C., 1998); George M. Fredrickson, *America's Caste System: Will It Change?* The New York Review of Books 68ff

(October 23, 1997); Andrew Hacker, *Goodbye to Affirmative Action?* The New York Review of Books, 21ff (July 11, 1996).

241. See Tom Wicker, *Tragic Failure* 155 (Morrow, 1996).

242. William Julius Wilson, *When Work Disappears* xiii, xxi–xxiii, 183–192 (Knopf, 1997); Wicker, *Tragic Failure* at 126–127 (cited in note 241).

243. Christina Hoff Sommers, *Who Stole Feminism?* 238–239 (Touchstone/Simon & Schuster, 1994).

244. U.S. Department of Commerce, *Statistical Abstract of the United States, 1998* (118th ed) at 436–437 (cited in note 240).

245. *Editor's Preface,* in Suzanne W. Helburn, ed, *The Silent Crisis in Child Care,* The Annals of the American Academy of Political and Social Science 8–19 (May, 1999).

246. William L. O'Neill, *feminism in America* 315 (Transaction, 2d rev ed 1989).

247. *Editor's Preface* at 8–19; John Morris, *Market Constraints on Child Care Quality* at 130–145; Mary Whitebook, *Child Care Workers* at 146–161, in Helburn, ed., *The Silent Crisis in Child Care* (cited in note 245).

248. Julia Wrigley, *Hiring a Nanny* at 162, 173, in Helburn, ed, *The Silent Crisis in Child Care* (cited in note 245).

249. *Editor's Preface* at 8–19, in Helburn, ed, *The Silent Crisis in Child Care* (cited in note 245).

250. Thernstrom and Thernstrom, *America in Black and White* at 499–504, 533 (cited in note 240); Orlando Patterson, *The Ordeal of Integration* 81 (Civitas/Counterpoint, 1997).

251. Christopher Edley Jr., *Not All Black and White* 42–46 (Hill and Wang, 1996).

252. Richard Epstein, *Forbidden Grounds: The Case Against Employment Discrimination Laws* (Harvard U Press, 1992) (demands repeal of Title VII); Richard A. Posner, *The Efficiency and Efficacy of Title VII,* 136 U Penn L Rev 512 (1987).

253. John J. Donohue, *Is Title VII Efficient?* 134 U Penn L Rev 1411 (1986).

254. Harry Holzer and David Neumark, *Assessing Affirmative Action,* 38 J of Economic Literature 483, 558 (September, 2000).

255. Fredrickson, *America's Caste System: Will It Change?* at 68ff (cited in note 240); Hacker, *Goodbye to Affirmative Action?* at 21ff (cited in note 240).

256. U.S. Department of Commerce, *Statistical Abstract of the United States, 1998* (118th ed) at 472 (cited in note 240).

257. Thernstrom and Thernstrom, *America in Black and White* at 183–184 (cited in note 240).

258. *Editor's Introduction to Chapter IV,* in Paul Burstein, ed, *Equal Employment Opportunity* 129, 130 (Aldine De Gruyter, 1994).

259. James P. Smith and Finis R. Welch, *Black Economic Progress after Myrdal,* in Burstein, ed, *Equal Employment Opportunity* at 155, 178 (cited in note 258).

260. John J. Donohue and James Heckman, *Continuous versus Episodic Change,* in Burstein, ed, *Equal Employment Opportunity* at 183, 202 (cited in note 258).

261. *Editor's Introduction to Chapter IV,* in Burstein, ed, *Equal Employment Opportunity* at 130 (cited in note 258).

262. Holzer and Neumark, *Assessing Affirmative Action* at 484, 553, 558 (cited in note 254).

263. Id at 503–504, 558.
264. Id at 504–508, 558.
265. Id at 506–507.
266. Id at 512–513.
267. Id at 507.
268. Id at 544, 558.
269. Id at 558.
270. Id at 559–560.

271. For example, in Edley, *Not All Black and White*, the author concedes that affirmative action has had only "a modest positive effect on employment," but contends that we are *morally* obliged to continue it. Id at 51 (cited in note 251).

272. Authors' note: Revised Order 4 has been replaced by regulations excerpted in appendix 3 of this chapter.

273. Authors' note: This document applies to larger service and supply contractors.

Chapter Four. Affirmative Action and the Primary and Secondary Schools

1. 163 U.S. 537.

2. Leonard W. Levy, *Plessy v. Ferguson*, in Leonard W. Levy, Kenneth L. Karst, and Dennis J. Mahoney, eds, *Civil Rights and Equality* 173–176 (Macmillan, 1989).

3. Karst, *Separate But Equal Doctrine*, in Levy, Karst, and Mahoney, eds, *Civil Rights* at 185–186 (cited in note 2).

4. 5 Cush (Mass) 198.

5. Levy, *Roberts v. City of Boston*, in Levy, Karst, and Mahoney, eds, *Civil Rights* at 80 (cited in note 2).

6. Karst, *Segregation*, in Levy, Karst, and Mahoney, eds, *Civil Rights* at 169 (cited in note 2).

7. Diane Ravitch, *The Troubled Crusade* 115 (Basic, 1983).

8. 109 U.S. 3.

9. *Buchanan v. Warley*, 245 U.S. 60 (1917).

10. *Guinn v. U.S.*, 238 U.S. 347 (1915).

11. *Nixon v. Herndon*, 273 U.S. 536 (1927); *Nixon v. Condon*, 286 U.S. 73 (1932).

12. 347 U.S. 483.

13. Karst, *Separate But Equal*, in Levy, Karst, and Mahoney, eds, *Civil Rights* at 185, 186 (cited in note 2).

14. Karst, *Brown v. Board of Education* (1954), in id at 212.

15. 349 U.S. 294.

16. Pub L 88–352, 78 Stat. 241, codified, as amended, at 42 USC § 2000d *et seq* (2000).

17. *Green v. The Board*, 391 U.S. 430 (1968); *Alexander v. Holmes County*, 396 U.S. 19 (1969); *Swann v. Charlotte-Mecklenburg*, 402 U.S. 1 (1971).

18. Ravitch, *Troubled Crusade* at 179 (cited in note 7).

19. 498 U.S. 237.

20. 515 U.S. 70.

21. Id at 120–121. Justice Thomas is strongly supported in this view by William H. Tucker, *The Science and Politics of Racial Research* ch 4 (U Illinois Press, 1994).

22. Steven C. Halpern, *On the Limits of Law* 167, 174, 270 (Johns Hopkins U Press, 1995).

23. 413 U.S. 189.

24. Jack Greenberg, *Civil Rights,* in Levy, Karst, and Mahoney, eds, *Civil Rights* at 10 (cited in note 2).

25. Ravitch, *Troubled Crusade* at 177 (cited in note 7).

26. 418 U.S. 717.

27. *Wessmann v. Gittens,* 160 F3d 790, 798, 796–800 (1st Cir 1998).

28. 195 F3d 698 (4th Cir).

29. Id at 707.

30. *Missouri v. Jenkins,* 515 U.S. 70.

31. Gary Orfield, et al, *Dismantling Desegregation* 20–21 (New Press, 1996).

32. U.S. Department of Education, *The State of Charter Schools, Third Year Report, 1999* at 42 (U.S. Government Printing Office).

33. Jodi Wilgoren, *2 Florida Schools Become Test Ground for Vouchers,* The New York Times, natl ed, A1, A18 (March 14, 2000); U.S. Dept. of Education, *The State of Charter Schools, Third Year Report, 1999* at 18 (cited in note 32).

34. Orfield, et al, *Dismantling Desegregation* at 21, 25 (cited in note 31).

35. 402 U.S. 1 (1971).

36. *Keyes v. School District #1, Denver,* 413 U.S. 189 (1973).

37. Hugh Davis Graham, *The Civil Rights Era* 366–375 (Oxford U Press, 1990).

38. K. B. Clark, *Effect of Prejudice and Discrimination on Personality Development* (Midcentury White House Conference on Children and Youth, 1950); Witmer and Kotinsky, *Personality in the Making* ch vi (1952); Deutscher and Chein, *The Psychological Effects of Enforced Segregation: A Survey of Social Science Opinion,* 26 J. Psychol. 259 (1948); Chein, *What Are the Psychological Effects of Segregation Under Conditions of Equal Facilities?,* 3 Int. J. Opinion and Attitude Res. 229 (1949); Brameld, *Educational Costs, in Discrimination and National Welfare* 44–48 (MacIver, ed., 1949); Frazier, *The Negro in the United States* 674–681 (1949). See generally Myrdal, *An American Dilemma* (1944).

39. 349 U.S. 294.

40. Id at 300–301.

41. 42 USC § 2000d *et seq* (2000).

42. 391 U.S. 430.

43. Id at 442.

44. *Alexander v. Holmes County Board of Education,* 396. U.S. 19, 20 (1969).

45. *Swann v. Charlotte-Mecklenburg,* 402 U.S. 1, 24 (1971).

46. David J. Armor, *Forced Justice* 158–160 (Oxford U Press, 1995).

47. Diane Ravitch, *Troubled Crusade* 176, 268,142–143, 162–165 (Basic, 1983).

48. *Keyes v. School District #1, Denver,* 413 U.S. 189 (1973).

49. Ravitch, *Troubled Crusade* at 177 (cited in note 47).

50. 418 U.S. 717.

51. Orfield, et al, *Dismantling Desegregation* at 12 (cited in note 31).

52. The authors' review of the books covered in this section is largely from their essay, *Affirmative Action and the Presidential Role in Modern Civil Rights Reform: A Sampler of Books of the 1990's*, 29 Presidential Studies Quarterly 175, 184–188 (March, 1999). © Center for the Study of the Presidency. It is reprinted here with the permission of Sage Publications. For an excellent recent appraisal of *Brown*, see James T. Patterson, *Brown v. Board of Education* (Oxford, 2001).

53. Halpern, *On the Limits of Law* (cited in note 22).

54. Id at ix, x, 133, 303–304, ch 1.

55. Id at ch 7.

56. 42 USC § 2000d *et seq* (2000).

57. Halpern, *On the Limits of Law* at ch 4, 50–80, 81–136, 231–235 (cited in note 22).

58. Peter Schmidt, *Clinton Civil-Rights Agenda Cloudy*, Education Week 1, 15 (January 25, 1995).

59. Gary Orfield, et al, *Dismantling Desegregation* (New Press, 1996).

60. Id at 344.

61. Id at 12.

62. Id at ch 12.

63. Id at 346–348.

64. *Milliken v. Bradley*, 418 U.S. 717.

65. Orfield et al, *Dismantling Desegregation* (cited in note 59) at 10.

66. 433 U.S. 267 (1977).

67. 515 U.S. 70.

68. Orfield, et al, *Dismantling Desegregation* at xxiii (cited in note 59).

69. Id at 21.

70. Id at chs 1–4.

71. Id at 14–16.

72. Hugh Davis Graham, *Civil Rights Era* 320–321 (Oxford U Press, 1990).

73. Steven Holmes, *At N.A.A.C.P., Talk of Shift on Integration*, The New York Times, natl ed, A1, A15 (June 23, 1997).

74. Armor, *Forced Justice* (cited in note 46).

75. Id at 158–160.

76. Ravitch, *Troubled Crusade* at 163 (cited in note 47).

77. Christine H. Rossell, *The Fulfillment of Brown*, in Richard Fossey, ed, *The Courts, and Equal Education*, in vol 15 of *Readings on Equal Education* 45, 47–48 (AMS Press, 1998).

78. Armor, *Forced Justice* at 76–98, 99–102, 174–188, 169–174 (cited in note 46).

79. Id at 172–188. Doubtless, the atrophy of "exposure" is also a function of mass minority immigration since the late 1960s, along with the high minority fertility rate. In many big cities, the non-Hispanic white student body has declined so dramatically that—in Stephan Thernstrom's view—" it has become absurd to bus white kids all over the place in the quest for an elusive racial balance." Letter from Professor Stephan Thernstrom to the authors, July 3, 1999.

80. David J. Armor, *Forced Justice* 228–233 (Oxford U Press, 1995).

81. Orfield, et al, *Dismantling Desegregation* at 82, 86 (cited in note 59).

82. Diane Ravitch, *Troubled Crusade* 179 (Basic, 1983).

83. Id.

84. The studies cited in *Brown I* have received harsh criticism. See, e.g., Yudof, *School Desegregation: Legal Realism, Reasoned Elaboration, and Social Science Research in the Supreme Court*, 42 Law & Contemp Prob 57, 70 (Autumn 1978); L. Graglia, *Disaster by Decree: The Supreme Court Decisions on Race and the Schools* 27–28 (1976). Moreover, there simply is no conclusive evidence that desegregation either has sparked a permanent jump in the achievement scores of black children, or has remedied any psychological feelings of inferiority black schoolchildren might have had. See, e.g., Bradley & Bradley, *The Academic Achievement of Black Students in Desegregated Schools*, 47 Rev. Educational Research 399 (1977); N. St. John, *School Desegregation: Outcomes for Children* (1975); Epps, *The Impact of School Desegregation on Aspirations, Self-Concepts and Other Aspects of Personality*, 39 Law & Contemp Prob 300 (Spring 1975). Contra, Crain & Mahard, *Desegregation and Black Achievement: A Review of the Research*, 42 Law & Contemp Prob 17 (Summer 1978); Crain & Mahard, *The Effect of Research Methodology on Desegregation-Achievement Studies: A Meta-Analysis*, 88 Am. J. of Sociology 839 (1983). Although the gap between black and white test scores has narrowed over the past two decades, it appears that this has resulted more from gains in the socioeconomic status of black families than from desegregation. See Armor, *Why Is Black Educational Achievement Rising?*, 108 The Public Interest 65, 77–79 (Summer 1992).

85. Ravitch, *Troubled Crusade* at 268–274 (cited in note 82).

86. Rachel F. Moran, *The Politics of Discretion: Federal Intervention in Bilingual Education*, 76 Cal L Rev 1249, 1288 (1988).

87. U.S. Congress, House of Representatives, *Reforming Bilingual Education*, Hearing before the Subcommittee on Early Childhood, Youth, and Families, of the Committee on Education and the Workforce, 105th Congress, 2d Sess, 208–209 (April 30, 1998).

88. Ethan Bronner, *Bilingual Education Is Facing Its Demise in California*, The New York Times, natl ed, A1 (May 30, 1998).

89. Hearing before the Subcommittee on Early Childhood, Youth, and Families, 105th Congress, 2d Sess at 209–211 (cited in note 87).

90. Id at 209.

91. Bronner, *Bilingual Education Is Facing Push toward Abandonment*, The New York Times, natl ed at A1, A6 (cited in note 88). Federal funding is authorized by 20 USC § 7401 *et seq.*

92. Cited by Moran, *Federal Intervention in Bilingual Education* at 1302 (cited in note 86).

93. Hearing before the Subcommittee on Early Childhood, Youth, and Families, 105th Congress, 2d Sess at 2–7 (cited in note 87).

94. Study reviewed in Moran, *Federal Intervention in Bilingual Education* at 1285 (cited in note 86).

95. Id at 1288.

96. Luis Rodriguez, *Discretion and Destruction: The Debate Over Language in California's Schools*, 4 Texas Forum on Liberties & Civil Rights 189, ns 244, 245 (Summer/Fall, 1999).

97. Cited by Moran, *Federal Intervention in Bilingual Education* at 1266 (cited in note 86).

98. 414 U.S. 563.

99. Id at 565.

100. Id at 567–568. Only four years after *Lau,* a conflict between Title VI's administrative regulations and the statute itself emerged. In *Bakke* (1978), a Court majority, deviating from the majority in *Lau,* interpreted Title VI as barring only intentional discrimination. This interpretation has been adhered to by the Court. But—curiously enough—Title VI's administrative regulations prohibit disparate-impact discrimination where bad intent does not have to be shown to exist. This tension between the statute and its "subordinate" administrative regulations is yet to be resolved. See *Alexander v. Sandoval,* slip op, 99–1908 (U.S. Supreme Court, April 24, 2001).

101. 414 U.S. at 565.

102. Moran, 76 Cal L Rev at 1280–1282 (cited in note 86).

103. Statement of James M. Littlejohn in Hearing before the Subcommittee on Early Childhood, Youth, and Families, 105th Congress, 2d Sess at 261 (cited in note 87).

104. 648 F2d 989.

105. Statement of Littlejohn in Hearing before the Subcommittee on Early Childhood, Youth, and Families, 105th Congress, 2d Sess at 261 (cited in note 187).

106. Rachel F. Moran, *Bilingual Education as a Status Conflict,* 75 Cal L Rev 321, 332–333, 341–349 (1987).

107. California Secretary of State, *Proposition 227,* in California Ballot Pamphlet for Primary Election, June 2, 1998 at 75–76.

108. Don Terry, *The Reply, It Turned Out, Was a Bilingual: No,* The New York Times, natl ed, A10 (June 5, 1998).

109. Id.

110. Statement of Richard W. Riley, U.S. Secretary of Education, in Hearing before the Subcommittee on Early Childhood, Youth, and Families, 105th Congress, 2d Sess at 243–248 (cited in note 87).

111. Meredith May, *Districts Give Final Say on Prop. 227,* The San Francisco Chronicle A15 (September 29, 1999).

112. Louis Sahagun, *L.A. Schools Are Abusing Prop. 227, Report Says,* Los Angeles Times B3 (July 1, 1999).

113. Don Terry, *California Bilingual Teaching Lives on after Vote to Kill It,* The New York Times, natl ed, A1, A17 (October 3, 1998).

114. Jacques Steinberg, *Arizona Teachers Look to End of Bilingual Era,* The New York Times, natl ed, A12 (December 18, 2000).

115. Abby Goodnough, *New York and Neighboring States Are Sticking by Bilingual Classes,* The New York Times, natl ed, A1, A20 (June 15, 1998).

116. Id at A20. Also see Scott S. Greenberger, *Bilingual Ed Loses Favor with Some Educators,* The Boston Globe A1 ff (August 5, 2001); *Bilingual on the Ballot,* The Boston Globe A12 (August 7, 2001).

117. Diane Ravitch, *Troubled Crusade* 228–266 (Basic, 1983).

118. James Brooke, *Minorities Flock to Cause of Vouchers for Schools,* The New York Times, natl ed, A1, A7 (December 27, 1997).

119. Jodi Wilgoren, *2 Florida Schools Become Test Ground for Vouchers,* The New York Times, natl ed, A18 (March 14, 2000).

120. L. Scott Miller, *Promoting Academic Achievement among Non-Asian Minorities*, in Eugene Y. Lowe Jr., ed, *Promise and Dilemma* 47, 71(Princeton U Press, 1999).

121. Id at 72–73.

Chapter Five. Affirmative Action in Higher Education

1. Pub L 92–318, 86 Stat 373, codified, as amended, at 20 USC § 1681 *et seq* (2000).

2. Diane Ravitch, *The Troubled Crusade* 268 (Basic, 1983).

3. Gary Orfield, *Campus Resegregation and its Alternatives*, in Gary Orfield and Edward Miller, eds, *Chilling Admissions* 1, 6 (Harvard Education Publishing Group, 1998).

4. 416 U.S. 312.

5. 438 U.S. 265.

6. Id at 316–318.

7. 78 F3d 932.

8. Id at 944–946. Cert denied at 518 U.S. 1033 (1996); 150 L Ed 2d 717 (2001).

9. Susan Welch and John Gruhl, *Affirmative Action and Minority Enrollments in Medical and Law Schools* (U Michigan Press, 1998).

10. Bernard Schwartz, *Behind Bakke: Affirmative Action and the Supreme Court* (NYU Press, 1988).

11. Welch and Gruhl, *Affirmative Action and Minority Enrollments* at 140 (cited in note 9).

12. Letter to the authors, July 3, 1999.

13. Linda Wightman, *Threat to Diversity in Legal Education,* 72 NYU L Rev 1 (April, 1997).

14. Id at 50.

15. Id at 2.

16. Stephan Thernstrom, *Diversity and Meritocracy in Legal Education: A Critical Evaluation of Linda F. Wightman's The Threat to Diversity in Legal Education,* 15 Constitutional Commentary 11, 37, 39 (Spring, 1998).

17. Id.

18. Richard D. Kahlenberg, *The Remedy* 98–101 (Basic, 1996).

19. K. Anthony Appiah and Amy Gutmann, *Color Conscious: The Political Morality of Race* 140–141 (Princeton U Press, 1996).

20. Id at 141 n 38.

21. Ronald Dworkin, *Affirming Affirmative Action*, The New York Review of Books 91ff (October 22, 1998). The cited essay now appears as chapter 11, *Affirmative Action: Does It Work?* in Dworkin's *Sovereign Virtue* (Harvard, 2000). Also see chapter 12, *Affirmative Action: Is It Fair?* in id.

22. William Bowen and Derek Bok, *The Shape of the River* (Princeton U Press, 1998).

23. These were Bryn Mawr, Duke, Princeton, Rice, Stanford, Swarthmore, Williams, Yale, Barnard, Columbia, Emory, Hamilton, Kenyon, Northwestern, Oberlin,

Smith, Tufts, University of Pennsylvania, Vanderbilt, Washington University, Wellesley, Wesleyan, Denison, Miami University (Ohio), Pennsylvania State, Tulane, Michigan (Ann Arbor), and the University of North Carolina (Chapel Hill).

24. Dworkin, *Affirming Affirmative Action* at 91, 91–93 (cited in note 21).

25. Id at 93, quoting original.

26. Id at 102.

27. Id at 94. Dworkin, Bowen and Bok found that application of race-neutral admission policies would have substantially reduced the number of blacks actually admitted to the elite schools. In Dworkin's view, there is no basis for assuming that the black applicants who would have been rejected if race-neutral tests had been used were less qualified than those admitted, given the closeness of the average test scores for both groups. Therefore, "while abolishing affirmative action would very greatly decrease the number of blacks who attended selective schools, it would not much improve the average scores of those who did." Id.

28. Id at 94–95.

29. Id at 95–96.

29a. Id at 96–97. Dworkin believes that the answers to Bowen and Bok's questionnaires tend to refute the notion that incidents of racial hostility on campus, and practices like "black" dining-hall tables, show that racial diversity not only does not reduce racial isolation and hostility, but even exacerbates them. Id. For contrary views to that of Dworkin, see, e.g., Abigail Thernstrom and Stephan Thernstrom, *America in Black and White* 386–388 (Simon & Schuster, 1997); Richard D. Kahlenberg, *The Remedy* 52–58, 236 ns 80, 86, 237 n 94 (Basic, 1996).

30. This is obviously a sore spot with many affirmative action supporters, but Dworkin reports that the overwhelming number of blacks canvassed by Bowen and Bok applauded their universities' race-sensitive policies. Ronald Dworkin, *Affirming Affirmative Action*, The New York Review of Books 91, 97–98 (October 22, 1998).

31. Id at 98.

32. Id at 98–100.

33. Id at 100. Dworkin claims that current versions of affirmative action in university admissions do not use quotas or require decisions "simply by virtue of race." Id.

34. Id at 100–101. Dworkin rejects the notion that it is impossible to distinguish between "invidious use of race to achieve results in themselves creditable from a so-called 'benign' use." Id at 100.

35. Id at 101.

36. Id at 94–95.

37. Thernstrom and Thernstrom, *America in Black and White* at 393 (cited in note 29a).

38. Id at ch 14.

39. Id.

40. Id at 409. Professor Thernstrom noted that the Dworkin 11% higher black dropout figure was in error. He wrote that Bowen and Bok calculate two sorts of graduation rates (and their converse dropout rates). Appendix Table D.3.1 [of the Bowen and Bok book] shows that the 1989 first-school dropout rate for blacks was 25.3[%] and for whites 14.2[%]. The overall dropout rate, including those who trans-

ferred and graduated elsewhere, was 20.8[%] for blacks, 6.3[%] for whites. In the former case, we do have a difference of 11 points, but that does not mean that the black rate was only 11 percent higher than that for whites; it was 78 percent higher!! 11 points higher would be correct. Letter to the authors, July 3, 1999.

41. Harry Holzer and David Neumark, *Assessing Affirmative Action*, 38 Journal of Economic Literature 483 (September, 2000).

42. Id at 558.

43. Id at 509.

44. Id at 510–512.

45. Id at 553, 558–559.

46. Id.

47. Id at 553, 559.

48. Id.

49. Id at 553–554, 559 (emphasis added).

50. Id at 553.

51. Id at 510–512.

52. 38 F2d 147 (4th Cir).

53. 78 F3d at 952–955 (5th Cir).

54. 91 F3d 1547 (3d Cir 1996).

55. *Brief for the United States as Amicus Curiae for Piscataway Township v. Taxman* in the Supreme Court of the United States, 1996, No. 96–679 at 8.

56. Id at 8–9.

57. James Traub, *The Class of Prop. 209,* The New York Times Magazine 44, 76 (May 12, 1999).

58. Greg Tanaka, Marguerite Bonous-Hammarth, and Alexander W. Astin, *An Admissions Process for a Multiethnic Society,* in Gary Orfield and Edward Miller, eds, *Chilling Admissions* 123, 125–126 (Harvard Education Publishing Group, 1998).

59. Julie Flaherty, *Notebook: A Case For Diversity*, The New York Times, natl ed, B8 (August 4, 1999).

60. Richard Cacon, *A Segregation Finding and a Squabble at Harvard*, The Boston Globe A1, A35 (December 31, 1997).

61. 233 F3d 1188. Cert denied, 149 L Ed 2d 1024 (2001).

62. Id at 1197–1200.

63. *Regents v. Bakke*, 438 U.S. at 324–325.

64. 122 F Supp 2d 811, 821 (E D Mich, Southern Div).

65. Id at 822–823.

66. Id at 823.

67. Id at 824–830.

68. 106 F Supp 2d 1362, 1371–1372 (S D Ga, Savannah Div). An 11th Circuit panel also found the University of Georgia diversity program unconstitutional on the ground that it was not narrowly tailored to fill a compelling governmental interest. *Johnson v. University of Georgia*, 263 F3d 1234, 1270 (2001)

69. 137 F Supp 2d 821, 849 (E D Mich Southern Div). The two diametrically opposed Michigan cases were appealed to the 6th Circuit whose judgment in favor of the law school was announced as this book went to press.

70. Id at 849, 869.

71. Id at 853.

72. Id at 851.

73. Linda Chavez, *Colleges and Quotas*, The Wall Street Journal A21 (Feb 22, 2001).

74. Traub, *Class of Prop. 209* at 51(cited in note 57). Traub writes that "[t]he vast majority of four-year institutions admit all or almost all students who apply." Id. For support of this view, see Thomas J. Kane, *Misconceptions in the Debate over Affirmative Action in College Admissions*, in Orfield and Miller, eds, *Chilling Admissions* at 18 (cited in note 58). Also see Stephan Thernstrom's comments at page 139.

75. Cited by Traub, *Class of Prop. 209* at 50 (cited in note 57).

76. Abigail Thernstrom, *The Flawed Defense of Preferences*, The Wall Street Journal, A19 (October 23, 1998).

77. Eugene Y. Lowe Jr., *Incorporating Racial Diversity in Selective Higher Education*, in Eugene Y. Lowe Jr., ed, *Promise and Dilemma: Perspectives on Racial Diversity and Higher Education* 19 (Princeton U Press, 1999).

78. Claude Steele, *How Stereotypes Shape Intellectual Identity and Performance*, in Lowe, ed, *Promise and Dilemma* at 92–128 (cited in note 77). On this theory, also see Elaine Woo, *Can Racial Stereotypes Psych Out Students?* Los Angeles Times A1, A14 (December 11, 1995).

79. James Traub, *The Class of Prop. 209*, The New York Times Magazine 76 (May 12, 1999).

80. Id.

81. Lowe, *Incorporating Racial Diversity*, in Lowe, ed, *Promise and Dilemma* at 5 (cited in note 77).

82. Kim Murphy, *Decision 98/The Final Count*, Los Angeles Times, Special Section, S1 (November 5, 1998).

83. California Secretary of State, *California Ballot Pamphlet, General Election* (November 5, 1996) at 94.

84. Ethan Bronner, *Minority Enrollment at the U. of California Will Dip in Fall*, The New York Times, natl ed, A20 (May 21, 1998).

85. Ward Connerly, *Why I'm Still Fighting Preferences in Florida*, The Wall Street Journal A26 (November 18, 1999); *Fla. Regents Endorse Plan to End Affirmative Action*, Los Angeles Times A26 (November 20, 1999).

86. Traub, *The Class of Prop. 209* at 44, 78 (cited in note 79); *U. of California Alters Admission Policy*, The New York Times, natl ed, A12 (July 20, 2001). Dual admissions are to start in 2003, but in recent years, the UC system had come to recruit more extensively from the junior colleges in the State. Rebecca Trounson, *UC Admits Record Number of Community College Students*, Los Angeles Times B10 (June 1, 2001).

87. Susan Wilbur and Marguerite Bonous-Hammarth, *Testing a New Approach to Admission*, in Gary Orfield and Edward Miller, eds, *Chilling Admissions* 111, 114–115 (Harvard Education Publishing Group, 1998).

88. Id at 116.

89. Id at 118.

90. Traub, *Class of Prop. 209* at 46 (cited in note 79).

91. Id.

92. *Grutter v. Bollinger,* 137 F Supp 2d 821, 870 (E D Mich, Southern Div, 2001).

93. Bronner, *Minority Enrollments at U. of California Will Dip in Fall* at A20 (cited in note 84).

94. Traub, *Class of Prop. 209* at 46 (cited in note 79).

95. See Thomas J. Kane, *Misconceptions in the Debate over Affirmative Action* at 17, 19; Jerome Karabel, *No Alternative,* in Orfield and Miller, eds, *Chilling Admissions* at 33 (cited in note 87).

96. Karabel, *No Alternative,* in Orfield and Miller, eds, *Chilling Admissions* at 38 (cited in note 87).

97. Amy Dockser Marcus, *New Weights Can Alter SAT Scores,* The Wall Street Journal B1, B8 (August 13, 1999).

98. Cited by Amy Dockser Marcus, *Colleges Back Recruiting Test for Minorities,* The Wall Street Journal B1, B4 (November 19, 1999).

99. Id.

100. Daniel Golden, *Language Test Gives Hispanic Students in California a Leg Up,* The Wall Street Journal A1, A6 (June 26, 2001).

101. Diana Jean Schemo, *Head of U of California Seeks to End SAT,* The New York Times, natl ed, A1, A11 (February 17, 2001).

102. Jeffrey Selingo, *Why Minority Recruiting Is Alive and Well in Texas,* Chronicle of Higher Education A34–36 (November 19, 1999).

103. Cited in id at A34.

104. Id at A35.

105. 38F 3d 147.

106. Chronicle of Higher Education A29 (June 2, 1995).

107. Scott Jaschik, *Education Dept. Sticks by Policy Upholding Minority Scholarships,* Chronicle of Higher Education A28 (June 9, 1995).

108. Cited at id.

109. Id.

110. U. S. Commission on Civil Rights, *The Black/White Colleges* 3–4 (Clearinghouse Publication 66, April, 1981).

111. Cited in id at 4 n 9.

112. Id at 8.

113. Id at 9–11.

114. Adapted from id at 13–24.

115. 391 U.S. 430.

116. Kenyon D. Bunch and Grant B. Mindle, *Testing the Limits of Precedent: The Application of Green to the Desegregation of Higher Education,* 2 Seton Hall Constitutional Law J, 541, 542–592 (1992).

117. Id, passim.

118. Id, passim.

119. 112 S Ct 2727.

120. Id at 2737.

121. Id.

122. Id at 2738–2742.

123. See *Ayers v. Fordice,* 879 F Supp 1419 (ND Miss 1995); 111 F3d 1183 (5th Cir 1997), cert denied, 139 L Ed 2d 768 (1998).

124. *Knight v. Alabama,* 900 F Supp 272 (N D Ala, 1995).

125. Southern Education Foundation, *Miles to Go: A Report on Black Students and Postsecondary Education in the South* 47–48 (Southern Education Foundation, 1998).

126. Eric Lichtblau, *Miss. to Pay $500 Million in Bias Case,* Los Angeles Times A1, A17 (April 24, 2001).

127. Southern Education Foundation, *Miles to Go* at xiv–xxxiii (cited in note 125).

128. 112 S Ct 2727, 2746.

129. Id at 2749.

130. Diane Ravitch, *Troubled Crusade* 179 (Basic, 1983). For a striking example of the impact of integration on an HBCU, see Diana Jean Schemo, *Discrimination Accusations Divide a Virginia University,* The New York Times, natl ed, A14 (August 26, 2001).

131. 20 USC § 1681 *et seq* (2000).

132. Mary Becker, Cynthia Grant Bowman, and Morrison Torrey, *Cases and Materials on Feminist Jurisprudence* 17, 23, 26 (West, 1994).

133. Id at 26.

134. See *United States v. Virginia Military Institute,* 518 U.S. 515, 532 (1996).

135. *Goesaert v. Cleary,* 335 U.S. 464 (1948).

136. 404 U.S. 71.

137. Id at 27.

138. 411 U.S. 677.

139. 429 U.S. 190.

140. 518 U.S. 515.

141. Id at 531–534.

142. Id at 535–546.

143. See *Cohen v. Brown,* 101 F3d 155, 183, 197 n 22 (1st Cir 1996) cert denied, 137 L Ed 2d 682 (1997).

144. 518 U.S. at 533 n 7.

145. Id at 553–557.

146. Tod Christopher Gurney, *Comment: The Aftermath of the Virginia Military Institute Decision,* 38 Santa Clara L Rev 1183, 1186–1194 (1998).

147. Id.

148. American Association of University Women Educational Foundation, *Separated by Sex: A Critical Look at Single-Sex Education for Girls* 1–10 (American Association of University Women Educational Foundation, 1998).

149. Cited by Connie Leslie, *Separate and Unequal?* Newsweek 55 (March 23, 1998).

150. 20 USC § 1681(a) *et seq* (2000).

151. Note: *Cheering on Women and Girls in Sports,* 110 Harvard L Rev, 1627–1644 (1997).

152. Id.

153. U.S. Congress, House of Representatives, *Hearing on Title IX of the Education Amendments of 1972* before the Subcommittee on Postsecondary Education, 104th Cong, 1st sess 78 (May 9, 1995).

154. Id at 79.

155. 101 F3d 155, 175–176 (1st Cir).
156. Id at 170–171, 174–176.
157. 20 USC § 1681 (b) (2000).
158. 101 F3d at 177.
159. Cited in 101 F3d at 166.
160. Id at 175–176, 178–181.
161. Id at 179–180.
162. 515 U.S. 200.
163. 101 F3d at 182.
164. Id at 183–184, and n 22.
165. Id at 184.
166. Id at 195, 197–198.
167. Id at 196.
168. Id.
169. Id at 190–191, 197.
170. Id at 198.
171. 864 F2d 881, 897–899 (1st Cir).
172. See *Meritor v. Vinson,* 477 U.S. 57 (1986); *Oncale v. Sundowner Offshore Services,* 118 S Ct 998, 1001(1998).
173. 526 U.S. 629, 651–652 (1999).
174. Daphne Patai, *Heterophobia* (Rowman & Littlefield, 1998).
175. Id at xxi, xv, 6, 12, 23, 24, 35, 57, 158, 161, 207.
176. Stephen Shulhofer, *Unwanted Sex* 148, 169, 186, 272–273 (Harvard U Press, 1999).

Chapter Six. Affirmative Action and the Political Representation of Minorities

1. Pub L 89–110, 79 Stat 437, codified, as amended, at 42 USC § 1973 *et seq* (2000).
2. *Reynolds v. Sims,* 377 U.S. 533, 538 (1964).
3. For an excellent account, see Alexander Keyssar, *The Right to Vote* (Basic, 2000).
4. Id at 256–266, 287; Chandler Davidson, *The Voting Rights Act,* in Bernard Grofman and Chandler Davidson, eds, *Controversies in Minority Voting* 7, 10–17 (Brookings, 1992); Samuel Issacharoff, Pamela S. Karlan, and Richard H. Pildes, *The Law of Democracy* 285, 286 (Foundation, 1998).
5. 383 U.S. 301, 308.
6. Id at 308–309.
7. 42 USC § 1973c (2000) (emphasis added).
8. Issacharoff, Karlan, and Pildes, *Law of Democracy* at 285, 286 (cited in note 4).
9. Id at 276.
10. 42 USC § 1973b (2000).
11. Chandler Davidson, *The Voting Rights Act,* in Grofman and Davidson, eds, *Controversies in Minority Voting* at 7, 43 (cited in note 4).

12. Id.

13. Id.

14. Keith J. Bybee, *Mistaken Identity* 28 (Princeton U Press, 1998).

15. David Lublin, *The Paradox of Representation* 22 (Princeton U Press, 1997).

16. For the statistics on this point, see id at 23–24; Laughlin McDonald, *The 1982 Amendments*, in Grofman and Davidson, eds, *Controversies in Minority Voting* at 66, 73–74 (cited in note 4). Also see, Lublin, *The Paradox of Representation* at 23–24 (cited in note 15).

17. Bybee, *Mistaken Identity* at 29 (cited in note 14).

18. Lublin, *The Paradox of Representation* at 23–24 (cited in note 15).

19. Davidson, *The Voting Rights Act*, in Grofman and Davidson, eds, *Controversies in Minority Voting* at 17–21 (cited in note 4); Bybee, *Mistaken Identity* at 18 (cited in note 14).

20. 347 U.S. 483 (1954).

21. Issacharoff, Karlan, and Pildes, *The Law of Democracy* at 285–286 (cited in note 4).

22. For a full description, see Davidson, *The Voting Rights Act,* in Grofman and Davidson, eds, *Controversies in Minority Voting* at 25–29 (cited in note 4).

23. *South Carolina v. Katzenbach*, 383 U.S. 301, 334–335 (1966).

24. 393 U.S. 544.

25. Id at 555.

26. Timothy G. O'Rourke, *The 1982 Amendments,* in Grofman and Davidson, eds, *Controversies in Minority Voting* at 85, 90 (cited in note 4).

27. 393 U.S. at 569.

28. *Reynolds* is located at 377 U.S. 533. It is referenced in *Allen* at 393 U.S. at 555–556. Since the equalization rule ("one man, one vote") is a constitutional mandate, antidilution plans under VRA must meet its requirements.

29. The applicability of the "purpose" prong is now uncertain, since, in *Reno v. Bossier Parish School Board,* 528 U.S. 320 (2000), the Court held that discriminatory intent is irrelevant to the preclearability of "nonretrogressive" redistricting plans.

30. Lublin, *The Paradox of Representation* at 5–6 (cited in note 15).

31. Id at 6, 28–29.

32. Kathryn Abrams, *Raising Politics Up,* 63 NYU L Rev 449, 470–471 n 139 (1988).

33. Lublin, *The Paradox of Representation* at 6, 7, 28 (cited in note 15).

34. Id at 6 and passim.

35. 425 U.S. 130 (1976).

36. Id at 134–135.

37. Id at 136 (emphasis added).

38. Id at 137.

39. Id.

40. Id at 141.

41. Id at 142.

42. See, for example, *City of Richmond v. United States,* 422 U. S. 358 (1975), upholding preclearance of an urban annexation plan which reduced the City's black population share by 10% but did not provide for carryover of its level of representa-

tion. The Court ruled that Section 5 did not mandate a carryover, but would be satisfied if the blacks' post-annexation "representation [were] reasonably equivalent to their political strength in the enlarged community." Id at 370.

43. Drew Days, *Section 5 Enforcement,* in Bernard Grofman and Chandler Davidson, eds, *Controversies in Minority Voting* 52, 56 (Brookings, 1992).

44. Keith Bybee, *Mistaken Identity* 20–21, 41 n 40 (Princeton U Press, 1998) referring to the well-known contrarian view of Abigail Thernstrom.

45. This is not to say that Section 5 has become a dead letter. Under the VRA 1982 extension, it remains in effect through 2007. It furnishes a major portion of DOJ's VRA-workload. Samuel Issacharoff, Pamela S. Karlan, and Richard H. Pildes, *The Law of Democracy* 293–294 (Foundation, 1998).

46. *Fortson v. Dorsey,* 379 U.S. 433, 439 (1965) (emphasis added).

47. 403 U.S. 124 (1971).

48. Id at 133, 149.

49. 412 U.S. 755.

50. Id at 766, 769.

51. See *Zimmer v. McKeithen,* 485 F2d 1297, 1395 (5th Cir 1973) listing the nine criteria of the "totality of the circumstances" test applied by the *White* majority. For analysis, see Issacharoff, Karlan, and Pildes, *The Law of Democracy* at 383, 386 (cited in note 45).

52. 446 U.S. 55.

53. *Thornburg v. Gingles,* 478 U.S. 30, 35 (1986) (emphasis added).

54. In this view, *Bolden* unjustifiably abandoned the *White/Zimmer* standard, and imposed an unfair burden of proof on minority plaintiffs. See McDonald, *The 1982 Amendments,* in Grofman and Davidson, eds, *Controversies in Minority Voting* at 68 (cited in note 43). For in-depth analysis, see Issacharoff, Karlan, and Pildes, *The Law of Democracy* at 405–407 (cited in note 45). It should be noted that, in *Rogers v. Lodge,* 458 U.S. 613 (1982), the Supreme Court held that discriminatory motive may be inferred from evidence of discriminatory results, thus, in the view of some authorities, mooting opposition to the *Bolden* ruling. See Issacharoff, Karlan, and Pildes, *The Law of Democracy* at 408–409 (cited in note 45).

55. *Thornburg v. Gingles,* 478 U.S. at 35 (emphasis added).

56. 430 U.S. 144.

57. Id at 159–161.

58. Id at 161.

59. Id at 162.

60. Id at 165.

61. Id.

62. Id at 186–187.

63. Section 2(a), 42 USC § 1973a (2000) (emphasis added).

64. Section 2(b), 42 USC § 1973b (2000).

65. See Thomas M. Boyd and Stephen J. Markman, *The 1982 Amendments,* as excerpted in Issacharoff, Karlan, and Pildes, *The Law of Democracy* at 412–434 (cited in note 45), for a narrative summary and excerpts from the Senate Judiciary Committee Report on the 1982 Amendments.

66. 446 U.S. 55.

67. See Boyd and Markman, *The 1982 Amendments,* in Issacharoff, Karlan, and Pildes, *The Law of Democracy* at 413, 426–428, 434 (cited in note 45).

68. Id at 427.

69. Id at 427–428. The Senate report regarding the amendment of Section 2 enumerated seven "typical factors" and described two "additional factors" that have had "probative value" in some cases; and said that "other factors" will indicate "the alleged dilution" in some cases.

70. Issacharoff, Karlan, and Pildes, *The Law of Democracy* at 434 (cited in note 45).

71. *Johnson v. De Grandy,* 512 U.S. 997, 1007 (1994), quoting *Voinovich v. Quilter,* 507 U.S. 146, 153–154 (1993) (emphasis added).

72. See chapter 3 at pages 40–49; and chapter 4 at pages 111–113 in this volume.

73. Hugh Davis Graham, *Voting Rights,* in Bernard Grofman and Chandler Davidson, eds, *Controversies in Minority Voting* 180–196 (Brookings, 1992). Professor Graham maintains that VRA, like Title VII in EEO law, has moved beyond color-blind equality of treatment to institutionalized racial preference. But cf *Editors' Postscript,* in id at 315 and n 36, questioning whether the VRA benefit of undiluted voting strength "fits the usual model of affirmative action case law."

74. See Steven Lawson, *Running for Freedom* 154 (McGraw-Hill, 1996).

75. 478 U.S. 30.

76. Samuel Issacharoff, Pamela S. Karlan, and Richard H. Pildes, *The Law of Democracy* 434 (Foundation, 1998).

77. 478 U.S. at 42, 80, 82.

78. Id 48, and n 15, 49.

79. Id at 47.

80. Id at 50–51(emphasis added).

81. Issacharoff, Karlan, and Pildes, *The Law of Democracy* at 464, 466 (cited in note 76).

82. See, e.g., *Johnson v. De Grandy* (1994) rejecting "packing" claims by Hispanic residents of single-member, majority-minority districts in Dade County, Florida. Based on the plaintiffs' existing power to elect "their chosen representatives in substantial proportion to their percentage of the area's population," the Court held that they were not entitled, under Section 2, to a proportionate number of majority-minority districts in the area. 512 U.S. 997, 1008. For analysis, see Issacharoff, Karlan, and Pildes, *The Law of Democracy* at 499–500, 506–509 (cited in note 76).

83. David T. Canon, *Race, Redistricting, and Representation* 71–72 (U Chicago Press, 1999).

84. 478 U.S. at 44, 49 n 17.

85. Alexander Keyssar, *The Right to Vote* 294–295 (Basic, 2000); Canon, *Race, Redistricting and Representation* at 70–73 (cited in note 83).

86a. 478 U.S. at 50 n 17.

86. Keyssar, *The Right to Vote* at 294 (cited in note 85); David Lublin, *The Paradox of Representation* 30 (Princeton U Press, 1997).

87. 478 U.S. at 96.

88. *Shaw v. Reno,* 509 U.S. 630 (1993); *Miller v. Johnson,* 515 U.S. 900 (1995); *Shaw v. Hunt,* 517 U.S. 899 (1996); *Bush v. Vera,* 517 U. S. 952 (1996).

89. Issacharoff, Karlan, and Pildes, *The Law of Democracy* at 148 (cited in note 76) (emphasis added).

90. Id.

91. *Davis v. Bandemer,* 478 U.S. 109, 164 (1986) (Powell concurring).

92. J. Morgan Kousser, *The Voting Rights Act,* in Grofman and Davidson, eds, *Controversies in Minority Voting* at 135, 144 (cited in note 73); Eric Foner, *Reconstruction* 590 (Perennial/Harper, 1988).

93. *Shaw v. Reno,* 509 U.S. 630, 670 (1993) (White dissenting).

94. See Lublin, *The Paradox of Representation* at 8, 30 (cited in note 86); Issacharoff, Karlan, and Pildes, *The Law of Democracy* at 546, 566–567, 582–588 (cited in note 76).

95. Lublin, *The Paradox of Representation* at 10–12 (cited in note 86). For *Shaw v. Reno,* see 509 U.S. 630.

96. 509 U.S. 630.

97. Id at 633–636.

98. Lublin, *The Paradox of Representation* at 7 (cited in note 86).

99. 509 U.S. at 636–637; Lublin, *The Paradox of Representation* at 7 (cited in note 86).

100. 509 U.S. at 642.

101. Id at 648.

102. 430 U.S. 144.

103. *Shaw v. Reno,* 509 U.S. at 651–653, 659–668, 670–673, 676–684, 685–686.

104. 509 U.S. 630.

105. 517 U.S. 899, 908–918.

106. 517 U.S. 952.

107. 515 U.S. 900 (1995).

108. 517 U.S. 952.

109. Id at 1000.

110. Id at 1060.

111. Id at 1062.

112. Id at 1070–1071.

113. Id at 1073–1074.

114. J. Gerald Hebert, *Redistricting in the Post-2000 Era,* 8 Geo Mason U L Rev 431, 437–438, 458, 475–476 (2000).

115. 149 L Ed 2d, 430.

116. 517 U.S. 899.

117. *Hunt v. Cromartie,* 149 L Ed 2d, 430.

118. Id at 445–446.

119. Id at 453.

120. Id at 444, 453 citing and quoting *Bush v. Vera,* 517 U.S. 952, 968 (1996) (O'Connor principal opinion): "If district lines merely correlate with race because they are drawn on the basis of political affiliation, which correlates with race, there is no racial classification to justify."

121. Id at 453 (emphasis added).

122. *Hunt v. Cromartie,* 143 L Ed 2d 731, 732–733 (1999) (*Cromartie I*).

123. *Hunt v. Cromartie,* 149 L Ed 2d, 430 (2001) (*Cromartie II*) illustrates the potential dangers of a fact-specific approach. This decision must be seen as something of a judicial mutant, considering that it came into being only because of Justice

O'Connor's as yet unexplained defection to the side of her former antagonists. There is no telling whether or when she may revert to her affiliation with the Court's rigorously race-neutral bloc.

124. *Hunt v. Cromartie,* 143 L Ed 2d 731(*Cromartie I*) at n 7, citing *Davis v. Bandemer,* 478 U.S. 109.

125. Hebert, *Redistricting in Post-2000* at 437–438, 449–450 (cited in note 114).

126. *Holder v. Hall,* 512 U.S. 874, 914 (1994) (Thomas and Scalia, JJ, concurring).

127. David Lublin, *The Paradox of Representation* 129 (Princeton U Press, 1997).

128. William L. O'Neill, *feminism in America* ch 8 (Transaction, 2d rev ed, 1989).

129. Ellen Fitzpatrick, *Afterword,* in Eleanor Flexner and Ellen Fitzpatrick, *Century of Struggle: The Women's Rights Movement* 326, 327 (enlarged ed, Harvard U Press, 1996).

130. David Lauter, *Emily's List,* in Alida Brill, ed, *A Rising Public Voice: Women in Politics* 217, 218 (Feminist Press, 1995).

131. Id.

132. Id at 221.

133. Beth Reingold, *Representing Women* 1 (U North Carolina Press, 2000).

134. Id.

135. Paul S. Herrnson, *Congressional Elections* 78 (CQ Press, 1998).

136. Reingold, *Representing Women* at 3–4 (cited in note 133).

137. Id at 251.

138. Id at 4.

139. Id at 6–7, 23.

140. Id at 240.

141. Laughlin McDonald, *The 1982 Amendments,* in Bernard Grofman and Chandler Davidson, eds, *Controversies in Minority Voting* 66, 74–75 (Brookings, 1992).

142. Id at 82; Davidson, *The Voting Rights Act,* in Grofman and Davidson, eds, *Controversies in Minority Voting* at 46 (cited in note 141).

143. McDonald, *The1982 Amendments* at 82 in Grofman and Davidson, *Controversies in Minority Voting* (cited in note 141); Davidson, *The Voting Rights Act* at 46.

144. Lani Guinier, *Voting Rights,* in Grofman and Davidson, eds, *Controversies in Minority Voting* at 283, 283–288 (cited in note 141).

145. For representative statements, see Abigail Thernstrom, *Whose Votes Count?* (Harvard U Press, 1987); Timothy G. O'Rourke, *The 1982 Amendments*; Hugh Davis Graham, *Voting Rights,* in Grofman and Davidson, eds, *Controversies in Minority Voting* (cited in note 141).

146. Graham, *Voting Rights* at 188 in id.

147. Id at 189.

148. See, for examples, in Grofman and Davidson, eds, *Controversies in Minority Voting* (cited in note 141): Drew Days, *Section 5 Enforcement* at 58–64; Laughlin McDonald, *The 1982 Amendments* at 77–79; Morgan Kousser, *The Voting Rights Act* at 166–176. For reasonably evenhanded critiques, see Davidson, *The Voting Rights Act* and Editors' *Postscript,* in id. Also see Keith J. Bybee, *Mistaken Identity* ch 3 (Princeton U Press, 1998).

149. J. Gerald Hebert, *Redistricting in the Post-2000 Era,* 8 Geo Mason U L Rev 431, 475 (2000).

150. In the past decade, the country's growth rate was the greatest in our history. See Eric Schmitt, *U.S. Population Has Biggest 10-Year Rise Ever,* The New York Times, natl ed, A10 (April 3, 2001).

151. Eric Schmitt, *Whites in Minority in Largest Cities, the Census Shows,* The New York Times, natl ed, A1, A15 (April 30, 2001); Jim Yardley, *Non-Hispanic Whites May Soon Be a Minority in Texas,* The New York Times, natl ed, A18 (March 25, 2001); Editorial, *America's Demographic Quilt,* The New York Times, (April 2, 2001).

152. Todd S. Purdum, *California Census Confirms Whites Are in Minority,* The New York Times, natl ed, A1, A16 (March 30, 2001); Yardley, *Non-Hispanic Whites May Soon Be a Minority in Texas,* at A18 (cited in note 151).

153. Purdum, *California Census Confirms Whites Are In Minority,* at A1, A16 (cited in note 152).

154. Editorial, *America's Demographic Quilt,* at A14 (cited in note 151).

155. See, for example, Melissa S. Williams, *Voice, Trust, Memory* (Princeton U Press, 1998).

156. See Abigail Thernstrom, *Whose Votes Count?* (Harvard U Press, 1987).

157. See, for example, David Lublin, *The Paradox of Representation* 10–11 (Princeton U Press, 1997).

158. Hebert, *Redistricting in the Post-2000 Era,* 8 at 437–438, 463–464 (cited in note 149) for a description of a hypothetical "functional majority" district in which minority voters comprise 40% of the voting age population.

159. Samuel Issacharoff, Pamela S. Karlan, and Richard H. Pildes, *The Law of Democracy* 722, 723–726 (Foundation, 1998); Davidson, *The Voting Rights Act* in Grofman and Davidson, eds, *Controversies in Minority Voting* at 48–51 (cited in note 141); McDonald, *The 1982 Amendments* at 83–84 in id.

160. Guinier, *Voting Rights,* in Grofman and Davidson, eds, *Controversies in Minority Voting* at 290–291 and n 16 (cited in note 141); see Issacharoff, Karlan, and Pildes, *The Law of Democracy* at 780–784 (cited in note 159).

161. 377 U.S. 533 (1964).

162. 478 U.S. 109.

163. Bruce Cain, *Voting Rights and Democratic Theory,* in Grofman and Davidson, eds, *Controversies in Minority Voting* at 262–263 (cited in note 141).

164. Alexander Keyssar, *The Right to Vote* at 290–291 (Basic, 2000).

165. David T. Canon, *Race, Redistricting, and Representation* 69–70 (U Chicago Press, 1999).

166. *South Carolina v. Katzenbach,* 383 U.S. 301, 308, 337 (1966).

Chapter Seven. Affirmative Action and Fair Housing

1. Pub L 90–284, 82 Stat 81, codified as amended, at 42 USC § 3601 *et seq* (2000).

2. 42 USC § 1982 (2000).

3. Institute on Race & Poverty, *Examining the Relationship between Housing, Education, and Persistent Segregation: Final Report, Part IV* at 1–2 (U Minnesota Law School, 2000).

4. Karl Taeuber, *Statement,* in Robert G. Schwemm, ed, *The Fair Housing Act after Twenty Years—A Conference* 33 (Yale Law School, 1988).

5. Gary Orfield, et al, *Dismantling Desegregation* 304 (The New Press, 1996).

6. Id at 306; John O. Calmore, *Spatial Equality and the Kerner Commission,* in John Charles Boger and Judith Welch Wegner, eds, *Race, Poverty, and American Cities* 309, 324–325 (U North Carolina Press, 1996).

7. Orfield, et al, *Dismantling Desegregation* at 304, 306 (cited in note 5).

8. As detailed by Eric Schmitt, *Analysis of Census Finds Segregation Along with Diversity,* The New York Times, natl ed, A15 (April 4, 2001). For segregation data on the pre–2000 census, see Douglas S. Massey and Nancy A. Denton, *American Apartheid* (Harvard U Press, 1993).

9. As noted, whites are less "isolated." Additionally, the Brookings Institution reports that census tracts with less than a 1% black population have decreased from 40% in 1960 to 23% in the last census, and that far fewer African Americans live in tracts that are 80% or more black. See Robin Fields, *Census Fuels Debate over Integration,* Los Angeles Times A1, A24 (June 24, 2001).

10. Robin Fields and Ray Herndon, *Segregation of a New Sort Takes Shape,* Los Angeles Times A1, A17 (July 5, 2001).

11. Eric Schmitt, *Segregation Growing Among U.S. Children,* The New York Times, natl ed, A 20 (May 6, 2001). Data for the article from the Mumford Center at SUNY-Albany.

12. Gary Orfield, *The Movement for Housing Integration,* in John M. Goering, ed, *Housing Desegregation and Federal Policy* 18, 20–21 (U North Carolina Press, 1986).

13. Boger, *Race and the American City,* in Boger and Wegner, eds, *Race, Poverty, and American Cities* at 3, 8–9 (cited in note 6).

14. William Julius Wilson, *When Work Disappears* 11–17, 37–42 (Knopf, 1997).

15. Cited by Boger, *Race and the American City,* in Boger and Wegner, eds, *Race, Poverty, and American Cities* at 9 (cited in note 6).

16. See, for example, Orfield, et al, *Dismantling Desegregation* at 331 (cited in note 5).

17. Wegner, *Notes and Reflections,* in Boger and Wegner, eds, *Race, Poverty, and American Cities* at 551, 552 (cited in note 6).

18. *Statements* by James A. Kushner, John Payne, and Robert Schwemm in Schwemm, ed, *The Fair Housing Act* at 48, 52–54, 81–89, 106 (cited in note 4); W. Dennis Keating, *The Suburban Racial Dilemma* 5 (Temple U Press, 1994).

19. *Statement* by Robert Ellickson, in Schwemm, ed, *The Fair Housing Act after Twenty Years* at 58–61 (cited in note 4).

20. See Neil A. Lewis, *For Black Scholars Wedded to Prism of Race, New and Separate Goals,* The New York Times, natl ed, A14 (May 5, 1997); Wendy Brown-Scott, *Does Sound Educational Policy Support the Continued Existence of Historically Black Colleges?,* 43 Emory L J 1ff (1994).

21. Massey and Denton, *American Apartheid* at 212–216 (cited in note 8).

22. *Arlington Heights v. Metropolitan Housing Development Corp*, 429 U.S. 252 (1977).

23. Earl Maltz, *Thirteenth Amendment*, in Kermit L. Hall, et al, eds, *The Oxford Companion to the Supreme Court of the United States* 869–870 (Oxford U Press, 1992).

24. 42 USC § 3601 *et seq* (2000).

25. See citations collected at *United States v. Starrett City Associates*, 840 F2d 1096, 1100 (2d Cir 1988).

26. Paul Boudreaux, *An Individual Preference Approach to Suburban Racial Desegregation*, 27 Fordham Urban L J 533, 539–540 (1999).

27. Id at 533–534.

28. 42 USC §§ 3613, 3614 (2000).

29. *Mountain Side Mobile Estate Partnership v. HUD*, 56 F3d 1243 (10th Cir 1995); *Betsey v. Turtle Creek Associates*, 736 F2d 983 (4th Cir 1984); *Huntington Branch NAACP v. Town of Huntington*, 844 F2d 926 (2d Cir 1988); *United States v. City of Black Jack*, 508 F2d 1179 (8th Cir 1974).

30. Statements by Roberta Achtenberg, Assistant Secretary, HUD Office of Fair Housing and Equal Opportunity, and Deval Patrick, Assistant Attorney General— Civil Rights Division, U.S. Department of Justice in House of Representatives, Sub-committee on Civil and Constitutional Rights, *Hearings on Fair Housing Issues*, 103d Congress, 2d Sess, 17–18, at 72–74 (September 28, 30, 1994).

31. Id at 61.

32. 245 U.S. 60.

33. 334 U.S. 1.

34. 392 U.S. 409.

35. 840 F2d 1096 (2d Cir 1988), cert denied, 488 U.S. 946 (1988).

36. *Town of Huntington v. Huntington Branch, NAACP*, 488 U.S. 15 (1988).

37. *Hills v. Gautreaux*, 425 U.S. 284 (1976).

38. Douglas S. Massey and Nancy A. Denton, *American Apartheid* 199 (Harvard U Press, 1993).

39. Id at ch 7; Keating, *The Suburban Racial Dilemma* at 34–36 (cited in note 18).

40. *Editor's Concluding Remarks*, in John M. Goering, ed, *Housing Desegrega-tion and Federal Policy* 327, 330 (U North Carolina Press, 1986).

41. Michael Selmi, *Public vs. Private Enforcement of Civil Rights*, 45 UCLA L Rev 1401, 1422–1427 (1998).

42. *Editor's Introduction*, in Goering, ed, *Housing Desegregation and Federal Policy* at 203 (cited in note 40).

43. W. Dennis Keating, *The Suburban Racial Dilemma*, part III (Temple U Press, 1994); Charles M. Haar, *Suburbs under Siege* 15–29, 166 n 20, 246–248 (Princeton U Press, 1996).

44. Id at 6.

45. See statement by Deval Patrick, Assistant Attorney General—Civil Rights Division, U.S. Department of Justice in *Hearings on Fair Housing*, Subcommittee on Civil and Constitutional Rights at 73 (cited in note 30). Here the Assistant Attorney General noted that the Justice Department focused primarily on the abolition of inten-tional discrimination in its fair housing pursuits.

46. Cited by Massey and Denton, *American Apartheid* at 215 (cited in note 38).

47. Orfield, *The Movement for Housing Integration,* in Goering, ed, *Housing Desegregation and Federal Policy* at 18–30 (cited in note 40).

48. See Peter Flemister, *Statement,* in Robert G. Schwemm, ed, *The Fair Housing Act after Twenty Years—A Conference* 116–120 (Yale Law School, 1988).

49. Rodney A. Smolla, *Integration Maintenance,* 1981 Duke U L J 891, 915–917 (1981).

50. 436 F2d 809 (3d Cir).

51. Id at 811–812.

52. Id at 820–821.

53. Robert W. Lake, *Unresolved Themes in the Evolution of Fair Housing,* in Goering, ed, *Housing Desegregation and Federal Policy* at 313, 315–318 (cited in note 40); Rochelle Stanfield, *The Split Society,* The National Journal 762ff (April 2, 1994); Kushner, *Statement,* in Schwemm, ed, *The Fair Housing Act after Twenty Years* at 49 (cited in note 48); Florence Wagman Roisman, *Long Overdue,* Cityscape 171–172 (vol 4, no 3, 1999); John Charles Boger, *Race and the American City,* in John Charles Boger and Judith Welch Wegner, eds, *Race, Poverty, and American Cities* at 15 (U North Carolina Press, 1996).

54. Lake, *Unresolved Themes in the Evolution of Fair Housing* in Goering, ed, *Housing Desegregation and Federal Policy* at 315–318 (cited in note 40).

55. Alexander Polikoff, *Sustainable Integration,* in Goering, ed, *Housing Desegregation and Federal Policy* at 43, 44–45 (cited in note 40).

56. Institute on Race & Poverty, *Examining the Relationship between Housing, Education, and Persistent Segregation: Final Report, Part IV* at 7 (U Minnesota Law School, 2000).

57. Smolla, *Integration Maintenance* at 891–939 (cited in note 49); Lake, *Unresolved Themes in the Evolution of Fair Housing,* in Goering, ed, *Housing Desegregation and Federal Policy* at 320–322 (cited in note 58).

58. Lake, *Unresolved Themes in the Evolution of Fair Housing* in John M. Goering, ed, *Housing Desegregation and Federal Policy* 320–323 (U North Carolina Press, 1986).

59. Cited by Stanfield, *The Split Society* at 765 (cited in note 53).

60. Goering, Helene Stebbins, and Michael Siewert, *Report to Congress: Promoting Housing Choice in HUD's Rental Assistance Programs* 79 (HUD Office of Policy Development and Research, April, 1995).

61. Id at 79–80.

62. Institute on Race & Poverty, *Examining the Relationship Between Housing, Education, and Persistent Segregation* at 7 (cited in note 56). This report at 7–8 describes a number of the special-mobility projects.

63. 169 F3d 973.

64. Id at 981.

65. Id at 983.

66. Id.

67. 484 F2d 1122.

68. Id at 1125, 1134, 1140.

69. Id at 1133, 1136.

70. 135 F3d 11.

71. Id at 12–18.

72. Id at 16.

73. 840 F2d 1096.

74. Id at 1098.

75. Id at 1102.

76. Id at 1103.

77. William Claiborne, *HUD, Chicago Ink Deal to Reconstruct Public Housing,* The Washington Post A2 (February 6, 2000).

78. *Rule to Deconcentrate Poverty and Promote Integration in Public Housing,* 65 Fed Reg 8124, 24 CFR § 903 *et seq* (2000).

79. W. Dennis Keating, *The Suburban Racial Dilemma* 200–210 (Temple U Press, 1994).

80. 935 F2d 868 (7th Cir).

81. Id at 887.

82. Id.

83. Charles M. Haar, *Suburbs under Siege* (Princeton U Press, 1996).

84. For examples, see articles collected at 27 Seton Hall L Rev 1268–1471 (1997).

85. Haar, *Suburbs under Siege* at 15–29 (cited in note 83).

86. Doctrine name derived from opinion title: *Southern Burlington County N.A.A.C.P. v. Town of Mount Laurel,* 67 N.J. 151 (1975).

87. Harr, *Suburbs under Siege* at 10 (cited in note 83).

88. Id.

89. Id at 190–191.

90. John M. Payne, *Statement,* in Robert G. Schwemm, ed, *The Fair Housing Act after Twenty Years—A Conference* 81 (Yale Law School, 1988); John Charles Boger, *Mount Laurel at 21 Years,* 27 Seton Hall L Rev 1450, 1455 (1997).

91. Harr, *Suburbs under Siege* at 166 (cited in note 83).

92. Id at 243 n 12.

93. The Institute on Race & Poverty, *Examining the Relationship Between Housing, Education, and Persistent Segregation* at 24 (cited in note 56).

94. Id at 3.

95. Id at 4.

96. Id at 2–4.

97. Id at 34.

98. In this epilogue, and throughout this chapter, the authors are particularly indebted both to Robert Lake's essay, *Unresolved Themes in the Evolution of Fair Housing* and the writing of John M. Goering, ed, *Housing Desegregation and Federal Policy* (U North Carolina Press, 1986) where the Lake essay appears at 313–326.

99. Wilhelmina A. Leigh and James D. McGhee, *A Minority Perspective on Residential Integration,* in Goering, ed, *Housing Desegregation and Federal Policy* at 31–42 (cited in note 98).

100. See E. Franklin Frazier, *Human, All Too Human: The Negro's Vested Interest in Segregation,* in G. Franklin Edwards, ed, *E. Franklin Frazier: On Race Relations—Selected Writings* 283–291 (U Chicago Press, 1968).

101. *Editor's Concluding Remarks,* in Goering, ed, *Housing Desegregation and Federal Policy* at 330–331 (cited in note 98).

Chapter Eight. Facing Affirmative Action's Future

1. Witness the following remarks by Senator Orrin Hatch: "I want to emphasize that *affirmative action means quotas* or it means nothing. It means discrimination on the basis of race or sex. It does not mean remedial education [or] special programs for the disadvantaged. . . . It has nothing to do with equality of opportunity. . . . Affirmative action is about equality of results, statistically measured. . . . All distinctions [between quotas and "goals," "targets," and "timetables"] dissolve in practice." Hatch, *Loading the Economy,* in Paul Burstein, ed, *Equal Employment Opportunity* 261, 262 (Aldine De Gruyter, 1994).

2. See appendixes to chs 1 and 3 in this volume.

3. Todd S. Purdum, *Shift in Mix Alters the Face of California,* The New York Times, natl ed, 1ff (July 4, 2000).

4. 488 U.S. 469.

5. 515 U.S. 200.

6. *Allen v. Alabama State Board,* 164 F3d 1347, 1353 (11th Cir 1999); *Duffy v. Wolle,* 123 F3d 1026, 1038–1039 (8th Cir 1997). See also *Raso v. Lago,* 135 F3d 11 (1st Cir 1998).

7. *Lutheran Church—Missouri Synod v. FCC,* 141 F3d 344, 351–353 (DC Cir 1998); *Monterey Mechanical Co. v. Wilson,* 125 F3d 702, 709–713 (9th Cir 1997).

8. *Bush v. Vera,* 517 U.S. 952, 958 (1996) (emphasis added).

9. *Adarand Constructors Inc. v. Peña,* 515 U.S. 200, 227 (1995).

10. Id at 237.

11. 438 U.S. 265, 307–309.

12. Id at 311–312, 314–315, 319–320. Justice Powell held that diversity was a "compelling interest," but that the set-aside was not "necessary to promote this interest," hence unconstitutional under well-settled strict scrutiny principles. The "fatal flaw" in the set-aside was not a failure to prove that it was intended to remedy past discrimination, but rather "its disregard of" the white applicants' individual Fourteenth Amendment rights to compete for the reserved minority seats. Id at 314–315, 321.

13. *Hopwood v. Texas,* 78 F3d 932, 944–946 (5th Cir 1996). The panel held, 2–1, that the State law school violated equal protection by applying lower LSAT and grade requirements for minority applicants. See also *Lutheran Church—Missouri Synod v. FCC I,* 141 F3d at 351–355, where a panel of the D.C. Circuit rejected the FCC's claim that it had a compelling interest in fostering racial diversity by requiring broadcast licensees to establish numerical minority-hiring goals.

14. *Wessmann v. Gittens,* 160 F3d 790, 796 (1st Cir 1998). See also *Eisenberg v. Montgomery County Public Schools,* 19 F Supp 2d 449 (S D Md 1998) refusing to follow *Hopwood.*

15. 233 F3d 1188. Also see *Gratz v. Bollinger,* 122 F Supp 2d 811 (E D Mich Southern Div 2000).

16. See Christopher Edley Jr., *Not All Black and White* 126–141 (Hill and Wang, 1996) for a comprehensive statement of the pros and cons of nonremedial preference in education and employment. Also see Nicholas deB. Katzenbach and Burke Marshall, *Not Color Blind; Just Blind,* The New York Times Magazine, 42ff (February 22, 1998).

17. For instance, law enforcement, prison administration, fire fighting, education, broadcasting, health care, and corporate administration. See *Wessmann v. Gittens,* 160 F3d at 795–798. Authorities on diversity successes are collected at Walter Dellinger, *Memorandum to General Counsels Re Adarand,* Office of Legal Counsel, U.S. Department of Justice 14–19 (June 28, 1995).

18. 509 U.S. 630 (1993).

19. 515 U.S. 900 (1996).

20. *United States v. Virginia Military Institute,* 518 U.S. 515, 531 (1996).

21. Pub L 92–318, 86 Stat 373 codified, as amended, at 20 USC § 1681 (2000).

22. 443 U.S. 193 (1978).

23. The statutory references are to those published in the year 2000 edition of the U.S. Code.

24. 401 U.S. 424 (1971).

25. Robert G. McCloskey, *The American Supreme Court* 212–213 (2d ed, revised by Sanford Levinson (U Chicago Press, 1994).

26. David Schoenbrod, *Power Without Responsibility* 3–21 (Yale U Press, 1993).

27. John E. Roemer, *Equality of Opportunity* 1 (Harvard U Press, 1998).

28. Id at 108.

29. Some theorists propose the alternative rationale of "distributive justice," under which disadvantaged persons, *regardless of race, gender, or ethnic affiliation,* are entitled to whatever they would have gained proportionally absent invidious discrimination. See Ronald J. Fiscus, *The Constitutional Logic of Affirmative Action* 8–14 (Duke U Press, 1992).

30. Roemer, *Equality of Opportunity* at 1 (cited in note 27).

31. Edley, *Not All Black and White* (cited in note 16).

32. Id at 84–106.

33. Id at 42–46, 122.

34. Id at 16–17, 21–24, 44–52, ch 4.

35. Id at 83, 121.

36. Id at ch 10.

37. Id at 50.

38. Id at 204.

39. Id at 140.

40. Id at 78.

41. Id at 67.

42. Id at 125.

43. Id at 123–141.

44. Stephan and Abigail Thernstrom, *America in Black and White* (Simon & Schuster, 1997).

45. Id at 424–426.

46. Id at 459.

47. Id at 459–461.

48. Id at 184–189.

49. Id at 188.

50. Id at 537–539.

51. Id at 533.

52. Id at 499–501, 661 ns 34–40.

53. Id at 501–504.

54. Id at 534.

55. Id at 540.

56. Id at 539.

57. Id at 234.

58. Id at 234–235.

59. Id at 264.

60. Id at 259, 264.

61. Id at 271–279.

62. Id at 274–277.

63. Id at 285.

64. Id at 443–449.

65. Id at 460–461.

66. Michael M. Weinstein, *America's Rags to Riches Myth*, The New York Times, natl ed, A30 (February 18, 2000).

67. Congressman Bernie Sanders, *Falling Behind in Boom Times*, Boston Globe, A15 (February 12, 2000).

68. Id.

69. Weinstein, *Rags to Riches Myth* at A30 (cited in note 66).

70. See Alfred W. Blumrosen, *Modern Law* 301–304 (U Wisconsin Press, 1993).

71. In the month of January, 2000, while the national unemployment rate fell to a 30-year low of 4%, the black rate rose from 7.9% in December, 1999 to 8.2%. Jeanine Aversa, *January Jobless Rate Falls to 30 Year Low of 4%*, Boston Globe C1 (February 5, 2000).

72. Debra A. Millenson, *Whither Affirmative Action*, 29 U Memphis L Rev 704, 731–738 (1999); *Affirmative Action Review: Report to the President* chs 3, 4 (July 19, 1995) submitted by George Stephanopoulos, Senior Adviser to the President and Christoper Edley Jr., Special Counsel to the President.

73. Tom Wicker, *Tragic Failure* (Morrow, 1996).

74. Id at 126–127.

75. William Julius Wilson, *When Work Disappears* (Knopf, 1997).

76. Id at 3–55.

77. Id at xv–xviii, 172–182.

78. A Wilson central finding is that "For the first time in the twentieth century most adults in many inner-city ghetto neighborhoods are not working in a typical week." Id at xiii.

79. Id at xxi–xxii, 183–192.

80. Id at 192.

81. Id at 186.

82. Id at 193.

83. Id at 197.
84. Id.
85. Id.
86. Id at 198.
87. Id.
88. Id.
89. Id.
90. Id at 205.
91. Id.
92. Id.
93. Id.
94. Id at 210–217.
95. Id at 218–220.
96. Id at 221–223.
97. Id at 223–224.
98. Id at 226–235.
99. Id at 235–238.
100. Wicker, *Tragic Failure* at 83, 62–73 (cited in note 73).
101. Richard D. Kahlenberg, *The Remedy* (Basic, 1996).
102. Id at 152.
103. Id at 83, 100–101, 124, 151–152. In the Kahlenberg scheme, even where the *Croson* standard for racial preferences is met, the employer or university would be subject to class-based affirmative action requirements. Id at 151–152.
104. Id at 186.
105. Id at 186, 203, 317 n 112, 151, 287 ns 158–162, 164–165.
106. Id at 80. For Kahlenberg's support of this claim, see id at 42–76.
107. Id at 44.
108. Id at 144.
109. Id at 156–160.
110. 404 U.S. 424.
111. Kahlenberg, *The Remedy* at 31, 159 (cited in note 101). See further, Alfred Blumrosen, *Modern Law* 254 (U Wisconsin Press, 1993): "the *Griggs* principle of 'adverse impact'. . . require(s) that an employer be 'race conscious.' The disparate impact concept requires an analysis of the effect of a selection procedure on race. . . . *It is impossible to analyze adverse impact without being race conscious*." (emphasis added.)
112. Kahlenberg, *The Remedy* at 166–171 (cited in note 101).
113. Id at 64–74.
114. Id at 171.
115. Id at 177.
116. Id.
117. Stephan and Abigail Thernstrom, *America in Black and White* 16, 18, 81–82, 199–198 (Simon & Schuster, 1997); William Julius Wilson, *When Work Disappears* 193 (Knopf, 1997); Tom Wicker, *Tragic Failure* xi, 19, 57, 155 (Morrow, 1996).
118. Thernstrom and Thernstrom, *America in Black and White* at 211–219 (cited in note 117). In *Grand Illusion*, The New York Review of Books 26, 27–28 (June 11, 1998), Andrew Hacker argues that the number should be higher, given the *threefold*

increase in the number of black families earning over $75,000, and that the claim that the suburbs are generally integrated is simply not true. He faults the Thernstroms for failing to observe that a "depressing number" of "mainly black" suburbs "are just a few steps from slums." Id at 28.

119. Wicker, *Tragic Failure* at 157 (cited in note 117).

120. Id.

121. John Charles Boger, *Race and the American City*, in John Charles Boger and Judith Welch Wegner, eds, *Race, Poverty, and American Cities* 41 (U North Carolina Press, 1996).

122. Wicker, *Tragic Failure* at 157 (cited in note 117).

123. Wilson, *When Work Disappears* at 194–195 (cited in note 117).

124. Wicker, *Tragic Failure* at xi (cited in note 117).

125. Thernstrom and Thernstrom, *America in Black and White* at 232 (cited in note 117).

126. Boger, *Race and the American City*, in Boger and Wegner, eds, *Race, Poverty, and American Cities* at 41 (cited in note 121).

127. Thernstrom and Thernstrom, *America in Black and White* at 501–505, 507–508, 519–528 (cited in note 117).

128. Id at 500, 499–501.

129. Id at 219–221.

130. Id at 224.

131. Wilson, *When Work Disappears* at 119–120, 183, 186–187 (cited in note 117).

132. Wicker, *Tragic Failure* at 188 (cited in note 117).

133. Christopher Edley Jr., *Not All Black and White* 47 (Hill and Wang, 1996).

134. Id at 50.

135. Id at 209.

136. Id. Other versions of the Doomsday scenario can be found in Derrick Bell, *Faces at the Bottom of the Well* (Basic, 1992) and Andrew Hacker, *Two Nations* (Scribner, 1992). On Bell and Hacker in this connection, see Wilson, *When Work Disappears* at 183 (cited in note 117).

137. Orlando Patterson, *The Ordeal of Integration* (Civitas/Counterpoint, 1997).

138. Id at ix.

139. Id at 2–5, 177–181.

140. Id at 81.

141. Id at 48.

142. Id at 43–48.

143. Id at 57–58.

144. Id at 15, 16, 18, 21.

145. Stephan and Abigail Thernstrom, *America in Black and White* 207 n 18 (Simon & Schuster, 1997).

146. Patterson, *The Ordeal of Integration* at ix, 5, 15–21, 48, 82–85 (cited in note 137).

147. Id at 28–42.

148. Id at 48–50, 77–81.

149. Id at 147.

150. Thernstrom and Thernstrom, *America in Black and White* at 533 (cited in note 145).

151. Id at 539.

152. Patterson, *The Ordeal of Integration* at 192–193 (cited in note 137).

153. Id at 173.

154. Id at 42–48.

155. Id at 157.

156. Id.

157. Id.

158. Edley, *Not All Black and White* at 9, 134, 141, 189 (cited in note 133).

159. Patterson, *The Ordeal of Integration* at 193–198 (cited in note 137).

160. Donald R. Kinder and Lynn M. Sanders, *Divided by Color* (U Chicago Press, 1996).

161. Id at 6–8, 11, 13–14, 31–34, 25–27, 68, 85–86, 90–91.

162. Id at 124.

163. Id at 191.

164. Id at 269.

165. Paul Sniderman and Thomas Piazza, *The Scar of Race* (Harvard U Press, 1993).

166. Thernstrom and Thernstrom, *America in Black and White* at 500ff (cited in note 145).

167. Kinder and Sanders, *Divided by Color* at 271 (cited in note 160).

168. Id at 272.

169. In *Grand Illusion*, The New York Review of Books 26, 28 (June 11, 1998), Andrew Hacker addresses the question of "how to account for the persistence of racial subordination . . . the feelings of most black Americans that white Americans continue to judge them unjustly." Id at 28. He disputes opinion research indicating that white opposition to affirmative action is based on principle, not aversion to the blacks who may benefit. In his view, whites, when interviewed, always try to convey a compassionate, unprejudiced, not necessarily truthful image. Id.

170. Randall Kennedy, *Race, Crime, and the Law* (Pantheon Books, 1997).

171. Id at 231.

172. Id at 9–10, 238–252.

173. Id at 19.

174. Thernstrom and Thernstrom, *America in Black and White* at 274 (cited in note 145).

175. Kennedy, *Race, Crime, and the Law* at 5–7, chs 4, 8 (cited in note 170).

176. *McCleskey v. Kemp*, 481 U.S. 279 (1987). In this case a black defendant was condemned to death by a Georgia court for killing a white man. On appeal, he contended that the sentence was unconstitutionally predicated on his race and that of his victim. As proof, he presented a professional statistical study which, after controlling for some 230 variables, concluded that the odds of being condemned to death in Georgia were 4.3 times greater for defendants who killed whites than for those who killed blacks. The Supreme Court, 5–4, rejected the appeal, on the ground that the requisite inference of *intentional* discrimination

directed at the defendant *individually* could not be drawn from the *group* data in the study.

177. For the Thernstroms' view as to bias, see *America in Black and White* at 268–279 (cited in note 145).

178. Alfred W. Blumrosen, *Modern Law* 326 (U Wisconsin Press, 1993).

179. Stephen Steinberg, *Turning Back* (Beacon, 1995).

180. Id at 164.

181. Id at 179–220.

182. Id at 212.

183. Id at 213.

184. Id at 218.

185. Id at 219.

186. Id.

Selected Bibliography

—⁂—

Abrams, Kathryn. 'Raising Politics Up': Minority Political Participation and Section 2 of The Voting Rights Act." *New York University Law Review* 63 (1988): 449–531.

Adams, Michelle. "The Last Wave of Affirmative Action." *Wisconsin Law Review* (1998): 1395–1463.

Affirmative Action Review: Report to the President. Submitted by George Stephanopoulos, Senior Advisor to the President and Christopher Edley Jr., Special Counsel to the President, July 19, 1995.

American Association of University Women Educational Foundation. *Separated by Sex: A Critical Look at Single-Sex Education for Girls.* Edited by Susan Morse. Washington, D.C.: American Association of University Women Educational Foundation, 1998.

Andrew III, John A. *Lyndon Johnson and the Great Society.* Chicago: Ivan R. Dee, 1998.

Appiah, K. Anthony and Amy Gutmann. *Color Conscious: The Political Morality of Race.* Princeton, New Jersey: Princeton University Press, 1996.

Armor, David J. *Forced Justice: School Desegregation and the Law.* New York: Oxford University Press, 1995.

Becker, Mary, Cynthia Grant Bowman, and Morrison Torrey. *Cases and Materials on Feminist Jurisprudence: Taking Women Seriously.* St. Paul, Minnesota: West, 1994.

Bell, Derrick. *Faces at the Bottom of the Well: The Permanence of Racism.* New York: Basic, 1992.

Belz, Herman. *Equality Transformed: A Quarter Century of Affirmative Action.* New Brunswick, New Jersey: Transaction, 1991.

Benedict, Michael Les. "Reconstruction, Federalism, and Economic Rights." In *The Oxford Companion to the Supreme Court of the United States,* edited by Kermit L. Hall, et al. New York: Oxford University Press, 1992.

Blumrosen, Alfred W. *Modern Law: The Law Transmission System and Equal Employment Opportunity.* Madison: University of Wisconsin Press, 1993.

293

Bobo, Lawrence. "Race, Interests and Beliefs about Affirmative Action: Unanswered Questions and New Directions." *American Behavioral Scientist* 41, no. 7 (April, 1998): 985–1003.

Boger, John Charles. "Mount Laurel at 21 Years: Reflections on the Power of Courts and Legislatures to Shape Social Change." *Seton Hall Law Review* 27 (1997): 1450–1470.

Boger, John Charles and Judith Welch Wegner, eds. *Race, Poverty, and American Cities*. Chapel Hill: University of North Carolina Press, 1996.

Boudreaux, Paul. "An Individual Preference Approach to Suburban Racial Desegregation." *Fordham Urban Law Journal* 27 (1999): 533–563.

Bowen, William and Derek Bok. *The Shape of the River: Long-Term Consequences of Considering Race in College and University Admissions*. Princeton, New Jersey: Princeton University Press, 1998.

Boyd, Thomas M. and Stephen J. Markman. "The 1982 Amendments to the Voting Rights Act: A Legislative History." *Washington and Lee Law Review* 40 (1983): 1347–1428.

Branch, Taylor. *Parting the Waters: America in the King Years, 1954–63*. New York: Simon & Schuster, 1988.

———. *Pillar of Fire: America in the King Years, 1963–65*. New York: Simon & Schuster, 1998.

Brill, Alida, ed. *A Rising Public Voice: Women in Politics Worldwide*. New York: Feminist Press, 1995.

Brown-Scott, Wendy. "Race Consciousness in Higher Education: Does Sound Education Policy Support the Continued Existence of Historically Black Colleges?" *Emory Law Journal* 43 (1994): 1–81.

Bunch, Kenyon and Grant B. Mindle. "Testing the Limits of Precedent: The Application of *Green* to the Desegregation of Higher Education." *Seton Hall Constitutional Law Journal* 2 (1992): 541–592.

Burstein, Paul, ed. *Equal Employment Opportunity: Labor Market Discrimination and Public Policy*. Hawthorne, New York: Aldine De Gruyter, 1994.

———. *Discrimination, Jobs, and Politics: The Struggle for Equal Employment Opportunity in the United States since the New Deal*. Chicago: University of Chicago Press, 1998.

Bybee, Keith J. *Mistaken Identity: The Supreme Court and the Politics of Minority Representation*. Princeton, New Jersey: Princeton University Press, 1998.

California Secretary of State. "Proposition 209: Prohibition against Discrimination or Preferential Treatment by State and Other Public Entities. Initiative Constitutional Amendment." *California Ballot Pamphlet, General Election*, November 5, 1996, at 94.

———. "Proposition 227: English Language in Public Schools. Initiative Statute." *California Ballot Pamphlet, Primary Election*, June 2, 1998, at 75–76.

Canon, David T. *Race, Redistricting, and Representation: The Unintended Consequences of Black Majority Districts*. Chicago: University of Chicago Press, 1999.

Chafe, William Henry. *The Paradox of Change: American Women in the 20th Century*. New York: Oxford University Press, 1991.

Civil Rights Act of 1964, Pub L 88–352, 78 Stat 241, codified, as amended, generally at 42 USC § 1971 *et seq* (2000).

Civil Rights Act of 1965, Pub L 89–110, 79 Stat 437, codified, as amended, at 42 USC § 1973 *et seq* (2000).

Civil Rights Act of 1968, Pub L 90–284, 82 Stat 73, codified, as amended, at 42 USC § 3601 *et seq* (2000).

Civil Rights Act of 1991, Pub L 102–166, 105 Stat 1071, codified, in scattered sections of 2, 29, and 42 USC (1999).

Congressional Research Service, American Law Division. *Compilation and Overview of Federal Laws and Regulations Establishing Affirmative Action Goals or Other Preferences Based on Race, Gender, or Ethnicity: A Report to Senator Robert Dole*, February 17, 1995. Washington, D.C.: Library of Congress, 1995.

Conway, David, ed. *Free-Market Feminism*. London: IEA [Institute of Economic Affairs] Health & Welfare Unit, 1998.

DeGroot, Morris, Stephen E. Fienberg, and Joseph B. Kadane, eds. *Statistics and the Law*. New York: Wiley, 1986.

Dellinger, Walter. *Memorandum to General Counsels Re Adarand*, June 28, 1995. Washington, D.C.: U.S. Department of Justice, Office of Legal Counsel, 1995.

Detlefsen, Robert R. *Civil Rights under Reagan*. San Francisco: Institute for Contemporary Studies, 1991.

"Developments in the Law, Employment Discrimination." *Harvard Law Review* 108 (1996): 1569–1692.

Drake, W. Avon and Robert D. Holsworth. *Affirmative Action and the Stalled Quest for Black Progress*. Urbana, Illinois: University of Illinois Press, 1996.

Dworkin, Ronald. "Affirming Affirmative Action." *New York Review of Books*, October 22, 1998: 91–102.

Edley Jr., Christopher. *Not All Black and White: Affirmative Action and American Values*. New York: Hill and Wang, 1996.

Edwards, Franklin G., ed. *E. Franklin Frazier: On Race Relations—Selected Writings*. Chicago: University of Chicago Press, 1968.

Epp, Charles R. *The Rights Revolution: Lawyers, Activists and Supreme Courts in Comparative Perspective.* Chicago: University of Chicago Press, 1998.

Equal Employment Opportunities Commission. *Affirmative Action Guidelines of the Equal Employment Opportunities Commission.* 29 CFR 1608 (2001).

Fiscus, Ronald J. *The Constitutional Logic of Affirmative Action.* Edited by Stephen L. Wasby. Durham, North Carolina: Duke University Press, 1992.

Fisher, Anne B. "Businessmen Like to Hire by the Numbers." *Fortune,* September 16, 1985: 26–30.

Flexner, Eleanor and Ellen Fitzpatrick. *Century of Struggle: The Woman's Rights Movement in the United States* Expanded edition. Cambridge: Harvard University Press, 1996.

Foner, Eric. *Reconstruction: America's Unfinished Revolution, 1863–1887.* New York: Perennial/Harper, 1988.

———. *The Story of American Freedom.* New York: Norton, 1998.

———. "The Strange Career of the Reconstruction Amendments." *Yale Law Journal* 108 (1999): 2003–2009.

Fossey, Richard, ed. *Readings on Equal Education, Race, the Courts, and Equal Education: The Limits of the Law.* Vol. 15. New York: AMS Press, 1998.

Franke, J. B. "The Civil Rights Act of 1991." *Southern Illinois University Law Review* 17 (1993): 267–298.

Franklin, John Hope. *Reconstruction after the Civil War.* Chicago: University of Chicago Press, 1994.

Franklin, John Hope and Arnold A. Moss Jr. *From Slavery to Freedom: A History of African Americans.* 8th ed. New York: Alfred A. Knopf, 2000.

Fredrickson, George M. "America's Caste System: Will It Change?" *New York Review of Books,* October 23, 1997: 68–75.

Genovese, Eugene D. *Roll, Jordan, Roll: The World the Slaves Made.* New York: Vintage/Random, 1974.

Glazer, Nathan. *Affirmative Discrimination: Ethnic Inequality and Public Policy.* Cambridge: Harvard University Press, 1975.

———. *We Are All Multiculturalists Now.* Cambridge: Harvard University Press, 1997.

Goering, John M., ed. *Housing Desegregation and Federal Policy.* Chapel Hill: University of North Carolina Press, 1986.

Goering, John M., Helene Stebbins, and Michael Siewert. *Report to Congress: Promoting Housing Choice in HUD's Rental Assistance Programs.* Washington, D.C.: U.S. Department of Housing and Urban Development, Office of Policy Development and Research, 1995.

Graham, Hugh Davis. *The Civil Rights Era: Origins and Development of National Policy, 1960–1972.* New York: Oxford University Press, 1990.

———. *Civil Rights and the Presidency: Race and Gender in American Politics, 1960–1972.* New York: Oxford University Press, 1992.

———. "Unintended Consequences: The Convergence of Affirmative Action and Immigration Policy." *American Behavioral Scientist* 41, no. 7 (April, 1998): 898–912.

Grofman, Bernard and Chandler Davidson, eds. *Controversies in Minority Voting: The Voting Rights Act in Perspective.* Washington, D.C.: Brookings, 1992.

Gurney, Todd Christopher. "Comment: The Aftermath of the Virginia Military Institute Decision: Will Single-Gender Education Survive?" *Santa Clara Law Review* 38 (1998): 1183–1222.

Haar, Charles M. *Suburbs Under Siege—Race, Space, and Audacious Judges.* Princeton, New Jersey: Princeton University Press, 1996.

Hacker, Andrew. *Two Nations: Black and White, Separate, Hostile, Unequal.* New York: Scribner, 1992.

———. "Goodbye to Affirmative Action?" *New York Review of Books,* July 11, 1996: 21–28.

———. "Grand Illusion." *New York Review of Books,* June 11, 1998: 26–29.

Halpern, Stephen C. *On the Limits of Law: The Ironic Legacy of Title VI of the 1964 Civil Rights Act.* Baltimore: Johns Hopkins University Press, 1995.

Hebert, J. Gerald. "Redistricting in the Post-2000 Era." *George Mason University Law Review* 8 (2000): 431–476.

Helburn, Suzanne W., ed. "The Silent Crisis in Child Care." *The Annals of the American Academy of Political and Social Science.* (May, 1999): 8–19.

Herrnson, Paul S. *Congressional Elections: Campaigning at Home in Washington.* 2d ed. Washington, D.C.: Congressional Quarterly, 1998.

Hill, Herbert and James E. Jones Jr., eds. *Race in America: The Struggle for Equality.* Madison: University of Wisconsin Press, 1993.

Hochschild, Jennifer L. "The Future of Affirmative Action." *Ohio State Law Journal* 59 (1998): 997–1037.

Holzer, Harry and David Neumark. "Assessing Affirmative Action." *Journal of Economic Literature 38* (September, 2000): 483–568.

Institute on Race & Poverty. *Examining the Relationship between Housing, Education, and Persistent Segregation: Final Report, Part IV.* University of Minnesota Law School (2000): 1–33.

Issacharoff, Samuel, Pamela S. Karlan, and Richard H. Pildes. *The Law of Democracy: Legal Structure of the Political Process.* Westbury, New York: Foundation, 1998.

Jaschik, Scott. "Education Dept. Sticks by Policy Upholding Minority Scholarships." *Chronicle of Higher Education*, June 9, 1995, A28.

Kahlenberg, Richard D. *The Remedy: Class, Race and Affirmative Action.* New York: Basic, 1996.

Katzenbach, Nicholas deB., and Burke Marshall. "Not Color Blind, Just Blind." *New York Times Magazine*, February 22, 1998: 42–45.

Keating, W. Dennis. *The Suburban Racial Dilemma: Housing and Neighborhoods.* Philadelphia: Temple University Press, 1994.

Kennedy, Randall. *Race, Crime, and the Law.* New York: Pantheon, 1997.

Keyssar, Alexander. *The Right to Vote: The Contested History of Democracy in the United States.* New York: Basic, 2000.

Kinder, Donald R. and Lynn M. Sanders. *Divided by Color: Racial Politics and Democratic Ideals.* Chicago: University of Chicago Press, 1996.

Koppelman, Andrew. *Antidiscrimination Law and Social Equality.* New Haven, Connecticut: Yale University Press, 1996.

La Noue, George R. and John C. Sullivan. "Presumptions for Preferences: The Small Business Administration's Decisions on Groups Entitled to Affirmative Action." *Journal of Policy History* 4 (1994): 439–467.

———. "Deconstructing the Affirmative Action Categories." *American Behavioral Scientist* 41, no. 7 (1998): 913–926.

———. "Gross Presumptions: Determining Group Eligibility for Federal Procurement Preferences." *Santa Clara Law Review* 41(2000): 103–159.

Lawson, Steven. *Running for Freedom: Civil Rights and Black Politics in America since 1941.* New York: McGraw-Hill, 1996.

Lemann, Nicholas. *The Promised Land: The Great Black Migration and How It Changed America.* New York: Knopf, 1991.

———. *The Big Test: The Secret History of the American Meritocracy.* New York: Farrar, 1999.

Levy, Leonard W., Kenneth L. Karst, and Dennis J. Mahoney, eds. *Civil Rights and Equality.* New York: Macmillan, 1989.

Litwack, Leon F. *North of Slavery: The Negro in the Free States, 1790–1860.* Chicago: University of Chicago Press, 1991.

———. *Trouble in Mind: Black Southerners in the Age of Jim Crow.* New York: Knopf, 1998.

Lowe Jr., Eugene Y., ed. *Promise and Dilemma: Perspectives on Racial Diversity and Higher Education*. Princeton, New Jersey: Princeton University Press, 1999.

Lublin, David. *The Paradox of Representation: Racial Gerrymandering and Minority Interests in Congress*. Princeton, New Jersey: Princeton University Press, 1997.

Maltz, Earl M. *Civil Rights, The Constitution, and Congress, 1863–1869*. Lawrence, Kansas: University Press of Kansas, 1990.

———. "Thirteenth Amendment." In the *Oxford Companion to the Supreme Court of the United States*, edited by Kermit L. Hall, et al. New York: Oxford University Press, 1992.

Mandle, Jay R. *Not Slave, Not Free: The African American Economic Experience since the Civil War*. Durham, North Carolina: Duke University Press, 1992.

Massey, Douglas S. and Nancy A. Denton. *American Apartheid: Segregation and the Making of the Underclass*. Cambridge: Harvard University Press, 1993.

McCloskey, Robert G. *The American Supreme Court*. 2d ed., revised by Sanford Levinson. Chicago: University of Chicago Press, 1994.

Millenson, Debra A. "Whither Affirmative Action: The Future of Executive Order 11,246." *University of Memphis Law Review* 29 (1999): 679–737.

Moran, Rachel F. "Bilingual Education as a Status Conflict." *California Law Review* 75 (1987): 321–362.

———. "The Politics of Discretion: Federal Intervention in Bilingual Education." *California Law Review* 76 (1988): 1249–1352.

"Note: Cheering on Women and Girls in Sports: Using Title IX to Fight Gender Oppression." *Harvard Law Review* 110 (1997): 1627–1644.

"Note: The Civil Rights Act of 1991 and Less Discriminatory Alternatives in Disparate Impact Litigation." *Harvard Law Review* 106 (1993): 1621–1638.

Nussbaum, Martha C. *Sex and Social Justice*. New York: Oxford University Press, 1999.

Office of Federal Contract Compliance Programs. *Affirmative Action Programs*. 41 CFR 60 (2001).

O'Neill, William L. *feminism in America: A History*. 2d rev. ed. New Brunswick, New Jersey: Transaction, 1989.

Orfield, Gary, et al. *Dismantling Desegregation: The Quiet Reversal of Brown v. Board of Education*. New York: New Press, 1996.

Orfield, Gary and Edward Miller, eds. *Chilling Admissions: The Affirmative Action Crisis and the Search for Alternatives*. Cambridge: Harvard Education Publishing Group, 1998.

Patai, Daphne. *Heterophobia: Sexual Harassment and the Future of Feminism*. Lanham, Maryland: Rowman & Littlefield Pub., 1998.

Patterson, Orlando. *The Ordeal of Integration: Progress and Resentment in America's 'Racial' Crisis*. Washington, D.C.: Civitas/Counterpoint, 1997.

Purdum, Todd S. "Shift in Mix Alters the Face of California." *New York Times*, Natl ed, July 4, 2000, 1 ff.

Rae, Douglas. *Equalities*. Cambridge: Harvard University Press, 1989.

Ravitch, Diane. *The Troubled Crusade: An American Education, 1945–1986*. New York: Basic, 1983.

Reingold, Beth. *Representing Women: Sex, Gender, and Legislative Behavior in Arizona and California*. Chapel Hill: University of North Carolina Press, 2000.

Roemer, John E. *Equality of Opportunity*. Cambridge: Harvard University Press, 1998.

Roisman, Florence Wagman. "Long Overdue." *Cityscape* 4, no. 3 (1999): 171–196.

Rose, David L. "Twenty-Five Years Later: Where Do We Stand on Equal Employment Opportunity Law Enforcement?" *Vanderbilt Law Review* 42 (1989): 1121–1139.

Schmidt, John R. *Memorandum to General Counsels Re Post-Adarand Guidance on Affirmative Action*. February 29, 1996. U.S. Department of Justice, Office of the Associate Attorney General, 1996.

Schoenbrod, David. *Power Without Responsibility: How Congress Abuses the People Through Delegation*. New Haven, Connecticut: Yale University Press, 1993.

Schulhofer, Stephen J. *Unwanted Sex: The Culture of Intimidation and the Failure of Law*. Cambridge: Harvard University Press, 1999.

Schwartz, Bernard. *Behind Bakke: Affirmative Action and the Supreme Court*. New York: New York University Press, 1988.

Schwemm, Robert G., ed. *The Fair Housing Act after Twenty Years—A Conference*. New Haven, Connecticut: Yale Law School 1988.

Selingo, Jeffrey. "Why Minority Recruiting Is Alive and Well in Texas." *Chronicle of Higher Education*, November 19, 1999, A34–36.

Selmi, Michael. "Public vs. Private Enforcement of Civil Rights: The Case of Housing and Employment." *UCLA Law Review* 45 (1998): 1401–1459.

Shull, Steven A. *A Kinder, Gentler Racism—The Reagan-Bush Civil Rights Legacy*. Armonk, New York: M. E. Sharpe, 1993.

Skrentny, John David. *Ironies of Affirmative Action: Politics, Culture, and Justice in America*. Chicago: University of Chicago Press, 1996.

Smolla, Rodney A. "Integration Maintenance: The Unconstitutionality of Benign Programs that Discourage Black Entry to Prevent White Flight." *Duke University Law Journal* (1981): 891–939.

Sommers, Christina Hoff. *Who Stole Feminism?: How Women Have Betrayed Women.* New York: Touchstone/Simon & Schuster, 1994.

Southern Education Foundation. *Miles to Go: Report on Black Students and Postsecondary Education in the South.* Atlanta, Georgia: Southern Education Foundation, 1998.

Southern Poverty Law Center. *Free at Last.* Atlanta, Georgia: Southern Education Foundation, 1989.

Stampp, Kenneth M. *The Era of Reconstruction, 1865–1877.* New York: Vintage/Random, 1965.

Stanfield, Rochelle. "The Split Society." *National Journal,* April 2, 1994, 762–767.

Steinberg, Stephen. *Turning Back: The Retreat from Racial Justice in American Thought and Policy.* Boston: Beacon, 1995.

"Symposium: Moments of Change: Transformation in American Constitutionalism." *Yale Law Journal* 108 (1999): 1917–2449.

Thernstrom, Abigail. *Whose Votes Count?—Affirmative Action and Minority Voting Rights.* Cambridge: Harvard University Press, 1987.

———. "The Flawed Defense of Preferences." *Wall Street Journal,* October 23, 1998, A19.

Thernstrom, Stephan. "Diversity and Meritocracy in Legal Education: A Critical Evaluation of Linda F. Wightman's 'The Threat to Diversity in Legal Education.'" *Constitutional Commentary* 15 (Spring, 1998): 11–43.

Thernstrom, Stephan and Abigail Thernstrom. *America in Black and White, One Nation, Indivisible: Race in Modern America.* New York: Simon & Schuster, 1997.

Title IX of the Education Act of 1972, Pub L 92–318, 86 Stat 373, 20 USC § 1681 (2000).

Traub, James. "The Class of Prop. 209." *New York Times Magazine,* May 12, 1999: 44ff.

Tribe, Lawrence. "Trial by Mathematics: Precision and Ritual in the Legal Process." *Harvard Law Review* 84 (1971): 1329–1393.

Tucker, William H. *The Science and Politics of Racial Research.* Urbana, Illinois: University of Illinois Press, 1994.

Uniform Guidelines on Employee Selection Procedures (1978). 29 CFR 1607 (2000).

United States Commission on Civil Rights. *The Black/White Colleges: Dismantling the Dual System of Higher Education.* Washington, D.C.: Clearinghouse Publication 66, 1981.

United States Department of Education. *The State of Charter Schools, Third Year Report, 1999.* Washington, D.C.: U.S. Government Printing Office, 1999.

U.S. Congress. House. Committee on Economic and Education Opportunities. *Hearings on Title IX of the Education Amendments of 1972 before the Subcommittee on Postsecondary Education, Training, and Life-Long Learning.* 104th Cong., 1st sess., May 9, 1995.

U.S. Congress. House. Committee on Education and the Workforce. *Hearing on Reforming Bilingual Education, April 30, 1998 before the Subcommittee on Early Childhood, Youth and Families.* 105th Cong., 2d sess., April 30, 1998.

U.S. Congress. House. Committee on the Judiciary. *Hearings on Fair Housing Issues before the Subcommittee on Civil and Constitutional Rights.* 103d Cong., 2d sess., September 28, 30, 1994.

Urofsky, Melvin I. *Affirmative Action on Trial: Sex Discrimination in Johnson v. Santa Clara.* Lawrence: University Press of Kansas, 1997.

Welch, Susan and John Gruhl. *Affirmative Action and Minority Enrollments in Medical and Law Schools.* Ann Arbor: University of Michigan Press, 1998.

Wicker, Tom. *Tragic Failure: Racial Integration in America.* New York: Morrow, 1996.

Williams, Melissa S. *Voice, Trust, and Memory: Marginalized Groups and the Failings of Liberal Representation.* Princeton, New Jersey: Princeton University Press, 1998.

Wilson, James Q. *Bureaucracy: What Government Agencies Do and Why They Do It.* New York: Basic, 1989.

Wilson, William Julius. *When Work Disappears: The World of the New Urban Poor.* New York: Knopf, 1997.

Wightman, Linda F. "Threat to Diversity in Legal Education." *New York University Law Review* 72 (1997): 1–53.

List and Index
of Selected Cases

—⁓⁓—

Topical Index

—⁓⁓—

To assist the reader, brief descriptions of central judicial opinions and statutes are provided herein. Except as otherwise noted, case citations are to the U.S. Supreme Court. Further, the Affirmative Action main entry is a cross-reference for all the other main entries. Main entries are in bold.

Adarand Constructors Inc. v. Peña (strict scrutiny held by the Supreme Court to be the test for racial/ethnic classifications in governmental affirmative action), 21, 54, 58, *71*, 77, 138, 225, 226, 228, 231, 234, 258 n 101
    analysis of, 70–83
    Clinton policy, 21–22
    intermediate scrutiny for gender discrimination, 78, 163–167, 169–171
    issues about, 79–83, 225–229
    See also Equal Opportunity in Employment and Contracting; Supreme Court

Affirmative Action
    acceptance: by business, 66–67, 83; in education, 66–67, 139, 150–158; by the public, 243–244
    antiaffirmative action laws and referenda, 154
    arguments for and against, 1–2, 34–38, 53–54, 206, 232–246

beneficiaries of, 1–2, 21–22, 31–32, 34–51, 53–54, 64–67, 83–86, 114–124, 138–143, 168, 174–176, 203–206, 220–221, 237–244
bilingual education, 129–134
Brown v. Board of Education as precursor of, 109–113
class-based assistance as an alternative for, 140, 155, 238–239
Clinton policy, 21–22
color (race/ethnic) blindness as basis for opposition to, 37, 49, 52, 154, 233, 235, 238, 242, 245
definition of, 1–2, 53–54, 247 ns 1–2
disparate (race/ethnic/gender) impact as rationale: background, 28–32, 41–48; in employment and contracting, 7–11, 41–52, 87–107, 230; in higher education, 138–150, 168–172; in housing, 203, 205, 208–212; in K–12 education, 111–114, 130–132, 134, 268 n 100; in military recruiting, 10–11; for voting rights, 175–195
disparate impact and treatment distinguished, 1–2, 28, 247 n 2
diversity rationale for, 53–57, 140–154, 225–227

307

Index of Selected Names